SPARE NONE:

THE FEDERAL OCTOPUS

How it Grew and Other Tales

CARL A. KEYSER

The Amherst Press

1972

To
F. A. Hayek, Ludwig von Mises, Frederic Bastiat, A. J. Nock, James Gibbons Huneker, Henry Grady Weaver, Dean Russell, Leonard E. Read, Henry Hazlitt, and countless more whose paths in print my eyes have trod, who sowed the seed that grew this book.

Amherst Press   Amherst, Massachusetts

PREFACE

"Individual activity must not do violence to the general interest, but must be exercised within the framework of the community and for the general good.

"We demand the nationalization of all trusts.

"We demand profit-sharing in large business enterprises.

"We demand massive expansion of aid for the aged.

"We demand a ruthless fight against those whose activities harm the general good. Those who commit crimes against the people, usurers, profiteers, etc. are to be punished by death without respect to race or creed.

"To open the doors of higher education—and thus to better jobs—to every capable and hard-working . . . man, the government must thoroughly restructure our entire educational system. The curricula of all educational institutions must be made relevant to the requirements of practical life. As soon as the mind begins to develop, the schools must promote the idea of civic responsibility. We demand education at public expense of intellectually gifted children of poor parents without regard to class or occupation.

"The government must see to it that national health standards are raised, by protecting mothers and children, by prohibiting child labor, by promoting physical strength through compulsory gymnastics and sports.

"The party as such combats the . . . materialistic spirit within us and around us, and is convinced that a permanent recovery of our people is possible only from within on the basis of
        The Public Interest Before Private Interest
"To implement these points, we demand the creation of a strong

Federal government, possessing unconditional authority over the entire nation and its subordinate divisions.

Munich, February 24, 1920." [1]

How thin is the barrier that separates sanity from insanity! Those governments which have been longest remembered in history are those that have inflicted the worst tortures, the foulest persecutions, and the most hideous barbarisms on humanity, all in the interests of the people.

Laissez-faire. Save me not from myself, but from you.

[1] A partial translation of the Program of the National Socialist German Workers Party. The first use of the ellipsis indicates the omission of the word *German*, and the second use the omission of the word *Jewish*. The complete translation in various forms is available from numerous sources.

TABLE OF CONTENTS

CHAPTER 1

OF POLITICS, POLITICIANS, AND POWER

When the LORD God formed man from the dust of the ground and breathed into his nostrils the breath of life, he created a unique animal who was at once a social being and an individual. Creating a single species having both strong herd instincts as well as strong individual instincts is even more miraculous than making dark light or cold heat. It is this paradox in man's nature which has caused the eternal struggle between the individual and the herd: the quest for freedom.

Freedom is like a flower struggling in a garden loaded with weeds. This book is mostly about the weeds and how they grew.

"A monkey with a microscope," said Henry George in 1876, giving us a hint about how the weeds can do so well, "a mule packing a library, are fit emblems of the men—and unfortunately, they are plenty—who pass through the whole educational machinery, and come out but learned fools, crammed with knowledge they can not use—all the more pitiable, all the more contemptible, all the more in the way of real progress, because they pass as educated men."

Those who pass as educated men are influential, but, educated as Henry George described them, their influence can hardly be good. It is they who have allowed the weeds to grow and threaten the flowers. A casual observer searching for such influential learned fools might first point to the politicians, even though all politicians have not passed through George's "whole educational machinery." Most politicians are really disqualified by their neutrality. They do no more than fertilize the garden, bestowing their favors equally on flowers and weeds. Others, who have failed to weed the garden, or who have even planted a few weeds of their own, are Henry George's learned fools. Lack of cultivation, rather than spreading too much fertilizer has been the real source of the damage.

Liberty and freedom of the person, products of human individuality, are thwarted by the power of government, product of the herd. It is commonly thought that politicians steer the country in one direction or another. This mistaken idea leads some persons, fighting the Federal Octopus, to jump into politics. The political leap has become increasingly fashionable as Federal interference has grown and personal frustrations have waxed. But leaping into politics is like spitting into the wind, and the leaper is often dismayed to find he has landed in a dung heap. Furthermore, although politicians may seem to give form to government, they are really more like machine operators who press buttons and pull levers. The product of the machine is designed elsewhere.

From the standpont of the professional, a successful politician is one who wins elections. Getting elected calls for the craft and cunning of the fox and the busy energy of the bee. It depends partly upon the genetic accidents which produce the biological bent and body chemistry that are responsible for a pleasant voice, charming personality, and handsome appearance. It depends partly, too, upon an abundance of cash, cash from father, from a labor union, from lobbyists, from businessmen, or even from taxpayers (who fund the political favors used to buy votes). It depends partly upon the vagaries of time, place, and chance. It depends partly upon the ability of the politician to harmonize with influential persons in the community: working newsmen, union bosses, welfare mothers, ministers, agitators, professors, old people, students, editors, columnists, and, on a sub-rosa basis, those untouchables of untouchables, the successful businessmen. Harmonizing with such a chorus becomes increasingly difficult for the politician as growing government intervention produces greater discord from the conflicting interests of each group. Today's politician needs the skills of the sleight-of-hand artist, the shell game player, and the snake charmer. Winning elections is *the* business of the politician. How he votes and how he seems to feel about issues are important to him only as they contribute to his election or his defeat.

How the successful politician might like to vote and how he really feels are suppressed by his need to be re-elected. Thus, although he may possess a philosophy he would like to follow, the opportunity for independent and original action is usually vetoed by the always imminent next election. This was shown by the behavior of Lyndon B. Johnson, a notoriously anti-civil-rights senator who became a zealous civil-rights president when he discovered that there were lots of voters living outside of Texas. It was also shown by the magic mutation of New York's Charles Goodell who changed from an upstate conservative congressman to a dull liberal senator when his constituency grew to include the predominantly liberal voters of New York City. Now these metamorphoses might lead one to conclude that politicians are unprincipled. They are not. They are just as attached to principles as you or I. They do, however, follow a different set of principles, of which, for them, the leading one is to get elected.

For instance, it has been stated that the men who served Harding were, apart from Herbert Hoover, "politicians who came up out of the soil of most practical Republican politics to serve a President who thought in political terms; to whom policies, measures, bills, and all the achievements of an administration were considered first in terms of elections, primaries, majorities, popular feeling, and public sentiment . . . It is the politician's job to get votes counted on the tally sheet of the election returns—and little more . . ." (1, p 417) [1] This is the way it will always be in a country where officials are elected by popular vote. And this being the case, political goals are more certainly achieved by influencing voters than by running for office.

"Every politician," wrote James MacGregor Burns, who has had more success as a political scientist than as a politician, "tries to win elections by simple 'followership'—that is by gauging carefully group attitudes, opinion trends, party activities, and then taking that position that will reap the most voters on Election Day." (2, p 197)

Walter Lippmann came to essentially the same conclusion twenty-one years earlier when he wrote *The New Imperative*. Lipp-

---

[1] Copyright notices for publications from which quotations have been reprinted by permission of the copyright holders are shown in the bibliography. The numbers in parentheses refer to the number of the book listed in the bibliography and the page number of the reference. For instance, (1, p 417) refers to reference number 1, page 417.

mann, in his ponderous philosophical way, compared Hoover with Roosevelt.

"They profess," concluded Lippmann, "to be deeply opposed. Would it not be reasonable to assume that where we find a new principle and a new function of government (*namely, Lippmann's proclaimed new imperative, by which government assumes responsibility for maintaining the standard of living*) common to both Mr. Hoover and Mr. Roosevelt, there is a strong presumption that we are in the presence of a change due to historical forces that transcend individual parties and their articulate programs?" (3, pp 10-11)

Mr. Lippmann, who is like those Russian writers who are paid by the word and never use five words if ten will do, might have written that politicians are the children of their times. They are followers. They adapt to current political fads and fashions, and the fads and fashions are styled by the opinion makers: teachers, writers, ministers, philosophers, social "scientists", and occasionally, by unsuccessful politicians. Successful politicians more often merely recycle the prevailing fancy and usually do not add much to it. Most of the public accepts, or at least does not question, what is served up to them as the written, spoken, or visual version of the gospel by the opinion makers. The politician who best personifies the gospel wins the election.

Thus, in the first years of the Roosevelt II administration there was only a gradual push toward applying the theories of the "new economics", which theories were put forth most effectively by opinion-making economists like Keynes and Hansen. Roosevelt as a candidate attacked Hoover's unbalanced budget with scornful orthodoxy. Even as president, Roosevelt first adhered to the goal of a balanced budget. But gradually the goal was given no more than lip service and deficit followed deficit. Real commitment to a balanced budget was finally quietly abandoned.

In his very interesting book, *Federal Budget and Fiscal Policy, 1798-1958*, Lewis H. Kimmel wrote that, "if for no other reason, the reluctance of the (*Roosevelt*) administration to accept an alternative theory could be justified on the basis of the maxim that public policy should not run too far ahead of, or diverge too greatly from, public opinion." (4, p 215) Policies can not be adopted by politicians who hope for re-election unless those policies are either accepted, or at least not opposed, by most of the electorate. Politicians walk in the shadows cast by others.

One of the paradoxes of politics is that the loser of an election is more influential in *altering* sentiment than the winner, since the winner merely reflects existing sentiment. Although the winner is considered successful, the loser has a valid claim to success by virtue of the leadership which cost him the election. This is true of parties as well as of individuals. The defeated contender or party may represent ideas that have not yet been accepted. The People's Party, for instance, was not a successful political party since it won few elections. At its peak strength in 1890 it held only nine seats in the House of Representatives and four in the Senate. However, the Populists prepared the way for the growing statism of the twentieth century. They called for a graduated income tax, popular election of senators, postal savings banks, laws favoring labor unions, and inflation of the currency. All of these have since been adopted under the auspices of either Republicans or Democrats. (The postal savings system has since been abandoned.) The most significant parts of the Populist platform have been accepted. Catholic Al Smith, a loser, helped put John F. Kennedy in the White House and sterilized Catholicism as a political issue. Winston Churchill suffered defeat and humiliation before the upheaval on the continent proved that his opposition to appeasement was right. Who knows who may become president on some distant day with an assist from Barry Goldwater's failure in 1964?

"I am," wrote William S. White, "a professional political writer of long experience, if nothing else, and very wide acquaintance among the practicioners of the art. And I never knew a truly able politician, liberal or conservative, Republican or Democrat, Northerner or Southerner, who was not deeply vain (if justifiably so) underneath—and quite tough enough, underneath, to cut down his own brother if that brother should become objectively expendable to his objectively higher demands." (5, p 46) Politicians, it would seem, have traits which are not usually admired: vanity and disloyalty to one's own. Whether they are endowed with these qualities and become politicians because of them, or whether they are born nice little children who develop these qualities after they become politicians is immaterial. The qualities are there and are cause for viewing politicians and their power with extreme suspicion. Limited government, diffusion of power, and checks and balances become more and more attractive when the traits of politicians are considered. But before considering further these traits let us digress to consider limited government and what makes it sensible.

Henry Watterson is a name that not one person in ten thousand would recognize today. Yet toward the end of the 19th century and the beginning of the 20th century, Henry Watterson was an editor and writer of great influence. Watterson was a Democrat and a Confederate veteran. Nevertheless he had opposed slavery and had stood for the Union, typifying in a special way the tragic dilemma of the Civil War. He was for many years editor of the Louisville *Courier-Journal* and a liberal in the original and classic sense of the term. Watterson served as a congressman from Kentucky although he considered himself a Tennesseean and was born in Washington, D. C.

Watterson was a strong supporter of limited government and checks and balances. "Government, like all else," wrote Watterson, "is impossible of perfection." (6, v I, p 225) In fact, Watterson concluded, "Of all human contrivances the most imperfect is government." (6, v I, p 271) Because he recognized the limitations of the beast he wrote: "Under the pretense of 'liberalizing' the government the politicians are sacrificing its organic character to whimsical experimentation; its checks and balances wisely designed to promote and protect liberty are being loosened by schemes of reform more or less visionary; while nowhere do we find intelligence enlightened by experience and conviction supported by self-control, interposing to save the representative system of the Constitution from the onward march of the proletariat." (6, v I, p 73)

The need for limiting the power of representative government rests not only upon the imperfection of the institution, but also upon the limitations of the electors. Consider three classes of adults eligible to vote.

First, there are many voters who do not bother to vote. These persons are not as harmful a factor in elections as one might first suspect from the silly slogan which recently has been badly overworked: *It doesn't matter how you vote, but vote!* Persons who lack the interest to vote probably also lack the energy to conduct even an elementary inquiry into issues and candidates. If all the disinterested nonvoters could be transported to the polls and coerced into voting they would probably vote randomly, in which case their votes would have no more weight than if they had stayed home and watched Buffalo Bob on television.

Second, there is a class of voters who might be called traditional voters. They regularly vote along party lines for almost any candidates put up by the party of their traditional choice. But a Democrat can win in a predominantly Republican area if he is willing to attach a Republican label to himself and make superficial noises that traditional Republicans like to hear. When he gets to Washington he can vote with the Democrats on almost everything excepting the organization of congress. He's likely to be in trouble if someone back home wises up the local folks.

Third, there is an enormous class of voters, reasonably well informed, who are not traditionalists and who nevertheless fail to support the candidates who could best represent their interests. The reason they do not do so is that they do not themselves recognize or have a clear idea of what their best interests are or should be. It is more often than not beyond the ability of the average citizen to discern that short-time benefits may be very costly in terms of long-time expense or that a government intervention intended to alleviate one social problem is likely to create new problems calling for additional interventions. As an example of the difficulty, most people believe that inflation is necessary for continuing prosperity, but if asked to explain why this is so, they can not respond. In fact they can not even differentiate between the cause and effects of inflation. Inflation, to most people, is a rise in prices, which in reality is an *effect* of inflation, whereas inflation itself is an unjustified increase in the amount of currency in circulation. It is caused solely by government action and its effects include a rise in prices. Few Americans are aware that an inflation which causes prices to rise 5 per cent in a year will cause an annual loss of 25 billion dollars in bank deposits (1970 figures). This amounts to a special tax on those who have money in savings banks or in commercial accounts. If the loss in the value of life insurance policies is considered, total losses are even more disastrous. Failure of honest, thrifty, and hardworking people to recognize inflation as one of the most serious threats to their own welfare is little short of astounding. This is clearly the result of inadequate education and knowledge and lack of serious reflective thought. What is surprising is that many people with sixteen or more years of schooling, fall into the category of those who are incapable of determining their best interests. The situation is not likely to grow better. In fact, it will probably grow worse if the Federal government continues to assume more and more of the responsibilities formerly borne by individuals, family units, and local government, since, with growing Federal intervention problem solving becomes both remote and obscure. The average citizen, struggling to earn a living for himself and his family, and in addition struggling to meet the tax burdens imposed by government, has neither the time nor the inclination to study in detail the multitude of problems on which Octopus Federalis operates.

Two possible solutions are suggested. First, raise voter qualifications so that only those capable of analyzing the problems and making wise choices are allowed to vote. This could be dangerous, resulting in a small elite making the decisions. It is a solution likely to be favored by those liberals who think of themselves as being somewhat elite, and hence automatically qualified to tell other people how to function. The second suggestion is to reduce the number and complexity of the problems which government seeks to solve. In other words, place limits on government activity. This is likely the solution to be favored by libertarians. With a strictly limited government voters will be asked to decide questions which are not beyond their capacity to judge. If government functions are restricted, individual responsibility and activity must expand. Problems are then transferred from government to individuals, becoming immediate rather than remote, and simple rather than complex.

But let us return to politicians and their traits . . .

Sam Houston Johnson was brother Lyndon's confidante during LBJ's years as congressman, senator, and vice-president. When his brother finally became president Sam lived obscurely in the White House and continued his service. Eventually he wrote *My Brother Lyndon* in which, apart from its predominantly gossipy style, he makes some interesting observations.

"There were," wrote Sam Houston Johnson, "a lot of dismayed

columnists who jumped on Bobby Kennedy for suddenly announcing his candidacy for President right after McCarthy's victory in New Hampshire (*1968*), calling him ruthless and opportunistic for robbing poor old Gene of his hour of triumph. I don't know why they were so surprised; Bobby was completely in character—a cool, ambitious politician who moved when he had to, and to hell with ethical considerations. Ambition and egotism are the twin names of the game; and without them no man enters public life." (7, p 14)

With ambition and egotism unrestrained by ethical considerations, we can be thankful for the periodic opportunities to "throw the rascals out."

"There isn't a single mayor, councilman, state legislator, governor, congressman, president, or any other elected official," wrote Sam Houston Johnson at another point, "who hasn't gotten a contribution from some fat cat expecting a government contract somewhere down the line. Some of these large contributions may not be solicited—perhaps even turned down by a rare office seeker—but I find it hard to imagine Joe Smith giving a ten-thousand dollar check to Congressman X's campaign without expecting something in return." (7, p 105)

If the above statement is substantially true, and it certainly seems reasonable, the blame for wrongdoing must rest with politicians who dispense contracts and favors, as well as with campaign donors. An additional injustice is also involved. Opponents of a politician are forced by circumstances to support his quest for re-election since the favors granted in return for major campaign contributions are paid for by all taxpayers, opponents and supporters alike. Herein lies a strong argument for limited government.

The opportunities for wrongdoing, corruption, and injustice are reduced, if not banished, when the functions of government are limited to guaranteeing the life, liberty, and property of its citizens against domestic and foreign transgressions. The original United States Constitution came closer to such a limitation of the powers of government than any document before or since written. Sadly, substantial alterations have been made not only by the legal process of amendment, but also by the extra-legal actions of congress and the executive branch, sanctioned by court con-

nivance. Most of these have tended to cancel the restraints originally placed on the power of the Federal government so that
the truth exceeds the humor in Mr. Dooley's conclusion that "th'
Constitution iv th' United States is applicable on'y in such cases
as it is applied to on account iv its applicability."

William Allen White has not been so long with the angels that
he has been forgotten by men. He was much more than the
Walter Lippmann or James Reston of his day, for he was far
more versatile and influential. He purchased the small newspaper
in his hometown in 1895 and his editorials in the Emporia *Daily*
and *Weekly Gazette* became famous throughout the country.
White was also the author of successful novels, short stories,
essays, and biographies. He was a liberal, somewhat, but not too
far, to the right of the Populists. In his *Masks in A Pageant,*
White wrote of himself this warning footnote: "Again the reader
should be warned that this book is written by a convinced liberal." (1, p 311) As a liberal, White's thoughts on the courts are
significant.

Depending upon the politics of the moment when they were
appointed and the politics of the moment when their judgment
is exercised, judges and justices may be somewhat more conservative or somewhat more radical than the general mood throughout
the country. Over the years, in spite of fleeting variances, the
courts do reflect changes in what the majority of the people seem
to believe. White cites numerous reversals and changes in Supreme Court decisions to prove this point, and concludes: "Moreover, in every case the court, whether consciously or not, was
following what, according to its lights, seemed to be real justice in
the matter; and because courts are human, it is more likely that
the court took its color of the right and wrong of the matter
from its environment, from the newspapers and magazines it
read, from men it met, from the public sentiment it felt. And in
so far as American convictions are deep-rooted, the courts—even
our Supreme Court—can not escape from these convictions, and
so ultimately the will of the people will prevail." (8, p 221)

White recognized and, one must conclude from his writing,
approved of the liberal view that there is nothing amiss in the
determination of justice by popular vote, that a government by
men is more desirable than a government by law. But he shows

himself not to be the complete liberal when he adds, "And the slowness of the courts to respond to public sentiment is the one real—though at times amply disguised-blessing of this government." (8, p 189)

The courts, according to White, "mark the bound beyond which democracy at any given time may not trespass. The bounds marked by the courts are changing. They are not the same yesterday, today and forever. And even though the Constitution is not formally amended, its interpretation changes as the people grow intellectually . . . The Constitution is amended by interpretation more than by formal amendment . . . Men take the color of their times. And the courts are men." (8, p 189)

Many judges, no less than most politicians, reflect the currently popular thinking, or at least what the opinion makers lead the judges to believe is the current popular thinking. The courts, instead of safeguarding us from the tyranny of the majority, play a major role in enforcing that tyranny when restraints on government power are weakened.

Only where the powers of government are strictly limited is an unlimited franchise safe. This is so partly because of the tyrannical notion that the majority is always right and can do no wrong. Such a concept ignores the fact that as the bonds on government power are loosened the majority choices become more and more tainted by ignorance, greed, and neglect. Furthermore, the majority is increasingly influenced by clever application of new means of communication to old propaganda techniques and to new techniques of propaganda applied to old means of communication. George Caleb Bingham's politicians who won elections with the aid of free whisky and hard cider have been replaced by a more cunning breed playing for higher stakes as restrictions which formerly limited government are broken down. Even as long ago as the turn of the century, before propaganda skills reached their present state, the voters almost chose William Jennings Bryan, a man of colossal ignorance, for president.

It is frightening to think that such a man was three times nominated by his party and three times came close to wielding the awesome power of the presidency. In every campaign, including his first in 1896, Bryan received more votes as a Democratic candidate than did Wilson, the Democratic winner in 1912. Had television or radio been available to Bryan he would doubtless have been the majority's choice.

Frederick Lewis Allen in *The Big Change, America Transforms Itself, 1900-1950*, describes Bryan with sympathy.

"Bryan was no demagogue," wrote Allen, "but a genuine lover of the people, a good man, an honest man, a natural defender of human rights. He had a shallow and opinionated mind, but he also had a magical gift of speech. In those days when there was no radio and no television and when oratory was a widely appreciated art, there was no one who could hold and sway an audience as Bryan could . . . when Bryan began they listened with skepticism; and how the organ tones of his glorious great voice and the rise and fall of his rhetorical cadences so captures them that when, at last, he came to the end of his peroration, they found themselves hardly able to move their cramped muscles: for two hours they had sat motionless under the spell of his tongue." (9, pp 19-20) Bryan later charmed the old ladies and gentlemen on the Chatauqua circuit. No doubt he was better qualified for that than he was for the presidency. It is appalling to think of what television, radio, and the press, with the help of their biases, could have done in the past and what they may hold for us in the future. Very depressing. If for no other reason than to counter the leverage of the communications media, the power of the Federal government should be contracted rather than expanded.

In addition to the defeated Bryan, consider the characters of some of the men who were not defeated. When you read what their friends as well as their enemies wrote about them, their frailties, foibles and fallibility come through. Teddy Roosevelt has been described as impulsive, boyishly immature, inconsistent, and a showman. Taft, in spite of his sunny disposition, was a first-class hater and stubborn. Wilson was said to have a tempermental instability and eventually knifed every man who had helped him along the way. He was an opportunist, void of conviction and indifferent to consistency. Harding lacked high or lofty morals, Coolidge was described as an opportunist and negative character. Hoover was considered a marvelous self-advertiser and publicity expert, Roosevelt II was a dabbler in revolution who understood neither revolution nor history and was bored by economics. And so on. Human were all these presidents and politicians. The same or worse descriptions could be applied to most of us. It is for this very reason, the humaneness of all politicians, that the power of government should be held in fear. At the same time we should rejoice that every few years we have the opportunity to exchange old rascals for new ones.

Remember, too, the words of that early-day liberal, William Allen White, who wrote: "Sometimes at the top in politics, the deadening sense of power callouses the qualities which give men leadership; the practice of omnipotence would make a tyrant of an angel." (1, p 417)

CHAPTER 2

LIBERALS, LIBERTARIANS, AND LAISSEZ-FAIRE

Modern liberals are not liberals at all. They are the descendants of Lord Byron who managed to work up a feverish hatred of kings but never learned to love the peasants. The new liberals are also hypocrites. They detest the wealthy, professing to love the common man, that fellow in the local tavern to whom most would never condescend to speak. They are really pseudo-liberals who have appropriated the name of a respectable philosophy which was popular during parts of the 18th and 19th centuries. The appropriation of names reminds one of the Communists for whom oppression has become freedom, dictatorship democracy, and slavery liberation. A recent absurdity of this kind is illustrated by the Kent State chemistry professor who, in Michener's *Kent State: What Happened and Why*, described himself as a "libertarian communist." A libertarian communist is as impossible as dry water or a universal solvent. Nevertheless, let us acquiesce to the perversion of current usage and call them henceforth, not pseudo-liberals, but liberals, although that we know they are not. *Pseudo-liberals* is awkward, but there is no suitable, printable four-letter substitute.

The moral bankruptcy of liberalism is shown by a quote from Eric Goldman's *The Tragedy of Lyndon Johnson:*

"Many of his (*Goldwater's*) speeches (*during the 1964 campaign*) sounded like those of a man who would much rather be right or at least a man, pretty sure he was not going to be President who saw no reason why he should not take the opportunity to be right." (10, p 220) The liberals, of whom Goldman is representative, have tried to picture "being right" as a sin, or if not a sin, as something stupid.

Something, too, is shown by liberal attempts to make John F.

Kennedy appear as an intellectual of refined tastes, when, in fact, he was a man who was predominantly pedestrian in his likes and dislikes. Victor Lasky, no liberal, told the story in his *J. F. K. The Man and The Myth:*

"The gulf between Jacqueline Kennedy and her in-laws was indicated by a 1960 yachting party: Jacqueline, Prince and Princess Radziwill—and Jack—sat in the stern partaking of *oeufs en gelee avec vin rosé:* while assorted Kennedys sprawled in the bow, munching on peanut butter sandwiches and cokes." No doubt Jack would have preferred the bow.

Lasky also reported:

"Jacqueline was crazy about the arts. Jack, however, never could dig all that cultural jazz. His wife's arty friends annoyed him, and he made no secret of his annoyance . . . The evenings really got rough when Jacqueline and her guests would converse in some foreign language. . . . In entertainment, Jack's tastes ran to big, gaudy musicals and horse operas . . . Jack was strictly a meat-and-potato man . . ." (11, p 261) You'd never guess it from reading the popular liberal columnists.

The writers who would commonly be classed as liberals embrace a statist philosophy. They generally believe that the organized coercion of government is the universal cure for all of men's problems. They have little or no faith in anyone's ability to act wisely in his own interest. Their gloom and pessimism is shown by the titles of their books and papers: *The Ordeal of Power, The Tragedy of Lyndon Johnson, The Crucial Decade, The Decline and Fall of American Foreign Policy, The United States in the World Arena,* etc, etc. They would be likely to title a book on the toilet training of children *The Crisis of Movement: A Pressing Problem,* and no doubt they would recommend more Federal aid as the solution to the problem.

The liberal writers are also impossible to please. This is not because of any principle or philosophy or conviction. For people who have adopted situation ethics as a standard there can be little room left for convictions. Their perpetual dissatisfaction must arise from other sources. Perhaps it is a form of self-righteousness born of a feeling that they stand close to the Lord (which seems anomalous since most of them have declared Him dead). Their grouchy dispositions have led them to assault Truman, Eisenhower, Taft, Goldwater, Kennedy, Johnson, Humphrey, and Nixon. Surely a few of these victims are also on the side of the Lord and could be called liberal. No doubt even Adlai Stevenson would have suffered the same abuse had he been unlucky enough to have become president.

As an example of liberal cussedness reflect upon Professor James Tobin's article: "The Eisenhower Economy and National Security: Defense, Dollars, and Doctrines," which appeared originally in the *Yale Review* (v XLVII, no. 3, Mar 1958, pp 321-324). Tobin approvingly reports a *New Yorker* cartoon showing a wife and husband talking together.

"It's a great week for everybody," says the wife. "The Russians have the intercontinental ballistic missile and we have the Edsel."

Tobin then proceeds to attack the Eisenhower administration for cutting the defense budget. (12, p 138) Yet it is the liberals, with an assist from the Communists, who have fought against the development and deployment of the anti-ballistic missile.

"The United States," wrote Tobin, "turned its back on the concept of limited wars, and on maintenance of costly manpower and conventional armaments to fight them. Taken seriously, the policy greatly reduces our freedom of action in case of local Communist aggression as in Korea."

Yet it is the liberals, again with Communist help, who mounted the drive to make us abandon our fight against local Communist aggression in Vietnam.

"For the defense of North America against nuclear attack from the air, the government has done almost nothing," wrote Tobin.

Yet it is the liberals who have come to fight defense appropriations most doggedly and who make noises about the need "to re-order our priorities."

Nevertheless the liberal writers include some fine craftsmen. They are interesting, humorous (in spite of the titles they choose for their books), sarcastic, light, powerful, and skillful. Only poor old Walter Lippmann, who has done us all a favor by retiring, was dull and ponderous. Perhaps he munched on a mouthful of dry oatmeal as he wrote, or perhaps it was the peanut butter sticking to his upper plate in later years. But Lippmann was not typical. Liberal writers are sharp observers and some of their observations are worth reading and noting.

The liberal policies which have been so warmly embraced by the country have failed miserably in many ways. By 1970 it was clear that political paralysis would again prevent the government from following monetary and fiscal policies which would have stopped inflation. Inflation has been the means by which liberals have achieved the booms of the last forty years, postponing inevitable adjustments and inviting worse catastrophes in the long run. Although for two years Richard Nixon made an effort to return to honesty in fiscal and monetary affairs, the effort was hastily abandoned after the mid-term elections of 1970 and the growing business slowdown. Inflation is here to stay and grow worse as long as the people fail to recognize that only the government can inflate the currency. When ordinary citizens try the same thing it is called counterfeiting.

The political paralysis which insures that inflation will continue derives from economic ignorance, from living on the myths of the past and failing to face the reality of the future. Prices tend to rise on the upside of a business cycle. The prices of raw materials, finished goods, hiring money (interest), labor, and management all increase. On the downside of the cycle reverse price movements tend to occur, and will occur, in areas where there is free competition. The more free is the competition the slower will be the adjustment on the upside and the faster on the downside. In the market areas mentioned above, the labor market is the one with the least freedom of competition. Through the efforts of unions, wage rates in most manufacturing enterprises are rigidly fixed. In many non-unionized enterprises the wage rates are fixed by minimum wage laws. Thus during the downward adjustment of business the prices of materials, management, goods and hiring money can and do fall. The government plays with interest rates, but apart from this, only wage rates remain rigidly high, immobilized by the near monopoly powers of organized labor. This being the case, the price of labor remains too high relative to the prices of the other factors of production. When the cost of something is too high it is not purchased—and this is as true of labor as it is of anything else. Therefore, workers are laid off. This is politically unacceptable. The only way the price of labor can be brought back into line is to inflate the currency, which has the effect of reducing real wages even though minimal wages are fixed. As real wages fall it again becomes profitable to rehire labor, and politicians face the next election with no more than mild nervousness.

Inflation is hard on creditors, and the term *creditors* includes anyone to whom others have obligations, such as persons with savings in the bank, persons with life insurance, and persons with bonds in safe-deposit boxes. *Creditors* also includes those on fixed income, pensions, or nearly fixed incomes such as social security beneficiaries.

Inflation is a form of taxation of capital. It has been called the cruelest tax of all because of its impact on creditors and because it is so well hidden. It strikes most viciously at the thrifty. Its magnitude is not recognized by most Americans.

"In the years from 1929 to 1933," states a report of the American Institute for Economic Research (Economic Education Bulletin, v IX, no. 8, Sept. 1969), "nearly 40 per cent (about 9,000) banks failed in the United States. The losses to the depositors totaled about $1.3 billion. Loud were the lamentations and allegedly devastating were the consequences."

"Since World War II," the report continues, "nearly $500 billion real wealth has been embezzled from American citizens as continued inflating (to September of 1969) has 'robbed', to use Mr. Nixon's term, them of a substantial portion of their savings, including the cash values of their insurance. If one were to include the loss in the buying power of the face value of life insurance policies, the loss would be nearly doubled.

"Losses in the three decades of *nearly 400* times the losses attributable to bank failures during the Great Depression, and losses in the current year (1969) 50 times the 1929 to 1933 . . . losses have been realized." Since 1969 the situation has grown worse.

The ultra-leftist liberals, Professors Gettleman and Mermelstein, wrote on the first page of their interesting book *The Great Society Reader: The Failure of American Liberalism* that "the Great Society is the self-conscious successor to John Kennedy's New Frontier, Harry Truman's Fair Deal, Franklin Roosevelt's New Deal, Woodrow Wilson's New Freedom and Theodore Roosevelt's New Nationalism." (13, p 1)

Many who think of themselves as Republicans, and therefore as conservatives, might agree with this genealogy if Teddy Roosevelt's New Nationalism had been left out. But not only are the authors correct to include Teddy Roosevelt's contribution (more commonly known as the Square Deal) as we shall see, but they should also have included Herbert Hoover's contributions, as we shall also see. The first resolute steps down the path of Federal statism were taken during the years of Roosevelt I. It was under Teddy Roosevelt that trust busting, control of the railroads, pure food and drug laws, the Employee Liability Act, and the establishment of the Department of Commerce and Labor were listed as accomplishments.

Do not be misled by the subtitle of Gettleman and Mermelstein's book: *The Failure of American Liberalism*. They are not libertarians who frown on liberalism. In the eyes of Gettleman and Mermelstein, American liberalism has failed because it did not go far enough, not because it went too far. In the eyes of a libertarian, its very existence is a mistake.

The author-editors have assembled an artful piece, cleverly packaged to trap the naive. This is reflected in the title itself. It should be kept in mind that these unabashed pro-Marxist editors served as organizers and officers of the extreme left radical Socialist Scholars Conference.

Gettleman and Mermelstein are professors of history and economics respectively, which has an interesting bearing on the common charge that radicalism in the United States originates with teachers rather than with students. At the time their book was published one or both of them had been on the staffs of the Polytechnic Institute of Brooklyn, Hunter College, Columbia, and Fairleigh Dickinson University.

There is always the danger when one becomes enamored of an idea or a philosophy that not only would it be nice for others to share it, it would be even nicer if they could be *forced* to share it. This has led philosophers, economists, and women's liberationists astray in the past. Take, for instance, the case of Count Henri de Saint-Simon.

Saint-Simon was a most unusual Frenchman. He fought in the American Revolution, proposed a canal to join the Atlantic and the Pacific, made a fortune as a land speculator, lost it, and spent the last years of his life as a philosophical writer on economics and other subjects. Saint-Simon is best remembered as the founder of French Socialism, something which occurred in the final eleven years of his life (after he had lost his fortune). Until this metamorphosis Saint-Simon had been a classical liberal, the antithesis of his later position.

Eight years before he died, Saint-Simon wrote a statement of principle which has become a fundamental tenet of Socialists, Communists, Fascists, and welfare statists.

"The philosophers," goes Saint-Simon's terrifying little statement, "of the nineteenth century will show the necessity of making all children study the same code of this world's morality, since the similarity of positive moral ideas is the one link that can unite men in society and since nothing but the perfection of the system of positive morality can bring about the perfecting of the social state." (14, p 34)

Presumably, under Saint-Simon's thesis, the state will first determine what is and what isn't moral. It will then legislate morality and enforce its conclusions, perhaps through Federal Child Care Centers. Morality will have been reduced to a political issue.

John Dewey restated Saint-Simon's tyranny nearly one-hundred years later. In *My Pedagogic Creed* (1897) he advocated as a primary goal of education the destruction of the child's individualistic traits. It is likely that William Allen White was familiar with Dewey's thinking, for by 1904 Dewey had tried his experiments at the University of Chicago and was en route to Columbia University's Teachers College. In *The Old Order Changeth* (1910) White, who was somewhat of a statist liberal, resurrected Saint-Simon's ideas: "Therefore . . . the first obligation upon those who would change the trend of our American democracy from the worship of property rights to the rights of men (*one wonders who, if not men, can have property rights*) should not be to change the laws and reform the courts; the first obligation of reformers should be to go to the bottom and make men and women who can think and feel and act justly and unselfishly. The mainspring of democracy is in the schools . . . If democracy is to go forward, it must begin to move in the schools of the country." (8, p 192)

William Allen White supported a scheme for paying parents for the loss of family income which resulted from a child going to school rather than working.

"A few states," wrote White in 1910, "notably in Ohio, make provision for the reimbursement of parents for the time children are in school. And eventually all the states must come to that plan. For the pittance that the child can earn is so little compared with the need of the state for that child's judgment formed by a trained mind in making public sentiment when he is grown, that it is folly to haggle over the expense account." (8, p 192)

The reference to "the need of the state" is bone chilling to the anti-statist. Reformers who write of "the need of the state" are, unwittingly perhaps, first cousins to every dictator and despot who ever lived.

The libertarian system operates at a disadvantage because, in truth, it is not a system at all. It is more nearly the antithesis of a system. The true libertarian believes in passing along his ideas only to those willing to receive them. Once he starts to force his doctrine on nonlibertarians, he ceases to be a libertarian. The pure libertarian, even if he could bring himself to justify public schools, could never agree to the teaching of his ideas while excluding contrary concepts. Not so the statists, and the stronger their interventionist tendencies the more rigid is their exclusion of competing philosophies. In communist and fascist countries the concepts of libertarianism, classical economic liberalism, and truly representative government are suppressed. The statists recognize the paradoxical weakness of libertarianism which makes it recoil from suppression of competing ideas. The statists, particularly the communists, favor the dissemination only of information which has state approval. Less militant statists may give lip service to freedom of expression but manage to control and manipulate the nongovernmental organs of power, such as the press, television, schools, and churches, so that a continuous barrage of interventionist propaganda drowns out hostile voices.

The libertarian philosophy also operates at a disadvantage because it presents another paradox. The basis of libertarianism is a strong desire to be left alone accompanied by an equally strong willingness to leave others alone. This would maximize freedom in a world occupied solely by libertarians. But the world is not

occupied solely by libertarians. Minding one's business is not
looked upon as a virtue by millions of militants. The libertarian
impulse to leave others alone puts his philosophy at a disadvantage since by not interfering with other people he in effect
abandons the field to the activists who make the most noise and
kick up the most dust. If the libertarian too actively promotes his
philosophy he is in danger of violating his philosophy.

In addition, libertarianism suffers from another cause: it operates from an unfavorable public relations base. If the libertarian
resists government encroachment upon what he feels is his right
to be left alone, he must oppose the proposals of the statist. Thus,
he is often accused of being against—against old folks, against
poor folks, against widows, against orphans, against education,
against, in short, progress. The statists have made it a sin to be
against whatever they propose, since they claim all rights and
title to progress. When asked by the statist what the libertarian
proposes as an alternative to the latest save-the-world scheme, the
answer is likely to be a shocking "Nothing!" He would leave
individuals and voluntary groups of people solve the problem
without government interference. He is against the government
coercing some individuals to solve the problems of others, for
such coercion is the essence of utopianism. His advocacy of
doing nothing is an advocacy of the *government* doing nothing,
not an advocacy that nothing be done. He is really advocating
the application of the ingenuity and energy of individuals and
voluntary groups of individuals to the improvement of mankind.
He is encouraging at the same time a rebirth of the charitable
impulses in human beings, impulses which have been atrophied by
the tax collector's long arm and grasping hand.

Walter Lippmann was known chiefly as a writer, but his real
ability was as a mental acrobat. He has been known at one time
or another, and sometimes simultaneously, to have been a Socialist,
conservative, liberal, New Dealer, internationalist, isolationist, and
perhaps even a Dukhobor. What other man can boast such spectacular mental agility? It is this quality which made it possible
for the former president of Harvard's Socialist Club to write a
defense of the free market of which almost any libertarian would
be proud. Read the 1943 post-Harvard Lippmann.

"And so I insist that collectivism, which replaces the free market by coercive centralized authority is reactionary in the exact sense of the word . . . in Russia . . . there have been two attempts to establish socialism, and two retreats, one in 1921 and another in 1931, from a planned and directed economy to an economy directed by the market. The first retreat was by Lenin in 1921 and was known as the New Economic Policy. It was regarded as a temporary repeal of communism. The second retreat was by Stalin in 1931 when he reintroduced differential wages, the conduct of enterprises for profit, the personal responsibility of licensed management, called 'socialist ownership', trading in open shops. Communism is now (*1943*) outlawed in Russia, its adherents being known as Trotskyites.

". . . the new mode of production (i.e. division of labor using sophisticated machines and capital) can not be made to operate, even by omnipotent dictators over a docile terrorized people, without re-establishment of at least relatively free markets . . . so when advanced nations adopt collectivism and its inevitable corrollary, the self-contained economy, they are doomed to a descending standard of life and are driven to unspeakable brutality in order to crush the ensuing discontent.

". . . there is no way of practising the division of labor and the harvesting of fruits of it, except in a social order which preserves and strives to protect the freedom of the market.

". . . the kind of revolution which would make obsolete the market economy would be a series of inventions which enabled men by their own self-sufficient effort to achieve a more satisfactory standard of life than they now aspire to . . . or it might be done by a medicine which would make men cease to want the diversified products of modern industry." (15, pp 205-209)

The last comment seems, some thirty years after it was written, to have prophesied the coming of the drug culture!

Walter Lippmann in 1935 was arguing for statism and more intervention in private affairs. From his lectures came his booklet *The New Imperative* in which he gave a liberal's concept of what is meant by *laissez-faire*. His comments, even libertarians would agree, fairly represent what the term meant then and what it means today.

The believers in *laissez faire* "recognize," wrote Lippmann, "the government has certain duties to perform, that it must defend the frontiers against aggression (*the liberals and the liber-tarians both agreed on this in the forties, but by 1970 the liberals seem to have abandoned this belief*) and domestic violence (*something the liberals seem to have traded for permissiveness since 1935*), that it must provide social services, such as education (*laissez-faireists of libertarian persuasion disagree*), that it must regulate many abuses (*such as fraud*). They hold it has no function to perform in governing the national economy as a whole, either to maintain it in a working equilibrium or to see to it that its products are well distributed. They insist that the vital balance is automatically self-regulating and that deliberate policy in regard to it is meddlesome, expensive, and subversive.

"On the major issues of the world they believe in masterly inactivity. This is the ideal that they would have schools and colleges profess. To the young men asking how they would save their country—how they can mitigate booms and depressions, maintain a healthy relation between agriculture and industry, conserve and develop the natural resources, prevent the congestion of population and prevent the concentration of wealth and power, the orthodox answer must be that these matters are not the concern of the state and that the only sound policy is to have no policy." (3, pp 42-43)

The statist movement has grown in the three and one-half decades since Lippmann described and attacked *laissez-faireism*. Although the growth of statism has not always been at a steady rate, there has not been any significant reversal of the trend. What have been the results of the increasing intervention Lippmann urged on the young collegians to whom he revealed the new imperative in 1935? Have we learned, as urged by Lippmann, to mitigate booms and depressions, maintain healthy relationships between agriculture and industry, conserve and develop natural resources, prevent congestion of the population and concentration of wealth and power? And if so, what price has been paid?

The Great Depression was not banished by the kind of intervention Lippmann had in mind, for this type of intervention was tried for more than eight years without success. The Great Depression was liquidated by the second World War. Since then we have had numerous depressions. True, none of them have been as severe as the Great One, and they have been given a more politically palatable name: recession. But what price have we paid? The 1950 depression was, like its predecessor, liquidated by a war and rearmament. (This is not to say that the war was not justified.) Successive depressions have been overcome by inflation-inspired booms brought on by massive Federal deficit spending. Each recession has been followed by a new burst of inflation. Inflation, if it follows the course of past inflations in other countries will accelerate until the ultimate collapse. Great turmoil and hardship far worse than any depression will follow. Then the claim will be made that laissez-faire capitalism has failed. It will in reality have been state-controlled capitalism that has failed, not *laissez-faire* capitalism which was long ago abandoned. Inflation transfers wealth from capital accumulation and replacement to consumption. Possibly technological advances will raise productivity enough to offset this increased consumption of wealth, but if this is not the case, the standard of living will fall as capital is consumed and not replaced.

How have we fared in regard to maintaining a balance between agriculture and industry? Federal intervention has been mainly directed at control of agricultural production so that farm prices would remain high. In order to do this farmers have been subsidized and have lost some of their freedom in the process. They have also been encouraged to remain "down on the farm" where they have continued to produce unneeded crops. This represents wasted manpower and natural resources which would either have been conserved or diverted to more useful purposes had intervention been avoided and free-market forces allowed to operate.

How about conservation and development of natural resources? The libertarian is specially troubled by the ravaging of resources to which there must be common title: air and water. Here the government should have intervened in force long ago, but being so preoccupied with matters beyond its legitimate interests it has failed to concern itself with pollution and waste. We are now faced with unpleasant and possibly future dangerous contamination of air and water supplies by the unchecked disposal of consumer and industrial wastes. It is worth pointing out here, that where ownership of something is shared by all it is likely to be abused by many and cared for by few. It is so with air and water to which private title can not be assigned. This principle should serve as a warning of the hazards of public ownership. What the public owns the public will profane.

Have we prevented the concentration of wealth and power with which Mr. Lippmann was so concerned? There are really two separate questions here, one involving wealth and the other power. In regard to the concentration of wealth is there any legitimate reason to prevent its concentration? In regard to power, it is contrary to *laissez-faire* principles to permit anyone to concentrate power at the expense of others: all men must be equal before the law. To put it another way, power acquired by political means is unacceptable to libertarians beyond the power needed for government to perform its minimum functions. But to return to wealth, wealth acquired by legitimate means in the absence of fraud and by the voluntary exchange of goods or services should, according to the principles of *laissez-faire* remain in the possession of the acquisitor until he desires to dispose of it as and how he sees fit. The interventionists have been successful in preventing accumulations of wealth comparable to the fortunes made at the turn of the century. No one today can earn and keep a yearly income of $23,000,000 as Andrew Carnegie did in 1900. Punitive taxation far beyond the amounts needed for what libertarians regard as the proper functions of government have prevented duplication of Carnegie's feat. But the graduated income tax which has accomplished this economic levelling of wealth has pyramided enormous concentrations of power in Washington. The power concentrated in the Federal government is far more threatening to more people than any power wielded by Carnegie, the Morgans, Ford or Frick. Furthermore, a government functioning as libertarians would wish it to function would permit no special political power to result from concentration of wealth.

Nor has interventionism prevented congestion and deterioration of the cities about which Mr. Lippmann spoke in the thirties. Through liberalized welfare programs it has encouraged the movement of large numbers of negroes from the South to the North. Welfare programs that were intended to care for local needy now offer support to persons for which taxpayers of a given locality did not previously have responsibility. As a result the cities are near bankruptcy, congestion is worse than ever, slums are growing faster than subsidized housing programs can replace them, and Mayor Lindsay has become a Democrat. Negroes who were said to be miserable in the South seem to be not much less so in the North. Additionally, rent control, where it has been adopted, has kept rents down to the point where property can not be profitably maintained, contributing to the slum problem.

The Federal government has throttled the railroads by its action in the field of labor relations and by its rulings requiring the continuation of unprofitable service. The railroads, like the cities, face or are already in bankruptcy. The story has been told in detail elsewhere. (16) The government has subsidized air transportation, paid for in part by taxes collected from the railroads and from persons who have never flown and will probably never fly. (17, pp 273-286) Having aided in slaying rail passenger service Octopus Federalis is now trying to revive it by Amtrak subsidies. The government has subsidized housing and the housing shortage is worse than at any time since World War II. In the five years between 1923 and 1927 when the population of the country was about half of what it was in the five years between 1960 and 1970, the housing industry built 860,000 dwelling units per year. (18, p 96) Between 1960 and 1970, "helped" by subsidies, urban renewal programs, and subsidized mortgages and rents, the housing industry built about 1,380,000 units each year. (*U.S. News and World Report*, v LXX, no. 5, Feb 1, 1971.) In terms of doubling the population in the years compared, we have been falling behind by about 340,000 units per year.

The Federal government has intervened in science and engineering. Billions have been spent on the space program and the experts (who have a conflict of interest since they benefit from it) tell us about the enormous benefits which have resulted from the research and development needed to put a man on the moon. The results are truly spectacular, including the overproduction of PhD's, engineers and scientists. Many are unemployed or working at jobs for which other training or education might have better prepared them. None of the experts who proclaim the benefits has assessed, in fact none can assess, the actual cost of the benefits. Therefore, it can not be determined if the same benefits might not have been achieved at lower cost by using other methods.

The Federal government has massively intervened in subsidizing education, and it appears to have contributed to school problems. Teacher training has been pushed by all kinds of Federal aid and in 1971-1972 there was a huge surplus of school teachers. It seems that whenever the government intervenes, some economic forces are stimulated and others are thwarted, economic distortion occurs, and an unexpected economic blight results.

Is it any wonder that the policy of libertarians is to do nothing?

The libertarian believes that in addition to the government's legitimate duty to provide protection against domestic violence and fraud there is a paired obligation to protect the nation from the attacks and threats of foreign predators. This obligation does not require the United States to see to the establishment of freely elected governments throughout the world. Nor does it require the United States to include among its exports democracy, republicanism, capitalism, libertarianism, or Rotarianism. The sole responsibility of the government should be to protect such liberties as remain in our country from the designs of other countries, at the same time that it expands liberty within our borders. Such a foreign policy would see us at times allied with despotic governments, dictatorships, and other unsavory movements, *when these alliances provide support of our own efforts to combat systems of greater danger to our own security*. Such a foreign policy will be called cynical by idealistic critics, and practical by more sensible realists. In any event it is not new. It has been practiced by the United States and other countries in the past. Such a policy, however, is not without risks and when approached recklessly can result in disaster.

The alliance with the Soviet Union in World War II was an example of this policy in practice. The great and immediate threat to our security in 1941 was clearly the Rome-Berlin-Tokyo coalition. The despotism of the Axis powers was no more or less vicious than that centered in Moscow. Such considerations should not enter into the choosing of sides. The significant difference was the relative strength of the two opposing despotisms and their relative threat to our security. The Axis was far stronger and potentially much more dangerous than the USSR. To be sure, the alliance with the Russians involved elements of accident rather than design, but it resulted in the elimination of the immediate major threat. Our initial failures in post-war foreign policy resulted from the failure to recognize that once the war was over our Communist ally would replace the Axis as the immediate and major threat. General Patton recognized this, but his voice was that of a man among the babble of children who deluded themselves with the romantic idea that the Communists were friends rather than allies. There is a difference.

The blame for post-war policy failures rests largely with Franklin Roosevelt and those who advised him. It is greatly to Harry Truman's credit that he at once recognized true Soviet aims. His reversal of our country's course was amazingly fast considering the suddenness with which he had to deal with the problem and the complete failure of his predecessor to prepare him for his task.

Examples of the type of disaster which is likely to result from a failure to follow a sensible foreign policy are our dealings with China in the '40's and Cuba in the '50's. With regard to China we abandoned a government which was alleged to be a corrupt oligarchy, allowing the power to fall into the hands of a ruthless Communist dictatorship. Even if it is assumed that allegations against Nationalist China were true, this government posed, relative to the regime which succeeded it, no threat to our security. Based on this, it is obvious that the United States should have continued its alliance with the Nationalists.

The error in China was repeated in Cuba ten years later. The United States withdrew support from Batista's dictatorship, which offered a minimal threat to our security, thus making possible the Castro dictatorship. Communism thus gained a foothold in the Americas. Our interests clearly rested with Batista regardless of any sympathy we may have had for Cubans under his misrule. As it has turned out, the repression, torturing, and murdering under Communist rule in both Cuba and China have been far worse than under the regimes which preceded them. This is not unexpected since the Communists have replaced the Nazis as the world's most efficient extermination service.

United States' post-war foreign policy, by failing to recognize that it is at times necessary to support undemocratic governments, has managed to replace imperfect governments with appalling governments. At the same time we have permitted the establishment of Communist staging areas in the Americas and in China.

Libertarians, like all sensible human beings, abhor war. Nevertheless, they are committed to a policy by which the nation has an obligation to defend itself against foreign marauders. Although no polls have been taken it is likely that most libertarians support United States' action against Communist aggression in Vietnam. Those who oppose American action claim that the Communists in Vietnam do not pose a danger to the United States. It is true that there is no direct threat, but the indirect threat is very real and very great. This conclusion is supported by the views of George F. Kennan, one-time ambassador to Moscow and generally held to be a liberal rather than a libertarian.

Kennan was the author of the containment policy from which the Truman doctrine developed, and for which Kennan was severely attacked by anti-Communists. Criticism of the containment policy was based upon its acceptance of the status quo: the illegal occupation and domination by the USSR of its Western neighbors. Nevertheless, Kennan's February 22, 1946 cable from Moscow to the State Department was accurate in predicting Communist behavior in the 'fifties and 'sixties, as quoted by B. J. Bernstein and A. J. Matusow in *The Truman Administration: A Documentary History.* (19)

Kennan stated that the Communist apparatus would "undermine the general political and strategic potential of major western powers. Efforts will be made to disrupt national self-confidence, to hamstring measures of national defense, to increase social and industrial unrest, to stimulate all forms of disunity. All persons with grievances, whether economic or racial, will be urged to seek redress not in mediation and compromise, but in defiant struggle for destruction of other elements of society. Here poor will be set against the rich, black against white, young against old, newcomers against established residents, etc."

In his message Kennan listed a variety of "national associations or bodies which can be dominated or influenced by Communist penetration. These include: labor unions, youth leagues, women's organizations, racial societies, religious societies, social organizations, cultural groups, liberal magazines, publishing houses, etc."

"In foreign countries," Kennan cabled, "Communists will, as a rule, work toward destruction of all forms of personal independence, economic, political, or moral. Their system can handle only individuals who have been brought into complete dependence on higher power . . ."

". . . particularly violent efforts will be made to weaken power and influence of western powers on colonial, backward, or independent peoples. On this level, no holds will be barred." (*Witness what has happened in Algeria, Egypt and the Suez Canal, Indo-China and other former colonies, and in China, Korea, and Cuba.*)

Knowing Communists as well as he did, it was surprising that Kennan defended Oppenheimer at the latter's security hearings. Yet, when he testified, Kennan stated that the Soviets "would have continued to lay their greatest hopes for the expansion of their power on police weapons, the capacity to absorb contiguous areas (*as they have done in eastern Europe, in Korea, and as they are trying to do in Indo-China*), and on the conventional armaments as a means of intimidating other people and perhaps fighting if they have to fight." (19, pp 207-208)

The charge is often made that the Vietnamese War is a civil war and as such the United States should not become involved. We are said to be immoral imperialists and so on. Similar charges were made regarding earlier U.S. foreign actions many years before. Eisenhower, writing about the Lebanese occupation of 1958 stated that "Sam Rayburn (*then Speaker of the House*) was fearful that we might be getting into something that was strictly a civil war. Most skeptical of all was (*Senator*) Fulbright, who seemed to doubt seriously that this crisis was Communist inspired . . . Congressman John M. Vorys . . . reminded the group that the Soviets had claimed back in 1947 that the Greek conflict, to which the United States had committed so much material and advisory help, was also nothing but a civil war." (20, p 272)

From the standpoint of the United States, intervention or non-intervention should not rest upon whether a conflict is or is not a civil war. There can conceivably be civil wars which would not call for United States action. These would be civil wars for which there was no Communist inspiration and from which no Communist gains could evolve, a prospect which has become increasingly unlikely since the end of World War II. The significant determinant is whether as a result of inaction by the United States the chances of Communist gain are improved. Not significant is the issue of whether the action does or does not involve a civil war. It is useless to protest Senator Fulbright's blindness to the facts for he is not blind. His consistently pro-Communist stands attest to his viewing the world through red-tinted glasses.

As long ago as March 16, 1950 Dean Acheson, who understood Communist strategy better than he knew how to deal with it, wrote in a State Department publication, *Strengthening the Forces of Freedom*, that we could not compromise with the basic theory of international Communism which, according to Acheson, states that "the end justifies the means, that any and all methods are therefore permissible, and that the dignity of the human individual is of no importance as against the interests of the state . . ." (19, p 290) Acheson was paraphrasing the message of the disillusioned Communist Arthur Koestler in Koestler's magnificent novel *Darkness at Noon*.

CHAPTER 3

L'ETAT, C'EST MOI

Statism is the parent of and older than other isms, past, present, and yet to come. On that long-ago day when some hairy primitive proved that he could yell louder and glower more menacingly than other inhabitants of the cave the first tribe surrendered to the first tribal chief and statism was invented. It has dominated the group affairs of most men for most of the time that man has existed on his planet.

The struggle for freedom has been a never-ending fight against the state, a fight which peaked in the late 18th century with the writing of the Constitution. Even with its obvious defect of sanctioning slavery, the Constitution, more than any other written document restricted the powers of a central government by balancing the powers of its three branches and by reserving to the people and the states those powers not specifically granted to the central authority.

Freedom flourished, too, in England during much of the 19th century. At the same time in Italy, in France, in Germany and in the other monarchies of Europe, freedom, though imperfect and fragile, gained ground. Before long, such freedom as existed was soon threatened by socialist ideas. It was in response to these ideas that Bismarck created the first welfare state. Wherever adopted the welfare state has resulted in socialism on the installment plan with loss of freedom as the down payment.

". . . the increasing use of government power," wrote socialist advocates Gettleman and Mermelstein, "does not define socialism." (13, p 122) It doesn't. It does, however, define statism which is the polar opposite of freedom. Statism is the prerequisite of socialism, fascism, national socialism, communism, the welfare state, the Great Society, and the New, Fair, Square, and

Raw Deals and all the other fantasies of political press agents. The main difference between these schemes is the degree of statism which each inflicts on its subjects. For instance, the National Recovery Administration in the days of the New Deal was similar to Il Duce's corporate fascism. Mussolini formed an alliance between business and government by which labor was disciplined and production was controlled and coordinated. Some naive Americans believed that private enterprise was being safeguarded in Italy, when in fact it was diminished to the extent that it relinquished its decision-making powers to the government. The control of, as well as the title to, productive property must remain in private hands if the free market is to function effectively and free enterprise is to flourish. A title to property without control is meaningless. True, the NRA was not Fascism. What distinguished the two was that the NRA relied on more subtle forms of persuasion than large doses of castor oil.

William Allen White in *The Old Order Changeth* described how private corporations, wealthy individuals, and voluntary private groups aided persons in need of financial, legal, or medical help and how private resources were applied to the study of economic and social problems. One glimpses from his account how such problems were attacked in the late nineteenth and early twentieth centuries. One can not help wondering what might have been accomplished had not the reformers, more and more convinced of their infallibility, moved steadily toward increasing government interventions.

White, an ardent reformer himself, did not seem to recognize the significance of his perceptive observation: "The Constitution was meant to suppress clamor, not sentiment; the difference between the two expressions being—broadly—that clamor is the desire to reform someone else, and public sentiment is the desire to reform one's self. Public clamor is essentially selfish—tyrannical. Real public sentiment is essentially unselfish—democratic." (8, p 131)

White's assignment of so personal a quality as sentiment to so impersonal a construction as the public is open to argument. Since White's time public sentiment has been renamed *public opinion*, measurable, supposedly, by public opinion surveys. The validity of this device is questionable since the privacy of one's views are compromised when revealed to a stranger. Under these conditions a person's "private" opinion is tempered by an attempt to conform to what the person thinks others would like him to hold as his private opinion. Public opinion becomes not what many people believe, but what some people believe most other people would like them to believe. The determination of public opinion on many issues is a massive guessing game.

White was also on shaky ground when he stated that "public sentiment is the desire to reform one's self." The desire to reform one's self may be affected by public sentiment, i.e. by what self guesses to be the overwhelming opinions of one's peers, but to equate public sentiment with a private desire is hardly justified. Only a private desire is capable of accomplishing self-reformation. If White meant that the Constitution was intended to suppress the tyrannical desire of some to reform others, but not to suppress the desire to reform one's self, he was on ground that any libertarian would be proud to defend, but it is not the ground that most liberals hold.

"It is the history of our government," wrote White, "that we have always taken over for government use any good thing developed by the people . . . First we have a society or organization; next comes the private establishment securing results; then follows the law, putting the whole matter under the Federal government. Our national government is jealous of large success outside of its domain in any public matter." (8, p 151)

The government, be it local or state, as well as national, is incapable of jealousy which is a feeling that only humans can have. It is the politicians, not government, that become jealous when they see a private solution to any general problem, for they wish to become a party to the success. Private sponsors made brash by the results of their efforts may also conclude that if fifty thousand dollars raised privately can do so much, then fifty million dollars raised by the coercive tax power of the state can do a thousand times more. (It ain't necessarily so!) The voluntary organization then becomes a lobby whose principal function is to act as a pressure group for tax money. At this point, attainment of public subsidy has become more important than the original objective of the private group. ". . . whenever the government finds an organization working unselfishly to an end that is unmistakedly for the common good," wrote White, "that organization eventually becomes a part of the Federal government." (8, p 152) And that's how mighty governments from little nuts grow.

Murray Rothbard, libertarian professor of economics at the Polytechnic Institute of Brooklyn, described the changes which have taken place since Roosevelt I's Square Deal.

"All of these assorted Deals," wrote Rothbard, "constituted a basic and fundamental shift in American life—a shift from a relatively *laissez-faire* economy and minimal state to a society in which the state is unquestionably king. In the previous century, the government could have been safely ignored by almost everyone; now we have become a country in which the government is the great and unending source of power and privilege. Once a country in which each man could by and large make the decisions for his own life, we have become a land where the state holds and exercises life-and-death power over every person, group, and institution . . . government once confined . . . has burst its feeble bonds to dominate us all."

In a footnote, Rothbard adds: "Recent . . . disclosures by economic historians that pure *laissez-faire* did not exist in the 19th century are beside the point; no one ever claimed that it did. The point is that state power in society was minimal, relative to other times and countries, and that the general locus of decision making resided in the individuals making up society rather than in the state." (13, p 503)

(Gettleman and Mermelstein's book, from which the above quote by Rothbard was taken, is a classic example of leftist polemic tactics: it grants token recognition to an anti-statist and sets a trap for the unwary. Rothbard was probably tolerated as an author-contributor, even though he is a libertarian, because he happened to oppose the war in Vietnam and this was the critical leftist issue at the time *The Great Society Reader* was published. One can not help being reminded of the liberals' concept of a balanced panel discussion: one conservative, six liberals and a Marxist moderator. Or a liberal's demonstration of academic freedom: arranging a "distinguished" lecture program which lines up as successive speakers Arthur Schlesinger, Hans Morgenthau, Tom Hayden, Bayard Rustin, Jules Feiffer, Sargent Shriver, Daniel Patrick Moynihan, Gettleman, Mermelstein, and Murray Rothbard (who would probably be booed). Incidentally, this list is a partial list of contributors to *The Great Society Reader*.

Rothbard is the only *one* of almost two dozen authors who does not rate as 110 per cent, or moreso, liberal-leftist.)

The renegade state is the political means by which everyone attempts to live at the expense of everyone else. Rothbard described it this way: "The path which avoids the necessity for production and exchange, is for one or more persons to seize other people's products by the use of physical force. This method of robbing the fruits of another man's production was shrewdly named by Oppenheimer [1] the 'political means'. Throughout history men have been tempted to employ the 'political means' of seizing wealth rather than expend effort in production and exchange. It should be clear that while the market process multiplies production, the exploitative means is parasitic, and as with all parasitic action, discourages and drains off production and output in society. To regularize and order a permanent system of predatory exploitation, men have created the state which Oppenheimer brilliantly defined as 'the organization of the political means.' " In a footnote Rothbard added: "Or as Albert Jay Nock, heavily influenced by Oppenheimer's analysis concluded: 'The state claims and exercises the monopoly of crime' in its territorial area." (13, p 504) For instance, inflating the currency, which, if you and I tried it, would be punishable as counterfeiting, is a state prerogative.

Albert Jay Nock wrote a gem of an essay called "The God's Lookout" which appeared in *Free Speech and Plain Language*. (21) In this essay Nock stated a basic law of human nature: "Man tends always to satisfy his needs and desires with the least possible exertion."

"A candid examination will show," he continued, "that this law is fundamental to any serious study of politics. So long as the state stands as an impersonal mechanism which can confer economic advantage at the mere touch of a button, men will seek by all sorts of ways to get at the button, because law-made property is acquired with less exertion than labor-made property. It is much easier to push the button and get some form of State-created monopoly . . . and pocket the proceeds, than it is to accumulate the same amount by work.

"At the time our government was set up . . . some political

[1] Not Robert! Franz Oppenheimer, *The State*, 1926.

thinkers, notably Franklin (*had the idea*) that it should be no function of the State to intervene upon society's economic life in a positive way, but only negatively as occasion required, to punish fraud and to safeguard the general regime of the contract. Aside from this the State's only function should be that of safeguarding the lives and liberties of its citizens." (21, pp 319-320)

To make statism, or state interventionism, acceptable to a free society an illusion must be created which convinces suitable numbers of voters that they are living at the expense of someone else, that they are getting something for nothing, or that they would be starving to death were it not for kind-hearted politicians in Washington. Thus, we have "free" education, "free" public health services, "free" polio shots, "low cost" housing, rent subsidies, farm price supports, "low cost" mortgages, "low cost" loans for risky small businesses, and on and on. All the "free" and "low cost" benefits the government bestows must be paid for in one way or another—a portion by the people who receive the benefits, a larger portion by those who don't receive them, and, on occasion, still another portion by printing money. The latter is known as inflation and amounts to a tax on any form of savings.

The tariff is a form of benefit bestowed on one portion of the total population and paid for by everyone. This outrageous device receives enough support to keep it going because of the ignorant fears of voters and the pressures of groups who benefit from restrictions on imports. When a tariff is imposed the cost of imports is raised to match or exceed the cost of domestic products, i.e. the prices paid by the consumer are artificially raised by the tariff. More must be paid for domestic products than would have to be paid for equivalent imported goods if the tariff had not been imposed. The benefits of the tariff are bestowed upon the owners and workers in the protected industries. The cost to the public is spread thinly and is hidden. Therefore, those who bear it can not be aroused to the point of organizing resistance to it. At the same time the beneficiaries of the tariff are organized to support actively those politicians who vote for tariffs and to oppose those who take a stand against tariffs.

Some persons who bear the cost of tariffs enjoy other kinds of government largess, paid for by yet others, including the beneficiaries of the tariff. In a parody of "you scratch me and I'll scratch you," the manufacturers subsidize the farmers, the farmers subsidize the railroads and truckers, the railroads and truckers subsidize the airlines, the farmers in the Northeast and West subsidize the farmers in the Tennessee River Valley via the TVA, and so on. Americans are panic-stricken at the thought of what would happen if this system should disappear because they think they could not manage their affairs without "free" benefits. This is an absurd fear. With abolition of the system the need for government help would vanish along with elimination of the taxes from which all benefits flow. Fear and ignorance guarantee the faithful return to power of those politicians who promise the greatest "benefits"—at the expense of fictitious "others".

"Once admit a single positive intervention 'to help business', as our euphemism goes," wrote Albert Jay Nock in 1932, "and one class or group after another will accumulate political power in order to command further interventions; and these interventions will persist in force and frequency until they culminate in a policy of pure Statism—a policy which in turn culminates in the decay and disappearance of the society that invokes it." (21, p 322)

One might think that in the end all the taxing and Federal "giving" would cancel out so that the question might be asked, "What difference does it make?" To that several objections must be raised. First, under taxing and "giving" it is impossible to know what you are paying for and how much it costs. The average citizen who has difficulty balancing his monthly bank statement would certainly get lost in the jungle of government statistics trying to figure things out. Second, all which is taken is not returned—some of it disappears in nonproductive tasks of collection, distribution, and accounting. And third, and most important, under statism the citizen loses his freedom to decide what goods and services *he* wants to buy and how much *he* wants to pay for them. Since this power has been delegated to politicians, the citizen may be forced to buy that which he does not want and do without that which he does want.

Soaking the rich contributes to the illusion of being able to live at someone else's expense. This has been politically popular because the wealthy are such a small minority of voters that they can not register effective opposition. The rich alone, however, can not supply enough dollars to suport all the schemes of the welfare state. The bulk of the money must come from the middle and lower income groups. Although soaking the rich will not supply the funds for near-socialism, it will shunt to consumer goods that portion of the national product which would otherwise go to capital goods. If some of our production is not set aside for capital replacement and expansion, productivity will suffer and the standard of living will decline accordingly.

The tradition of freedom is neither old nor durable. The early experiments of the United States and the later experience of 18th and 19th century England came under assault of the authoritarian welfarism of Bismarck. Élie Haélvy described what happened.

"The ideal of English liberty in the nineteenth century was the idea of a Parliament strictly controlling the aristocracy and the monarchy, the paradoxical idea that the basis of society was not to obey those who governed but to disobey them, control them, and make things difficult for them. Then came the political economists Adam Smith, Ricardo, and their propagandists, Cobden and Bright, who added something to the definition of English liberalism in making the state practically evanescent—by the bold idea of reducing the functions of the state to as little as possible, aim at what Huxley called 'administrative nihilism'—giving the state nothing to do but to abdicate and simply allowing individuals freely to interchange the products of their respective labour. I think you will agree that it was in the 'forties and 'fifties of the nineteenth century that this new idea of English liberalism reached its acme and England was admired all through Europe as the center of Western civilization. Even our French tyrant, Napoleon III, fell victim to the propaganda of the English free traders. Then began the rise of Bismarck and, little by little, as the German Reich impressed the world with its organization, Bismarckian methods gained the better of the English ideal of liberty and the Hegelian idea of the state gained the better of the idea of the evanescent state." (14, p 261)

Thus, the West, including the United States, had a fleeting look at liberty. Since the turn of the century we have been sinking backward more and more rapidly into statism, all because of the ignorance and the fiction of hoping to be able to live at the expense of the other fellow. We are, all of us, other fellows.

CHAPTER 4

POWER TO THE PEOPLE:
THE MASK OF DESPOTISM

There is a specially apt paragraph in *The First Leftist*,[1] a pamphlet by Dean Russell, which is worth quoting.

"The rallying cry," wrote Russell, "of this new left (*the Jacobins in 18th century France*) was: all power to the people. And as always it sounded good to the people. But the point that the French people missed is the same point that haunts the world today (*1951*). It is this: The people can not themselves individually exercise the power of government; the power must be held by one or a few persons, whether the form of government is a kingdom, a dictatorship, a democracy, or whatever. If the people truly desire to retain or regain their freedom, their attention should first be directed to the principle of limiting the power of government itself instead of merely demanding the right to vote on what party or person is to hold the power. For is the victim of government power any less deprived of his life, liberty, or property merely because the depriving is done in the name of—or even with the consent of—the majority of the people?"

According to Élie Halévy in *The Era of Tyrannies, Essays on Socialism and War* (14) socialism was considered by its advocates as a natural evolution of liberty, a fulfillment of the revolution of 1789, the end of the subjection of labor by capital.

"But on the other hand," wrote Halévy, "it is also a reaction against individualism and liberalism; it proposes a compulsory organization in place of outworn institutions destroyed by the Revolution." (14, p 260) Thus, old despotisms were to be replaced

---

[1] Russell, Dean, *The First Leftist* which appeared in *In Brief*, v 7, no. 3 Foundation for Economic Education, Irvington-on-Hudson, New York, 1951, p 7.

by new ones. Men were again to surrender themselves to the tyranny of the state.

In the years following the Napoleonic wars Charles Comte and Charles Dunoyer founded a periodical called *Le Censeur* (The Censor) in France. The observations made in 1815 have permanent validity.

"The first way," wrote Dunoyer, "that occurs to man to satisfy his needs is to take; plunder was the first industry, as it was the first end of human association; history hardly knows a society that was not first formed for war and pillage." (14, p 29)

"The first need of man," stated Charles Comte along the same line of thought, "is to provide for his subsistence, and, as we have already seen, he can do so only by the spontaneous product of nature, or by what he seizes from his fellows, or by the produce of his industry." (14, p 29)

The justification for peaceful government is to prevent the seizure of one man's life and property by another. Today our Federal government is subverted to perform the very function the prevention of which justifies its existence: pillage. This occurs when the government attempts to fulfill what are commonly called social needs: it takes from some and gives to others.

"In their present state," according to Dunoyer at the start of the nineteenth century, "the nations can be compared to swarms made up equally of hornets and bees, swarms in which the bees agree to produce torrents of honey for the hornets, in the hope of keeping at least a few combs for themselves. Unhappily, there is not always even a small part left for them . . . Man's concern is not with government; he should look on government as no more than a very secondary thing—we might almost say a very minor thing. His goal is industry, labor, and the production of everything needed for his happiness. In a well-ordered state, the government must be only an adjunct of production, an agency charged by the producers, who pay for it, with protecting their persons and their goods while they work. In a well-ordered state, the largest possible number of persons must work, and the smallest possible number must govern." (14, p 31)

The same thought was expressed by Count Henri de Saint-Simon, a brilliant but somewhat erratic and eccentric philosopher-economist, who was cognizant of the work of Comte and Dunoyer and who ironically later became the founder of French socialism.

"Society," stated Saint-Simon, "needs to be governed as little as possible, and there is only one way to accomplish that—to be governed as cheaply as possible." (14, p 32)

Later Saint-Simon and his followers forgot this advice and advocated a tyrannical industrial state ruled by a scientific elite.

Dunoyer and Comte divided society into two classes: those who wish to plunder and those who wish to produce and exchange in peace. Dunoyer wrote of the struggle between these two classes.

"We must not forget," wrote Dunoyer of the peaceful, producer class, a sort of minority nineteenth century silent majority, "that its members are still few in numbers and isolated from each other; that there are few means of communication and defense; in a word it is not organized, while, generally speaking its enemies are organized." (14, pp 32-33)

These and similar thoughts made their way via Saint-Simon to Auguste Comte, the founder of positivism, to Buckle, the historian, and finally to Herbert Spencer, the economist and philosopher. The philosophy was accepted in England, the United States, and elsewhere, playing a major part in the mid-nineteenth century economic expansion of the American West.

But by the turn of the century socialism was making plunder respectable, claiming to be a new liberalism. It took hold first in Germany, later in England and the Scandinavian countries, and then in violent form in Russia. Finally it evolved into the Fascism of Italy, the National Socialism of Germany, and the welfare state in England and the United States. The struggle between the peaceful producers and plunderers still goes on. The peaceful producers are "isolated from each other . . . there are few means . . . of defense . . . ," they are "not organized, while, generally speaking its enemies are organized."

Toward the end of the critical Appendix II to *The Era of Tyrannies*, Élie Halévy asked, "Am I going to be told about a future state of the human race, when a perfect socialism will be united with a perfect freedom? What freedom? The freedom to do nothing, as in the abbey of Thélème, or the absence of obedience to a master, along with incessant labor like an ant or a bee? This ultra future . . . goes beyond the limits of my vision. And when I see men giving themselves up to these dreams, I can not help but think of Kant's dove trying to fly in the void or of Hegel's swimmer without water." (14, pp 313-314)

Socialism ends, although the end may be many years away, in tyranny and loss of freedom. The French Socialists of the nineteenth century were followed by Napoleon III, Kerensky and the Socialists of Russia lasted a few months and yielded to Bolshevism, the post-war Socialists of Italy were followed by Mussolini's Fascists, and after a dozen or so years the Socialists of Germany succumbed to Hitler's terror. In Spain, Franco was Socialism's heir. Once the terror takes over, only a war seems able to bring about a change and there is no assurance that a new terror will not replace the old. Under some forms of terror vestiges of private ownership were allowed to remain as attempts were made to gain social security without completely extinguishing economic freedom. But freedom is indivisible and freedom compromised is freedom lost.

Henry Watterson, whom we have met earlier in this book, was rightly fearful of unlimited government, even if it was the choice of the people.

"We are told by Herbert Spencer," wrote Watterson, "that the political superstition of the past having been the divine right of kings, the political superstition of the present is the divine right of parliament and he might have said of peoples. The oil of annointing seems unawares, he thinks, to have dripped from the head of the one upon the heads of the many, and given sacredness to them also, and to their decrees."

"That the Proletariat, the Bolsheviki, the People are on the way seems plain enough," he wrote in 1919 with unusual foresight. "How far they will go, and where they will end, is not so clear. With a kind of education—most men are taught to read, very few to think—the masses are likely to demand more and more for themselves. They will continue strenuously and effectively to resent the startling contrasts of fortune which opportunity and aptitude have created in a social and political structure claiming to rest upon the formula 'equality for all, special privilege for none.'"

"The law of force," continued Watterson, "will yield to the

rule of numbers. Socialism, disappointed by its Utopia, may then repeat the familiar lesson and reproduce the man-on-horse-back, or the world may drop into another abyss, and, after ensuing 'dark ages' . . . emerge with a new civilization and religion." (6, v II, pp 289-290)

At another point in *Marse Henry*, Watterson nevertheless wrote: "As poorly as I rate the reign of majorities, I prefer it to the one-man power, either elective or dynastic." (6, v II, p 158-159)

James Gibbons Huneker was a connoisseur of music, the arts, and literature. He lived from 1860 to 1921 and witnessed the socialist drift of the Western world, including the Red revolution in Russia. His biographer, Arnold T. Schwab, claims that Huneker was "the most versatile and one of the most entertaining and influential American critics . . ." Huneker's interests ranged far beyond the arts into political ethics and lead him to spend time in the greasy restaurants of New York arguing communism with avant-gardists like Emma Goldman.

The last book Huneker wrote, *Variations*, was a collection of essays published posthumously in 1921. (22) In his powerful essay "Socialism and Mediocrity" Huneker quotes the French laissez-faire economist Yves Guyot (1843-1928): "There are three words which socialism must erase from the facade of our public buildings, the three words of the republican motto: Liberty, Equality, and Fraternity. Liberty because socialism is a rule of tyranny; equality because it is a rule of class; fraternity because its policy is that of class war." Huneker himself then goes on to write: "M. Guyot might have quoted Napoleon, a realist, a cynic in politics, for he knew its seamy side, who said: 'Tell men they are equal and they won't bother about liberty.' How true—if we are all reduced to the level of slaves and live in filth and depravity, we shall not be concerned with freeing ourselves from this condition, providing we all equally enjoy the same conditions of our non-existence.

"Guyot . . . attacks Karl Marx on his weakest flank, and, incidentally, proves him not to have been a proletarian, but the son-in-law of a Prussian Junker. The selfishness of Marx, his tyrannical behavior, his unphilosophical wrath when opposed by two such intellectual giants as Bakunine [2] and Lasalle [3]; his jealous attitude toward Ferdinand Lassalle, especially after his tragic death are all well known. Able but frequently unscrupulous men amuse the idle and attract the multitudes—such are the leaders . . . These leaders are plagiarists, with some variations, of all the communist romances inspired by Plato."

Not only did Marx and Lenin plagiarize Plato, but, according to Huneker they "built up their theories upon a sentence of Saint-Simon and three phrases of Ricardo's.[4] Our author (*Huneker is quoting Guyot*) gives these examples: 'German socialism is derived from two sources: (1) The French doctrine of Saint-Simon; '*The way to grow rich is to make others work for one,*' which in Proudhon's mouth becomes '*the exploitation of man by man.*' (2) Three formulas of Ricardo, viz.: (a) '*labor is the measure of value;* (b) '*the price of labor is that which provides labor in general with the means of subsistence, and of perpetuating his species without either increase or diminution*'; (c) '*profits decrease in proportion as wages increase.*' " Saint-Simon and Proudhon are guilty of vicious distortions and Ricardo of abject assininity unworthy of yet another tiresome refutation.

"No Socialist," Huneker continues, "has succeeded in explaining the conditions for production, the remuneration, and the distribution of capital in a collective system. No Socialist has succeeded in determining the motives for action which an individual would obey. When pressed for an answer, they allege that human nature shall be metamorphosed, but that the individual remains a constant quantity! Rank materialism, all this, and absolutely without vision . . .

"It may be said that man is ready for every form of sacrifice save one: nowhere and at no time has he been found to labor voluntarily and constantly from a disinterested love for others. Man is only compelled to productive labor by necessity, by fear of punishment, or by suitable remuneration. The Socialists of to-day, like those of former times, constantly denounce the waste

---

[2] Russian anarchist, nihilist, and terrorist who believed in anarchy excepting in organizations *he* controlled. 1814–1876.
[3] German socialist and economist. 1825–1864.
[4] Ricardo was an English economist. He was not a socialist. 1772–1823.

of competition. Competition involves losses, but biological evolution, as well as humanity proves that they are largely compensated by gain. Furthermore, there is no question of abolishing competition in socialistic conceptions; the question is merely one of substitution of political for economic competition. If economic competition leads to waste, and claims its victims, it is none the less productive. Political competition has secured enormous plunder to great conquerors such as Alexander, Caesar, Tamerlane, and Napoleon; it always destroys more wealth than it confers on the victors. The Socialist formulates a theory of robbery and calls it 'restitution to the disinherited.' Disinherited by whom? Disinherited of what? Let them produce their title deeds . . . Georges Bernard says that 'socialism will be a regime of authority.' On this point Guyot grimly agrees with him. In reality it will be the most oppressive spiritual and material system ever intended by man.

". . . The future—which is said by some to belong to socialism —will work out the problem of mediocrity, especially if socialism is involved; mediocrity and socialism are not poles asunder. Concrete houses filled with concrete people who will eat, drink, and think alike will cover the land. Everything will be concrete, even our opinions. In his concrete Capitol a concrete President will devise concrete laws. Art, music, literature will be so concrete that our native Gradgrinds, hungry for hard facts, will be ravished into the seventh concrete heaven . . . And this coming age of concrete, wherein all must walk and look alike, is it not a dream compared with which Dante's Inferno would be a Garden of Armida?" (22, pp 111-120)

Boris Pasternak would probably have answered, "Yes."

Socialism, according to the classic definition, concerns itself with the collective ownership of the means of producing and distributing goods, under democratic government control. In practice socialism has been expanded to cover state ownership, operation and control of all the facilities and institutions which, even indirectly, contribute to the production and distribution of goods. Additionally, socialist governments have assumed responsibility for providing those services which are used by most citizens, and for providing material security for all of their citizens.

According to this concept the government of the United States has been engaged in socialist activities ever since it was established.

Post-offices and post-roads were authorized in the Constitution under Article I. Certainly this would represent ownership and control of facilities which contribute indirectly to the production and distribution of goods. Additionally, the provision of a service used by most citizens is involved. (The argument is often made that services used by all citizens should be provided by the government since this will take the profit out of the activity. How about breathing, for instance?) Eventually the Congress made the handling of mail a government monopoly, and after 182 years of dismal deficits, the socialistic postal service has been changed to an independent government agency which is supposed to resemble a private corporation and which is supposed to be self-supporting. It remains, however, a government agency, presumably owned by the people, and it is not less socialistic than it was before, nor has it yet proved more efficient.

The big-government liberals, who double as humanitarians when they dispense the money they have stolen from the thrifty, until recently revered Thomas Jefferson as a near-God, which, of course, he wasn't. Then one of his biographers made the rather unremarkable disclosure that Jefferson had been a Negro slave-holder and this relegated him to the position of a latter-day leper. Some years earlier Clinton Rossiter wrote that Jefferson regarded government as "inherently corrupt, oppressive, and malevolent." (4, p 3) This should have forewarned the liberals, including Mr. Rossiter, and caused some anguish, but it didn't. Perhaps it was because, in spite of Jefferson's mistrust of government, he was responsible for several early American socialist sorties.

The first Jeffersonian socialist endeavor was the Louisiana Purchase of 1803, by which the United States became a dealer in real estate. This was an atypical socialist activity in that it proved enormously profitable. (This seems to tell us that, if we are going to go socialist, let's have a few Thomas Jeffersons run the show, rather than Franklin Roosevelts.) The profits from the sale of Louisiana Purchase land helped to pay the cost of running the government for the second fifty years of the country's existence. Although the international legality of the enterprise was authorized under the treaty-making powers granted by the Constitution, there is nowhere a clear authorization for the United States to engage in a real estate development the size of the Louisiana purchase. Acquisition of territory on a limited scale for purposes of defense would certainly be permissible, but it is questionable whether a big purchase could be justified under the general welfare clause. In any event, who was to question the constitutionality of such a step? This and later real estate ventures of the United States have proved to be quite generally profitable in spite of their socialist nature. Perhaps it all proves that even socialists can make money in real estate!

By 1806 the income of the Federal government had grown beyond what was needed for the limited government the nation then enjoyed. Small amounts of money were needed for service of the national debt and for national defense, the major government activity. Unbelievable as it now seems, there was great concern over what to do with surplus funds! Handling this problem, Jefferson showed himself to be the eternal politician. Instead of recommending that customs duties, the major source of Federal income, be reduced, he sought ways to increase spending. "Congress," he wrote, "should explore the possibilities of Federal appropriations for the great purposes of Federal education, roads, rivers, canals, and such other objects of public improvement as may be thought proper." (4, p 216) It is to Jefferson's everlasting credit that he was enough of a constitutionalist to have felt that an amendment would be needed to permit such a socialist invasion of fields heretofore largely private. In this he was unlike 20th century politicians who increasingly agree with Mr. Dooley that "th' Constitution iv th' United States is applicable on'y in such cases as it is applied to on account iv its applicability."

It is noteworthy that for 82 of the first 112 years preceding World War I surpluses were a problem. (4) What a lovely problem! This brings to mind the 1970 row over Federal-state revenue sharing. If the states are in need of more money and the Federal government is so overburdened with cash that it can afford to give some to the states, why not simply reduce Federal taxes and allow the states to raise their own funds? Under this scheme the money would be raised where it is spent and the local taxpayers could better watch how it was spent. Under revenue-sharing the Federal government will parcel out its favors subject to the influence of political pressures far removed from the people who fill the till. This is hardly likely to contribute to careful taxing and spending.

The socialist proposal of Jefferson that Congress consider Federal support of education have led many to consider him as father of publicly-supported education. Not until about sixty-five years later did this become a reality. In 1862 the first Morrill Act, known as the Land Grant Act, was passed providing for the establishment and maintenance of state colleges. Republican president, Rutherford B. Hayes (1877-1881), later proposed that Federal grants be made for public education.

"Whatever government can fairly do," wrote Hayes, "to promote free popular education ought to be done. Wherever general education is found, peace, virtue, and social order prevail and civil and religious liberty are secure." (4, p 47)

Hayes was not a very reliable prophet, as the recent riots, turmoil and general breakdown of the legal and social traditions of the country have proved. Events in the 1930's in Germany, where public education was an even older tradition, also seem to show that education isn't the answer to all men's problems.

Republican presidents Arthur (1881-1885) and Harrison (1889-1893) continued pressing for Federal support. In 1890 the second Morrill Act was passed granting $25,000 annually to each of the land grant colleges. In 1971 Congress appropriated 18 billion dollars in aid to education. Socialist enterprises have a way of growing on you.

In spite of all, socialist intrusions by the end of the nineteenth century represented a miniscule portion of American endeavor. The twentieth century has been quite different.

The Federal government entered the field of social security under President Franklin Roosevelt. Social security was not an invention of Roosevelt nor of his braintrusters, Bismarck having imposed it in Germany many years before. From Germany the idea spread to the countries north and west of Germany until it reached the United States. In this country the material security an individual might attain was, prior to Roosevelt II, largely a private matter attended to by individuals themselves or by their relatives and friends, the latter often acting through churches and charitable or fraternal organizations. In addition to these private sources of material security, tax-supported services such as local "poor farms" were provided by towns, cities, counties, and states. Herbert Hoover and the Republican leaders of the 1920's and 1930's endorsed *local* tax-supported efforts and private charity as the solution to helping the needy. The socialism represented by tax-supported welfare was on a state or lower level. Roosevelt's contribution to socialism consisted of Federalizing the old-time local socialist endeavors. Accompanying the Federalization and wild expansion of these socialist activities there was a simultaneous and enormous transfer of power from individuals and local communities to Washington.

The socialism that has been with us almost since the founding of the republic has been sponsored at times by the political ancestors of both Democrats and Republicans. Since the turn of the century, and particularly in the middle third of the century, both parties have accelerated their sponsorship. But it must be remembered that the politicians do not lead the people. They follow. Let us see how.

CHAPTER 5

THAT DAMNED COWBOY IN THE WHITE HOUSE

By the turn of the century the country had survived the anarchists of the 1880's, the union agitators of the 1890's, and the financial panic of 1893. The Spanish-American War and the Populists had come and gone. Waves, however, do not rise, pound the shore, and then quietly slip back into the sea without leaving their marks on the beach.

The Spanish-American War extended American influence far beyond the continent and gave the country a popular hero who, by accident, soon became its president. It spawned the Philippine Insurrection and momentarily aroused imperialist passions.

The Populist movement was recast as a new liberalism which was in reality the antithesis of the classical liberalism whose name it usurped. As Populism was absorbed by both major political parties the new liberal influences brought forward men like Bryan and LaFollette. Spokesmen for the new view included the liberal Republican editor from midwestern Kansas, William Allen White, and the liberal Democrat editor from the east, New Yorker Oswald Garrison Villard. Other members of the chorus included Upton Sinclair, a Socialist who was given to gross exaggeration and sensationalism if not to outright dishonesty, Ida Tarbell, and Lincoln Steffans. These and others like them pushed the country leftward toward statism.

The Populist movement in the last decade of the nineteenth century was strongest in the midwest, specially in Kansas and Nebraska. Kansas was also the birthplace and home of William Allen White, progressive Republican and, by his own definition, a liberal. Although White gained national fame in 1896 when he blasted Populism in an editorial entitled "What's the matter with Kansas?" there is no doubt that Populism rubbed off on him just as it became the fountainhead of progressive Republicanism of the early 1900's.

The Populist Party may have been the child of distress and poverty, but it was well fed on the envy from which it gathered strength. It blithely ignored the Tenth Commandment and encouraged its followers to covet their neighbor's houses, slaves and slave girls, asses, and et cetera. The condition of the poor was not, of course, made poorer in the nineteenth century by increasing numbers of nonpoor nor by the increasing wealth of the wealthy. Rather the condition of the poor *seemed* to grow worse as the general standard of living rose and differences between the poor and nonpoor became greater and hence more noticeable. The Populists were the original share-the-wealth party and their offspring has included progressive Republicans, liberal Democrats, New Dealers, Huey Long, Dr. Townsend and other assorted and unassorted oddballs, eccentrics, demagogues, and do-gooders of the twentieth century. The Populists believed the majority could do no wrong and that taking from the rich to give to the poor via majority rule, with the government as middleman, made this form of robbery legal and provided a convenient mask of anonymity for the thief.

The Populists called for a graduated income tax, popular election of United States Senators, direct nominating primaries, direct presidential preferential primaries, adoption of the initiative, referendum, and recall, government ownership of railroads, telegraph, and telephone companies, laws to protect labor unions, corrupt practices acts, and cheap money, i.e. inflation.

By 1910 William Allen White was a popular and widely read author, spreading rather than attacking the propositions of Populism. His writing reflected and also helped to create the mood of the moment. One of the confusions that White helped spawn was that property rights are apart from and rivals of human rights. "As the rights of man enlarge," wrote White, in *The Old Order Changeth*, "the rights of property in so far as they are antagonistic to human rights are clipped." (8, p 93) This is a fiction for property of itself has no rights. The right *to own* property is unique to human beings, possession granting the *owner* the right to use or dispose of his property as he wishes so long as he does not harm others in the process. When the *human right* to own property is increasingly diminished by acts of the state, humanity and freedom are debased. This fact is demonstrated by a study of the spectrum of statist societies: welfarist, socialist, fascist, and communist.

A reading of *The Old Order Changeth* will show that William Allen White campaigned for many Populist proposals including the infallibility of majorities. For instance, White wrote: "Each of these innovations, the secret ballot, the primary, and the re-formed primary is a step toward Democracy—a step toward the Declaration of Independence and *away* from the Constitution, which so feared majority rule that the majority was hedged about with checks and balances at every point." (8, pp 50-51) The Populists and White shared the view that majorities could do no wrong since they were so obviously divinely inspired.

White also favored recall, the graduated income tax, inheritance taxes, and public revelation of party finances. The fight for party reform "began in a demand that campaign contributions be accounted for. Then the people prohibited corporation contributions, thereby taking refined bribery from politics. This drove money from the ballot box . . ." (8, pp 66-67)

Corporate money, that is. Not union money. And unfortunately, union members can not withdraw from a union which contributes money to candidates of whom they disapprove, for desertion of the union would mean loss of job. The corporate shareholder who objects to his company's politics does not suffer the same disadvantage for he can always sell his shares of Xerox or Midas Muffler and invest elsewhere.

"With the breaking of these shackles upon democracy—," White continued, "direct bribery, party bribery, machine rule, and unresponsive legislative control of the states—democracy is now setting out upon its real mission: to define the rights of the owner and user of private property according to the dictates of an enlightened public conscience." (8, p 71)

In reference to federal courts striking down state laws regulating rates, White wrote: "The opposing forces of greed are manifest in the judicial worship of property rights as against human rights. The worship of shear property rights as such is still found lingering . . . in the judicial theory that a legislative act is not 'due process of law.' " (8, p 203)

White would have us believe that legislative authority is not to be questioned, that legislative authority is without limit, and that whatever the legislature enacts in response to the will of the majority is moral, right, and legal. This brings to mind the state legislature which, seeking to make life simpler for its constituents, decreed in 1896 that henceforth the circumference of any circle would be exactly equal to three times the diameter of the circle!

White's attacks on property rights led to a general attack on business. The federal courts represented the forces of greed in the late 19th century by their worship of property rights, according to White, and this was because the judges were appointed by politicians who were beholden to businessmen.[1]

"The men who named these courts were interested in business prosperity," intoned White, implying that there was some kind of nonbusiness prosperity. "This was our national god during the closing years of the nineteenth century." (8, p 206) White suggested that "business" prosperity is bad, because businessmen, who are obviously greedy (excepting those in the newspaper business), can prosper only if nonbusinessmen suffer. Have businessmen at any time generally prospered when the balance of the population came upon hard times? Most businessmen may be better off than most wage earners during depressions, but both groups share the misery. It is for this reason that neither businessmen nor wage earners shun prosperity. White, and the liberals who have followed him, have erroneously assumed that no man can become wealthy unless it is at the expense of someone else. One man's wealth is said to result from another man's poverty. This, of course, is false, wrong and foolish.

In White's account of Roosevelt's handling of the 1902 anthracite coal strike, White continued his assault upon private property and at the same time confirmed that politicians' hands are guided by others.

[1] The liberals and the statists want an unlimited government subject to the momentary whims of the majority rather than a limited government restrained by law. To this end the courts have been persistently assaulted, particularly for their insulation from the will of the majority. Robert La-Follette, Sr., campaigning in 1924, proposed that federal judges be elected and that Congress be granted the power to override the courts on questions of constitutionality. The supreme attack was Franklin Roosevelt's court-packing plan.

"When President Roosevelt," wrote White, "interfered [2] in the anthracite coal strike early in his administration, he did not create the sentiment which backed him so loyally for his extra-constitutional act. A score of organizations for a decade had been making sentiment which recognized the common good as paramount to the private right. The right of property as against the right of the people was a shell. It was worm eaten by public sentiment . . ." (8, p 142)

In order to understand how Roosevelt the man responded to the mood, we must examine the man. Opinions of contemporary newsmen who knew Roosevelt personally, of Taft who served Roosevelt and succeeded him in the presidency, and of LaFollette who was one of the original Republican progressives, can be compared with the opinions of later observers who never had personal contact with Roosevelt. The results are consistent. Roosevelt was a politician first and foremost, with the usual personality traits of successful politicians spiced with a few eccentric deviations from the norm.

Henry Watterson, Democrat and grand old editor of the Louisville *Courier-Journal* personally observed Theodore Roosevelt. In spite of his political leanings, Watterson was an objective reporter who was just as critical of Democrat Woodrow Wilson as he was of Republican Theodore Roosevelt.

"The inconsistencies," Watterson wrote in his autobiography, "and quarrels in which Theodore Roosevelt was now and again involved were largely temperamental. His mind was of that order which is prone to believe what it wants to believe. He did not take much time to think. He leaped at conclusions, and from his premise his conclusion was usually sound." (6, v II, p 167)

Frank I. Cobb was the liberal editor of the New York *World*. His appraisal of Roosevelt appears in Pringle's *The Life and Times of William Howard Taft*.

"Always more law, more law, like the daughters of the horseleech crying 'Give! Give!' When will the President's clamor for

[2] Roosevelt brought about a meeting of the leader of the union and the operator's representative. His threat to have the army operate the mines forced acceptance of arbitration and eventual settlement of the strike. Roosevelt, the Republican, set the precedent for later interventions by Democrats Wilson (railroads) and Truman (railroads and mines).

new legislation end? When will he give the legitimate business interests of the country a breathing spell? The grave defect of Mr. Roosevelt's corporation policy is that he has no policy . . . More legislation has been passed in a single year than the courts can dispose of in the next three years. . . . It is folly to invent new schemes of regulation and excite new unrest when acts already passed are yet to be worked out in the courts.

"Nothing is settled. Nothing is certain," continued Cobb. "The demand for new experimental legislation goes on before the older experimental legislation has been tried and tested. Confidence is shaken, and confidence is the mother of credit. Credit is weakened, and without credit the business of the nation cannot be carried on. . . . It is a time to call a halt. It is time to give business a breathing spell and to permit the restoration of confidence and credit. The country needs a rest from agitation." (29, pp 478-479) There was a depression in 1907.

No doubt the Roosevelt era was one of turbulence and unrest. The noise drowned out the melody.

Edward P. Mitchell was a former editor-in-chief of the New York *Sun*, an associate of and later a successor to the famous Charles A. Dana. Mitchell was a gentle man with a gentle sense of humor. His assessment of Teddy Roosevelt is given in a few paragraphs in his *Memoirs of an Editor, Fifty Years of American Journalism.*

". . . Colonel Roosevelt . . . in his characteristic desire to be a good fellow and old friend with all his well-wishers . . . was at times suspected of consulting, at least figuratively, a shirt-cuff memorandum before producing the name of the voter. . . . This trick of pretended remembrance is a venial sin with politicians and headwaiters, great and small, no more damning than some of the amenities of polite society. (24, p 314)

"It has been said that he could never admit a mistake personal to himself. That was true in a certain sense, but only when the admission involved a confession hurtful to his pride. When the cut went deep beneath the skin . . . no matter how strong the case seemed to be, he possessed, apparently, all docketed and ready for use at a moment's notice an incredible amount of material for argument or rejoinder or evidence in rebuttal, which he proceeded to use ruthlessly; and no man then living had a quicker more accurate perception of strategic principles in personal controversy. He was as bold as a lion and persevering as the almanac, but he could be as agile as a rabbit and know when and how to retreat. Yet it was always hard for him to modify a course to which his pride of opinion had publicly committed himself.

". . . The eternal boy that rejoiced beneath Theodore Roosevelt's jacket, frock, or dinner coat, military uniform, hunter's shirt, and toga of state as long as he lived was one of the secrets of the charm he wrought on friends and acquaintances, on supporters and adversaries." (24, p 426)

Oswald Garrison Villard is not so well remembered as William Allen White. He was, however, probably just as influential as White, reaching a more sophisticated group of readers through his editorship of *The Nation*.

Villard's background is interesting. His grandfather was William Lloyd Garrison, a reformer, anti-slavery editor, and publisher of the *Liberator*. So effective was Garrison as an abolitionist that the State of Georgia offered a reward of $5000 for his body, and The Vigilance Association of Columbia, South Carolina offered a $1500 reward for the apprehension and conviction of any white person distributing or circulating Garrison's anti-slavery newspaper.

Villard's father was Henry Villard who came to America when he was eighteen years old from Germany. He worked as a journalist for the Cincinnati *Daily Commercial*, the New York *Herald* and the New York *Tribune*. German investments in American business were growing during this period and Villard became the American agent for German bondholders of the Northern Pacific Railroad. Eventually he acquired control of the company and was its president when the "Golden Spike" was driven at Gold Creek, Montana. Henry Villard continued to have an interest in publishing, purchasing *The Nation* and the New York *Evening Post*. Later he founded the Edison General Electric Company and was its president when it became the General Electric Company in 1893.

Oswald Garrison Villard was raised as a rich man's son. The family estate *Thorwood* at Dobb's Ferry on the Hudson was a magnificent establishment with a Georgian manor house, landscaped gardens, coachmen, grooms, nursemaids, butlers, and a private-secretary manager. Villard went to private schools and the family travelled in a private railroad car. Friends and guests included Lord Russell, who was the Chief Justice of England, English earls, countesses, German professors and generals, ambassadors, and American generals, politicians, and presidents. Such a background enabled young Villard to make contacts and observe people and events which were beyond the reach of his journalist contemporaries. Villard's comments on Theodore Roosevelt are valuable.

It should be kept in mind Villard claimed to be a liberal, which put him on the same side of the ideological fence as Roosevelt. Villard's claim was more authentic and genuine than was Roosevelt's whose progressive leanings grew as a matter of political convenience rather than of sincere conviction. Villard was a Democrat and Roosevelt a Republican and this may have flavored some of Villard's observations. However, Villard, like Watterson, was equally critical of Wilson, who was, like Villard, both a liberal and a Democrat.

In Villard's book *Fighting Years—Memoirs of a Liberal Editor*, there is an account of Roosevelt, the politician.

"But the editors (of the New York *Evening Post*)," wrote Villard, "were under no illusions as to Roosevelt and insisted up to the time that he became President that he had a boyish and unstable mentality. Horace White (*an editor*) had been well aware of the Roosevelt propensity for not telling the truth when it served their (*sic*) purposes . . . coming out of the Republican convention in Chicago (*1884*), Mr. White . . . met . . . Theodore Roosevelt and Henry Cabot Lodge. He found them as entirely outraged by the nomination of James G. Blaine as he was himself. Both told him that they had decided to bolt the ticket. When Mr. White asked Roosevelt if he might telegraph what the latter had said, he replied 'By all means.' Before Mr. White could reach New York, however, the press received a telegram from Mr. Roosevelt . . . to the effect that Mr. White's published statement that he proposed to bolt Blaine was erroneous. Said he: 'I shall not bolt the convention by any means. I have no personal objections to Blaine. I think you will find there will be no fatal disaffection . . . I have been called a reformer but I am a Republican.' On talking it over further, Roosevelt and Lodge had decided that they, as young and rising politicians, could not afford to break with the party machine. This incident is the key to Roosevelt's entire political career; the reformer in him always surrendered to the politician and to his ambition when it came to a tight place and he never hesitated to twist the truth." (25, pp 145-146)

When Roosevelt returned from Cuba in 1898 he was offered the Independent nomination for governor of New York, on the condition that he would not withdraw if later the Republicans should also nominate him. Senator Thomas C. Platt, Republican boss of New York, put pressure on Roosevelt who was a politician first and reformer last. Roosevelt reneged on his pledge and withdrew as an Independent. He was elected governor as a Republican with a slim majority of slightly less than 18,000 votes.

As the Republican convention of 1900 grew closer, Roosevelt continued to issue statements disclaiming any interest in the vice-presidential nomination. He issued the now standard statement that he would be most useful continuing in his job as New York's governor. "I very earnestly ask," wrote Roosevelt, "that every friend of mine in the convention respect my wish and judgment in the matter." (25, p 148) Platt and the New York Republicans were anxious to get rid of Roosevelt, who had by this time become a nuisance to them, and they couldn't think of a better way to geld the stallion than to send him to the vice-presidential stall. Platt controlled the convention and Roosevelt was nominated.

Yet in spite of his shallowness, Roosevelt had an engrossing personality. Villard described him in these words: "But one thing is certain: few people could resist his buoyancy of spirit, his extraordinary vitality, the force of his ego, and his cheery good nature. I know that I could not any more than I can escape the, to me, even greater charm of Franklin Roosevelt . . . If ever a man led an exemplary family life it was Theodore Roosevelt . . . He was as clean 'as the hound's tooth' in his habits, as he urged everybody else to be." (25, p 152) His political life obviously was not as chaste as his family life. For instance, he was not reluctant to attempt buying the Civil War veteran's vote with an annual increase of $5,000,000 in veterans benefits.

On April 14, 1902, Villard was invited to the White House for a luncheon to discuss army matters with the President and his

Secretary of War, Elihu Root. An army officer, a minister from
the diplomatic corps, Mrs. Roosevelt and three of the children
were present. Villard reports that in the midst of a serious discussion among the adults, Theodore, Jr. "jumped up and disappeared
into what was then a nearby conservatory. He returned bearing a
vicious-looking yellow, red, and blue macaw. The minute he
hove into sight the President burst out with: 'Take it away, take
it away.' In calm defiance of the Presidential order, Teddy, Jr.
came nearer and nearer with the menacing bird. Meanwhile Alice
Roosevelt had set up a chant: 'Father's afraid, father's afraid, father's afraid, father's afraid.' That was more than the President
could stand. The boy in him came to the surface, he leaped from
his chair, went over and took the bird, rather gingerly, and,
showng his teeth, turned upon his offspring and said: "Now who's
afraid, now who's afraid, now who's afraid.' He then handed
the macaw back to Teddy who bore it off without a word, took
his seat at the table, and we resumed the discussion of the fate of
nations. I looked at Secretary Root and the minister during the
episode but they never moved a muscle of their faces. I came to
the conclusion that that was a familiar sort of happening." (25, p
152) What a wonderful scene this would have been for *Father
Knows Best.*

   In the presidential campaign of 1904 Roosevelt bitterly attacked big business and its leaders. Before the election Roosevelt
became worried that he might be defeated. He sent for Daniel
Lamont (President of the Northern Pacific Railroad), Edward
H. Harriman (President of the Union Pacific Railroad and father
of New Dealer Averill Harriman), Hamilton M. Twombly (a
director of fifty corporations), and Henry C. Frick (director of
the Pennsylvania Railroad and the U.S. Steel Corporation) and
begged for a quarter of a million dollars. He told them that if he
got the money and was re-elected they would have nothing to
fear from him as president. His Democrat opponent, Judge Alton
B. Parker, learning of the story, made general charges but could
not give names, dates, and the place of the meeting. Roosevelt, of
course, vehemently denied the charges calling them a "wicked
falsehood." But in 1912 the story was confirmed, indirectly by a
friend of Twombly's, and verified by Henry Frick, who described
the incident: "He got down on his knees to us. We bought the
son of a bitch and then he did not stay bought." (25, p 181) On

the advice of Frick's attorneys, the story was not cleared for publication. Of course it was of no credit to Frick, Harriman, and Twombly that they had made such a deal with the President, but it was even more unconscionable of Roosevelt to do so for he held a public trust.

Before 1912 was over Roosevelt vengefully attacked his personally chosen successor, Taft, left the Republican party and ran as a Bull Moose. This insured Taft's defeat and Wilson's election. It is likely that Roosevelt originally merely intended to eliminate Taft as a Republican power in the 1916 election and did not himself intend to run in 1912. Further treachery came in 1916 when Roosevelt urged the Progressive and Republican conventions to nominate Henry Cabot Lodge as a compromise candidate. Both conventions rejected the suggestion, the Republicans nominated Hughes and the Progressives Roosevelt. Sensing another defeat in the coming three-way battle, and unable to suffer it again as he had in 1912, Roosevelt declined the nomination. According to Villard this insured the death of the Progressives which Roosevelt had helped create four years earlier to serve his own purposes. (25, pp 315-316) Roosevelt's fight with Taft and serious flirtation with the Progressive movement was the result of his 1904 declaration that he would not be a candidate in 1908.

Roosevelt soon regretted his 1904 statement, but he could not gracefully renege on his promise. He had, however, said nothing that would prevent his running in later years and he was soon ruthlessly driving ahead. The story, while out of chronological sequence in an account of the Roosevelt presidency is so revealing of the character of the man and politician that it deserves retelling here. For this, LaFollette's autobiography is the source of information.

Robert LaFollette, Sr. is best remembered as a progressive Republican senator from Wisconsin. He was a leader in the progressive movement in the Republican party and later a founder of the Progressive party. Teddy Roosevelt started out as a New York reform Republican and cautiously slithered into progressivism. For a time he and LaFollette were allied but eventually they fought each other for progressive support. LaFollette was a progressive of conviction, Roosevelt was a progressive of convenience.

"Speak softly and carry a big stick" has long been a part of the

Roosevelt myth. And a myth it was as LaFollette's description of the presidential performance shows: "His administrative policies as set forth in his recommendations to Congress were vigorously and picturesquely presented, but characterized by an absence of definite economic conception. One trait was always pronounced. His most savage assault upon special interests was invariably offset with an equally drastic attack upon those who were seeking to reform abuses. These were indiscriminately classed as demagogues and dangerous persons. In this way he sought to win approval, both from the radicals and the conservatives. This cannonading, first in one direction and then in another, filled the air with noise and smoke, which confused and obscured the line of action, but, when the battle cloud drifted by and quiet was restored, it was always a matter of surprise that so little had really been accomplished. Roosevelt is deserving of credit for his appeals made from time to time for higher ethical standards, social decency, and civic honesty. He discussed these matters strikingly and with vigor, investing every utterance with his unique personality. He would seize upon some ancient and accepted precept—as, 'Honesty is the best policy'—and treat it with a spirit and energy and in a manner that made him seem almost the original discoverer of the truth. He often confessed, however, a distaste for and lack of interest in economic problems, . . ." (26, pp 478-479)

It would seem that a more appropriate motto for Roosevelt would have been "Speak loudly and carry a small stick."

Roosevelt was a political chameleon whose conscience was never bothered by taking different positions on the same subject. One of the issues of the time was the Payne-Aldrich tariff bill which was unpopular in the Western wheat belt but was favored in the industrial Northeast. When he campaigned in 1910 in the West he showed his prepared speeches to a progressive senator who was accompanying him. These had been written in the East and endorsed the tariff bill. The progressive senator reminded Roosevelt of the disastrous Western reaction to a similar earlier endorsement by Taft.

"But this did not at all embarrass ex-President Roosevelt," LaFollette stated in his autobiography. "He promptly adjusted himself to Western ideas upon the tariff, by cutting out of his speeches in Iowa, Kansas, and other Western states the approval of the Aldrich bill which had been written in when the speeches were prepared for delivery. Thus he made the right impression upon the West for the time being. But it was a distinct shock to his admirers beyond the Mississippi a little later when Roosevelt joined with the New York standpatters in the Republican State Convention in praising the Payne-Aldrich Tariff Bill . . ." (26, p 491)

This seems incredible for a man who, according to LaFollette, made stirring speeches about ethics and civic honesty and gave the impression that he had personally discovered that "Honesty is the best policy."

In January 1911 progressive Republicans in the House and Senate formed the National Progressive Republican League. The League adopted a number of proposals the Populists had put forth twenty years earlier. Among these were direct election of senators, direct nominating primaries, preferential presidential primaries with direct election of delegates to national nominating conventions, adoption of the initiative, referendum, and recall, and adoption of a corrupt practices act.

"Roosevelt was invited," according to LaFollette, "to become a member of the . . . League . . . but he had not become enough of a Progressive . . . to be willing to identify himself with the organization, and therefore declined. He was urged to join the League for several reasons. The name of a former President would give strength to the organization. It would help, sooner or later, to place him in open opposition to the Taft administration. It would commit him to a clear-cut and definite position upon the five propositions embodied in the Declaration of Principles. This would be very important, as it is his political habit so to state and qualify his positions that you are never quite sure of him." (26, pp 496-497)

As the 1912 election approached Roosevelt became increasingly bitter about the man he had chosen as his successor. He favored letting Taft win the Republican nomination, feeling certain that Taft would be defeated, leaving the way open for a Roosevelt victory in 1916. Progressives felt that a candidate should run against Taft who, even though he might be defeated by the president, would hold progressive elements together. Roosevelt had suffered the 1910 defeat of Stimson, his hand-picked gubernatorial candidate at the New York state convention, and could not bear the thought of another humiliation. He was not about to offer himself as a sacrificial lamb, and he knew that if he were defeated in 1912 his chance in 1916 would be lost.

When Roosevelt returned from touring Africa and Europe in June of 1910 he found, according to LaFollette, "the Progressive movement . . . far in advance of him; he neither understood it, nor was he in sympathy with its manifest purposes . . . *Roosevelt was still looking to 1916*, and as the political situation developed in the following year (1911), in his political philosophy, which is always personal, Taft's renomination and defeat in 1912 fitted admirably into his plan." (26, pp 510-511)

In the Spring of 1911 Roosevelt made a speaking tour of the country in an attempt to restore his prestige. "It fired his blood," wrote LaFollette. "There were the old crowds, the music, the cheers. . . . But everyone saw the uncertainties of 1912. Roosevelt clearly saw them. He could take no chance. He could not afford to become a candidate against Taft and fail. Why not put forth another man, and feel out the Taft strength?" (26, p 512)

Even if Taft could not be beaten in the convention, a contest would weaken him and contribute to his eventual defeat. If, on the other hand, it appeared that Taft could be beaten in the convention, Roosevelt could jump in at the last moment and seize the nomination and the stalking horse would be forgotten. This thinking brought about a change in Roosevelt's interest in a progressive challenge to Taft. He urged LaFollette to run. Although Roosevelt could not attack the man *he* had picked to succeed him, he agreed to promote LaFollette's virtues. (26, p 513)

Duplicity seems to have been a trait of both Roosevelt presidents,[3] for at the same time Teddy urged LaFollette to challenge Taft, he also told Secretary of War Stimson that he was not really opposed to Taft's nomination. (26, p 514)

The politicking was similar to the Bobby Kennedy-Gene McCarthy sham in 1968, and is convincing evidence that politicians are as slippery as greased eels.

Just before the 1912 convention Roosevelt was visited by Gilson Gardner, a progressive, supporter and friend of LaFollette,

[3] See the account in Chapter 11 of F.D.R.'s maneuvers in the 1944 election.

and an even closer friend of the ex-president. Gardner was a syndicated Washington correspondent and his mission was to urge Roosevelt to increase his efforts for LaFollette. Roosevelt, instead, used him to administer the coup de grace.

Returning to LaFollette to report the results of his talk with Roosevelt, Gardner stated that "Roosevelt is not only surprised at the development of your candidacy, but he is disappointed as well." He continued: "Roosevelt wants to be President again, but you know it has heretofore been his judgment that Taft could not be beaten. However, he now believes that he will be beaten. This change of opinion is not due alone to my report of the conditions in the West, but others have seen him; and then this Chicago conference has been very informing to him. He begins to see that this Progressive movement is a whole lot bigger than he has ever believed it to be. Now you are developing such strength that being nominated in 1912 becomes a possibility. And even if you should fail in the nomination, your leadership of the Progressive movement would become so established that you would be in the way in 1916." [4] (26, pp 535-536)

When the Republicans finally met on June 18th, 1912 in Chicago, Roosevelt did not have a majority of honestly chosen delegates. His tactics against Taft were identical to the tactics used against Taft's son by the Eisenhower forces under Henry Cabot Lodge fifty years later. "Thou shalt not steal" chanted the Lodge lackeys in 1952. In 1912, according to LaFollette, "Roosevelt made a loud outcry against the fraud which he professed to believe the National Committee intended to perpetrate in passing upon the contests to be brought before it." (26, p 646) After Taft's renomination the Roosevelt delegates met again to consider the formation of a new party, justifying their action by the contention Roosevelt delegates had been fraudulently denied their seats.

" 'Thou shalt not steal!' was made the keynote of the Republican-bolting convention. 'Thou shalt not steal—from *me*,' would

---

[4] LaFollette stayed in the fight until the end but was not nominated. Oswald Villard claimed that LaFollette's chances died when he spoke in Philadelphia on February 2, 1912 at the annual banquet of the Periodical Publisher's Association. Villard stated that LaFollette appeared to have had too much to drink and spoke endlessly, and this agrees with press reports. LaFollette claimed that he was overtired from campaigning and worried about an imminent operation on his daughter. In his autobiography (pp 608–609) he admitted to a poor performance. In any event, his candidacy died at this point.

have been more in keeping as a Roosevelt slogan," wrote La-Follette. (26, p 647) Roosevelt won the Bull Moose nomination.

"The true psychology of the Roosevelt proceedings," declared LaFollette in a final judgment, "became perfectly plain. He was there to force his own nomination or to smash the convention. He was not there to preserve the integrity of the Republican party, and make it an instrument of Progressive principles . . ." (26, 669)

So the terrible-tempered egotist finally won the Bull Moose nomination. By this act he assured the end of his political career and the defeat of Taft and the Republican party. This twist of history gave the country its first Democrat president in 16 years.

Only after Roosevelt's personal attacks in the 1912 campaign became incessant did Taft finally reply, but he was never able to match Roosevelt's verbal venom. Taft wrote his Aunt Delia an appraisal worth quoting: "I have a sense of wrong in the attitude of Theodore Roosevelt toward me which I doubt I can ever get over. (*Taft got over it. He and Roosevelt were reconciled just before the latter's death.*) But I have an abiding confidence . . . in the eventual justice of the American people, and I am quite sure that in the end the hypocrisy, the insincerity, the selfishness, the monumental egotism . . . that possesses Theodore Roosevelt will make themselves known to the American people in such a way that his place in history will be accurately defined." (27, pp 256-257)

Emil Ludwig, the German expatriate author (1881-1948) wrote a mawkish 1938 biography of Franklin D. Roosevelt in which he described the relationship of the two Roosevelt cousins, Theodore and Franklin, and the similarity of the paths they followed to the White House. Theodore did not receive Ludwig's blessings as shown by the following quotes from *Roosevelt: A Study in Fortune and Power.*

"Like the Fascists of today (*1938*)," wrote Ludwig, "Theodore took as his own the so-called manly ideals and virtues of the strong fighter and hunter, training himself obstinately in that direction; from this sprang everything that later determined his nationalistic, anti-spiritual principles, which made him threaten to disinherit a son who did not feel like risking a broken leg for the sake of a football victory . . ."

"As Police Commissioner of New York he played a nocturnal Harun-al-Rashid role in fantastic costumes, as President he had in attendance a mounted adjutant, and at the age of fifty he planned for his European journey a glittering uniform which only his wife prevented him from actually having made."

"Theodore's eccentricities had their root in the first convulsions of a childish heart, in that struggle to become what Nature had not wanted him to be," concluded Ludwig, referring to T. R.'s bad eyesight and general poor health as a youngster.

"Not having been born a country squire, Theodore always wanted to appear one," Ludwig claimed, "and phrases such as 'I intend to belong to the ruling class,' and 'I belong to the ship of the doers' could never have crossed Franklin's lips or entered his heart . . . he (*Theodore Roosevelt*) wrote that he had been lightweight champion of Harvard, a distinction which he passionately sought but had in reality never achieved (see *The New York Times*, Mar 23, 1879, p 1) . . . in Theodore Roosevelt we have a man of whom one of his closest friends wrote: 'Don't you know that the President is only just six years old?' "

T. R. wrote, according to Ludwig, ". . . that there had never before been such a Governor of New York as himself . . . that no one could have led the regiment (*of Rough Riders*) in war as well as he." (28, pp 122-128)

According to Roosevelt's own letters he was recommended for the Congressional Medal of Honor by Generals Wood, Wheeler, and Shafter. But the medal was not forthcoming. Undaunted, Roosevelt pursued the medal with as much vigor as he had pursued the Spaniards up Kettle Hill at San Juan, but the medal proved more elusive than the Spaniards. He wrote letters to Senator Henry Cabot Lodge, of which the one dated December 6, 1898 reveals his egotism. (*The Letters of Theodore Roosevelt*, E. E. Morison, ed, v 2, p 892, Harvard University Press, Cambridge, Mass, 1951)

"Dear Cabot:—

Hearty thanks! The attitude of the Secretary (*of War*) of course simply means that the War Department does not intend that I should have the Medal of Honor. If I didn't earn it, then no commissioned officer can ever earn it . . ."

Roosevelt then recounts, without the least trace of modesty, how he on his own initiative led his brigade, "being the first man on the Hill, and killing a Spaniard with my own hand."

Of the Medal of Honor, he wrote "I don't ask this as a favor—I ask it as a right . . . Remember that though I had commanded a brigade, and though I had been singled out in reports for special commendation, I was given no brevet rank. For this I don't care, but I am entitled to the Medal of Honor, and I want it." Roosevelt never got it.

But egotism should not be confused with cowardice. On the night of October 14, 1912 in Milwaukee, Roosevelt was shot by a crazed man named John Schrank. Even though a bullet was lodged in his rib cage and he was losing blood he refused to go to a hospital until he had delivered a scheduled speech. Roosevelt was a man of great drive, fortitude and bravery, which his egotism should not be permitted to mask.

How did Theodore Roosevelt, the late-coming liberal, end up in power in an era of growing liberalism while the leading liberal of the day, William Jennings Bryan, faded into obscurity? After all, Bryan had been *nationally* recognized as a true-blue liberal at about the same time that Roosevelt was receiving *local* recognition as President of the Police Board in New York City. But Roosevelt had fate and personality as allies.

Roosevelt and Bryan were both Colonels, but Roosevelt was the one who got to Cuba, where reporters, attracted by the colorful, made him a much bigger hero than he really was. Later, as governor of New York, he was such a nuisance to the Republican machine that he was neutralized by being nominated for vice-president. Finally, President McKinley was shot, and when he died eight days later on September 14, 1901, Roosevelt's fame was firmly insured.

William Allen White describes Roosevelt's path to power in a few paragraphs of *Masks in a Pageant.*

"Roosevelt's star was rising in that day, and Bryan's leadership, even in his own party was declining. The independent liberal group left Bryan for a number of reasons: First because Roosevelt was obviously more erudite, more generally intelligent than Bryan; second, because Roosevelt, when he became President, had the prestige of his office behind his liberalism. Third, because Roosevelt was more energetic, more pugnacious, more clamorous than Bryan." (1, pp 255-256)

Although White quotes Roosevelt as having said, "Well I drowned him (*Bryan*) out in 1900. I talked two words to his one," he concluded that "Probably Roosevelt did not regard Bryan as a windbag, but Roosevelt always had a lively sense of Bryan's intellectual capacity, his abyssmal unintelligence about things in books. But fundamentally it was because there was more wind in Roosevelt's trumpet than in Bryan's that the independent liberals left the Democratic party and began voting with the Republicans." (1, p 256)

During the Roosevelt administration the base for Federal intervention in private economic affairs was expanded. Two laws interfering with the free market as it relates to the railroads were passed: the Elkins law (1903) which forbid railroad rebates and the Hepburn rate bill (1906) which granted rate-setting powers to the Interstate Commerce Commission. Pure Food and Drug legislation and The Employee Liability Act also were passed.

Not only was the base for action expanded, but actual interventions increased, although perhaps not as fast as the more rabid statists wished. The attorney-general initiated Sherman Act antitrust suits against the American Sugar Refining Company, the United States Steel Corporation, the Standard Oil Company, and, most notably, the Northern Securities Company (a railroad holding company).

But Roosevelt's most significant intervention and break with tradition was the role he played in settling the anthracite coal strike in 1902. Forcing the union and operators to accept arbitration was an unprecedented government involvement in private affairs which opened the door for political settlements of labor disputes. Since there are more voters who are workers than there are who are owners, and even more voters who are consumers, it doesn't take much imagination to predict the biases of political intervention. Roosevelt's coal strike action was popular and should, therefore, have been expected from a man with his political motivation.

McKinley, who was Roosevelt's predecessor, had said only two years before the coal strike that he "believed, quite sincerely, that the government oughtn't to intervene in business affairs unless criminal activities were involved." (9, p 84)

Presidents, no doubt, assume that the men they appoint to the

Federal courts, and particularly to the Supreme Court, will support them. This is not always the case. It is to the eternal credit of the authors of the Constitution that the term of judicial office is independent of the president and that confirmation of appointment must be made by an independent Senate. Two of Teddy Roosevelt's letters to Henry Cabot Lodge make one quake at the thought of a less safe arrangement.

"In the ordinary and low sense which we attach to the word 'partisan' and 'politician'," Roosevelt wrote to Lodge, "a judge of the Supreme Court should be neither. But in the higher sense, in the proper sense, he is not in my judgment fitted for the position unless he is a party man, a constructive statesman . . . and . . . (*keeps*) . . . in mind also his relations with his fellow statesmen who in other branches of the government are striving in cooperation with him to advance the ends of government." Given Roosevelt's character it is safe to interpret the phrase about advancing "the ends of government" as meaning advancing Roosevelt's concepts of the ends of government.

On another occasion, concerning an appointment to fill a court vacancy, Roosevelt wrote of the candidate that he was "right on the Negro question . . . right on the power of the Federal government . . . right on the insular business . . . right about corporations . . . right about labor." (29, p 239) "Being right" no doubt meant being right in agreement with Roosevelt. Fortunately, once men are raised to a Federal judgeship they are free to exercise judgment independently of the president, the senate, and the voters.

Roosevelt's role as a statist was recognized by Walter Lippmann: "The reforms of Theodore Roosevelt and of Woodrow Wilson brought under some regulation large areas of private enterprise: the railroads, the central banking function, the public domain and natural resources, food and drugs." (3, p 32) Of these, only control of the central banking function should be credited to Wilson; the rest are Theodore Roosevelt's.

Roosevelt's Square Deal, according to William Allen White "advocated an income-tax amendment, postal savings banks, parcel post, regulation of the railroads, prosecution and breaking of the trusts, a pure-food-and-drug law with state laws to support it, extension of laws promoting public health and hygiene, shorter hours for labor, collective bargaining—and this was the catch phrase, 'with representatives of their own choosing'—workmen's compensation laws, state and national extension of civil service, the movement for good roads, the regulation and control of insurance companies, banks and savings institutions." (30, p 423)

In 1910, after he was out of the White House, Roosevelt moved further in the statist direction and proposed the New Nationalism which went beyond the Square Deal. This was to be a program for "social justice and popular rule," no doubt with power to the people! It included some Populist proposals that had not been included in the Square Deal and added a few new ideas. The New Nationalism would have provided for recall of elective officials by popular vote, the referendum, direct primaries, and the recall of court decisions.

On one issue Roosevelt was against Federal intervention. The question of prohibition came up in the 1908 campaign when Taft was asked to support the drys. He refused and asked Roosevelt if he agreed with his stand. Roosevelt replied in a letter dated July 16, 1908:

"Of course your position is absolutely sound. If ever there was a wicked attitude it is that of those fanatic extremists who advocate a law so drastic that it cannot be enforced, knowing perfectly well that lawlessness and contempt of the law follow . . . I favor the local option plan . . . But to pass prohibition laws that govern localities where the sentiment does not sustain them is simply the equivalent of allowing free liquor plus lawlessness, and is the very worst way of solving the problem." (29, p 375)

This statement is both interesting and ironic. It is ironic because the Republicans eventually inherited the blame for the failure of a Constitutional amendment which their leadership originally opposed and which became law under Wilson's Democrat administration. The statement is interesting because it has to do with the attitude of Americans toward limited government. Note that Roosevelt saw nothing wrong in local prohibition laws as long as local sentiment would sustain them. To Roosevelt, and growing numbers of Americans, unlimited government seemed acceptable providing it represented the will of the majority, local or national. Although Roosevelt was sensible in opposing a Federal law which was unenforceable, libertarians would oppose prohibition as a state intervention in private affairs, an attempt by the government to protect people from their own folly, and a step toward unlimited government, particularly unlimited Federal government.

The libertarian view on this and similar government controls of drugs can be attacked. If libertarians believe that a legitimate function of government is to protect citizens from the predatory acts of others, shouldn't the government act to make supplies of alcohol, hallucinogens, and narcotics illegal? What of the wives and children of drunkards, the victims of drunken or drugged drivers, etc.? The answer, of course, is that the libertarian takes the view that the use of alcohol or any disabling drug can not be taken to excuse an act that harms others. The drunk and the drug addict must be held responsible for their acts and punished as severely as any other predator, but it is beyond the responsibility of the government to make drug use or possession illegal.

There is one item that must be entered on the credit side of history's ledger under Roosevelt's name. The Panama Canal is probably his greatest accomplishment. The canal has been of enormous strategic importance as an instrument of national and hemispheric defense. It has also been of great economic value. With the development of aircraft and missiles its defense value has diminished somewhat but by no means has it been rendered obsolete. Furthermore, in the years to come, as fossil fuels become scarce and are replaced by nuclear energy, a resurgence of the importance of surface transportation may restore some of the canal's lost defense value. It is true that the methods employed to acquire the rights to construct the canal have been criticized. But apart from this blemish, Roosevelt served his country well in making the canal a reality.

Frederick Lewis Allen in his *The Big Change, America Transforms Itself, 1900-1950,* views with reserved approval the drift toward statism. Allen could probably be classed as a liberal, but not a passionately blind one. He is, in fact, representative of many of the liberals who, by the middle of the century were beginning to have some doubts about liberalism.

Of Teddy Roosevelt, Allen wrote: "It has been pointed out again and again . . . that Roosevelt's bark was much worse than his bite; that the legislation which he actually put through—such as the Hepburn Act for further regulation of the railroads, for example—did not pack much of a wallop; that never again in his seven and a half years in the White House did he do anything so bold as to attack the Northern Securities Company; that the conservative Taft administration which followed his was much more active in bringing prosecution under the Sherman Act than he was; and furthermore that Roosevelt had a limited and uncertain knowledge of economics (*this was equally true of the other Roosevelt*) and was impulsive, boyishly immature, inconsistent, and unduly addicted to the delights of political showmanship (*how like his cousin!*) all of which is true—but overlooks Roosevelt's most vital contribution to American history.

"For what this dynamic President did was to advertise and dramatize to the whole country a point of view on business, government, and the public interest that was refreshingly new, exciting and contagious." (9, pp 96-97)

Here, then, we have the successful politician who was unable *during* his term of office to advance toward liberalism at a pace faster than public opinion and practical politics would permit, and who, *after* his term in office, as an *unsuccessful* politician, recycled what the opinion makers were making popular, and in so doing became somewhat of an opinion maker himself, paving the way for further steps toward statism by later presidents.

Roosevelt's record was the product of White's "national mood," the politics and the politicians around him, and his personal peculiarities. It was these peculiarities of character, his bubbling exuberance, his supreme egotism, his zeal and his immaturity which led McKinley's mentor, Marc Hanna, to describe him as "that damned cowboy in the White House." And we should be grateful for the checks and balances which kept the cowboy from running away with the horse.

"In our time," wrote William Saroyan, perhaps thinking of other political cowboys, "with the number of people in the world increasing all the time, it isn't likely that any person will seem significant for longer than a moment, and his significance will be of an order that will not permit him to be confused about who he is and what he is doing. That includes politicians. *Especially*, one might add." (23, p 105)

CHAPTER 6

THE RELUCTANT PRESIDENT

William Howard Taft was a genuine intellectual from a family of intellectuals in the days before widespread circulation of academic counterfeits cast suspicion upon the species. Taft was an excellent student who graduated second in his class from Yale. His scholarly brother Horace, who supported Grover Cleveland and free-trade, founded the Taft School in Connecticut. His daughter became dean at Bryn Mawr College. His older son Robert, the senator, graduated number one from Yale and later number one from Harvard Law School. Younger son Charles, a liberal of sorts, graduated magna cum laude from Yale Law School. No members of the family have been expelled from school for cheating on tests, they all wrote their own dissertations, and none are recorded as having been arrested for disturbing the peace or smoking pot. All in all, a solid heritage.

Although Cincinnati-born, Taft had strong family ties to New England. His father, a well-to-do lawyer, was born in Vermont. Taft's mother was from Massachusetts. Father Alphonso Taft was a Unitarian of broad-minded religious views, strongly anti-slavery, and ahead of his time in recognizing that women were able to do more than bear children. Alphonso Taft served as Secretary of War in Grant's cabinet and was the United States Minister in Vienna and later in Moscow. As a judge, he acted to ban religious instruction and bible reading in Cincinnati's public schools, for he did not believe that moral and religious instruction were the responsibility of government. Nor did he believe that religious partisanship had a place in public schools. (27, p 54)

In contrast to Theodore Roosevelt's truculence, William Howard Taft was pacific. He became Roosevelt's Secretary of War with almost as much reluctance as when he later became President. As he was about to return from the Philippines to assume his new duties, he wrote, "I have no particular aptitude for managing an army, nor do I know anything about it." (29, p 256) He took the new position only on the condition that he could continue to supervise reconstruction of the Philippines. His peaceful nature is shown in a letter he wrote to his sister Helen on October 24, 1909. He mentioned his lack of enthusiasm for a hunting trip on the ranch of his sister Fanny: "I hate to kill things anyhow, and I am content to be a tenderfoot." (29, p 155) Taft's advocacy of peace throughout his life led him at times to dangerous isolationism. In a 1903 letter he wrote: "I find it hard, myself, to subscribe to the Monroe Doctrine and to deem it of sufficient importance to warrant, as Bismarck said with respect to the Turkish question, 'the loss of the bones of one Pomeranian grenadier' . . ." (29, p 256)

Taft's amiability is well known, and he had the face to match his personality. He went to the Philippines as the first civilian governor and was soon greatly loved by the natives. The feeling was mutual. Pringle, in his not always complimentary book, described Taft as follows: "He was as patient as he was large in frame. He was tolerant. He could be stubborn when stubbornness was a virtue. Above all, he had a vast capacity for affection and before very long he had become very fond, indeed, of the little men (Filipinos) . . ." (29, pp 164-165)

Edward P. Mitchell, the editor, described a note from his friend Murray Crane, a leader of the Republican party in Massachusetts, referring to a dinner the night before at the White House, where "he and I sat with Archie Butt (*Taft's and formerly Roosevelt's aide*) at the family table and President Taft urged turkey and cranberry sauce, and bubbled with his contagious good nature." (24, p 430)

In spite of Taft's sunny disposition he had some strong dislikes. Among these were Joe Cannon, speaker of the house, Senator Robert LaFollette and, at least originally, Senator Nelson Aldrich. Archie Butt, who served both Taft and Roosevelt wrote early in Taft's term that Taft was "persistent in his antipathies . . . Mr. Roosevelt once said that Mr. Taft was one of the best haters he had ever known . . ." (29, p 431) Coming from a man with Roosevelt's reputation for personal attack that's quite a statement!

President Taft's huge bulk was the butt of many jokes. Supreme Court Justice David Brewer in an address at Yale said, "Secretary Taft is the politest man alive. I heard that he recently arose in a streetcar and gave his seat to three women." (29, p 334) While in the Philippines he had occasion to ride twenty-five miles on horseback. He cabled Secretary of War Elihu Root that he had stood the ordeal very well. Root cabled back his reply: "Referring to your telegram. How is the horse?" Then there is the famous story about Senator Chauncey M. Depew and the Secretary of War at a banquet. Depew, who was known for his wit, was serving as toastmaster. In his introduction of Taft he hinted that his size was the result of his being with child. "You have heard the Senator refer to the fact that he believes me to be pregnant," responded Taft. "If this is so and it is a boy I shall name him William, and if it is a girl she shall be known as Nell, but if, as I strongly suspect, it is merely wind I shall name it Chauncey, after the well known Senator from New York."

Taft's size, in addition to furnishing material for jokes was also a nuisance and a health problem. He was so huge that special chairs were needed to accommodate his broad beam and weight. When he was governor of the Philippines he had a special bathtub installed in the Malacanan Palace, the governor's residence. A photograph in Ishbel Ross's book shows the abandoned tub with eight Filipino boys splashing in it. Miss Ross claimed it could hold a dozen! (27, p 132) In December 1905 Taft weighed 314 pounds, but after working with a nutrition specialist for several months he got down to a healthy 255 pounds. Ishbel Ross claimed "The experiment cost him $400 for the alteration of his clothes, which he . . . said was a small price to pay for his improved physical condition." (27, p 175)

Taft's tendency to gain weight drove him to walk four or five miles daily around the decks of the ships which took him on his many overseas trips. It was also the reason for his frequent golf games. Walking and exercise were an absolute necessity for him. Another health problem was his susceptibility to colds and sore throats. In the days before public address systems he found speech making a painful chore. His tendency to cat-nap in public, specially when his weight went up, his fondness for golf, his bulk and hearty appetite, and his distaste for speech making and speech writing led to erroneous charges that he was lazy. Taft was anything but lazy. He was, along with Truman and Nixon among the most conscientious and hard-working presidents.

Law and the administration of justice were the real passions of William Howard Taft. He steadfastly aimed for the Supreme Court but was repeatedly sidetracked by being asked to perform duties which moved him toward the presidency instead. When President McKinley asked him to head the commission to administer the Philippines, Taft, who did not approve of their acquisition and felt that he lacked the qualifications of a colonial administrator, said the President might as well have asked "me to take a flying machine." But Taft was very effective and soon became the first governor of the islands. He did such an outstanding job that after Roosevelt succeeded McKinley he asked Taft to serve as his Secretary of War. In this position he was responsible for the construction of the Panama Canal. His work brought him closer to President Roosevelt who ultimately picked Taft as his successor.

Taft was lukewarm to the idea of the presidency since he lacked basic political instincts. When he was asked by Roosevelt to become his Secretary of War he hesitated because it would involve him in a political campaign "which would," as he put it himself, "be most distasteful to me, for I have no love for American politics." (27, p 150) His wife Nellie, who kept pushing him toward the White House, succeeded in having him accept the appointment since she felt that a cabinet appointment would move him closer to *her* goal. She was right. But Secretary of War Taft did not perform well as a politician. Ishbel Ross described it this way: Roosevelt ". . . found him to be too mild a campaigner . . . One of his letters brought the Secretary to the point of resigning. Taft had no heart for the bellicose touch and he felt he was not by nature a campaigner or spellbinder . . . Nellie and Horace (*Taft's brother*) both spoke to him frankly about the length and dullness of his speeches . . ."

". . . His family suffered with him as he left his addresses to the last minute, and then rushed them out under pressure, a life-long habit . . ." (27, p 159)

Nellie reported to her husband that President Roosevelt wanted him as a successor, but that the president might have to support

Charles Evans Hughes in the event that Taft could not muster enough backing from the party. On this occasion Taft's "reaction was to write . . . to Roosevelt saying if he . . . should decide to support Hughes it would be no disappointment to him. Two weeks later Taft told Root (*Roosevelt's Secretary of State*) that it 'would be a great thing for the country to have another term of Roosevelt.' Nellie was profoundly irritated by her husband's determination to push the cause of Roosevelt, Hughes, Root, or any but his own." (27, p 177) It is obvious that the reluctant president-to-be did not have a reluctant wife.

In spite of Taft's reserve he became the Republican nominee and won the election. The campaign, according to Ishbel Ross "was all bewildering to Taft, who rejected the public clamor that he wear a Rough Rider hat and frankly admitted that he could not be more aggressive . . . The aura of Roosevelt's dynamism threatened to swamp him . . . But if Taft did not have jubilant crowds as he moved from place to place he made a good impression and added to his own popularity by his temperate views on many issues and his self-evident honesty." (27, p 202)

A man, otherwise qualified, who did not want or seek to become president might be the ideal man for the job. Such a person would lack the hunger for power that is a source of danger. In the hands of such a man the liberty and freedom of the people should be secure—providing the reluctant president was strong enough to resist the attempts of truculent usurpers from seizing power. Taft, of all the presidents of the twentieth century came closest to this ideal. At least he resisted the temptation to seek the office until the last moment. Even after he was elected he showed little enthusiasm for re-election.

Both Ishbel Ross and Henry F. Pringle in their books on Taft describe his longing for a judicial rather than a political career. Taft was several times offered an associate justiceship on the Supreme Court. It was refused because he felt a strong obligation to finish work he had already undertaken. First it was his task in the Philippines, later it was his work in the War Department which included not only administration of the Philippines but also supervision of the building of the Panama Canal. In addition Taft was under great pressure from his ambitious wife to try for the presidency. Nellie mortally feared the judiciary as a dead

end. Taft's family was always consulted when he was offered
a place on the Court and, with the exception of his eighty year
old mother, they always advised against acceptance. But as Taft's
work continued as Roosevelt's Secretary of War, acting Secretary
of State, confidante, advisor, and, at times, as virtually the acting
president, Taft was drawn more and more into the political
arena. He took an active part in the 1906 congressional campaign
as the administration's chief spokesman and defender. In 1907,
still wavering, Taft slowly surrendered himself to the pressure
and by August of 1907 was actively helping the organization
that would get the nomination for him. Taft disregarded the final
prophecy made in his mother's letter of January 21, 1907: ". . .
the malice of politics would make you miserable." (29, pp 319-
320) Which proves that, on occasion at least, mom knows best.

William Howard Taft had critics aplenty who transformed
trivial incidents into genuine disasters. For instance, when campaigning for president Taft forgot it was Sunday and innocently
played cards, an incident which caused a violent explosion. On
another occasion he mentioned Grant's victory over intemper-
ance. Meant as a compliment, this was taken as a slur by the late
general's followers. On yet another occasion he said, in regard to
labor that "even a rat will fight when driven into a corner." [1]
Had he instead said "any living thing will fight when driven into
a corner" he would have remained unscathed. Perhaps he suffered
from the prejudices of some newsmen who, at this time were beginning to be pampered and coddled by ambitious politicians.
Taft was not enough of a politician to know how to manipulate
people in this way. Ishbel Ross wrote that "It was clear at once
that he lacked Roosevelt's relish for publicity. He disliked the
constant snapping of cameras and sometimes lost patience with
photographers." (27, p 195) The press has ways to get back at
those who refuse to cooperate or who are critical. When Taft
was tired from campaigning and dozed off while on the platform
or in public it was sure to be mentioned.

---

[1] This seems to have been an expression he used without malice. Henry
Stoddard, in his book, *As I Knew Them, Presidents and Politics from Grant
to Coolidge*, wrote that Taft used the same phrase in explaining why he
finally decided to campaign against Roosevelt for the Republican nomination in 1912. p 376. Unless Taft also thought of himself as a rat it should
not be concluded that he thought of labor in terms of rats.

After he became president, Taft proposed a reciprocal tariff reduction with Canada. In his message to Congress in 1911 he said that the Canadians were "coming to a parting of the ways." This was taken out of context and interpreted as meaning that Canada was about to desert the British Empire and become an appendage of the United States. This misinterpretation of one of Taft's statements was typical. It contributed to the defeat of the Liberal Party in the Canadian election and rejection of the reciprocal tariff agreement at the polls.

Many Republican politicians did not have a high regard for Taft's political abilities. Senator Henry Cabot Lodge was one of these. He wrote to Roosevelt that the "one thing which surprises me about Taft is that he does not know more about politics . . . he does not seem to have gotten hold of the elements of politics which must enter into so many matters, especially appointments." (29, p 427) According to Pringle, Taft at first refused to use patronage to achieve a legislative program: ". . . he believed . . . that the executive could not properly, under the Constitution, adopt such a policy." Pringle quotes Taft from a 1915 lecture on the presidency as having said "our President has no initiative in respect to legislation given him by law except that of mere *recommendation* and no *legal or formal method* of entering into the argument or discussion of the proposed legislation while pending in Congress." (29, p 425) In this respect Taft's thought closely parallels that of Calvin Coolidge, a lawyer-president who strongly believed in separation of the responsibilities of the legislative and executive branches. Coolidge, however, was not as hesitant as Taft about the use of patronage.

Taft viewed as dangerous Teddy Roosevelt's statement that he "did and caused to be done many things not previously done by the President . . . I did not usurp power, but I did broaden the use of executive power." (29, p 425) This was, according to Taft, an "unsafe doctrine" and, as if giving an uncanny warning about things to come eighteen years later under another Roosevelt, he said "The mainspring of such a view is that the executive is charged with the welfare of all the people in a general way: that he is to play the part of a universal providence to set all things right." (29, p 425) In 1915, at least, Taft was on the side of the anti-statists.

Taft won the 1908 election in spite of his inept politicking and his failure to match Bryan's platform performances. According to Pringle, Bryan insured his own defeat by calling for the nationalization of the railroads. Until that time there had been charges that Roosevelt had adopted many of Bryan's proposals and that he and Taft, Roosevelt's hand-picked heir, were no less radical than Bryan. After Bryan's call for nationalization, Wall Street decided that Taft was quite acceptable.

Nevertheless, Bryan, the unsuccessful politician, was instrumental in moving both his own party and the Republicans leftward. William Allen White told the story of Bryan's influence.

"Bryan had led his party to two consecutive defeats, and in 1904 the Democratic pendulum swung back to conservatism . . . The convention nominated Alton B. Parker, an old-fashioned, high-collared, tail-coated gold-standard Democrat . . . Roosevelt would have defeated Judge Parker, probably, without the Bryan defection (in a convention squabble about the gold standard), but the defeat of Parker was rather overwhelming. Obviously the Conservative wing of the Democratic party could not win, so the party turned to Bryan again, and in 1908 nominated him for President for the third time . . . William H. Taft supported by Roosevelt and his liberal followers, defeated Bryan easily. For four years, during the Taft administration, while Roosevelt was advocating the liberal cause in his party, Bryan went up and down the land converting the Democratic party also into a liberal organization . . .

"Without the prestige of the presidential office, Bryan, almost single-handed, kept his party from becoming merely a critical Conservative party . . . In every Democratic state, Bryan created by his influence Bryanesque Governors, and in Congress followers of Bryan, who were Roosevelt's allies against the Conservative East." (1, p 260)

By 1964 White's Conservative East was covered by a thick layer of liberalism which had gradually oozed outward from New York by way of articulate publishers and broadcasters and from New England's universities and lecture halls. It was this liberal-coated East which Goldwater in 1964 wanted to chop off so that it could quietly float to sea. A few sons of rich easterners, bored with money and its dwindling prestige, had discovered that

political power was more titillating. Teddy Roosevelt was the
first of these wealthy political triflers, but he soon was followed
by men like Colonel House, Averill Harriman, Franklin D. Roosevelt, Nelson Rockefeller, the second-generation Kennedys, and
others. Closely allied were a new line of liberal intellectuals,
mostly men of narrow experience, limited backgrounds, and comfortable, if not wealthy, circumstances, such as Woodrow Wilson,
and later, Archibald MacLeish, and Arthur Schlesinger, Jr. Taft
fit neither group, being neither rich nor liberal in the new sense.
Rather he was caught in the changing tide and swept away by the
progressive current. He was, in fact, a conservative intellectual
by nature.

As an undergraduate at Yale, William Howard Taft made an
interesting speech. It is interesting because Taft, who inherited
his Republicanism, praised the Democratic party and because it
shows that Taft was not a philosophical relative of Teddy Roosevelt. Taft's speech was quoted in Pringle's biography: "In a
Republic like ours where the powers are so nicely adjusted, because the resources of the general government are so much
greater than those of any single state, there is always the danger
that the former may gain preponderance. A close watch, therefore, must always be kept over the encroachments of the general
government. In other words, the state's rights principle is a constant quantity in the politics of the country so long as the Republic continues to exist as it ought. The party, therefore, which
takes this as its fundamental principle has an everlasting principle
on which to base its party faith.

"Such a foundation has the Democratic party . . ." (29, p 43)

Additional evidence of Taft's native anti-statist views is given
by his senior oration, made in 1878. Taft warned, according to
Pringle's summary about "political corruption, the growth of un-
sound radical thought, and the too-great centralization of government . . ." (29, p 44)

William Howard Taft's views on labor's right to strike were
courageous and just. They were stated in 1894 while he was Judge
of the United States Sixth Judicial Circuit. The occasion was the
decision to sentence Frank Phelan, the leader of a secondary railroad boycott, to six month's imprisonment for contempt of court.

"Now it may be conceded at the outset," read Taft's decision, "that employees . . . had the right to organize into or join a labor union which should take joint action as to their terms of employment. It is of benefit to them and to the public that laborers should unite in their common interest and for lawful purposes. They have labor to sell. If they stand together, they are often able, all of them, to command better prices for their labor than when dealing singly with rich employers, because the necessities of the single employee may compel him to accept any terms offered him." (29, p 137)

Phelan was then sentenced, not because of his legitimate union activities, but because of the coercion involved in the secondary boycott. Taft's stand took great courage since the action was an outgrowth of the violent Pullman strike and his courtroom was filled with hostile strikers. The Mayor and Chief of Police of Cincinnati had sent word that they feared a riot if Phelan was jailed. For years after this, Taft was held in low esteem by organized labor leaders.

Taft's attitude toward negroes and minorities were liberal in the original sense of the word and far in advance of the common views of his time.

"Whenever possible he took a strong stand in behalf of negroes wrote Ishbel Ross. "He felt that they needed highly educated leaders to plead their cause and on different occasions he expressed indignation over the 'blind and unreasonable assaults' on innocent people because of their color. Later as President, he tried to find places for them, an old interest of his . . . 'The prejudice against them is so strong that it makes few places available, and yet I must do something for the race, for they are entitled to recognition,' he wrote to Mrs. Taft." (27, p 187)

In the Philippines as head of the civilian commission sent to take over administration from the army, Taft broke down the army's color line and won the admiration and friendship of the Filipinos. Later as Secretary of War he was wrongly held responsible for indiscriminate wholesale punishment of negro soldiers of a unit stationed in Brownsville, Texas. One man was killed and two wounded in a shooting spree involving some negro troops. Since the guilty persons could not be identified, President Roosevelt ordered the discharge and forfeiture of benefits for one hundred sixty blacks. Taft rightly protested against this injustice without success and then, as Secretary of War, carried out the order.

Taft was also broadminded and tolerant with respect to religious views. He was a Unitarian and in later years attended the famous All Souls Unitarian Church in Washington. He was also a long-time active supporter of the YMCA. Ishbel Ross stated that "Taft was so liberal in his views that he was welcomed as a speaker by all religious organizations, Protestant, Roman Catholic, and Jewish." (27, p 281) When Al Smith ran against Hoover, Taft could not bring himself to support Smith, but this was because of Smith's Tammany Hall background. "For the bigots," wrote Pringle, "who objected to Smith's religion, the Chief Justice had deep contempt." Pringle quotes a letter Taft wrote on April 17, 1927 to Charles C. Marshall which read, in part, "Were Al Smith to be elected president, his defects would not appear in his Catholicism but they would grow out of his origin in Tammany Hall and the most vulgar and coarse political atmosphere of lower New York." (29, p 1064)

As president, Taft faced the perpetual problem of taxes. In the last decade of the nineteenth century, Federal expenditures and receipts seemed to be approaching a permanent state of unbalance. Tariffs, the chief source of income, were becoming increasingly unpopular, and income taxes were again considered as a substitute and supplement.

The first Federal income tax was called the Civil War Tax. Initially it called for a flat three per cent tax on personal annual incomes between $600 and $10,000. Ten years later in 1872 when it was abandoned, the rate had more than tripled to ten per cent. In 1893 an income tax law was again passed but before Uncle Sam could get his hand into his nephews' pockets the Supreme Court ruled it unconstitutional.

William Howard Taft advocated an income tax before he became president and continued to do so after taking office. However, he opposed a simple congressional enactment of the tax in 1909 since such a law had previously been judged unconstitutional. "I think it exposes the court to very severe criticism, whatever it does," stated Taft, "and the best thing to do is to accept the opinion of the court and submit to the people the question of a constitutional amendment." (29, p 433) Tariff problems brought the issue to a head.

Tariffs were enacted originally as a source of revenue for the Federal government, and during Taft's term they were, as they had been during most of the country's existence, the chief source of revenue. Taft's dilemma was caused by his promises to reduce the tariff as a means of reducing the high cost of living. Unfortunately even the very high rates set by the Dingley Tariff Act of 1897 permitted a Federal deficit of $100,000,000. Since the proposed revision called for a reduction in tariffs the deficit promised to grow larger unless new sources of revenue could be found. (It apparently never occurred to anyone that a reduction of expenditures would have achieved a balance.) The populist Democrats and the progressive Republicans proposed re-enactment of a three per cent income tax and a test of the Supreme Court. This prompted Taft's statement of objection.

Taft suggested, instead, an inheritance tax and a corporate exise tax. The latter was really a one per cent corporate income tax, but it was described as an excise tax on the privilege of doing business. The president finally won approval of the corporate income tax and submission of a constitutional amendment legalizing income taxes for individuals. The income tax amendment was proposed by Congress in July of 1909 and by February of 1913 it had been approved by the required number of states. Thus, it was under Taft's guidance that the Federal power to tax incomes was granted. A floodgate for Federal spending and taxing was about to be opened. Unfortunately there was no provision in the amendment to prevent a *graduation* of the tax rate. This later became the blank check for Federal sponsorship of any social "reforms" the majority might vote in the future. "So that one who looks at the large national movements of the decade now closing," wrote White ominously in 1910, "will find that those movements which have become national laws are laws looking to the distribution rather than the accumulation of national wealth." (8, p 143) For the first time taxes were to be collected for achievement of social rather than fiscal goals.

Thus, Taft's hand was on the knob when the door to Federal interventionism was opened. No doubt he never visualized the confiscatory income taxes which would come thirty years later. Nor did he realize that the Federal income tax would provide the means by which, under Franklin Roosevelt, the Democrats would emerge as the advocates of a domineering central government. Nor could he foresee that there would be an eventual reversal in the traditional positions of the Democrats and Republicans on the matter of states rights. His undergraduate admiration of the Democratic party would have to be revised.

During Taft's administration there was growing opposition to the high tariffs of the Dingley Act. It was generally recognized that the high rates contributed to the rising cost of living. Since the Republicans had promised revision of the tariff (they did not actually specify whether the revision would be upward, downward, or sideways) Taft favored an overhaul of the tariff schedule. President Taft was no hard line free-trader even though he did say in his inaugural address that in "the making of a tariff bill the prime motive is taxation and the securing of a revenue." (29 p 423) But Taft strayed from this principle and advocated a schedule which would equalize the *costs* of production at home with *costs* of competing foreign industries. This is a goal which can not be reached because manufacturers, particularly foreign ones over which there is no control, are not likely to reveal their true costs. Even if they could be persuaded to do so, standardization of cost-accounting methods would be required and this would be another almost impossible task. The real objective was to raise the *prices* of foreign goods so that domestic producers could raise their prices enough to be assured a "fair" profit. A subsidy is obviously involved which requires the impossible job of determining and legislating "fair" profits. There is no such thing as a legislated "fair" profit. The only kind of fair profit is that which can be realized by a voluntary exchange in a free and open market. Any attempt to establish "fair" profits by law makes the concept of a fair profit meaningless.

The Payne-Aldrich tariff revision which was finally approved by Congress and which Taft signed into law, and by which he obtained approval of the income tax amendment as a corollary, was attacked throughout the country. It was attacked by manufacturers and union leaders who lost tariff protection and benefits. It was attacked by the wool-producers of the West who wanted a higher tariff on wool. It was attacked by consumers who claimed that the remaining tariff on wool would show up in the prices paid for clothes. (It would and did.) But most important, it was attacked by the newspaper publishers who wanted a lower rate on newsprint. When Taft stumped the country in support of the bill even *he* seemed to abandon the aim of reducing the cost of living when he said "I did not agree, nor did the Republican party agree that we would reduce rates to such a point as to reduce prices by the introduction of foreign competition." (29, p 453) Thus, Taft supported the forces of interventionism and the free market was given another jolt. The public, of course, paid the bill.

The United States was originally conceived as a union of sovereign states. It was logical that the member states, acting through their popularly elected legislatures should choose the senators who would represent them in the national legislature. The ratification of the XVIIth amendment destroyed in large part the vestige of sovereignty which the states still retained in 1913.

The XVIIth amendment was the response to charges that state legislatures were bought and controlled by large corporations and trusts, particularly the railroads. This allegedly enabled business interests to "purchase" the election of United States Senators and thus to dominate the Senate. If there was such business domination it was not strong enough to prevent passage of the anti-trust laws long before Roosevelt's term and subsequent laws restricting and controlling business during both Roosevelt's and Taft's terms.

A half century later it would seem that, judging from the passage of laws favored by organized labor, that labor unions play a much more dominant role than business ever achieved. How has this been accomplished? A look at the record of labor contributions to liberal senators in the 1970 elections may supply a part of the answer: Tunney (D-Calif) $104,140; Williams (D-NJ) $150,966; Symington (D-Mo) $103,060; Hartke (D-Indiana) $93,-531. (Reported in *Human Events*, v XXXI, no. 24, June 12, 1971, p 14.) These are amounts openly acknowledged. It is possible that actual contributions, well disguised, were larger, and possibly significantly larger. Has labor purchased the U.S. Senate? Is the quality of the Senate any better now that some senators are obligated to labor unions whereas previously they were obligated to State Legislatures?

The original scheme for the election of senators worked well and would have continued to do so had there been sufficient interest in the local politics of choosing state legislators. Direct election, on the other hand, has resulted increasingly in a Senate more easily manipulated by organized minority pressure groups. Indirect election insulated senators from these groups and provided a check on the more responsive and more sensitive directly elected House of Representatives. With the ratification of the XVIIth amendment in 1913 Federal government intervention was accelerated and the pace of national social legislation quickened.

Republicans who think that their party has a conservative tradition should be reminded that both the income tax amendment and the amendment for direct election of senators were passed and ratified during the Republican administration of Taft and following sixteen years of Republican control.

Nosy prying of the Federal government into private affairs was not an invention of Roosevelt's New Deal in the thirties. Conservative Republicans may be surprised to read what President Taft wrote about his corporate income tax proposal of 1909: "The things that were required in the bill were two: first, the tax as an excise upon corporations, and, second, a certain degree of publicity with reference to the returns. *That publicity gives a kind of Federal supervision over corporations,* which is quite a step in the direction of similar reforms I am going to recommend at the next session of Congress." The act, Taft continued, "will give the Federal government an opportunity to secure most valuable information in respect to the conduct of corporations, their actual financial condition." (29, p 521) More than reluctance to be president is required of a man if he is to resist the temptations of power.

The Hepburn Act which was passed in 1906 during the Roosevelt administration give the Interstate Commerce Commission power over railroad rates. However, the ICC rulings were subject to court review and accompanying delays. This was intolerable to the progressives who in their time were just as impatient as today's liberals, demanding that today's edict be executed yesterday.

Taft and his attorney-general pushed for extension of ICC power, including supervising the issue of railroad stocks and bonds, suspension of higher rates until their "fairness" could be determined, and establishment of a special Commerce Court which could immediately review and enforce ICC orders. Appeal from the Commerce Court decisions could only be made to the Supreme Court. Taft considered this interventionist measure "second only to the corporation tax among the accomplishments of the Sixty-first Congress." (29, p 526)

Theodore Roosevelt made trust busting the favorite indoor political sport. But Roosevelt's performance resembled that of the swimming coach who couldn't swim. Even Taft's progressive foes admitted that Taft acted more and talked less than Roosevelt.

At the same time Taft did not knuckle under to Bryan's socialistic demagoguery. In 1907, just before leaving on a tour of the Orient, Taft spoke at Columbus, Ohio. According to Ishbel Ross, ". . . Taft calmly held his ground in defending the capitalist system. He deplored William Jennings Bryan's wholesale approach to the subject and his desire 'to extirpate trusts, root, and branch', since his own view was that there were benign trusts and evil ones . . . 'I believe that such large combinations, legitimately conducted greatly add to the prosperity of the country . . . The captains of legitimate industry . . . are entitled to large reward, and it is impossible to impose a fixed limitation on the amount which they may accumulate.'

"Instead of jailing those who had been found guilty of monopolistic practices he argued in favor of curbing their operations by injunction . . . Taft's views, as always, were dictated entirely by his respect for the law . . ." (27, p 186)

Taft obviously lacked the vindictiveness of Roosevelt and the sensationalism of Bryan.

Aunt Delia Torrey was William Howard Taft's durable and influential auntie. She was responsible for moving Taft to establish a Children's Bureau to oversee the industrial employment of children. It was not Taft's natural inclination to do so. Pringle states that Taft "protested that interest 'in the education of children and their development is one thing, but recourse to the national government for a bureau of this sort is another thing.' He deprecated the 'disposition to unload everything on the Federal government that the states ought to look after.' " (29, p 622) Taft was alarmed by the growing trend in this direction, but he succumbed to the wiles of his beloved Aunt Delia and eventually the Children's Bureau was established.

Aunt Delia's Children's Bureau was typical of the growing tendency for the Federal government to involve itself in social causes. In coming years agitation would nudge the Federal government into attempts to control wages, hours, and conditions of work, at first for children and women, and eventually for all workers. The pay for labor has increased, children are no longer employed in factories, hours of work have decreased, and conditions of work have improved. Hence, one may conclude that the improvement is the result of what the politicians and the government have done. But is it? William Allen White, our liberal editor, gave an incomplete explanation of what happened.

"What has given the democracy of the twentieth century," asked White in his 1910 book, *The Old Order Changeth*, "such an enormous store of capital, as evidenced in our national wealth, compared with the democracy of our fathers? They worked more hours, wore homespun clothes, bought few books, had few amusements, lived in primitive simplicity; certainly they should have saved more. (*White was wrong here. They produced barely enough to sustain themselves. There was little left over for saving.*) Yet we are richer, man for man, than they were. Something happened . . . It revolutionized us. It was some great force —elemental, dynamic.

"The force was steam—the thing that happened was the common use of steam," White concluded. "The nineteenth century will be known as the century made marvelous by the use of steam. Steam lightened the strain on human muscles; soon the hours of labor were shortened. The working man got more daylight in which to look about and see how the world is put together. With leisure came reflection, with reflections came opinions, with opinions came revolt against the inequalities of men, and with that revolt modern democracy is coming," said White, whose rhetoric, at this point was getting as steamy as his subject. "Steam annihilated distance, fostered understanding between men, set them in good houses, fed them nourishing food, made men of them. It multiplied their thrift ten and a hundredfold, and while it made them men . . . it put their accumulated savings into the hands of trustees who became masters of men."

Momentarily lapsing into an illogical choice of combatants, White continued, "And when one sees the struggle between democracy and capital, it must not be conceived to mean a struggle between the rich and the poor, but it must be recognized as a struggle in every man's heart between the unselfish and selfish instincts of his nature for supremacy. Democracy is struggling for the rights of man," wrote White returning to a favorite theme, "against the rights of property. The rich man is often democratic; the poor man, intensely selfish," (8, pp 4-6) he concluded, again becoming a little wobbly in his logic as he equated democracy and unselfishness.

White attributes economic progress in nineteenth century America to the growing use of steam. It is true that until steam power was developed, water power provided most of the energy with an assist from men and animals. It is also true that the contribution of steam power was vital. But White inexplicably ignores the other branches of technology which were also making progress and without which progress in the development and use of steam power would have ceased. Machines were designed and produced which increased the output of the men operating them. At the same time more useful products were designed to be produced by the machines. Conversion of steam power to electrical power made transmission of power a practical reality. And finally, better materials became available for the manufacture of improved machines and superior products. For instance, in the ferrous metals industry technology went beyond cast iron to wrought iron to small batches of crucible steel, finally arriving at the capability to produce multi-ton ingots of fine alloy steel without which development, transmission, and utilization of steam power would have remained at a most primitive level.

But White's failure to recognize these other contributions of technology is a minor deficiency compared to his failure to recognize the contributions of the political and economic systems under which the country operated, and which systems, White, a liberal in his day, so often attacks in his writing. The influence of the politico-economic system on productivity and the standard of living can be appraised by a comparison of nineteenth century Russia with the United States.

During the period when, according to White, steam was responsible for the tremendous accumulation of capital in the United States, the country was, excepting for the slaves, a free country. There were 3,000,000 slaves out of a total population of 32,000,-000 when Lincoln issued the emancipation proclamation in 1863. In Russia about 15,000,000 serfs were freed by Czar Alexander II in 1861 out of an estimated total population of 75,00,000. There were, it is true, distinctions between serfs and slaves: slaves were considered personal property whereas serfs were required to perform services for a master who did not own the serf and whose powers over the serf were limited. Serfs could be free of their bondage if they could pay off their indebtedness to their landlords, but since this was almost impossible the serfs could be considered for all practical purposes to be the equivalent of slaves. The proportion, then, of nonfree to free men in the population was about 10 per cent in the United States and about 20 per cent in Russia at the time of the emancipation. Here is the first of the major differences between Russia and the United States: until freedom was granted, there were proportionately twice as many people in bondage in Russia as in the United States.

At this point, it is worthwhile to quote a short passage from the *Encyclopedia Britannica*. (14th ed, v 20, p 360, 1938.) "Private enterprise and the free application of capital were hindered in every way by the bondage of the peasant class (*in Russia*). Even such a necessary measure as that of moving cultivators to the rich soil of the south was thwarted by the adherence of the northern peasantry to the glebe." But what about the free men, that is, those who were neither bonded in Russia nor enslaved in the United States? What was their status?

Probably the Russian landowners came closest to being free men in the nineteenth century. Until 1803 they lacked even the freedom to free their own serfs, not that there was a strong inclination to do so. In 1803 Czar Alexander I granted the noblemen permission to liberate their serfs, but only 47,000 were freed. In 1810 all legislative initiative rested with a Council of State presided over by the Czar. Elected assemblies in the cantons, districts, provinces, and states existed which could pass motions but not laws. The courts were susceptible to bribery and they operated in secrecy. Rule of the land was by the arbitrary action of an officious bureaucracy. Under Nicholas I the same autocratic, arbitrary rule continued. Higher education was permitted only for children of noblemen and officials. Censorship of the press and speech were very strict. Alexander II, Nicholas I's son, was an absolute monarch who, in response to revolutionary threats, freed the serfs without payment to the landlords. In addition, the serfs were granted allotments of land for which they paid a fixed rent to their landlords, with an option to buy, financed by government bonds. After freeing the serfs, local government was reformed by establishment of new provincial councils. Forty-eight per cent of the seats were assigned to landowners, forty per cent to peasants, and the balance to town residents. Not until 1864 was trial by jury and an independent judiciary established. The reign of Alexander II was an era of reform and progress in spite of the fact that the country remained an absolute monarchy, essentially without freedom of press, speech, and even thought, and with no guarantee of person and property from the whim of the autocrat.

By 1889, under Alexander III who had come to power in 1881, much of the progress made under Alexander II was erased. The provincial councils were placed under civil service and became subservient to the provincial governors. The representation of landowners was raised from 48 to 57 per cent in the councils while the peasant holdings dropped from 40 to 30 per cent. The press was ruthlessly silenced and taxes increased by 29 per cent in the ten years from 1883 to 1892.

At the beginning of the nineteenth century the United States and Russia were both agricultural countries, the one young and sparsely settled with people who sought to escape European autocracy and the other slightly, but only slightly more densely populated, an old country with a tradition of centralized power and despotism. Both countries were almost incalculably rich in natural resources.

Expansion of the United States westward was by natives seeking the opportunities of undeveloped land and by immigrants who chose freely and voluntarily to come to the new country. On the other hand, expansion of Russia eastward into Siberia was by

Cossacks whose interests were military rather than productive, by political and criminal prisoners exiled to the virgin land as laborers, by religious dissenters, and by fugitives escaping conscription in the Czar's army. Between 1823 and 1898, 700,000 exiles and 216,000 voluntary emigrants settled in Siberia, a region which had enormous wealth in timber, furs, and minerals.

Both the United States and Russia were open to the influence of steam which so captured the imagination and rhetoric of the man from Emporia, both were exposed to the effects of the industrial revolution, both had access to the development of technology and advances in science, and both had vast areas of undeveloped land and other resources.

From the beginning of the nineteenth century to the beginning of the 20th century Russian progress was minimal, while the United States changed from a weak agricultural state to one of the most productive and powerful countries of the world. The American miracle, and it was a miracle, was accomplished because of our vastly greater individual and personal freedom, imperfect though it may have been.

At a later point in his book, White credits national legislation and labor unions for the progress made by American labor: ". . . whatever there is of unselfish justice in the demands of labor for a humane day, a clean environment, a living wage, will come to them under national law. For when one considers how far labor has come in fifty years in this country, how large has been its actual as well as its comparative betterment as the result of organization (*White was referring to the American Federation of Labor*), the future becomes something more than a guess." (8, p 149)

Here and in subsequent passages concerning the abolition of child labor, White neglects the fact that the prerequisite for improved wages and working conditions, shorter hours, abolition of child labor, and so forth, is greater productivity. Greater productivity results from improved technology, from the use of machines which can perform most of the tiresome and many of the difficult tasks formerly accomplished by people, from the harnessing of energy sources, and from the accumulation of capital which results in the manufacture of the tools of production rather than in the manufacture of consumer goods. And lastly, greater productivity results from the government guaranteeing the safety of producers and their goods and investment; from the release of energy and ingenuity when the innovative among us are insured that they will be allowed to keep a fair share of the results of their efforts as determined by a free market and not by the dictates of the state. All the agitation of demagogues and do-gooders, the strikes of workers, and the laws of the politicians can not improve wages and working conditions unless first there is an improvement in productivity. The improvement in productivity is what makes the pie a little larger as the years go by so that the slices can be a little larger, too.

Differences between Roosevelt and Taft in personality and political philosophy ordained the eventual break between the two men. The behavior of Gifford Pinchot, a Roosevelt holdover in Taft's administration, and Taft's handling of Pinchot make clear how different Taft was from his predecessor. Pinchot was the Chief of the United States Forest Service. He was a great favorite of Roosevelt, and, like the man who appointed him, a zealous reformer with the reformer's typical imperial stance. Early in his administration Taft wrote that he was glad to have Pinchot's services even though he thought that Pinchot was "a good deal of a radical and a good deal of a crank." (29, p 480) The Chief Forester had the authority to license transmission lines through national forests as a fire prevention measure. Under Roosevelt and with Roosevelt's knowledge, Pinchot used this power to regulate power rates. If the power companies would not agree to what Pinchot declared to be "fair" rates, licenses would be withheld. When this outrageous usurpation of authority, which had been condoned by Roosevelt, came to Taft's attention he immediately stopped it. Eventually Taft had to fire Pinchot, but for other reasons, and Roosevelt gained another ally in his fight against Taft.

H. H. Kohlsaat was a journalist and editor of the Chicago *Record-Herald* and the author of *From McKinley to Harding, Personal Recollections of Our Presidents*. Kohlsaat was a very close friend of Roosevelt and a staunch Republican. Nevertheless, in Kohlsaat's story of the Roosevelt-Taft rift, Taft ends up as a man of integrity whereas Roosevelt is pictured as childish, immature, and egocentric, as well as dishonest. The story is worth retelling.

Kohlsaat wrote that he personally told Roosevelt that the trouble started in 1904. "You foolishly issued a statement," he said to the ex-president, "the night of your election . . . saying you would not be a candidate in 1908 for what you called a 'third term' . . . You could have been renominated easily if it had not been for that declaration . . ." (31, pp 184-185)

After Taft was elected Roosevelt was picqued because attention shifted away from Roosevelt to his successor. Roosevelt told Kohlsaat "that more than half of Loeb's (*Roosevelt's secretary*) time was taken by people calling, writing, or telephoning for an appointment with Taft. He said senators and congressmen dropped him completely and hunted for Taft. They paid no attention to him and took no interest in bills he was anxious to have passed before the end of his term." (31, pp 184-185) Roosevelt also claimed that Taft gave credit to both his brother Charles as well as to Roosevelt for his nomination and election. Roosevelt sent word back to Taft that "his brother Charley gave him money, but I gave him the Presidency." (The reference was to Charles Taft's personal financial help to William Howard Taft during the years he was in public office before he became president.) Roosevelt was also mad because Taft did not retain James Garfield and Oscar Strauss in his cabinet.

Kohlsaat went on to tell the results of his visit to Taft to get his version of the break. Kohlsaat claimed that at first he was no great admirer of Taft although he thought that he was competent and had many good qualities. Kohlsaat very sympathetically reported Taft's distress, sorrow, and bewilderment at the falling out. When Kohlsaat presented Roosevelt's version of the dispute without revealing his source, Taft replied, "I don't know where you got your information, but you are entirely wrong." (31, p 188) Taft then produced a file of Roosevelt-Taft letters to substantiate his claim. Kohlsaat wrote "Colonel Roosevelt's letters were so at variance with what he told me the day before, I was dumbfounded." (31, p 188) Roosevelt was known to handle the truth carelessly. Roosevelt later broke with Kohlsaat for equally nonsensical reasons but, as with Taft, the two men were reconciled when the United States entered the World War.

William Allen White visited Taft in the White House after Roosevelt had left for his game-hunting trip to Africa. It was obvious to the progressives that Taft was not going to carry out the program which Roosevelt had been pushing as his Square Deal, White claimed. White, as the leading progressive editor, attempted to get Taft to commit himself to progressive proposals. He described Taft as disagreeable, tactless, and edgy, but nevertheless could not deny his good humor. White's mission was unsuccessful.

"Many progressives," wrote White of his visit, "felt that his (*Taft's*) detachment from our group was a result of a lazy desire to avoid disagreeable encounters.

"It was not that. He was convinced that we were mad. He was a consistent, honest, courageous, most intelligent conservative. He believed in the existing order. He was nice about it, almost felicitous, and could at times smile indulgent condescension." (30, p 426)

LaFollette, another progressive, comparing Taft with Roosevelt wrote that "Taft's course was more direct, Roosevelt's devious . . . Taft's talk was generally in line with his legislative policy. Roosevelt's talk was generally at right angles to his legislative policy." (26, p 484) He felt the progressive movement made more real progress when Roosevelt was out of the country on his grand tour "than in all the seven years he was president." This he attributed to Roosevelt's shortcomings of character and conviction (26, pp 543-544) and to Taft's unwitting political ineptitude which united the progressives in opposition to any conservatism Taft displayed.

The general political philosophy of William Howard Taft was rated by Pringle as being "a little left of the center. He may have been fractionally closer to that center than Theodore Roosevelt, but that was all." (29, p 343) Although Taft believed himself to be a conservative (29, p 341) he had Federal statist tendencies. This is not surprising for conservatism and Federal statism are not mutually exclusive. As a statist, for instance, Taft favored setting rates for the railroads and forbidding rebates, he favored new antitrust laws which would achieve competition through legislation rather than through the play of economic forces, and he felt that government snooping via the corporate income tax was justified. To his credit he also favored the free market by pushing for tariff reductions, he opposed overt socialism, and he opposed secondary boycotts and the closed shop of labor unions.

The closed shop he felt was an infringement on the right of every man to work for whom he pleased, without duress. Labor, he felt, should have the right to organize, strike, and enforce its demands by any peaceful and nonviolent means, (29, pp 341-343) a stand with which no libertarian could argue. But Taft also encouraged an extension and continuance of Roosevelt's statist policies. He did not, however, become increasingly radical, as did Roosevelt, after leaving the White House.

After Taft's defeat in the 1912 election he was not very popular. Had the bitter Taft-Roosevelt feud not erupted, and had Roosevelt not split the party, Taft would probably have been re-elected. This would have contributed to a more favorable popular view of his ability. It would also have led to a course in international affairs quite different than the one followed by Wilson, and possibly much more fruitful.

"His brother Horace, who understood him as no one else but Nellie did," wrote Ishbel Ross, "considered the key to his unpopularity the fact that he was a poor politician; that he loathed the methods involved and was clumsy in practising them; that he underestimated the power of publicity and forbade any grand-stand play in attacking the trusts; that his speeches were too long and dull; that he talked indiscreetly about prominent politicians, and that his reliance on his great capacity for work sometimes led him to put things off until the time had passed for effective action. He scorned personal controversy until forced into it by Roosevelt's attacks." (27, pp 265-266)

In retrospect many of these qualities would be looked upon as desirable and admirable in a man. In a reluctant president they proved to be his undoing.

CHAPTER 7

THE MAN FROM OLYMPUS

Not many people know that Woodrow Wilson had a first name and fewer know what it was. The truth of the matter is that Wilson's first name was Thomas; his boyhood companions called him Tom. Had this been common knowledge he might never have become president—either of Princeton University or of the United States, for Tom Wilson, which is a perfectly good name, seems more to describe the 1920 operator of a marvelous flying machine or a magic electric rifle than it does a man from Olympus. It just doesn't have that imperious presidential ring.

Woodrow Wilson went to Princeton where, as a student, he was interested in politics and debating. He joined the American Whig Society and founded the Liberal Debating Club. Lest one be misled into thinking that young Wilson was a liberal in the current sense of the word it should be recalled that Wilson was at Princeton in the 1870's. At that time the liberal tradition and philosophy more nearly resembled what is now known as conservatism.

While Wilson may have favored a conservative view of society and of the functions of government, he did not extend this view to the organization of government. As an undergraduate he wrote an article which appeared in *International Review*. In this, Wilson proposed that members of the cabinet be given seats in congress and that congressional elections be patterned after British parliamentary elections. He also favored full publicity for congressional committee hearings. He thought that the separation of the legislative and judicial branches of government led to unresponsiveness and inefficiency. About constitutions he said that "They're outgrown, that's all. If you button them over the belly, they split up the back." (33, p 224) Checks and balances, intended to prevent tyrannies are never popular with people in pursuit of personal dreams of power. Without restraints the dreamers become tyrants.

Wilson eventually returned to Princeton as a professor, a trade at which he was very successful. For years he was the most popular professor at his alma mater. Adjectives commonly used to describe him were witty, genial, gracious, charming, brilliant, and stimulating. Professors, dealing year in and year out with students who are ignorant in special fields of knowledge, sometimes come to think of themselves as real first cousins to the Lord, and this entitles them to be downright contemptuous of all us second cousins. In Wilson's case these traits did not show up until after he became Princeton's president, and even then he was able to hide them most of the time behind a peekaboo woven of charm and grace.

When Francis Landry Patton resigned as president of Princeton, Wilson was ready and waiting. As Princeton's president, Wilson showed what his friends called flexibility and his enemies called guile. He served in a period when gifts to the university increased greatly, and initially his term was an era of good will and peaceful, pleasant days. But as James Kerney, editor and publisher of the Trenton *Evening Times*, wrote in his book *The Political Education of Woodrow Wilson*, "he was not made for long honeymoons." (32, p 8)

Under Wilson some expensive new programs were started. First, he instituted a paternalistic preceptorial system by which young instructors were assigned to oversee where undergraduates lived, what they talked about, what books they read, with whom they associated, and even the ideals they were expected to live up to. Then he attacked the club system. This degenerated into a form of class warfare between members of the eating clubs, who were predominantly wealthy, and the nonmembers, who were predominantly less wealthy. In turn, Wilson was attacked and called "a confiscator, a leveller, and (*although it had nothing to do with the issue*) a Socialist." (33, pp 136-137)

Wilson's ideas cost money. The preceptorial system and replacement of the eating clubs required construction of dormitory quadrangles. The money for this was diverted from the Graduate College to which it had previously been pledged by Wilson.

His prior support of the graduate program was documented in its prospectus, the preface of which had been written by Wilson himself. When Wilson was asked to justify his switch he claimed he had written the preface before he had read the prospectus. Flexibility. Later a copy of the page proofs were obtained showing notes in Wilson's handwriting. Guile—or a faulty memory. As Kerney wrote "Wilson was human like the rest of mankind." (32, p 9)

Wilson eliminated the eating clubs, but Princeton eliminated Wilson—with the help of Colonel George Harvey. Harvey was a colonel by appointment of a pre-Wilsonian governor of New Jersey. He was also President of Harper and Brothers, publishers, editor of *Harper's Weekly* and of other journals. Harvey, a conservative, was attracted to Wilson in 1904, when Wilson himself was still quite conservative. Once attracted to him Harvey found it hard to break the habit even though Wilson became increasingly liberal in later years. Harvey, a literary man, may also have been captured by Wilson's gift of expression. In any event, Wilson responded to the courtship of the conservative Democrats and by 1910 he was panting as eagerly for the gubernatorial nomination of New Jersey as he was to get out of the Princeton mess. Different versions of the story have been told by Edward P. Mitchell, James Kerney, and Oswald Garrison Villard.

"Everybody knows," wrote Mitchell, "or ought to know, that it was the discerning mind and political sagacity and loyal friendship of Colonel George Harvey that relieved Mr. Wilson from the embarrassments of the Princeton situation and put his eager feet upon the first round of the ladder by which he climbed to the White House . . . It was not until 1906, however, that the president of Princeton was publicly nominated by Colonel Harvey for President of the United States at a banquet of the Lotos Club. Mr. Wilson, there as a guest of honor, responded gracefully, as always, and receptively, as always, to the proposal of his name.

"I am not aware of any previous publication of the fact that two years before the event of the Lotos Club Mr. Wilson's qualification for the Democratic candidacy had been scrutinized in advance of the convention of 1904 by a self-constituted committee of investigation and selection, acting in behalf of a conservative Democracy as against the Bryanized variety . . . Mr. Wilson needed no urging when he was invited to meet at the Wyeth (Dr. John A. Wyeth) house in Lexington Avenue . . . Mr. Wilson talked freely and alluringly to conservative sentiment, as if he were conscious of the inspection he was undergoing. But the general judgment was so far from being favorable that not long afterward . . . the spokesman of the group was addressing to Judge Alton B. Parker a most respectful but very searching questionnaire . . ." (24, pp 386-388)

As the elections of 1910 approached, Harvey persuaded Senator James Smith to support Wilson for the governorship of New Jersey. Smith was a bank president, newspaper publisher, and was the head of several leather companies. Smith, like Harvey, was typical of the conservatives who controlled the Democratic party in New Jersey and when they asked Wilson to run they had no reason to believe he was any less conservative than they were. Wilson was not, of course, really interested in the governorship as such. He looked upon the governor's job as an escape from Princeton and as a springboard to the presidency. Ascent to high places, Wilson knew, was often, as Bacon put it, "by a winding stair."

Wilson had three reform competitors for the nomination for governor. They were regular Democrats who had come out openly for rate setting by public utility commissions, direct primaries for state and local offices, direct election of U.S. senators, restrictions on the size of campaign contributions, and establishment of employer's liability laws. All of these were popular liberal causes. They had been urged upon the people of New Jersey by the newspapers and were, according to Kerney, popularly accepted by the voters of both parties. They were not accepted by the men who dominated the parties nor by the rank and file party politicians. Wilson's lofty interests were really far beyond these mundane issues for it was he who grandly advocated a reorganization of the United States government along British lines; it was he who had little use for constitutions. Kerney claimed, however, that he had on various earlier occasions spoken or written against most of the more earthy reform issues. (32, p 50) But by merely keeping silent on them for the moment he got the support of the party machinery, and simultaneously he did not antagonize the members of his party who favored the reforms.

Hale in his biography reported (33, pp 136-137) that the nominating speech for Wilson was interrupted by catcalls, jeers, and wisecracks. Although there was serious opposition to him before and during the Trenton convention in that summer of 1910, Wilson was nominated. James Smith, boss of the state party machine, saw to it that the "right" delegates were seated. He ultimately achieved victory for Harvey's choice when he frankly admitted that although Wilson was really a stranger to him he was the one man who could win the election for the Democrats. Winning an election was to Smith, as it is to most politicians, more important than how it was won. For Wilson, the nomination provided a graceful egress for a graceful man from a graceless predicament at Princeton.

Once elected it became apparent to Wilson that the people, under the influence of the newspapers, supported reform, and Wilson soon reversed himself and became a somewhat radical progressive. During his two years as governor, business regulatory laws, the strictest to date, were passed by the New Jersey legislature and signed into law by him. (25, p 57)

"Between the time of his election in November and his inauguration in January," Kerney wrote, "he found himself discarding most of the petty political theories he had been teaching his students. Within three months he had completely shifted from the conservative that Harvey and Smith had so gleefully nominated and was fitting into his program much of the radical political doctrine of the day. In less than a year he was publicly apologizing for having been wrong in his university attitude against the initiative, referendum, and recall." (32, p 97) Flexibility or guile. Take your pick.

Although Wilson responded to the roar of the crowd, he was not a part of it. The Trenton *Evening Times*, of which Kerney was the editor, viewed Wilson "as a man of unusual ability and opportunity who had failed to take any interest in the public life of the community." (32, p 36) In over twenty years of residence in Princeton he owned no real estate, and until nominated for governor, attended no county, state, or national political convention, and took no part in the politics of Princeton Borough. He did not even vote in the 1909 election the year before he was nominated for governor.

And yet Wilson had for years harbored political ambitions, and by his own admission looked upon his work as a historian as training for his political career. (32, p vii) He stated his positions on the issues of the day, and in the manner of the hermit who has never ventured far from his cave, he was able to see the problems of the world with greater clarity and visualize the solutions with more ease than the rest of us. The reason why so many of his one-time supporters, Smith, Harvey, Villard, Nugent, Bryan, Lansing, and even House, to name a few, were betrayed and dumped is that Wilson was a politician, and as a politician he felt little conpunction to act as he had written or spoken. He fulfilled William S. White's portrayal of the truly able politician as being ready "to cut down his own brother if that brother should become objectively expendable to his objectively higher demands." (5, p 46)

In history's eye Woodrow Wilson was as much an accidental president as was Theodore Roosevelt. A special confluence of events and men made Roosevelt president: a deranged man, a gun and a bullet in the hands of the man, and a wound which would not have been fatal had the medical competence of 1901 been a few years advanced.

The circumstances of Wilson's ascendancy were less brutal but no less dramatic. Roosevelt's ego bred his bitterness, ambition, and demagoguery which became the three tools by which fate shaped Wilson's triumph. Roosevelt was bitter at Boston on August 17th, 1912 and when someone in the crowd yelled, "Tell us about Taft," he shouted back, "I never discuss dead issues." (32, p 245) Roosevelt's vindictiveness was exceeded by his unlimited personal ambition. LaFollette said that Roosevelt had "as great an opportunity to serve the progressive cause as Bryan had at Baltimore but would not accept it because he was serving himself only." (32, p 246) The third instrument used by fate to shape Wilson's victory was Roosevelt's demagoguery. According to Kerney "Roosevelt's appeals to discontent and class hatred so badly demoralized the Republican vote that the election resulted in Wilson receiving 435 electoral votes, while Roosevelt got 81, and Taft but 15." (32, p 247) Even so Wilson was a minority president: the Democrat received about 1,400,000 votes less than the combined total of his opponents, or about 45 per cent of the total vote.

Wilson's political heritage was that of a Southern Democrat. He was born in Virginia, educated in private schools in Georgia and North Carolina and did graduate work at the University of Virginia and Johns Hopkins in Baltimore. He practiced law briefly in Atlanta. Before entering active political life he had written and spoken against women's suffrage, terming it "foolishness." (32, p 32) He vigorously opposed state or federal commissions as regulatory bodies for public utilities and corporations, preferring instead to rely upon the courts, and he blamed the financial panic of 1907 on "the aggressive attitude of legislation toward the railroads." (32, pp 33-34) In general, he opposed government interventions and controls, unionism, and giving publicity in its entirety to everything done by corporations. All this, Kerney's evaluation.

Villard reported that Wilson leaned toward political bossism, favored fiercely the open shop (which is not the equivalent of opposing unionism), opposed generally the organization of labor and was very hostile to government regulation of public utilities. The latter probably accounts for his being picked by business interests as their choice for the Democratic gubernatorial candidate in New Jersey. (25, 219)

Did Wilson's stated political convictions reflect his Southern Democrat heritage? Some did and some didn't. For instance, he was a staunch segregationist in spite of what he wrote in *The New Freedoms*. When he left the White House negroes in the government were more discriminated against than when he entered. Negro clerks in the Treasury Department were segregated from the white clerks and whites replaced the traditional black ambassadors to Haiti and the Dominican Republic. (25, p 237) The progress that had been made under Taft was reversed.

In 1913 Wilson wrote A. Mitchell Palmer (who was to serve as Wilson's attorney-general) that he considered the one-term president plank in the Democrat platform as nonsense, but when he accepted the nomination in 1912 he had stated that he squarely supported the entire platform. Even before his first inauguration he notified Palmer that he would be ready to run again should the people and his party demand it. (25, p 306) Wilson, like Franklin Roosevelt and Richard Nixon after him, endorsed a platform which he cast aside after he became president.

Wilson referring to Teddy Roosevelt's elaborate promises in

1912 "declared," according to Kerney, "that no man had a right
to go so far afield. 'You have no right to promise Heaven, unless
you can bring us to it, for, in making promises you create too
much expectation and your failure brings with it only disappointment and sometimes despair. As a candidate for the Presidency, I
do not want to promise Heaven unless I can bring it to you.' . . ."
Kerney, realistically appreciating that politicians often follow
more than they lead, added that "the successful leader ought not
to keep far in advance of the mass he is seeking to lead, for he
will soon lose contact with them. No unusual expectation ought
to be created by him." (32, pp 244-245)

Villard commented on Wilson's erratic course and unstable
convictions, writing that by April of 1916 Wilson had changed
his opinions on the "initiative, referendum, recall, women's
suffrage, the tariff commission, tariff for revenue only, a permanent diplomatic service beyond politics, the merit system in
Civil Service . . . (although he had been a vice-president of the
Civil Service Reform Association) . . . Tammany Hall, Bryan,
on a Continental Army, on preparedness, and then finally, on
child labor legislation." (25, pp 311-312) The latter he had originally opposed as unconstitutional.

Villard was convinced that Wilson's conversion to women's
suffrage did not represent a change of conviction, but rather was
the result of the fact that "he wants re-election, must win the
suffrage states, and can not allow Theodore Roosevelt to have a
monopoly of suffrage support."

According to Villard, "those were the only reasons for the
change. He was no more convinced than before, that woman
suffrage was the right thing." Earlier when Wilson was told by
Villard that he was loosing thousands of votes because of the
suffrage issue, he said that he couldn't change his opinions in
order to get votes and that he was not like Roosevelt. "Women,"
concluded Villard, "no more than blacks figured in his vision of a
really democratic society." (25, pp 290-291)

Teddy Roosevelt's opinion of Wilson comes from the book
Presidents I've Known by Charles Willis Thompson, the reporter
and editor. Roosevelt looked upon Wilson, according to Thompson, as an academician, a professor lecturing his class, and therefore unable to reach the voters. Formal, cold, without passion

and human understanding he went to the Paris Peace Conference
as a tenderfoot in a poker game, but to Roosevelt, the difference
was that Wilson was playing "with other people's chips." (39,
p 171) Unfortunately Wilson did not enjoy beginner's luck.

"It was Theodore Roosevelt," wrote Edward P. Mitchell, another editor, "who styled Woodrow Wilson 'a Byzantine logo-
thete', a description which for originality and the somewhat
mystifying quality of its offensiveness deserves a place in the
bright lexicon of censure . . ." (24, p 385)

Ex-president Taft, in keeping with his peaceful nature, had
hoped the United States could avoid involvement in the war.
Nevertheless, once war was declared he supported the president.
He also backed Wilson's efforts to establish an international peace-
keeping body similar to the League of Nations. Yet "at different
times," wrote Ishbel Ross, "in letters to his intimates, Taft characterized Wilson as stubborn, thick-skinned, hypocritical, Jesuiti-
cal, a purist, an academician, and the 'most unblushing and most
ruthless opportunist' that he had ever met." (27, p 278)

William Howard Taft focused sharply on his successor's foibles. It is tempting to dismiss his comments as the product of
opposition party politics, but they agree with the opinions of
many of Wilson's fellow Democrats and one-time friends.

"How a man . . ." wrote Taft to a friend in 1918, "can absolutely exclude from his councils the members of Congress and of
the Senate, both of his own party and the party that is standing
so loyally behind him, I can not understand except by attributing
to him a peanut soul and a gross self-absorption that exceeds
anything we have had in our political history. When he sends
for senators he never confers with them at all—he just tells them
what he wants. He doesn't know the meaning of conference or
counsel. He has a conception that he is the arbiter of the universe
and that he knows everything by intuition." (29, p 912) The
disasters Wilson suffered at the Paris peace conference and later
when he returned home were failures of execution rather than
failures of concept, and the failures of execution stemmed from
Wilson's personality.

Kerney reported that William Jennings Bryan, who helped get
the presidential nomination for Wilson and who later served as
Wilson's Secretary of State, believed that Wilson was a "natural

autocrat who had spent his life dealing with school-boys and who had become unable to meet anyone on a basis of equality." Bryan, virtually ignored as Secretary of State, later resigned in disagreement over Wilson's policies.

"Always his test was not what he (*Wilson*) could do for the other fellow," wrote Villard in an appraisal of Wilson, "but what that fellow had to give him and in answer to that question he felt himself upon an Olympian height looking down. He made great trouble for Tumulty (*his press secretary*) through his refusals to see people because they had, in his judgment 'nothing to give' him." (25, p 289) Wilson's treatment of Bryan certainly supports this judgment.

At the Gridiron Dinner in Washington in 1915, President Wilson watched, without amusement, an amusing parody on his break with William Jennings Bryan. Edward P. Mitchell was there and he described the scene.

"His face did not move a muscle while the friendly tormentor sobbed and sang; Mr. Wilson certainly did not smile to himself . . ." as the "Secretary" ended each stanza with "God bless you! Mr. President."

"When it came to be the President's turn to speak I was charmed by the grace of his bearing and the felicity of his utterance. Every phrase seemed so apt, every period so elegantly conceived, . . . The impression was of frank sincerity saying something immensely important; when he was finished it would not have been the easiest thing for the delighted listener to reconstruct the substance, or to decide whether the phrases grew out of the ideas or the ideas grew out of the phrases. Some doubts of this kind, I think, always existed in the minds of those closest to Mr. Wilson. I remember at this dinner, Mr. Franklin K. Lane, one of his cabinet, sat beside me. At the most impressive passages of Mr. Wilson's rhetoric Secretary Lane, whom I knew well and who was always a man of unquenchable humor and unterrified judgment, would nudge me in the back and look at me quizically as if to say, 'Well, now, what do you think of *that* great truth?' " (24, p 385) [1]

---

[1] William B. Hale was an admiring biographer of Wilson who outlived his admiration for his subject. Hale, who prepared *The New Freedom* from Wilson's speeches, later published *The Story of a Style*, a caustic criticism of Wilson's use of words.

Villard in *Prophets, True or False* also records Lane's opinion. Before Wilson was inaugurated, his Secretary of Interior wrote of him "he is apt to prove one of the most tremendously disliked men in Washington that has ever been here." Seven years later, in 1920, Lane wrote that "The American-born did not like Wilson because he was not too frank, was too selfish and opinionated . . . I have served with (*Wilson*) long and faithfully under very severe circumstances. It is hard for him to get on with anyone who has any will or independent judgment." (34, pp 222-223)

For a long time Woodrow Wilson was a hero to many intellectuals and latter-day liberals. By the 1960's some of these same types were beginning to have second thoughts. But the original, classic liberals were never fooled by Wilson's charm and gifts as a speaker. Henry Watterson's comments, written in 1919 attest to this fact. Watterson was a Jefferson-Jackson-Tilden Democrat who criticized Bryan as an inflater and even criticized Cleveland as a *high-tariff protectionist!* He was just as critical of his fellow Democrat, Wilson.

"In all that he does," wrote Watterson of Wilson, "we can descry the schoolmaster who arrived at the front rather late in life. One needs only to go over the record and mark how often he has reversed himself to detect a certain mental and temperamental instability clearly indicating a lack of fixed or resolute intellectual purpose. This is characteristic of an excess in education; of the half-baked mind overtrained. The overeducated mind fancies himself a doctrinaire when he is in point of fact only a disciple." (6, v II, p 273)

"When the history of these times," wrote Watterson in 1919, "comes to be written it may be said of Woodrow Wilson: he rose to world celebrity by circumstance rather than by character. He was favored by the gods. He possessed a bright forceful mind.[2] His achievements were thrust upon him. Though it sometimes ran away with him, his pen possessed extraordinary facility. Thus he was ever able to put his best foot foremost. Never in the larger sense a leader of men . . . he was an opportunist void of conviction and indifferent to consistency." (6, v II, pp 288-289)

Superstition has not been slain by scientific enlightenment although it has been badly bruised. It still survives in athletes,

[2] Previously Watterson had indicated it was a half-baked mind.

politicians, and children. Who can't remember skipping the cracks in the pavement, or something equally odd? In most educated adults superstitions tend to be forgotten or disregarded. There was one which Woodrow Wilson never seemed to bury.

Henry L. Stoddard, the editor, describes Woodrow Wilson's fondness for the number 13. He wrote that around the White House this was well known and that Wilson saw some mysterious significance in the fact that there were thirteen letters in Woodrow Wilson and that there were thirteen original colonies. This superstitious quirk was responsible for Wilson's orders to slow down the *George Washington* en route to France so that he could land on December 13th rather than on the 11th or 12th. (35, pp 501-503) In this case arriving on the 13th seemed to bring more bad luck than good!

H. H. Kohlsaat, friend of Roosevelt and acquaintance of Taft who wrote about their famous feud claimed that he had "been more or less intimate with the Presidents for nearly forty years," and did "not believe any other President so completely ignored his official family." Kohlsaat suspected that even Treasury Secretary McAdoo, who was Wilson's son-in-law, finally resigned because of Wilson's aloofness. (31, p 215)

Colonel Edward M. House was Wilson's confidante for many years. It was partly Wilson's heavy reliance on House which made so many of Wilson's cabinet feel neglected and ignored. But House suffered, eventually, the same fate of all the other spirit wrestlers, holy rollers, and politicians who served Wilson.

Wilson's break with Colonel House, about whom more will be said later, was reminiscent of Roosevelt's break with Taft. Both Roosevelt and Wilson were egotists of the first order and could not stand being upstaged. House was as much bewildered by Wilson's behavior as Taft was by Roosevelt's behavior. Kohlsaat believed that Wilson's rejection of House began at the Peace Conference. In the course of a single meeting with Wilson, House was called out, first to greet Lloyd George, the Prime Minister of England, then Clemenceau, the Premier of France, and finally Orlando of Italy. (31, p 224) Stoddard told how, on another occasion, Wilson called on House at his hotel to find Lloyd George in conference there with the Colonel. Wilson "excused himself for interrupting and said he would call again when House was at leisure. The latter call was never made." (35, p 510) No doubt it seemed to Wilson that House had become more important to the negotiations than the President himself. Wilson's ego required that henceforth House be largely ignored.

It is almost impossible to look at a picture of Woodrow Wilson without seeing the wispy little figure of the Colonel lurking in the shadow of the man from Olympus. Gilbert and Sullivan, Simon and Schuster, Laurel and Hardy. Why not Wilson and House?

Arthur D. Howden Smith was Edward Mandell House's reverent biographer. His *Mr. House of Texas* is a saccharine treatment of his subject. On page one we learn that "Mr. House detested the honorary title of Colonel which he never earned and never sought . . ." On page 270 we learn that in the spring of 1918 a syndicated series entitled *The Real Colonel House* was published. This was written by Smith based on material furnished by House. The Colonel read and checked the proofs for accuracy and made whatever changes he felt were needed. Now it is *possible* that he never saw the title given the series and therefore he could not register his protest to the use of *Colonel*. But when the series was later published as a book by the George H. Doran Company, it *still* bore the *same* title. It wasn't until 1940, a dozen years later, that the Colonel got around to resigning a commission he never had, said he detested, and became just plain Mister.

Howden Smith at the end of his explanation on page one about House's objections to being called *Colonel* wrote ". . . It was one of those little traits which furnish the essential clue to a man's inward being."

The flavor of Smith's biography and of the man who provided the information can be judged from a passage on page 17.

When House was twenty-one years old, in 1879, "he had gone to visit a college friend at Breckenridge, Colorado, a mining camp. He was wearing an overcoat, and for that reason carried his revolver in his side pocket. A man he had never seen before entered a saloon and without warning commenced to villify him in violent terms. Ed House had his gun cocked and was about to shoot from his pocket, when the bartender vaulted between the two. It was a case of mistaken identity. 'In five seconds more I would have killed him,' he remarked of the incident in 1917." (36, p 17)

The idea of killing a man with a concealed weapon did not

seem cowardly to either House or his biographer. At least, there
was no apologia. Nor did taking a man's life for verbal abuse
seem to them to be overly severe. In fact there was not even a
trace of embarrassment at revealing that a supposedly sophisticated man and later presidential adviser had almost killed a man,
if you could believe him, in a barroom brawl. But then, Mr.
House was, as we shall see, a reformer.

House staged-managed the elections of governor's Hogg, Cul-
berson, Sayers, and Lanham in Texas before moving on to
greater things in Washington. But he was chairman only of Cul-
berson's campaign committee. "For the life of me," said House,
"I can't see why I did it. The chairman of political committees
are usually figureheads. Most of them are forgotten by the public
a few months after their candidates have won or lost. And the
publicity was a nuisance to me." (36, p 28) House's movement
toward the shadows was already evident. It seems that he was
not satisfied with being a mere figurehead. It is telling, too, that
in one breath the Colonel laments the fact that as a campaign
manager he would soon be forgotten and in the next bemoans the
publicity that went with the job.

In 1912 House published anonymously a novel, *Philip Dru:
Administrator*. Howden Smith, even though he admired House,
could not bring himself to deny that it was a sorry attempt. He
described it as "probably one of the worst (*novels*) ever published, but it is of abiding interest as a statement of his political
philosophy . . . as a forecast of the important domestic legislation he helped the Wilson Administration to put through Congress
within the next two years." (36, p 23)

Much of *Philip Dru: Administrator* was set in Texas and it is
obvious that Colonel House was playing a Walter Mitty role.
Before the novel ends, Dru has become a heroic general, van-
quished the Mexicans (p 285), become savior and dictator (only
until things have straightened out) of the United States (p 221),
and divided the world into spheres of interest among England,
Germany, Japan, and the United States (p 273).

Two sample paragraphs will serve to show that the novel was
in fact probably "one of the worst ever published."

In Chapter XL, entitled "A Departure in Battleships," Dru's
rich girlfriend engages in some romantic talk. Sample: "Perhaps

their (*i.e. rich employers of female labor*) profits are on a narrow basis, Philip; but the volume of their business is the touchstone of their success, for otherwise how could so many become millionaires? . . . I want to give you all the facts so that in recasting the laws you may plan something to alleviate a grievous wrong." (37, p 234)

Forty-four pages later the General has still not succumbed to all this sweet talk, but he has managed to redesign the battleships.

"One day when the three of them (*that's right, the three of them, Dru, his best girl and still another girlfriend*) were together she (*the other girlfriend*) said, 'Mr. Administrator, why don't you marry? It would add enormously to your popularity and it would keep a lot of us girls from being old maids." (37, pp 278-279)

Was Dru being urged to marry several of these gals at once? We'll never know.

That *Philip Dru* was written by House there is no doubt. In addition to Howden Smith's acknowledgment of the fact there are at least two clues in the book. On page 73 the line appears ". . . but if you will dine with me in my rooms at the Mandell House tonight," and on page 74, "When he reached the Mandell House . . ." Perhaps Walter Mitty craftily concealed these little hints so that if, just if, fame was later forthcoming the true author could rip off his false mustache and dark glasses and claim the work as his own. House was 53 years old when the book was published, which is a pretty old age to be playing Walter Mitty games.

House displays a touch of Fabian Socialist strategy when, in connection with working among the rich to convert them to the welfare state, he has Dru say, "Do your work gently, so that some at least may listen. If we would convince and convert we must veil our thoughts and curb our enthusiasm, so that those we would influence would think us reasonable." (37, p 64)

House's father was a wealthy man. When he died in 1880 the estate was divided among his three sons, and Colonel House inherited the cotton plantations. His income was $25,000 a year from this source—a princely sum in 1880. With this security House was able to dabble in politics, write a bad novel, and dream about reorganizing the world.

It is sometimes suspected that rich revolutionaries are moved by a sense of guilt. Not many, however, feel so guilty that they want to distribute their own wealth. They are, instead, modestly content to do the job for others. This is a major theme of *Philip Dru: Administrator,* and the guilt feelings of House peep through the sticky rhetoric from time to time. Dru claims that the "most selfish . . . will be the first to realize the joy of it all (*i.e. sharing the wealth*), and in this way they will redeem the sins of their ancestors." (37, p 160) Particularly if their ancestors owned a Texas cotton plantation.

Philip Dru, like his creator, Colonel House, never fled from problems which would make ordinary men cringe. The variety of topics upon which Dru had opinions is staggering.

For instance, on revising the judicial system, "General Dru took the matter in hand . . . He pointed out that heretofore the laws had been made for the judges, the lawyers, and for those whose financial or political influence enabled them to obtain special privileges, but that hereafter the whole legal machinery was to be run absolutely in the interest of the people." (37, p 175)

The General also was 58 years ahead of Nixon in proposing Federal revenue sharing. He suggested "that such a system would be devised as would render it unnecessary for either municipalities, counties, or states to require any further revenue." (37, p 177) How was this to be done? Through graduated Federal income and inheritance taxes. The Federal income tax would start at one-half of one per cent with no exemptions and would go to seventy per cent on incomes of ten million dollars, or more. The inheritance taxes would be "graduated at the same rate as the income tax" and would provide safeguards against "defrauding the Government by gifts before death and other devices." (37, p 180)

On labor, the General declared "the rights of labor to have one representative upon the boards of corporations and to share a certain percentage of the earnings . . ." He did not mention sharing the losses. "In turn it was to be obligatory upon them not to strike, but to submit all their grievances to arbitration." George Meany wouldn't like that! "The law was to stipulate that if the business prospered, wages should be high; if times were dull, they should be reduced." This is quite at variance with Keynes' proposals for prosperity.

But House must have written part of Keynes' script for he had General Dru proclaim ". . . the formulation of a new banking law, affording a flexible currency . . ." Even before he would die the currency grew a little too flexible to suit Colonel House's taste.

General Dru looked longingly at the prosperous and growing telephone and telegraph companies and proposed the "Postmaster General . . . (be) . . . instructed to negotiate . . . for their properties at a fair valuation. They were to be under the absolute control of the Post Office Department, and the people were to have transmission of all messages at cost, just as they had their written ones." (37, p 190) May the Good Lord forbid!

Even Women's Liberation was anticipated by the General. "It had long seemed to Dru absurd that the ignorant and, as a rule, more immoral male, should have such an advantage over the educated, refined, and intelligent female. Where laws discriminated at all, it was almost always against rather than in favor of women," (37, p 219) said the General, implying that discrimination in favor of, rather than against, women would be acceptable. Nor did the Administrator neglect sex education. (37, p 271)

If Women's Liberation did not escape Dru's attention you would certainly expect no neglect of so serious a subject as burial reform. Sure enough, Chapter XLV, entitled "Burial Reform" plumps for private interments, doing away with "the unsanitary custom of burial," cheap funerals, etc., etc.

In a chapter entitled "The High Cost of Living" General Dru states "I have thought long and seriously how to overcome the fixing of prices by individuals and corporations . . ." Let the government do it! The government would be entitled to a seat on every board of directors of every corporation "and the books, and every transaction, would be open to the public . . . If a single corporation, by its extreme efficiency, or from unusual conditions, should constitute a monopoly so that there was practically no competition, then it would be necessary . . . for the government to fix a price reasonable to all interests involved." (37, pp 256-259)

It took General Dru, who seemed to be growing ever more forgetful, less than 167 pages to forget his own advice to "do your work gently so that those we would influence would think us reasonable." Came the not so gentle *revolution*, and after it, "everything seemed about as usual, further than there were no legislative bodies sitting and the function of law making was confined to one individual, the Administrator himself." (37, p 221) Oh, boy!

Barely three pages later the Administrator said that "there never has been a time in our history when a majority of the people have not thought right on the public questions that come before them, and there is no reason to believe that they will think wrong now." (37, pp 224-225) Which is hardly a good reason for confining the lawmaking to "the Administrator himself." Consistency is not a political virtue.

A little further on Dru, the dictatorial administrator, damns the power of the presidency in these words: "The framers of the old Constitution lived in an atmosphere of autocracy and they could not know, as we do now, the danger of placing in one man's hands such enormous power, and have him so far from the reach of the people, that before they could dispossess him he might, if conditions were favorable, establish a dynasty." (37, p 229)

Colonel House, in true liberal fashion, had little respect for the Constitution. He speaks through Philip Dru.

"Our Constitution and our laws served us well for the first hundred years of our existence, but under the conditions of today they are not only obsolete, but even grotesque." (37, p 222)

House devoted a whole chapter to The New National Constitution, Dru style. It proposed a structure similar to, but not the same as, the British government, with ceremonial president and a separate chief executive selected by the lower house.

Dru also propsed social security, old-age pensions, workmen's compensation, an eight-hour day, a Federal employment service, and "that every indigent person that is honest and industrious shall be given employment by the . . . government . . ." (37, p 227)

Howden Smith gives the impression that House's political philosophy influenced the course of the Wilson administration. If the Wilson term followed a similar path it was not because of any originality or force of House and his ideas. Little, if any, of House's political testament was original. His novel merely restated a body of thought that had been popularized in varying degrees over the years by the muckrakers, populists, progressives, and those opinion makers who supported them. That which the public was willing to accept was also accepted by Wilson the politician. House's importance rested upon the fact that, as an advocate for these ideas, he was at the seat of power.

Before dismissing the Colonel's role in domestic affairs a note about his murky demise is in order. There was some cooling of relations between the man from Olympus and the little Colonel which set in when Wilson took his second wife on December 18, 1915. Mrs. Elizabeth Bolling Galt, the Washington jeweller's widow who became the new Mrs. Wilson, had already lost one husband and she wasn't about to lose another, specially one who was the president. Mrs. Wilson was a strong-willed, possessive woman who shut her husband off from the world during his illness in the closing months of his term. She has even been accused of usurping his power, and if this is true, the Women's Liberation group might claim she was out first lady president, even if only an acting one. But while the deterioration of the Wilson-House friendship may be partly charged to Mrs. Wilson, the major cause was probably the President's bruised ego in Paris. It was there that House was assigned as a permanent delegate to Limbo, from whch he never again ascended to Heaven. The Walter Mitty in him kept him trying, however.

House gave a copy of his book, *Philip Dru*, to Felix Frankfurter, a confidante of President Franklin D. Roosevelt. Frankfurter had good taste in literature and it is not believed that he ever recommended House to FDR. Furthermore, Roosevelt was known to like detective stories rather than romantic novels that mixed politics, battleships and burial reform. In any event, House never achieved status in New Deal circles.

According to Howden Smith, (36, p 369) House "found himself increasingly out of sympathy with the ballyhoo and hustle policies of the New Deal . . . he knew from experience that over-haste in legislation makes for frustration of valid accomplishment." This from the one-man legislature, Philip Dru, is wryly amusing.

"He thought the Blue Eagle sensationalism of the NRA was the sort of thing he might expect of a pack of Boy Scouts. He thoroughly disapproved of the attack on the Supreme Court." Philip Dru had scornfully written that checks and balances were outmoded and that one of the chief obstacles to "progress" was the Supreme Court. Apparently by the time of the New Deal, Administrator Dru had matured to the point where he believed that some checks and balances to thwart "social reform" weren't so bad, after all.

"He thought Mr. Roosevelt's purge politics against Senators who disagreed with him was nothing more than bad, cheap politics," but Howden Smith wrote that House did not entirely disapprove of New Deal policies, however.

"Now an amusing aspect of the Roosevelt policies," wrote Howden Smith, "was that according to internal evidence, Mr. House was mainly (*one might question the use of so strong an adverb here; others were no doubt involved*) responsible for the most challenged and debated of them. He was hoist by his own petard. And that petard was *Philip Dru* and its radical preachments delivered two decades previously."

Thus, ends the tale of General Philip Dru, Administrator, friend of the oppressed, and stuffed-shirt reformer, whose creator lived out his remaining years cashing dividend checks and clipping bond coupons. Which proves that even if you dye a black crow white, he remains a rogue.

House's influence in foreign affairs was probably more important than his influence in domestic affairs. Wilson and his first Secretary of State, Bryan, had little in the way of international experience or outlook. House was equally provincial, but he had gained Wilson's confidence and he had no obvious reservations about his ability to fill a vacuum.

"Wilson felt," according to James Kerney, "that in House, who loved to roam the world, he had a complete foreign service of his own. Wilson did not have any particular regard for the diplomatic agents of the country and when he desired information he never hesitated to send his own personal agents. House was recognized as the voice of Wilson, having the confidence of the President as none other, save Tumulty, ever had it, and superseding American diplomats wherever he turned up. Personally, Wilson, like many men of genius, was not a glutton for work and he was glad to turn over . . ." his burdens to others. "Making speeches and inditing the messages was his part of the great program." (32, pp 316-317)

Oswald Garrison Villard dealt with House in *Prophets True and False,* published in 1928. (34) According to Villard *The Intimate Papers of Colonel House* were published as a reply to the published letters of Walter Hines Page, who was Wilson's ambassador to London. In the House papers, the Colonel has "bared himself, retaining not even a fig leaf, and the picture is not one to enchant in so far as his political activities are concerned."

Of House, Villard wrote, "Shrewdness, the ability to draw others out, a tremendous power of sympathy and quick understanding, of eager friendliness, of apparent unselfishness, of profound interest in world problems—all of these combined, in addition to his personal attractiveness, to fit Colonel House for the role of king-maker and king-director.

". . . he obtained precisely what he wanted, namely the position of being the power behind the throne, and it flattered his vanity and caressed his ego far more than would have been the case had he accepted the Secretaryship of State and been held accountable to the country and the press for his official acts—had he been compelled to face constant press criticism.

". . . He was errand boy, court chamberlain, buffer extraordinary, minister plenipotentiary, chief justice, writer of presidential notes, opinions, and speeches, chief of the secret service, the perfect counsellor, and finally the self-appointed arbiter of the world's destiny.

". . . There can be no doubt that no other private citizen ever wielded greater power; and it, of course, could only have been wielded by a wily and able man. This he did by consent of the President, conscious and unconscious.

". . . Moreover, the position that House assumed compelled, I am inclined to think, insincerity and double dealing, and more so as time went on. He became more and more Machiavellian. Thus, he claimed to be a pacifist—Prof. Seymour (*Sterling Professor of History at Yale, Wilson's biographer, and editor of House's papers*) even dares to say that this man who approved the slaughter of men, women, and children at Vera Cruz, the lawless invasion of Mexico by Pershing, and the murder of over three thousand Haitians under President Wilson's orders, 'was himself, perhaps the most sincere pacifist in all America' . . .

His (*House's*) real attitude he reveals when he boasts that he stirred up a controversy between a group of pacifists '*as usual . . . which delights me.*' [3]

". . . Subsequently he always appeared to sympathize with those who came to him protesting against the infringement of American rights and liberties after the outbreak of the war, and particularly against the maltreatment of conscientious objectors, and to regret those official excesses. It is impossible now to believe that he was else than a complete hypocrite, that he was not in accord with what actually took place . . .

". . . This official-unofficial intriguer had grown so great in his self-esteem and his power that by 1916 he did not hesitate to gamble with lives of American citizens as if they were his pawns . . . on his own authority House brushes aside the Congress of the United States and repeatedly notifies Sir Edward Grey [4] that in certain contingencies the United States will join forces with the Allies.

"The history of statecraft," wrote Villard, "surely contains no record of anything approximating the naivete and the innocence and self-conceit with which House tackled the European problem. Never having had anything to do with foreign affairs in any capacity heretofore, he assured the Kaiser on June 1, 1914 that the President and he 'thought perhaps an American might be able to better compose the difficulties here and bring about an understanding with a view to peace than any European, because of their distrust and dislike for each other.'

" '*I have undertaken the work,*' he continued, '*and that is my reason for coming to Germany.*' "

In only two years, Walter Mitty's dreams were become realities.

"But when it came to the Presidential election in 1916," continued Villard, "Colonel House was all for trumpeting the fact aloud that Mr. Wilson had kept the country out of war and for concealing the fact still further that he (House) had done his best at times to put the country into it and still believed it inevitable . . . Professor Seymour thinks it would have been 'rather

---

[3] General Philip Dru's assault on Mexico and plans for central America were prophetic of House's part in later history.
[4] Sir Edward Grey was the British Foreign Minister and later Ambassador on Special Mission to the United States.

Quixotic' for House to fail to take advantage of this peace-desiring American mood . . ." (34, pp 169-183)

Wilson's atrocious treatment of his cabinet might have been predicted from the casual way he selected his official family. He had barely heard of and did not know Lindley M. Garrison who became his Secretary of War. Garrison was chosen because Wilson needed a man from New Jersey. He had never talked to or even seen, until they were introduced to him at his inauguration, Franklin K. Lane, a California newsman who became his Secretary of the Interior, James C. McReynolds, a Tennessean who became Attorney General, or Congressman William B. Wilson of Pennsylvania who served as Secretary of Labor! (25, p 31)

"His cabinet," wrote Villard, "was not there for consultation or deliberation with the President but merely to pass upon his views submitted to it by him with the expectation that there would be a prompt vote of complete approval. Only a minority of the cabinet was brave enough occasionally to dissent or go counter to the President's views, for the members realized that if they did so often they would lose what influence they had with the Chief Executive—some had none at all." (25, p 259)

But the Wilson-House relationship was ultimately responsible for the President's notoriously poor relationships with his cabinet and ambassadors. He failed to keep his subordinates informed, not only in foreign affairs but in domestic affairs as well, relying instead upon Colonel House. His similarly cavalier treatment of senators and congressmen led to the eventual defeat of his plan to participate in the League of Nations.

Much has been written about America's "drift" into the first World War. A reading of Stoddard's *As I Knew Them, Presidents and Politics from Grant to Coolidge* casts doubt on the "drift" theory.

The papers of Colonel House and the memoirs of Sir Edward Grey both mention the agreement signed on February 22, 1916 which stated that the United States would propose a peace conference. The agreement further stated that if Germany refused to attend "the United States would probably enter the war against Germany." With complete disregard for the responsibilities of Congress, the agreement added cynically that should Germany attend the conference and fail to agree to terms "not unfavorable to the allies . . . the United States would leave the conference as a belligerent on the side of the allies if Germany was unreasonable." (35, p 491) This was a "heads you lose, tails I win" proposition.

Although Wilson did not originate the slogan "He kept us out of war," [5] he did not shrink from the benefits it bestowed upon him and he cynically accepted the votes and plaudits of those who believed he had kept the country at peace, even while secret arrangements had been made, with House's connivance, for our entry. As early as October 26, 1916, a full year before the "He kept us out of war" election, Wilson said, "I believe that the business of neutrality is over." (See Baker, Ray Stannard and William E. Dodd, eds, *Public Papers of Woodrow Wilson*, v 2, p 381.)

Wilson's tacit assent to the use of the "He kept us out of war" slogan may have led the Germans to a miscalculation of American intentions. There is nothing more dangerous in international relations than leading a potential enemy to believe they have a carte blanche to do as they please. On January 31, 1917, a little more than a month before Wilson's second inauguration and *three months after the campaign in which the slogan played a key part*, the German Ambassador informed the Secretary of State that unrestricted submarine warfare would be resumed on February 1st. Diplomatic relations were broken on February 3rd by Wilson and on the same day the German foreign minister told the U.S. Ambassador in Berlin that "America will do nothing because Wilson is for peace and nothing else." (38, p 204) Just a month earlier Wilson, in a message to Congress, stated that "this country does not intend to become involved," and according to Stoddard "orders became more and more rigid against any preparation of our army and navy . . ." (35, p 495) Wilson succeeded not only in convincing the American people that he was committed unreservedly to peace, he also succeeded in convincing the Germans. This was a mistake.

Congressman Claude Kitchin was the most powerful Democrat to oppose Wilson's war policies. He was majority leader of the House of Representatives and Chairman of the Ways and Means

[5] Governor Martin Glynn used the slogan in his keynote address at the 1916 Democratic National Convention. Wilson edited the speech beforehand and promoted later use of the slogan. (25, pp 314–315).

Committee. Professor Alex Mathews Arnett details in his book, *Claude Kitchin and the Wilson War Policies* (pp 118-119), the struggle of the genuine neutralists to keep the United States out of the war, including the steps taken by the Wilson administration which could only have led us to war on the side of the allies.

So America went to war. Whether it was with Wilson's witting or unwitting help probably will never be firmly established. But the disaster of the Peace Conference rests firmly on his shoulders. After 106,000 American deaths and about 200,000 casualties, the world was not made safe for democracy. Monarchies, which had been moving toward democratic government, were replaced by the most oppressive dictatorships, and freedom was in retreat. At the peace conference the costumes and the props were merely assembled for the next, more tragic act. The Germans lost, but we did not win.

Of Wilson's opening address at Paris, Villard wrote, "Even the graceful speech of President Wilson, who was plainly the only barrier between a peace of folly, rapacity, and vindictiveness, failed to dispel my deep depression. I knew Woodrow Wilson, knew his cowardice, knew his egotism, knew his readiness to compromise, and to persuade himself that surrendering to your opponent was, in a tight place, the height of political skill . . ." (25, p 386)

Villard's depression was justified, even if some of his strong language wasn't. American correspondents were excluded from sessions of the peace conference and from private sessions of the leaders. "The President's first yielding was on his 'open covenants, openly arrived at.' " (25, p 387)

William Bullitt, the American diplomat, wrote a scathing letter of resignation as an attache of the American Peace Commission. "I am sorry," wrote Bullitt, "you did not fight our fight to the finish and that you had so little faith in the millions of men like myself in every nation who had faith in you." (25, p 452)

Wilson's grand failure in foreign affairs was accompanied by growth of the Federal Octopus. Even in the absence of any design to push the country in this direction, the war would have catalyzed the development. There were designs, however, and they were drawn by the political twins of progressivism and reform.

Woodrow Wilson and the Democrats were firmly in control

when the XVIIIth amendment was proposed by Congress and ratified by the states. However, all Democrats were not in favor of prohibition, and it is true that the Democrats were back in control when the amendment was repealed. But it is ironic that between times the Republicans took most of the blame for the damage caused by prohibition.

Henry Watterson, the Jefferson-Jackson-Tilden type Democrat, made this farsighted libertarian assessment of prohibition in 1919: "The challenge underlying prohibition is twofold: Does prohibition prohibit, and if it does, may it not generate evils peculiarly its own?

"The question hinges on what are called 'sumptuary laws'; that is statutes regulating the food and drink, the habits and apparel of the individual citizen. This in turn harks back to the issue of paternal government. That, once admitted and established, becomes in time all-embracing.

"Bigotry is a disease . . . Bigotry sees nothing but itself, which it mistakes for wisdom and virtue. But bigotry begets hypocrisy. When this spreads over a sufficient area and counts a voting majority it sends its agents abroad, and thus we acquire canting apostles and legislators at once corrupt and despotic.

"They are now," wrote Watterson as the XVIIIth amendment was ratified, "largely in evidence in the national capitol and in the various state capitols." (6, v II, pp 207-208)

Albert J. Nock perceived the dangerous trend set by the XVIIIth amendment. "For example," he wrote, "expediency suggested that the evils of liquor traffic be suppressed by coercion. It got results, after a fashion, but it got them for us at the price of making corruption and hypocrisy respectable . . . Again, expediency suggested that the care of the poor be made a government job. It got results, but at what price? First, the organization of mendicancy and subvention into a permanent political asset. Second, the indoctrination of our whole citizenry with a false and dangerous idea of the State and its functions—that the State is something to be run to in any emergency, trivial or serious, to settle matters out of hand.

"This idea," continued Nock, "encourages, invites, nay, insists upon what Professor Ortega y Gasset rightly calls the gravest danger that today threatens civilization: the absorption of all spontaneous social effort by the State." (21, p 271)

The Democratic attack on the prohibition amendment was launched, to his everlasting credit, by Al Smith. It was a libertarian attack. Franklin Roosevelt carried it on, but his grounds were economic, not libertarian: booze was supposed to restore prosperity.

The XVIth amendment to the Constitution was proposed by Congress on July 12, 1909 and was proclaimed ratified by the Secretary of State on February 25, 1913, a week before Wilson's inauguration. Although Wilson did not play a major role in adoption of the amendment, he wasted no time making use of its powers. In his first year in office the Congress, in response to Wilson's prodding, enacted an amendment to the tariff act which provided for the first graduated tax on incomes. The XVIth amendment and the taxes it permitted were beyond doubt the most significant legislation since the Constitution and Bill of Rights were first adopted.

The graduated federal income tax gave the Federal government prior claims to the income of all citizens. Since money is the source of government power, the Federal government took giant steps toward ascendancy over its citizens and the states. To be sure, the states had been permanently subordinated to the central authority by the results of the Civil War, but they still retained responsibility in the general areas of education, welfare, public health, and regulation of business. The reason for this is that the Federal government had insufficient means to raise the money to perform these tasks until the XVIth amendment was passed. From now on, the government in Washington would increasingly control more and more areas of life. Once the combination to the safe was sent to Washington the contents would no longer be secure. The power to tax grants the power to control, the power to dominate, and, of course, the power to destroy independence and freedom. The lesser socialism of the states was to be replaced by the vastly more ruthless, remote and comprehensive socialism of the Federal government.

Although Wilson had the Federal income tax as a new source of revenue, his fiscal policies remained essentially sound. His pre-presidential views on creation of Federal debt were that "appropriation without accompanying taxation is as bad as taxation without representation . . . taxation and appropriation must go hand in hand." (4, p 485) Wilson was entirely correct in criticizing appropriation without accompanying taxation. It is not only, as Wilson stated, "as bad as," it actually is, taxation without representation. It is a tax imposed by a present generation on a later generation as yet not represented. Twenty-seven years later, when he was president, Wilson still held that Federal borrowing is "short-sighted finance." Kimmel quoting from *Messages and Papers of the Presidents* reported Wilson as saying that borrowing can be justified "only when permanent things are to be accomplished which many generations will certainly benefit by and which it seems hardly fair that a single generation should pay for." (4, p 87) By 1935, this policy was discarded by Wilson's Democrat successor in the White House. Wilson was not, however, as ignorant of economics as was Franklin Roosevelt. In fact Wilson collaborated with two authors on an unpublished book concerning the history of American economic thought.

Among the interventions of the Wilson administration was the establishment of the Federal Reserve System. This was largely inspired by Senator Carter Glass of Virginia. The intent of the system was well meaning and some aspects of the system were sound. However, the system has been politically abused. It no doubt contributed to the inflation of the twenties and to the subsequent depression. It has also made possible the manipulations upon which perpetual deficit financing depends and which in turn has resulted in the continuing dangerous inflation since the New Deal. Such abuses are to be expected from political interventionist activities. The end results of inflation are likely to be price and wage fixing, rationing, and eventual serious erosion, if not complete destruction, of personal freedom. The cure that the Federal Reserve System was supposed to provide for financial instability may well prove to be worse than the original illness.

Another intervention of the Wilson administration was the establishment of the Federal Trade Commission. It has grown to be a Federal monstrosity with frightening power over business. It is prosecutor, judge, and legislature all rolled into one, as is the case with so many Federal commissions. Enforcement of anti-trust legislation was placed in the hands of the Federal Trade Commission and the anti-trust laws were expanded by passage of the Clayton Act.

Seizure of the railroads on December 21, 1917 led to gross and lasting government interventions. Under Wilson's Railroad Administration the Federal government massively intervened in the affairs of labor and capital. It forced the eight-hour day, raised wages and freight rates (the latter by 25 per cent), and introduced collective bargaining. The railroads were returned to their owners by 1920, but they remained under the restrictive rule of the Interstate Commerce Commission. The Transportation Act of 1920 required that the ICC fix "fair" rates, a task as likely to succeed as designing a perpetual motion machine. Railroads earning more than what the ICC determined was "fair" were required to give half their "surplus" to "weak" railroads, thus subsidizing and rewarding inefficiency. From this we have gone to the point where, by 1971, the government has taken over all passenger service, subsidizing the losses with taxes taken from all taxpayers regardless of whether they do or don't use the system. In the years since 1920 numerous railroads have gone bankrupt or are on the verge of bankruptcy. These are the rewards of government interference. The whole story is documented in Professor Clarence Carson's "Throttling the Railroads," which appeared in *The Freeman* starting with the May 1970 issue.

The Farm Loan Act was yet another Wilsonian intervention. This gave the farmers advantages that were not theirs by virtue of free-market conditions. The act was justified as a wartime measure and was partly responsible for expansion of the farm production which later created the farm relief issue and led to subsidy programs which are still with us.

James Kerney, the New Jersey newspaper publisher and editor, was one of Wilson's earliest supporters and later his most impartial biographer. According to Kerney, Wilson, the minister's son turned politician, found it necessary to compromise, to trade, to surrender, and to retreat in order to advance. He no longer believed in applying the inflexible moral tests to himself which he recommended to his students. He did the very things which he, as a moralist professor, had earlier uncompromisingly condemned. Kerney called him a "super politician, who when he had finished using politicians discarded them." (32, p XIV) Wilson himself is quoted as having said, "No man in whom you . . . look . . . for leadership is made up altogether of gentle qualities . . . You do not want sweetness and merely light in men who lead you." (32, p XII) Wilson, according to Kerney, "had an enormous capacity for dressing ideas, original or borrowed, into beautiful language . . . but . . . we saw him change from a conservative Democrat to a very militant two-fisted Radical, and with the coming of the war, into an equally two-fisted Autocrat." (32, pp XIII-XIV) Charles W. Elliot, who had been president of Harvard University wrote that "Wilson like most reformers and pioneering folks, had a fierce and unlovely side." (32, p 333)

Wilson also assumed the arrogance of the politician in power. Kerney's appraisal matches that of Villard. Kerney claimed that Wilson was guilty of "seldom admitting he was wrong; those who differed with him either became 'wilful' or 'they did not know what they were talking about.' He mostly saw man, the individual, in his littleness, and was intolerant, impatient, and disgusted with him . . . 'He has a bungalow mind,' was a favorite description," applied to the common man. "Like many men who accomplish great things, he was disposed," wrote Kerney, "to regard the virtues as his own, while the mistakes and conflicts became readily blamable on others. And like most men in places of power he, in time, came to accept as truth the fulsome praise and personal propaganda of the professional promoters and boosters." (32, p XI) Wilson was a man whose natural inclination toward arrogance was fed by the power of the presidency.

Kerney also stated that Wilson "was a lonely man, a dreamer with the type of intellect that found it difficult to tolerate ordinary mortals." (32, p 333) At another point he wrote that "He could not temper his demands . . . He was bent on saving the whole world at once." (32, p 483) This is typical of the reformer's impatience.

"Marse Henry" Watterson recognized the shift of his Democratic Party away, under Wilson, from the concept of limited government, particularly at the Federal level. He valued checks and balances and diffusion of power. Watterson's party changed from the party of decentralized power to the party of centralized power.

"The death blow to Jeffersonian democracy was delivered," he wrote, "by the Democratic Senators and Representatives from the South and West who carried through the prohibition amendment. The *coup de grace* was administered by a President, elected as a Democrat, when he approved the Federal suffrage amendment to the Constitution.

"The kind of government for which Jeffersonian democracy successfully battled for more than a century was thus repudiated; centralization was invited; States' rights were assassinated in the very citadel of States' rights. The charter of local self-government became a scrap of paper, the way is open for the obliteration of the States in all their essential functions and the erection of a Federal government more powerful than anything of which Alexander Hamilton dared to dream." (6, v II, pp 287–288)

One may misjudge Watterson because of what appears to be his opposition to women's suffrage. He was not opposed to women's suffrage *per se*. "Let me repeat," Watterson wrote, "that I have been fighting women's battles in one way and another all my life. I am not opposed to Votes for Women . . . It is feminism rather than suffragism which is dangerous." (6, v I, p 197)

"The woman," he wrote later in his book, "is becoming over much a professional female. It is important that we begin to consider her as a new species, having enjoyed her beauty long enough. Is the world on the way to an organic revolution? If I were a young man I should not care to be the lover of a professional female . . ." (6, v I, pp 221-222)

Watterson's fight was not with the vote for women, but with the expansion of Federal authority which demanded uniformity of the States regarding women's suffrage.

". . . it looks as though the United States, having exhausted the possibilities of reasonable democracy," wrote Marse Henry in 1919, "is beginning to turn crank . . ." And then after a blast at the Constitutional amendments on women's suffrage and prohibition he feared that "tobacco was next to walk on the plank (*it did in 1970*); and then!—Lord, how glad I feel that I am nearly a hundred years old and shall not live to see it!"

"The fanatic," Watterson wrote, "is never either very discriminating or very particular. As a rule, for him taking any "ism" will suffice. Today (*1919*) it happens to be 'whiskey.' Tomorrow it will be tobacco. Finally having established the spy system and made house-to-house espionage a rule of conventicle it will become a misdemeanor for a man to kiss his wife." (6, v II, p 284)

"This is merely to note the mortal fallibility of man, most fallible when herded in groups and prone to do in the aggregate what he would hesitate to do when left to himself and his individual accountability . . ." (6, v II, p 286)

Thus, A would never singly and openly face D and demand money to educate A's children, to care for A's parents, or to provide for A's needs when times were hard. Nor would B, nor C, openly approach D for satisfaction of these same needs. But if A, B, and C can combine and hide behind the anonymity of a government they are no longer bound by personal accountability and their individual timidity becomes the ruthlessness of a lynching mob.

"Mobs," wrote Watterson, "have seldom been tempted, even had a chance to go wrong, that they did not go wrong." (6, v II, p 285)

"Under a wise dispensation of power, despotism, we are told, embodies the best of all government. The trouble is that despotism is seldom, if ever, wise. It is its nature to be inconsiderate, being essentially selfish, grasping, and tyrannous," (6, v II, p 286) concluded "Marse Henry."

Thus it was with the French revolutionists, with Napoleon, with Mussolini, with Hitler, with Lenin, and with Stalin. Thus it will ever be.

When the shackles which bind government are broken the monster ravishes.

Wilson was the instrument by which a few shackles were broken and many more loosened.

CHAPTER 8

FALLEN ANGEL

Charles Willis Thompson wrote for the New York *Times*, the New York *Herald-Tribune*, *The American Mercury*, and *The Commonweal*. Thompson was a writer-reporter who had personal contacts with many prominent men at the close of the nineteenth century and in the first thirty years of the twentieth century. Toward the end of his career he wrote a delightful and interesting book, *Presidents I've Known and Two Near Presidents* relating his first-hand experiences of a half-century. Thompson did not rely on his memory. Rather he drew upon detailed diaries in which he had recorded his day to day impressions and confrontations. Thompson tells more about Warren G. Harding's character in eighteen pages than most biographies reveal in several hundred.

The future president borrowed the money to buy The Marion *Star* when he was only nineteen and for a while the going was hard. It was Harding's foreman, Billy Bull, who told Thompson, "why Mr. Harding would often see to it that his employees all got their money on Saturday night, and then go home himself without a cent left. He has men in his plant who have been working for him for twenty or twenty-seven years. You couldn't drive them away if you cut their salaries down. I never heard him talk cross or speak rough to any man. He has another way of getting what he wants—kindness is his way." (39, p 339)

Almost all writers, even Harding's antagonists, agree that Harding was a kind-hearted man. Bull told Thompson that Harding "never fired anyone. Once in a while, in the last thirty years, he had said to me, 'I don't like that man.' But he never fired the man, nor gave me orders to fire him; he always let the man stay on the paper till he went away on his own accord." (39, p 338)

Beyond the people who worked for him, Harding was equally generous. When a printer came to town down on his luck Harding would give him a job if he could, and if he couldn't, he'd give him enough money to get to the next town. He had the reputation of giving more to poor and needy persons in Marion than any other resident of the town. But his generosity and kindness had to do with more than money. For instance, Thompson quotes one of his editorial rules: "If any item comes in that will cast ignominy or reproach on some innocent woman or child, don't wait for somebody to suppress it, suppress it." (39, p 339)

Harding's kindness was not, originally at least, calculated. Even later, when it became the basis of his success as a politician, generosity was a basic part of his nature. Harding's strategy for political victory was to make many friends and to avoid making any enemies. Those who were his political opponents he fought without animosity, and often he could count on their help when needed later.

"Weary of striving onward and upward," wrote the slightly liberal Frederick Lewis Allen of the Harding phenomenon, "the electorate chose for President in 1920 the handsome Warren G. Harding, a senator whose greatest assets, aside from his magnificent good looks, were his kindness, folksiness, and humility. An amiable man of no lofty intellectual or moral stature, he had no conspicuous urge to improve anything; he preferred to talk about what he called "normalcy," meaning "normality." (9, p 132)

Harding was at heart a newsman. Even as a United States senator he couldn't resist the lure of his *Star* office. Thompson tells how a state senator came to visit Harding at his home. He found him at the *Star*, down in the composing room, "peeled to his shirt, with his sleeves rolled up and his hands and arms smeared with ink, was the next President." The visitor "gazed at him in astonishment for a few moments and then stepped up to him. At his approach Harding turned around, laid down a slug, and extended a grimy hand. 'Well,' said the state senator, drawing a deep breath, 'you are certainly a hell of a United States senator.' " (39, p 340)

Harding was not just a newsman, he was a successful working newsman. For a time he was his paper's only reporter, its editorial writer, and its make-up man. He had the reputation, according to Thompson, of being an "easy writer," linotype operator, advertising salesman, and, in the business office, a first-rate buyer. (39, p 340) Had fate left this happy man to pursue his natural talents and wishes he probably would have lived a longer life as owner of the *Star*. He certainly would have been happier in Marion than in Washington.

Henry L. Stoddard, whose lengthy career as a political reporter started with the old Philadelphia *Press*, talked with Harding two days before the President left on his final fatal trip. Harding had just signed a contract for the sale of his newspaper.

"This is the most distressful day of my life," Harding said sadly to Stoddard. "It tears at my heart. But what else is there for me to do? I do not expect ever to live in Marion again . . . It is hard for me to think that my days as an editor are over. An editor has the finest job in the world—I envy all you fellows. You've got a better job than I have." (35, p 472)

Stoddard's assessment of Harding's character generally matches that of Thompson.

"There was gratitude," wrote Stoddard, "there was friendship, there was a comradic warmth about Warren Harding that in every presence made him less a Senator, less a President, and more a genial understanding companion . . . He greeted every dawn with the sunny, cheery smile of the man who loved life and his friends, and whose record is made up only of kindly acts." (35, p 474)

Edward P. Mitchell, the late editor of the New York *Sun* said in a concurring comment that Harding was "the kindest-hearted of (*the*) Presidents of the United States." (24, p 441)

But a kind heart alone is not enough. Just as Taft's reluctance failed to produce, by itself, an outstanding president, Harding's kindness did not prevent the failures of his presidency. In fact his friendliness and warmth were at the root of his troubles, for Harding, like Grant before him, was betrayed by those he trusted. There is greater reason to excuse Grant's mistakes because the General was not experienced in politics and, until he became president, he had little contact with politicians. Harding as a former senator, newsman, and editor should have known better.

The awful heat of Chicago in August 1920 was an omen of the

hell that Harding's devilish friends would make of the last three years of his life. Mrs. Harding, older and more ambitious than her husband, pushed him ahead in Ohio politics until he found himself at the Republican National Convention as a favorite son. When it appeared that he might be nominated she had some last minute second thoughts about the presidency.

"I can't see why anyone should want to be President," she said. "I would rather have him stay in the Senate. I can see only one word written over his head if they make him President, and that word is 'Tragedy.' " (40, p 132)

Harry Daugherty, who later disgraced Harding's administration as Attorney-General, was not daunted by Mrs. Harding's reservations. Harry Daugherty's prediction, made four months earlier, that the convention would nominate a man picked by a dozen or so men "at two o'clock in the morning, in a smoke-filled room," (40, p 136) came true. The fact became more famous than the prediction. It was the work of the "Senate Soviet."

The Senate Soviet was a term used by Charles Willis Thompson to describe a clique of Senators led by Lodge, Smoot, Wadsworth, and Penrose. (Senator Penrose was not in the smoke-filled room. He was ill in Philadelphia at the time.) The Senate Soviet was fed up with battling the chief executive. Starting with Teddy Roosevelt, "that damned cowboy in the White House," and continuing with a slight respite during Taft's term, fights between the senate and president grew increasingly bitter in Woodrow Wilson's second term. What better solution than to choose one of their own? Harding was picked by the Senate Soviet because he was known as a thoroughly trusting man. The senators knew they could "shuffle him and deal him like a pack of cards." (39, p 331) Daugherty's dark vision probably extended far beyond such honest political manipulation.

In any event, according to Thompson, "Friday night had come with the convention at sea, with delegates tired and bored, dismayed by their mounting hotel bills, and with no interest in anything but the overpowering desire not to be stuck in Chicago over Sunday."

When the deadlocked convention met at ten-thirty Saturday morning, "everybody was sore and mutinous, but anxious to end it all and get home." (39, p 326) The delegates accepted the Senate Soviet's choice and Harding, the dark horse, was nominated.

Harding was not, according to Thompson, a popular man. He was not popular with the senators who picked him and he was not popular with the delegates who nominated him, and he was not popular with the voters who finally elected him. Sinclair reported that Harding ran behind the three leading contenders for the nomination, and even behind Charles Evans Hughes, the Republican candidate in 1916, who wasn't even a candidate in 1920. (40, p 132) He was picked by his fellow senators because he was bland, he was picked by the delegates because he gave them a chance to escape from a torrid Chicago, and he was picked by the voters who were not voting *for* Harding but were voting *against* the legacy of Wilson.

And what about Harding himself? A mere twenty-four hours before he was nominated he wanted to telegraph the Secretary of State of Ohio to put him on the ballot for re-election to the Senate. The deadline for filing was Friday night.

"Why, Harry (*Daugherty*), it's my last chance," Thompson quotes Harding, "You don't want me to give up the Senatorship, do you? And," continued Ohio's favorite son who was unable to capture all of his state's delegates, "I haven't a ghost of a chance at the presidency." (39, p 326) Harry Daugherty helped to prove Harding was wrong, even though Andrew Sinclair reported that Harding had but 39 of Ohio's 48 favorite son votes. (40, p 132)

Not to be neglected as a factor in the election were Harding's relations with the press. Harding as a working newsman understood what made news and he understood reporters' problems in gathering it. He made special efforts to be available, to answer their questions, and to bend elbows with them. He was down to earth and sociable, but the "incongruity between himself and his pretensions" Thompson, who was on the scene, reported was a source of irritation to some reporters. (39, p 333) Nevertheless most reporters were on his side. They reported on him favorably and this was of tremendous value. His mastery of the press was matched only by FDR's later mastery of the radio and JFK's mastery of television.

"A special bungalow with three rooms . . ." was erected in Marion, according to Andrew Sinclair, Harding's liberal English biographer, "for the use of the journalists. Once or twice a day,

Harding would wander in, greet them personally by name, borrow a plug of tobacco or a stogie and say 'shoot!' He would then answer all questions in a friendly way, without evasion. . ." (40, p 161) But he would specify which remarks were "off the record." He gave out copies of speeches in advance of delivery, he pitched horseshoes with the reporters and swapped stories with them. Even though much of this came naturally to him and was not contrived he certainly appreciated its value. The contrast with Wilson's teacher-student type press conferences and Taft's innocent bungling was astounding. It is no wonder that he captured the press.

The corruption which sullied Harding's reputation resulted from poor selections for his cabinet and from other equally faulty political appointments. The most disastrous choice was Albert B. Fall, who became the Secretary of Interior. However, Harding was not the only president deceived by Fall. Teddy Roosevelt thought so highly of him that he once chose Fall to nominate him for the presidency. (40, p 188) Harding was also criticized for being fooled by such a rogue as Harry Daugherty, his Attorney-General. But Daugherty fooled not only Harding, he also gulled Taft. Ishbel Ross told the story.

After William Howard Taft was appointed Chief Justice of the Supreme Court, he came to Washington. "His old friend, Harry Daugherty," wrote Ross, "now attorney-general, welcomed him . . ." Later that night "the President read the bonus message to him for comment and criticism, and he and Daugherty persuaded Harding to make some changes in it." (27, p 325-326)

"When Daugherty was in the deepest trouble he (*Taft*) wrote to Horace (*William Howard Taft's brother*): 'I am still of the opinion that Daugherty is honest personally.' The Attorney-General, in his opinion was 'one of the finest fellows I know . . . loyal, hard-working, disinterested, honest and courageous,' but he also considered him a man of boundless ambition who was never fitted for the post he held in the Cabinet." (27, p 345)

Fall was eventually convicted of accepting bribes in connection with the leasing of government oil reserves and served a jail sentence. Daugherty was suspected, as attorney-general, of trading presidential pardons for pay and of accepting favors, financial and otherwise, for dispensing alien property seized during the war.

Edwin Denby was the honest but woefully naive Secretary of the Navy. There were unreliable appointments of political cronies to lesser jobs than cabinet positions such as the Director of the Veteran's Bureau and the Alien Property Custodian. Both of these appointees were convicted and sent to the Federal penetentiary.

John W. Davis, the Democratic nominee for the presidency in 1924, summed up the public horrors of the Harding administration in his acceptance speech on August 12th, a little more than a year after the president's death.

". . . a Senator of the United States convicted of corrupt practice in the purchase of a Senatorial seat; a Secretary of the Interior in return for bribes granting away the naval (*oil*) reserves so necessary to the security of the country; a Secretary of the Navy ignorant of the spoilation in progress, if not indifferent to it; an Attorney-General admitting bribe takers to the Department of Justice, making them boon companions and utilizing agencies of the law for purposes of private and political vengeance; a chief of the Veteran's Bureau stealing and helping others to steal millions . . . Such crimes are too gross to be forgotten or forgiven."

Harding's record was used with gleeful gusto by the liberals as a club with which to flay conservatism. The people were not allowed to forget the scandalous public behavior of some of his appointees. Nor were they allowed to forget his own private misbehavior, his affairs with Nan Britton and Mrs. Carrie Phillips, his poker playing and his drinking in violation of a law for which he had voted as a senator. Conservatism became synonymous, in the eyes of many, with public corruption and private scandal. Other than venality what does the record of Harding's years really show?

Harding's basic political philosophy tended toward conservatism. It was tempered by the even more basic political creed that winning elections may require some bending of a politician's principles. This is not to say that even if he had remained a stalwart conservative he would also have been an anti-statist. After all, Republican conservatism and anti-statism have never been identical. Furthermore, Harding ran at times with the liberal or progressive Republicans. He was said to be "sanely progressive" when he bowed to political expediency. But in spite of statist tendencies which grew out of both business-biased conservatism and expedient progressivism, Harding recognized the desirability and advantages of limited government.

He knew that government tends to be inefficient, and he gave his reasons in May of 1921 when he spoke to the Academy of Political Science in New York.

"Government . . . ," he said, "is under obligation to give the greatest service for the lowest possible cost. But it is for certain obvious reasons difficult to do this, because government is not under the necessity to earn profits, nor to obey laws which regulate competition." (4, p 89)

This is certainly true of the Post Office, the oldest socialist operation of the Federal government. In 1860 the postal deficit was $9,900,000 or almost 16 per cent of total federal expenses of $63,100,000. (4, p 57) For the fiscal year ending June 30, 1908 the postal deficit was $17,500,000. The deficit resulted from low rates for magazines and newspapers, and rural free delivery. Second class mail was being delivered at a cost of nine cents a pound, but the charge was only one cent a pound. The loss from the unprofitable classes of mail delivery was $63,000,000, equal to total Federal expenses in 1860. Profits from first class delivery reduced the deficit by $45,500,000. Politics prevented correcting the situation.

President Taft asked congress to adjust rates to reflect more nearly the cost of the various types of service. For this he was attacked by the newspaper and magazine publishers, those lofty crusaders against privilege, who are no less biased in their own interest than any other pressure group which seeks to live at someone else's expense. They resorted to the irrelevant and still prevalent fiction that they are educational enterprises. This is not only an insufficient reason for public subsidy, but it disregards the fact that a major portion of the information disseminated, including advertising, cartoons, features, and society news could hardly be considered education. In apparent anticipation of this criticism rates had been set for the "reading portion" and the "advertising portion" of publications. But the rates (in the 1st and 2nd zones) have been identical for both portions for most of the time since 1884! When individuals (transients), rather than publishers, mail the *identical* newspapers no distinction is made between reading and advertising portions. Furthermore, there is a mysterious loss of educational value which entitles the Post Office to collect more from transients, in fact quite a bit more, per pound than it collects from publishers. Table 8–1 tells the tale. Between 1900 and 1971 non-local first class rates went from 2¢/oz to 8¢/oz and more than half of this increase has occurred in the last thirteen years of the seventy year period. The cost of post card service has increased from 1¢ to 6¢ in the same seventy year interval, and two deliveries a day are only a dim memory. Keep in mind that in 1900, even at the low first-class rates then prevailing, first-class service was helping to pay the cost of the other services.

TABLE 8–1

Publishers rates, per pound, 1st and 2nd zones [1]

	1885	1920	1921	1952	1971
Reading Portion	1¢	1½ ¢	1½ ¢	1.65	4.0
Advertising Portion	1¢	1¼ ¢	2¢	1.65	6.0

Transients (individuals) rates, per pound

	1884	1925	1952	1971
Reading and Advertising Portions	4¢	16¢	9¢	21¢

It is interesting to compare the cost [2] of delivering messages by mail with the cost of delivering messages by telephone since 1919. For instance, a three-minute, station to station, day rate call from Boston to Denver cost $17.05 in 1919, $9.25 in 1930, $4.00 in 1940, and $1.35 in 1971. Corresponding night rates were $8.50 in 1919 and $0.85 in 1971! From 1910 to 1925, one-party, unlimited residence service in Boston cost $3.25/month. In 1971 the same service had slightly more than doubled to $6.75/month (private communication, New England Telephone and Telegraph Company), but the area served was much larger than in 1919, and service much faster and more reliable. The increase was also less

---

[1] Source: *United States Domestic Postage Rates, 1789–1956*, United States Post Office, Washington, D.C., 1956; for 1971 rates see Post Office *PS Form 3541, May 1971*.
[2] *Cost* is used loosely. The charge paid by the mailer does not represent the cost, since mail delivery is a deficit operation. The total cost is partly paid by the user and partly by tax subsidy.

than needed to compensate for loss in the purchasing power of the dollar.

The Post Office can not match this record [3] because of politics and pressure groups, because of faulty cost accounting, and because of the lack of the dollar discipline that exists only in the free market and comes from the need to show a profit. Harding, as a businessman in politics, recognized these facts as impelling reasons for limited government.

Harding's administration took steps to restore civil liberties which had been violated as a result of the war. At the close of Wilson's administration 197 persons convicted of obstructing the war effort in one way or another remained in prison. Among them was Eugene Debs, the Socialist, who, while imprisoned in 1920, received nearly a million votes for president. Debs, who had admitted his guilt, was convicted under the Espionage Act for obstructing the draft. On Christmas day 1921, President Harding granted executive clemency to Debs. Many other prisoners were either released or deported. When Harding died in August 1923 all but twenty-one of the prisoners had been freed.

In October 1921 Harding went to Birmingham, Alabama, and spoke before a segregated audience of 20,000 whites and 10,000 negroes. He urged, in a statement that was bold for the place and the times, that "politically and economically there need be no occasion for great and permanent differentiation, for limitations of the individual's opportunity, provided that on both sides there shall be recognition of the absolute divergence in things social and racial." (40, p 231-232) He expressed the view that although racial partnership was needed, when negroes had equal opportunities in separate education they would develop their own leaders in favor of segregation. The radical blacks, including W.E.B. DuBois, who later left the United States and became a Communist, opposed this "inconceivably dangerous and undemocratic demand for social inequality." (40, p 232) Harding did not, of course, demand social inequality—he advocated "absolute diver-

---

[3] It is true that two totally different ways of communicating are being compared and the results must be interpreted in this light. Nevertheless, the telephone companies have managed to show profits, pay taxes, and improve the speed, reliability, and quality of service and at the same time reduce costs (in terms of constant value, noninflated dollars). Can the postal service make the same claim?

gence," or separation, or *laissez-faire*. At the time, probably most negroes, as well as most whites, supported the president's views on "natural segregation."

Harding's prediction that negro leaders would eventually press for segregation seems to have come true for at least some militants. In the last few years black militants have demanded separate dormitories, separate black social centers, separate political parties, and even a separate country. This is a black reaction to forced integration which is seen by them as an admission that blacks are inferiors who have something to gain by association with superior whites. It is the exact reverse of the white attitude that integration must be prevented because superior whites will be degraded by associating with inferior blacks. Both attitudes are ridiculous for it is obvious that some whites are superior to some blacks, and vice versa. This is true for the whole range of negro and white characteristics and abilities such as truthfulness, industry, athletic ability, ability to solve problems, musical ability, social graces, and so forth. It is true for individuals regardless of what may be shown by tests of large numbers of people and by *average* accomplishments of blacks and whites. People therefore should be free to associate or not associate, free to trade or not trade, free to sell or not sell, as they see fit, without governmental coercion. *Laissez-faire* is the solution to all the problems of race. Although libertarians may oppose some tax-supported facilities and services, such as public schools, hospitals, and the postal service, and support others, such as the courts, police, and defense establishment, they would certainly agree that *all* public facilities and services should be available to *all* citizens on an equal and unhindered basis. In private affairs and relationships, the libertarian holds that those who wish to segregate should be allowed to do so and those who wish to integrate should be allowed to do so without either government interference or encouragement. If the government is to be color blind in regard to *public* affairs it is inconsistent for it to suddenly become color conscious in *private* affairs. It can neither force nor prevent voluntary association or voluntary exchange of goods or services on the basis of similarity or dissimilarity of color *unless it looses its color blindness*. In other words, the government can not interfere in private affairs as long as it remains color blind.

Harding proposed in his Birmingham speech that literacy tests be applied uniformly to all citizens. "Let the black man," he said, "vote when he is fit to vote; prohibit the white man voting when he is unfit to vote." Here Harding is proposing color blind government. If the right to vote on this basis had become fact rather than remaining a fiction, it is likely that Southern racial problems would have reached earlier solutions. Voting rights alone will not guarantee racial peace, however, as seen from turmoil in the North where voting rights have not been infringed upon. But Bastiat asks a valid question in his book *The Law*. If the functions of government were limited to "nothing more than the organized combination of the individual's right to self-defense . . . is it likely that we citizens would argue much about the extent of the franchise?" (Bastiat, F., *The Law*, published originally in France in 1850, and by the Foundation for Economic Education, Irvington-on-Hudson, N.Y., 1968, p 16)

During and right after the first World War American agriculture was called upon to supply a major part of the food for countries of the Western hemisphere. This required both a major expansion of the land under cultivation and capital investment financed and promoted largely by Federal interventions during the Wilson years. The increased demand for food forced prices upward. In addition, prices rose because of inflationary policies of the governments at war. By the beginning of 1922, three years after the war ended, demand for American farm products had dropped greatly and inflation had been virtually stopped in the United States. There was a general decline in prices as a result of these changes, and the drop was specially severe in the farm market. Farmers were badly squeezed as they tried to meet interest and fixed charges on farms which had been greatly overexpanded in terms of domestic needs. The interventionism which created the problem was now expected to solve it. Harding, who stood to lose the farm vote, was facing a serious political problem, for the farm vote was of much greater significance then than now. For instance, total farm employment dropped from 13.4 million in 1920 to 4.6 million in 1969. Expressed as a percentage of votes cast in the 1968 presidential election, farmer workers represented 6.3 per cent of the vote cast. In 1920 they represented 53 per cent of the vote cast.

Harding's response to the problem was to call a National Agricultural Conference. At the opening session the President said that farming had always been a risky business and that farmers had never before looked for government to aid them. Although that was not strictly accurate, he added, "It can not be too strongly urged that the farmer must be ready to help himself." With this statement no libertarian could argue, but there evolved from the conference the principle that the government had an obligation to "subsidize farm prices in order to give the farmer a fair return for his labor." (40, p 249) To Harding's credit he resisted this principle which, when it was adopted ten years later, exchanged new problems for existing ones. This is typical of statist solutions—they do not improve the overall state of affairs —they merely remove a burden from the shoulders of one group, in this case the farmers, and place it on the shoulders of other groups, in this case the taxpayers and consumers. (Since the farmers are taxpayers and consumers, as well as farmers, they have paid part of the cost of their own subsidy.)

Although Harding acted as a libertarian in rejecting direct farm subsidies, he succumbed to statism by settling for the highest tariff rates ever imposed by the United States. These were supposed to restrict farm imports and improve demand for domestic produce. Tariffs were also applied to many manufactured products with the same intent. The farm population was supposed to buy manufactured American goods and the urban population was supposed to respond by buying American farm produce. Since the cost of foreign products to American buyers included the tariff, imports were priced out of the market. The result was the same as for all tariffs: consumers were denied access to lower-cost, more economically produced items. This is another way of saying that the tariff succeeded in lowering the standard of living by requiring more sweat and effort to produce or acquire the same quantity and quality of goods. High tariffs are at the crossroad where libertarians and many conservatives part company, since high tariffs are favored by conservatives with a statist bent. Interventions by statist conservatives are just as much rejected by libertarians as are interventions by statist liberals.

Sinclair provided some interesting information regarding Harding's personal feelings about the farm problem. He quoted a letter from Harding to his friend Malcolm Jennings. Jennings was a Marion businessman and one of the president's few friends who never sought favors from his friendship. Harding's letters to him revealed his real attitude on a variety of subjects.

"Of course," wrote Harding, "the agricultural world can not go on with such a disparity between agricultural compensation and the present wages to industrial workers. If the adjustment does not come in any other way many of the men will leave the farm and diminish agricultural production and turn to employment in the industrial centers."

Harding's statement is a realistic prediction of what would have happened had economic pressures been allowed to operate on the problem. Surplus labor would have left the surplus farms and excess production of farm products would have stopped. In addition, more manufactured products would have resulted, leading to a better balance between what is needed and what is produced. Economic pressure was, however, eventually thwarted by subsidies which tended to stabilize the unbalance and perpetuate the problem.

After the war, Wilson's nationalized railroads were restored to "private control" under the Interstate Commerce Commission and the Railway Labor Board. Nationalization being the ultimate in socialism, a restoration to "private control" was a step backwards from a socialist viewpoint. (Steps backward are, however, a part of Fabian socialist strategy.) Faced with this new kind of "private control" President Harding appointed men to the ICC who were at least sympathetic to railroad ownership. Nevertheless, railroads under "private control" continued to be hamstrung by the heavy hand of government.

The Federal Government got into the chemical and power industry via the Muscle Shoals project during the war. Harding attempted to have the complex sold to private industry, but he was thwarted by Republican insurgent George Norris. Senator Norris was the man who, during Franklin Roosevelt's term, finally succeeded in expanding government production of power under the guise of flood control and navigation in the Tennessee River Valley. The Norris Dam is a memorial to statism.

President Harding favored an open-shop labor policy. He stated

that "every American citizen, whether union or nonunion, should
have the privilege of working where and when he pleases and
should be guaranteed by the government in the exercise of this
right as an American citizen." (40, p 254) Harding's stand on
labor was more forthrightly libertarian than those of Coolidge
and Hoover, and, needless to say, of Franklin D. Roosevelt.

Striking coal miners murdered twenty strikebreakers at Herrin,
Illinois during Harding's term. Harding lacked Federal authority
to prosecute them. (They should have been prosecuted and judged
by the state in which the crime was committed, but they were
not.) He also lacked the authority to use Federal troops to seize
the mines and protect the strikebreakers. Nevertheless he threatened to do so and the strikers went back to work. Had there
been an actual seizure this would have been a usurpation of state
responsibility. The state should have protected strikebreakers
from the violence of strikers, just as it has an obligation to protect strikers from armed company police and to protect company
property from damage by strikers. The states should be the agents
which prevent all violence not in violation of Federal law, but the
precedent for Federal intervention had been set by Teddy Roosevelt in the coal strike of 1902.

When railroad workers went out on strike, the interventionist
pattern was followed again. A Federal injunction was obtained
against the strikers which forbid interference with the operation
of the railroads and forbid both picketing and encouraging of
picketing. The strike was broken two days after the injunction
was issued, but the denial of peaceful picketing is an unwarranted
invasion by the Federal government into private affairs. Harding
was again on the side of the conservative statists.

In the 1920 campaign Harding "proposed easier credits for
farmers and cooperatives, . . . a Federal public welfare department . . . government efforts to solve the housing problem, . . .
and a protective tariff." (42, pp 127-128) After the 1922 midterm
elections Harding moved toward a more progressive, and less
business-biased type of interventionism. He became interested
in "social justice." (Plato and Socrates, who had a hard time de-
fining *justice*, would certainly have been stumped by *social justice*.) Harding now came out for ending child labor, for "cheap"

money for farmers, and "cheap" (presumably subsidized) transportation. Earlier he had pressured the steel companies to abandon
the twelve-hour day. All excepting "cheap" money are worthy
goals. None are the *proper* goals of the Federal government.
Harding died before his progressive ideas made much headway.

Warren G. Harding, had he not been a politician concerned
with the always imminent next election, would probably have
opposed most progressive interventionist goals. As a business man
he would be expected to oppose labor unions because of the obstacles they can place in the way of an entrepreneur's freedom
of action. Likewise, he would be expected to favor high tariffs and
to oppose restrictions on child labor and twelve-hour days. The
libertarian would oppose government action on all of these questions, excepting to prevent the use of violence in their settlement,
because the libertarian holds that economic forces and the working of the free market will at the most opportune time provide
the best answers. In the cases, for instance, of child labor and the
twelve-hour day, legislation alone can not bring about the desired
results without lowering the standard of living. Child labor and
long working hours are eliminated only by technology advancing
to the point where equivalent or superior production is achieved
by machines or power equipment. Bargaining and the free market
for labor will then eliminate children in factories and sixty-hour
weeks. By this time legislation is no longer needed. Otherwise,
why not define children as persons under twenty and make employment of such persons illegal? If this is successful why stop at
twenty years of age? Why not forty or fifty years? Why press
for only an eight-hour day if a legal four-hour day would make
life that much more pleasant?

A few months before he died Harding became aware that his
friends had betrayed him, as William Allen White learned when
he visited Harding early in 1923. (30, pp 615–627)

"My God," cried Harding, "this is a hell of a job! I have no
trouble with my enemies. I can take care of my enemies all right.
But my damn friends. My God-damn friends, White, they're
the ones that keep me walking the floor nights." (30, p 619)

Herbert Hoover, who served as Secretary of Commerce, also
observed that just before Harding's death the president showed

concern over the behavior of his friends. On the final fatal trip to Alaska and the west coast Hoover was asked by Harding what he would do if he "knew of a great scandal" in the administration. Harding mentioned the Department of Justice and Jesse Smith [4] but did not reveal further details. (18, p 49)

Harding, the fallen angel, died a few days later.

[4] Jesse Smith was Attorney-General Daughterty's private confidante and accountant who occupied government office space near Daugherty's office. He shot himself as he was about to be arrested.

CHAPTER 9

COMPLETE YANKEE

Rural Plymouth in Vermont remains almost as rural as it was a century ago. A few important dirt roads have been hard-surfaced, school buses now take children to school, and some abandoned farms have surrendered to the resurgent forest. But Plymouth is basically the same as it was almost a century ago when John Calvin Coolidge was born on July 4th, 1872.

At the center of Plymouth the country store, which Calvin's father owned and operated, and the post-office still function. Nearby are several houses and barns. A roadside sign tells the infrequent traveler that, from the age of four, Calvin Coolidge lived in one of the houses across from and slightly behind the store until he moved south to Massachuetts. The possibilities of another sign, this a huge one stretching across the side of a barn which looks down on the Coolidge homestead, have surely been overlooked by the sophisticates who have so gleefully ridiculed the man who served as the 29th president. It reads *Plymouth Cheese.* John Coolidge, the late president's son and a part time resident of Plymouth, is president of the Plymouth Cheese Corporation.

When Nature created the Plymouth countryside the only riches she bestowed upon it were its unsurpassed beauty. She made no arrangements for an easy life from the soil. A century ago survival depended upon self-reliance, shrewdness, and self-discipline, all traits of the Coolidges who were successful in the hostile environment. After scratching for food and warmth, for clothing and shelter, little or nothing was left over for high-priced fun. The frugal Yankee substitute was homemade wit which cost nothing. Today a ski area a few miles down the road probably enriches Plymouth more than the remaining farms, the cheese factory, and the store all combined.

Many biographies have been written about Calvin Coolidge. Probably the most complete and best documented one (41) was written by Claude M. Fuess, former Headmaster of Phillips-Andover Academy, and published in 1940. A later, but somewhat more critical, study (42) was written by Professor Donald R. McCoy and published in 1967. These have been used as principal sources for the biographical background on the man who is probably ranked first among the twentieth century presidents by many antistatists as well as by many conservatives.

The Coolidges were the most prominent family in Plymouth. Father John Calvin Coolidge worked as a carpenter, mason, carriage maker, farmer, and proprietor of the local general store. At various times he served as a schoolteacher, commissioner of schools, superintendent of schools, selectman, state representative, tax collector, deputy sheriff, colonel on the staff of Governor William Stickney, and justice of the peace.

The Coolidges were also the wealthiest family in town. Even so, their standard of living was well below the lower limits of what is now considered the poverty level. Poverty, in those days, before it was discovered by politicians and sociologists, seemed to breed pride instead of shame, ambition instead of despair, industry instead of indolence, and obedience instead of crime.

The Coolidges were not only prominent and prosperously poor, they were a family blessed with a closeness and warmth which, like the horse and buggy, are long gone, replaced by the individual pursuit of pleasure and doing one's own thing. Calvin's affectionate letters home are a witness to this warmth. Obviously young Calvin was never instructed in the mysteries of the Oedipus complex, sibling rivalries, and Freudianism. It is clear that he behaved, simply because he had never been told by those who knew better that he was expected to misbehave. The generation gap had not yet been institutionalized.

His mother's death, when Calvin was twelve, affected him greatly as did the death of his sister, whom he loved dearly, six years later. The year after his sister's death, Calvin's father remarried. His talented and well-educated stepmother was devoted to her husband and stepson and her love was abundantly returned. At this time Calvin, having completed Black River Academy and attended St. Johnsbury Academy for a few months, entered Amherst College.

During his first two years at Amherst, Coolidge made little social or academic progress, but in his junior year his Yankee wit and personality were finally recognized and appreciated, and in his senior year he helped establish a chapter of a national fraternity in which he maintained a lifelong loyal interest. By the time Coolidge graduated in 1895 he had established a reputation as a serious, hardworking, unobtrusive student, a good debater, and somewhat of a wit and humorist. He was not elected to Phi Beta Kappa (until 1921) but he did graduate *cum laude*. Rural Vermont had not prepared him for an easy conquest of the academic world, but honest effort made up for his lack of background.

With his baccalaureate in hand, the young graduate moved to Northampton where he read law in the office of Hammond and Field, attorneys. He lived at Rob Weir's boarding house, down the hill from the Clarke School for the Deaf. It was here that the future president met his future wife, a young lady from Bennington, Vermont. The hilarious circumstances of that meeting are pure Yankee and worth repeating.

Grace Goodhue, who was to become Mrs. Coolidge, taught at the Clarke School and lived on the hill just above Rob Weir's house in the Baker House, a teacher's residence hall.

"One day," according to the account in McCoy's book, "as she was sprinkling the flowers around Baker Hall, she happened to glance up at Weir's place. There she saw a strange sight. At the window stood Coolidge, shaving, wearing a hat, and apparently in his long underwear. Grace laughed spontaneously, and then, partly in embarrassment and partly to control her laughter, she quickly turned back to watering the flowers. Coolidge heard her laughter and inquired about her. Weir arranged for them to meet. When they were introduced Coolidge explained that he had an undisciplined lock of hair that got in the way while he washed and shaved. To solve the problem he had to anchor the lock with the hat." (42, p 130)

If there was ever a complimentary match between husband and wife it was the Coolidge-Goodhue union. And if there ever was a woman who was appropriately named it was Calvin Coolidge's wife, Grace. Her name matched her manner and looks, and she rightfully won the reputation as the most attractive, delightful, and gracious first lady of the twentieth century. The president's plainness, shyness, and his outstanding oddity, his silence, were completely offset by Grace Goodhue Coolidge's natural charm and bouyant good nature.

Coolidge saw the humor of a man who was chided constantly about his silence marrying a teacher of the deaf. Ishbel Ross in *Grace Coolidge and Her Era* (Dodd, Mead and Co., N.Y., 1962, p 9) reported Rob Weir joked "that having taught the deaf to hear, Miss Goodhue might perhaps cause the mute to speak." In this she was unsuccessful, as two tales from Fuess' book illustrate.

Fuess quotes from a letter of Frank W. Stearns, Coolidge's original Boston booster, to his sister. "Mr. Coolidge," wrote Stearns, describing a dinner party, "was put beside the brightest and most attractive lady in the bunch. After it was over, she was asked how she got along. 'Well,' she said, 'I tried my very best. In the first place, I tried to be serious. Not a word from Mr. Coolidge. Then I tried to be frivolous, and you know I can be very frivolous when I try. Not a word from Mr. Coolidge. Finally, as the dinner was about over, I said to Mr. Coolidge, '*There is only one of those macaroons left, and they are good.*' Not a word from Mr. Coolidge. I turned to speak to a gentleman on the other side, and when I looked back, my macaroon was gone. I charged him with having taken it. He said, '*Oh that is yours, is it? Well you may have half of it.*' And that was the total result of the evening.' " (41, pp 470-471)

A second tale is included in Fuess' book. Fuess wrote that "the best story—probably authentic—is that of the prominent society woman who said as she sat down next to him, 'Oh, Mr. Coolidge, you are so silent. But you must talk to me. I made a bet today that I could get more than two words out of you.' 'You lose,' was the Vice President's reply." (41, p 300)

Brevity was the basis of the Coolidge style. It was his strength as well as his trademark. The point was never missed, whether he was serious or light, sarcastic or sentimental. He felled his quarry with a well-aimed single shot from a flintlock, not with a burst from a machine gun. If he set out to squelch someone, the victim was not merely maimed, he was killed.

Fuess quotes the effusive lady from Boston who said to Coolidge, "I come from Boston." Coolidge, who was never really accepted, or impressed, by Boston Brahmins, unexpectedly replied, "Yes, and you'll never get over it." (41, p 5) Fuess also wrote "about the dinner at the White House for a new member of the cabinet, who arrived inexcusably late, after the others had sat down. The lady turned to Mr. Coolidge and said, 'Mr. President, I knew my husband and I would do something perfectly awful before we'd been very long in Washington.' 'You have,' " was Coolidge's reply. (41, p 479)

"Coolidge had himself," wrote Fuess, "no affectations and despised people who, as he said, 'put on airs.' Once at a White House luncheon the only guest beside Mr. Stearns was an American diplomat home on leave, who easily dominated the conversation, describing his intimate social relations with the rich and aristocratic classes in the country to which he was an ambassador. When he had paused, the President looked over to his wife and said, 'Mother, those dogs have crossed the end of the room four times in the last ten minutes.' The guest collapsed like a punctured balloon and was restrained in his talk for the remainder of the meal." (41, p 485)

Calvin Coolidge who was frugal with money, both his own and the public's, was a spendthrift when it came to wit. Will Rogers, who was qualified to judge if anyone was, "insisted that Coolidge wasted more humor on people than anyone he knew." (39, p 376) He was not a master of the long anecdote and the careful build up. His best wit was brief like his best squelches. In August 1928 he took a vacation in Wisconsin and did some fishing in between official visits. In response to a press conference query about his activities, the President said, "I have been so busy at the lodge catching fish—there are 45,000 out there—I haven't caught them all yet, but I have them all pretty well intimidated. They have had to restock one lake."

Fuess told the story about Coolidge's first presidential salary check. "In all their personal expenditures the Coolidges were careful, although not penurious, and the accounts were systematically checked. Mr. Coolidge paid all his bills himself and probably saved money while he was in the White House . . . It was rumored that when a messenger brought him his first salary check, he pondered it carefully, put it in his vest pocket, and said drily, 'Call again.' " (41, p 324)

His humor and wit extended to practical jokes and teasing. McCoy quotes Colonel Edmund W. Starling of the Secret Service. "If the mood suited him," according to Starling, "he would press the buzzer which notified everyone he was on his way to the White House (*from the executive offices*). Then, while ushers, policemen, doormen, and elevator operators were rushing about getting things ready and snapping to attention, we would stroll out West Executive Avenue and leave them." (42, p 158) McCoy also claimed that Coolidge was an exasperating tease to his family. His love, however, was just as deep for his family as it had been for his parents, his stepmother, and his sister.

Guests were no more immune to Coolidge's jokes than were his family and the White House staff. The Coolidges frequently entertained at informal early morning breakfasts. At one of these small affairs the food and coffee was served and the several guests present waited for the President to commence. Finally he poured the cream and coffee from his cup into his saucer and blew on it. The guests looked at each other in nervous embarrassment for a moment and then poured *their* coffee into their own saucers. The President, without changing his expression, then leaned over and put his saucer on the floor for his cat.

As a youth, President Coolidge was saddened and deeply affected by the death, first, of his mother, and then of his little sister Abbie. The cycle of sadness ran full circle when the President's own son died at the age of 16. According to McCoy "The President's feelings were best expressed in a story told by Colonel Starling, his Secret Service body guard:

'Very early one morning when I came to the White House I saw a small boy standing at the fence, his face pressed against the iron railings. I asked him what he was doing up so early. He looked up at me, his eyes large, and round, and sad.

' "I thought I might see the President," he said. "I heard that he gets up early and takes a walk. I wanted to tell how sorry I am that his little boy died."

' "Come with me, I'll take you to the President," I said.

'He took my hand and we walked into the grounds. In a few minutes the President came out and I presented the boy to him. The youngster was overwhelmed with awe and could not deliver his message, so I did it for him.

'The President had a difficult time controlling his emotions. When the lad had gone and we were walking through Lafayette Park he said to me: "Colonel, whenever a boy wants to see me always bring him in. Never turn one away or make him wait." ' (42, pp 251-252)

The Coolidge brevity which made his wit and humor so pointed also enabled him to express deep feelings unspoiled by slush. Fuess wrote (41, p 473) that "When Edward K. Hall (*a friend of Coolidge's*) lost a son just as he was coming into a promising manhood, Coolidge sent him a book with this inscription:—

To E.K.H.
Whose boy, and my boy, by the grace of God,
Will remain boys through all Eternity."

Five years after he died Grace Coolidge wrote a poem in memory of her son, entitled "The Open Door." Her graceful poignancy is in sharp contrast to her husband's brief inscription in the book he sent to Hall, but it shows the same depth of feeling. Feuss quoted (41, pp 351–352) the poem and it is worth repeating as a measure of the woman who so perfectly complimented her husband.

> "You, my son,
> Have show me God.
> Your kiss upon my cheek
> Has made me feel the gentle touch
> Of Him who leads us on.
> The memory of your smile, when young,
> Reveals His face,
> As mellowing years come on apace.
> And when you went before,
> You left the gates of Heaven ajar,
> That I might glimpse,
> Approaching from afar,

The glories of His grace.
Hold, son, my hand,
Guide me along the path,
That, coming,
I may stumble not,
Nor fail to show the way
Which leads us home."

Calvin Coolidge's reticence and silence, while natural more than part of a conscious scheme, were appreciated by him as being useful. When he was President of the Massachusetts Senate he told a fellow Senator that "They can't hang you for what you don't say." Later when he became President he advised his Secretary of War, "You know, Mr. Secretary, I have found in the course of a long public life that the things I did not say never hurt me." (41, pp 473) When he was no longer president he advised Dwight Morrow, his Amherst College classmate who was running for senator from New Jersey, to "talk as little as you can, but if you have to talk, talk about patriotism. They seem to like it."

Yankees are like Cheshire cats. They smile in silence. Not talking too much is a good Yankee trait, and Calvin Coolidge, the complete Yankee, owed some of his political success to his silence. Keeping quiet is a Yankee tactical weapon against garrulous protagonists who talk themselves into a hole if given the chance. A man who talks and talks and talks is bound to say something wrong. Not so the man who is quiet. Calvin Coolidge did not proclaim himself the savior of Boston during the police strike. He wasn't. He was only an ex post facto savior as we shall see. He also did not deny the paeans of his patrons who proclaimed that he *was* the savior. He just sat silently like a Cheshire cat. He sensed when it was right to be quiet. And he smiled, and smiled, and smiled.

There is a corollary to Yankee silence. It is similar to an old navy saying: "When in danger, when in doubt, don't run in circles, scream and shout. Drop down to the wardroom for a cup of coffee." Calvin Coolidge was never in the navy, but he had the same philosophy. "If you see ten troubles coming down the road," he was fond of saying, "you can be sure nine of them will run

into the ditch before they reach you." And yet Coolidge at times
had doubts about his silence and lack of immediate action. Once
he said to his chief benefactor, Frank W. Stearns, "I wonder if I
have not a little overdone the plan of taking no position on some
public questions?" (41, p 165)

In addition to his brevity, his teasing and practical jokes, and
his silence, Coolidge was known for his sulking and rages. He
sulked if Grace did something to displease him, but Grace's good
nature always brought him out of his mood. "Ike" Hoover, the
chief usher at the White House, wrote that Teddy Roosevelt,
who resembled an erupting volcano at times, "in his worst temper
. . . was calm compared with Coolidge." (41, p 488) Like other
presidents, Calvin was not without his shortcomings, for presidents are, after all, human.

Boston blue-bloods, Lodge Republicans, snobs, and intellectuals
did not look upon Coolidge kindly. These antagonists were
sources of honest criticism, covert hostility, and overt ridicule.
Gamaliel Bradford, author of *The Quick and the Dead* and who
was called by McCoy "The self-appointed psychoanalyst to the
nation" relished ridiculing Coolidge. He wrote about "probing
the dry and unprofitable soul of Coolidge." (41, p 467)

Henry Cabot Lodge, the elder, who was Murray Crane's chief
rival for control of the Republican Party in Massachusetts, was not
particularly fond of Coolidge, the Crane protege with whom
leadership of the party had to be increasingly shared as Coolidge
climbed the political ladder. Lodge, who at one time had presidential ambitions, declined to seek the vice-presidential nomination which led Coolidge to the White House. This, too, must
have affected Lodge's relations with Coolidge. Although he was
respectful of and courteous to the president, Lodge, the majority
leader of the Senate, fought many administration proposals, and
when told by newsmen that Harding was dead, blurted out, "My
God! That means Coolidge is President!" (42, p 147) Louis Coolidge, a Boston Brahmin Republican leader and distant relative of
the president unsuccessfully tried to change Lodge's attitude
from latent hostility to open warfare. (42, pp 266-267)

Walter Lippmann concluded that Coolidge was the anchor
which held the ship of state against the tide of progress. "Mr.
Coolidge's genius for inactivity is developed to a very high point

. . . Inactivity is a political philosophy and a party program with Mr. Coolidge." (41, p 467) He also lamented that Coolidge stopped the "nationalizing tendency," (42, p 418) an expected reaction and a cause for lusty rejoicing among anti-statists.

Frederick Lewis Allen's summary of Calvin Coolidge is fairly typical of liberal opinion. ". . . Calvin Coolidge, an honest, careful, prudent man but one of the most negative characters ever to attain American high office. Coolidge didn't grapple with any national problem until it was forced upon his attention, could sit through a prolonged social occasion without opening his mouth to utter more than an occasional monosyllable, and liked to take afternoon naps in the quiet of the White House—naps which according to Chief Usher 'Ike' Hoover lasted from two to four hours." (9, p 132)

In 1940 Coolidge's friendly biographer Fuess wrote ". . . since his death all the Bright Young Men have had their turn disparaging Coolidge. The Revolt against Respectability, so widespread in some quarters during the Great Depression, did his reputation temporary damage. In an age where assertive literary groups made Decency synonymous with Dullness, Calvin Coolidge was a proper target for ridicule. He had never been unfaithful to his wife or come home blind drunk or betrayed a friend. . . . His heroisms and renunciations were unspectacular, not advertised for the benefit of the public." (41, pp 467-468)

Calvin Coolidge's record in practical politics is remarkable. He started at the bottom of the political ladder and by a display of service, hard work, thrift, honesty, and courage, he managed, helped along by luck, in spite of an unglamorous manner, to reach the top. He was elected successively to the Northampton Republican City Committee, the city council, three terms as state representative, four terms as state senator, president of the state senate, lieutenant governor, and vice president of the United States, before he was finally elected president. In the years from 1897, when he won his first election, until he retired 32 years later, he was rejected by the voters only once. In 1905 he was defeated for the School Committee in Northampton. All of this is quite a contrast to the political record of Woodrow Wilson, an earlier president, who never voted in an election before he moved from Princeton's presidency to the governorship in Trenton.

What was Coolidge's position in the political spectrum as he moved up the political ladder? Was he conservative, progressive, or liberal? Was he statist or anti-statist? Was he stable or did he change his philosophy, as did Teddy Roosevelt and Woodrow Wilson, in order to meet the demands of getting elected? Or did he have a ready-made philosophy that happened to harmonize with what the majority of voters wanted? Was he a politician or an idealist, or both?

When Calvin Coolidge was in Boston as a state representative during 1907 and 1908, his record showed him to be progressive on most of the popular issues of the day. McCoy reported that he supported "a six day week for workers, limiting the working hours of women and children, direct election of United States' senators, female suffrage, pensions to firemen's families, half-fares for school children on street cars, and the equipment of factories with basic surgical instruments." (42, p 38)

He returned to Boston in 1912 as a state senator and swam with the progressive political currents of the day, continuing to support direct election of United States' senators. He also supported the initiative, referendum, recall, workmen's compensation, widows pensions, minimum wages for women, and aid to needy mothers. During his terms in the state senate the XVIth (income tax) and XVIIth (direct election of senators) amendments were ratified by Massachusetts and became a part of the United States Constitution. He also voted for a state income tax. Many of these measures are statist, but most represent state intervention on a local rather than national scale. He remained firmly in favor of economy and thrift in government, certifying him as a conservative, but not necessarily as an anti-statist.

Upon election to the presidency of the state senate in 1914 Coolidge made the most famous of his speeches: "Have Faith in Massachusetts." This effort showed Coolidge to be a reflective man, somewhat of a philosopher, and a writer of some competence. At this point in his career Coolidge wrote all of his own speeches.

"Men do not make laws. They do but discover them," wrote Coolidge. "Laws must be justified by something more than the will of the majority. They must rest on the eternal foundation of righteousness . . ."

At this point Coolidge almost, but not quite, entered the realm of natural law and morality. Natural laws, such as the laws of classical mechanics by which, for instance, bodies respond to the forces applied to them, existed before they were discovered by men. Moral codes, such as the Ten Commandments attributed to Moses, evolved over many centuries of human behavior. They achieved the status of law because men observed the mutual benefits which came from obedience to them. Moses' genius, like Newton's, was in recognizing laws which already existed. Moral codes and wise laws rest on Coolidge's "eternal foundations of righteousness;" they are formulations of fruitful experience, they commend us to behave properly, i.e. to be expedient. (Expedient is used here as meaning advantageous or wise.) People who believe that right, truth, and morality are flexible and must be judged relative to the needs of the moment or of a special situation lose sight of what William James wrote in his treatise on pragmatism: ". . . expedient in the *long run and on the whole,* of course; for what meets expediently all the experiences in sight won't necessarily meet all further experiences satisfactorily."

"That state," continued Coolidge, "is most fortunate in its form of government which has the aptest instruments for the discovery of laws. The latest, most modern, and nearest perfect system that statesmanship has devised is representative government. Its weakness is the weakness of us human beings who administer it."

More than any other president of the twentieth century, including William Howard Taft, Coolidge respected the separation of powers and the mutual restraints placed on the three branches of government by the Constitution. His respect came from his awareness of human fallibility, from his knowledge of the "weakness of us human beings" who must administer the government. Since men were seen to be imperfect, it was essential that no man or group of men be allowed to become dominant through their activities in any single branch of the government, state, Federal or local. Coolidge has been criticized as weak, a do-nothing, a man of narrow vision because he did not provide congress with a steady flow of legislative suggestions and demands. This is an unjustified criticism even though it is true that he proposed very little legislation. His strong adherence to his basic philosophy and his self-discipline did not permit him to do so, for this would have been an encroachment of the executive upon the legislative branch, opening the door to the errors of "imperfect human beings." Rather, by maintaining the separation of powers and by permitting the checks and balances to operate, the imperfections and weaknesses of human beings were to some extent levelled and cancelled out.

It should be kept in mind that Coolidge, as a popular politician, did not come to power by convincing the people that his philosophy was right. This was done by others and by circumstances before Coolidge became president. It is correct to say Coolidge's ideas coincided with the concepts of the majority, and Coolidge in action was doing what the majority wanted.

"The people can not look to legislation generally for success," Coolidge stated. "Industry, thrift, character, are not conferred by act or resolve. Government can not relieve from toil. It can provide no substitute for the rewards of service."

Coolidge then acceded to one of the socialist tenets acceptable in the United States: "It can, of course, care for the defective and recognize distinguished merit. The normal must care for themselves . . ."

Thus, while he recognized individual responsibility, he accepted public welfare as a necessity. But remember his address was made to a state senate in 1914. He was not proprosing Federalization of welfare, but merely continuation and extension of locally controlled welfare. Gross socialism on the Federal level was not yet popular.

"Do the day's work," Coolidge admonished the state senators and the people of Massachusetts. "If it be to protect the rights of the weak, whoever objects, do it. If it be to help a powerful corporation better to serve the people, do that. Expect to be called a stand-patter, but don't be a stand-patter. Expect to be called a demagogue, but don't be a demagogue. Don't hesitate to be as revolutionary as science. Don't hesitate to be as reactionary as the multiplication table. Don't expect to build up the weak by pulling down the strong. Don't hurry to legislate. Give administration a chance to catch up with legislation."

Even Coolidge's most severe critics must concede that he followed to the end his stated political philosophy with honesty and consistency rare for most politicians. This was much in contrast to Theodore Roosevelt and Woodrow Wilson who were unbothered by infidelity to a stated position if they calculated that it would help win an election. Had it happened that Coolidge's political philosophy was unpopular he probably would have been a political failure, for it is unlikely that he would have bargained away his convictions for victory at the polls. His positions were determined by reason and belief rather than by a Gallup or Harris poll. It was Coolidge's good fortune that both he and most voters chanced to hold the same ideas on what government should be and do.

Calvin Coolidge was elected governor of Massachusetts on November 5, 1918. The first world war ended six days later. When he took office on New Year's Day in 1919 the wartime economy was changing to a peacetime economy and millions of servicemen were returning to civilian life. There were serious economic dislocations, and in Massachusetts a shortage of housing was a serious problem. Coolidge urged the General Court to legislate in favor of tenants. City and town governments were authorized to seize property under eminent domain in order to provide emergency housing, courts were granted power to stay evictions up to six months, rent increases were limited to 25 per cent per year, and landlords were penalized for failing to provide utilities promised to tenants. All of these provisions tended to prolong the housing shortage since each discouraged the flow of new capital into housing. Here is an example of good intentions exercised through the coercive power of government aggravating, rather than alleviating, a problem. Had the politicians of the day been as zealous as their successors during the second world war they would not even have permitted the 25 per cent rental increase. In this case, the shortage would have continued for an even longer time and would have been even more severe.

As governor, Coolidge approved an ineffective law which made it illegal to profiteer from dealing in the necessities of life. Profiteering can not be outlawed and fairness legislated because a fair trade or exchange can not be defined objectively: a fair trade or exchange of goods for goods or of goods for money is subjectively determined by the principals to the exchange. Any voluntary exchange is fair to the parties involved regardless of how outlandish it may seem to persons not participating. Although the law existed on the books it was useless. Had it been successful in preventing a rise in prices it would have produced shortages, to which a rise in price is the natural economic response by which production increases and shortages are relieved. Price controls not only produce shortages, they lead to a breakdown of respect for law by encouraging black market transactions. Furthermore, price controls in Massachusetts could not be effective unless all five bordering states passed similar laws.

The Boston police strike opened the door to national fame for Calvin Coolidge, since the governor was generally credited with breaking the back of the strike and preventing anarchy in Boston. The strike occurred when the police commissioner suspended nineteen leaders of a local police union who sought to affiliate with the American Federation of Labor. The police commissioner of Boston was a Republican appointed by the governor, in this case by Coolidge's predecessor, and not by the mayor of the city, a Democrat named Peters. The commissioner could not be directed to reinstate the nineteen policemen nor could he be fired by the mayor. A strike vote was overwhelmingly adopted by the policemen on Monday, September 8, 1919. At the end of the workday on Tuesday two-thirds of Boston's 1544 policemen left their posts. Coolidge, characteristically, took the position that this was not a gubernatorial problem, but one to be solved by the mayor and the police commissioner. In this he was correct although he was wrong in delaying the steps needed to insure order. Tuesday night brought rioting and looting. In the absence of an order from Coolidge mobilizing the Commonwealth's national guard, Mayor Peters boldly ordered to duty those guard troops who lived in Boston and asked for additional guardsmen from the governor. On Thursday afternoon, *after* order had been restored by the combined efforts of local police, local guardsmen and volunteers, Coolidge anticlimactically mobilized the entire guard. Coolidge's reputation was enhanced not so much by the mobilization as from his continued backing of the police commissioner's refusal to reinstate the striking policemen and, even moreso, from his famous telegram to Samuel Gompers, president of the American Federation of Labor: "There is no right to strike against the public safety by anybody, anywhere, anytime."

When Coolidge accepted the vice-presidential nomination, he

stated clearly his belief that the three branches of government were "separate and distinct and neither one directly nor indirectly exercises any of the functions of either of the others." This had been his philosophy while president of the Massachusetts senate and governor of the state, and later it was his guide when he became president. Coolidge also spoke for cutting taxes and public expenditures, for he recognized that taxation meant a transfer of wealth from private hands to the state and correspondingly reduced the freedom of the persons taxed. He also attacked profiteering and inflation as threats to the security of property. Just what he meant by profiteering was probably not clear in his own mind. It is possible that he felt that rapidly rising postwar prices penalized the holders of dollar savings. It is also possible that he confused the results of inflation, i.e. rising prices, wages, and rents, with inflation itself, i.e. an increase in the money supply. In any event, his economic proposals were sensible: increase the supply of goods by increasing production while simultaneously reducing the supply of money. These steps would not only stop inflation but would eliminate the rise in prices which it causes.

As vice-president, Coolidge's power was limited, but his dedication to liberty and freedom were not. For blacks, Coolidge urged in 1920, that they "be relieved from all imposition, to be defended from lynching, and to be freely granted equal opportunities." But Coolidge could do little about the problem. As vice-presidents before and since, Coolidge was annoyed by the limitations of the office.

Coolidge, as governor of Massachusetts and later as president of the United States, adhered to the concept of separation of powers. The legislators were to legislate. The executive was to administer. It was not in Coolidge's view a primary duty of the executive branch to propose legislation and press for its passage. For this he was criticized by the statists who believe that progress requires that the people be directed by a strong leader of a strong central government.

William Allen White, in his very interesting book, *Calvin Coolidge, The Man Who is President*, wrote that Coolidge ". . . was not master of the legislative situation, as Wilson was, or Roosevelt, or even at times Grover Cleveland. Congress seemed to be as determined that Coolidge should be a constitutional president as Mr. Coolidge himself was. His inaugural address had announced no legislative program, beyond economy, tax reduction, and participation in the World Court. He had staked off no fighting ground. Legislation evidently meant little in his idea of a successful administration . . . He enjoyed his work, freed from the pest of Congress. He went into the reorganization of Federal departments. He took a superintendent's joy in coordinating and consolidating bureaus. Not in years had the government had as its head a man who was so devoted to the problems of administration." (44, pp 156-157)

Coolidge generally took the anti-statist position that people free to make their own decisions make more progress than when their freedom to act is restricted by the coercive tax power of the state, which forces them to support that which the state deems important. Coolidge was more than dimly aware that the net economic aid given any one group by the government must be paid for by the sacrifices of all who are not members of the group. Government aid to farmers is paid by nonfarmers, aid to negroes is paid by non-negroes, aid to old is paid by the young, aid for the sick is paid by the healthy, aid for the businessman is paid by the nonbusinessman, and so on without limit. But the payments are not voluntarily made in a free market where individual choices are exercised. They are compelled by the police power of the state. Coolidge's failure to show the "leadership" wanted by the interventionists was, from a libertarian standpoint, his most laudable characteristic and his greatest contribution to freedom. In practical terms, his first message to congress in December 1923 proposed a reduction in government expenses and a corresponding reduction in taxes. In so far as the extent of taxation is probably the best indicator of the extent of statism, Coolidge was on the side of the anti-statists.

And yet Coolidge was to some extent an interventionist. His first congressional address praised the protective tariff, a benefit bestowed upon segments of the business and labor community and paid for by all who are not members of these favored minorities. He also stated, according to McCoy, that the government should be concerned with "character development, frugality, industry, and education. He asked for a new Cabinet department to encourage such things." (42, p 200) One wonders whether a Fed-

eral Department of Frugality and Character Building would have
supplied the answer!

In 1924 American farmers were in trouble. Production was far
in excess of that needed when European farming was disrupted
as a result of the war and postwar convulsions. American farmers,
having heavy overhead expenses to meet, strove to earn more by
producing more. This increased supplies and lowered prices,
aggravating rather than solving the problem. Senator Charles L.
McNary of Oregon and Congressman Gilbert N. Haugen of
Iowa proposed that the government purchase surpluses at average
prewar prices and dump the surpluses abroad in the open market.
This would have prolonged the surplus problem and shifted the
burden from farmers to taxpayers since the latter would be forced
to make up the losses. Coolidge opposed the McNary-Haugen
bill. His reasoning was expressed in a question to Senator Burton
K. Wheeler: "When a man can't make any money in a business,
what does he do?" Obviously he should get out, take his loss,
and contribute to the achievement of balance between supply and
demand which makes for the most economic and efficient use of
energy and resources.

By 1927 the McNary-Haugen proposals to buy surplus commodities at a profit and dump them overseas at a loss had won
the support of Dawes, Coolidge's politically ambitious vice-president. The proposals were also supported by the Republicans from
the farm states, who wanted to regain their strength in congress,
by influential business men such as Bernard Baruch, a speculator
and adviser to President Wilson, and by Owen D. Young, of the
General Electric Company. The proposals were, of course, supported by the farmers, a coherent pressure group of significant
size who wanted solace at the expense of the non-farming taxpayers. In his cabinet, Coolidge's opposition was backed only by
Andrew Mellon, his Secretary of the Treasury. In spite of the
pressure and lack of support, President Coolidge had the courage
to veto the bill. In his veto message he criticized "the employment of the coercive powers of government to the end that certain special groups of farmers and processors may profit
temporarily." Coolidge recognized that the bill would maintain
and increase surpluses and disrupt world markets, leading eventually to dumping of surpluses by other countries. Coolidge

showed a sound knowledge of economics in his veto message: "Instead of undertaking to secure a method of orderly marketing which will dispose of products at a profit, it proposed to dispose of them at a loss. It runs counter to the principle of conservation, which would require us to produce only what can be done at a profit, not to waste our soil and resources producing what is to be sold at a loss to us for the benefit of the foreign consumer."

Calvin Coolidge, sneered at by the liberals who accused him of being a negative character of narrow vision, put his finger on the insidious nature of Federal grants to the states. In his budget message of 1926, Coolidge stated that "while Federal taxes have been reduced, state and other government taxes have been steadily increasing. (*This was at a time of rapid and steadily rising prices*). Federal aid to states has influenced this latter condition . . . Roads should not be constructed faster than taxpayers can afford to pay for them. The amount that taxpayers can afford to pay can best be determined by the citizens of each state." (4, p 94) Would that this had been remembered years later when proposals were made to "help" the states with Federal subsidies for welfare, education, urban renewal, hospitals and a hundred lesser causes.

Calvin Coolidge observed prophetically in a letter to E.T. Clark, dated May 28, 1932 that "almost every Democrat thinks the sovereign remedy for any of our ills is an appropriation of public money. A good many Republicans think so, too." Forty years later the situation is essentially the same, excepting that there are now more Republicans in the ranks of the big spenders than there were then.

In a final assessment, McCoy, who is a British liberal, repeated the stock criticisms of American liberals: Coolidge did too little, he did not exert moral leadership, his policies were those of do nothing and drift. For instance, McCoy wrote: "Coolidge's signal fault was his pursuit of policies approved by most Americans." (42, p 418) But isn't this generally true of successful politicians? It is true that the president can buck majority opinion on a few issues indefinitely, and he can for a time buck majority opinion on many, if not all, issues. But if the administration does not, in a general way and in the long run, reflect public opinion, it will be defeated. The people can be manipulated to a certain extent by the politicians in power, but majority opinion results from what people read, see, and hear. Thus, although politicians contribute to the mix, the major input comes from commentators, lecturers, writers, teachers, ministers and other men of verbal influence. By the time the politician arrives on the scene the die has been cut. The job for most politicians who want to win elections is to sense what is wanted and to give the impression that they can deliver the goods. In the case of Coolidge this required little effort because he happened to ride the same wavelength as most voters.

William Howard Taft thought that Coolidge was "nearly as good a politician as Lincoln." (41, p 481) Massachusetts Judge Henry P. Field concluded that Coolidge's "greatness did not lie in his contacts with men. But as a politician he was brilliant. He seemed to know what people were thinking and how they would act." (41, p 481)

Coolidge, who was acclaimed as a master in sensing and expressing what was popular, made some significant mistakes. Unfortunately, general sentiment was sometimes wrong in the middle and late twenties. And when the president deviated from his general battle plan of silence and echoed erroneous popular notions he was just as wrong as those whose views he returned. In January, 1928, when the president "in response to a direct question, made a statement to the effect that brokers' loans were not too high", he helped encourage further speculation and gambling in the stock market. (41, p 433) This was a serious error for the stock market gyrations of the twenties helped prepare the way for the collapse of the thirties.

McCoy, in spite of criticizing Coolidge for lack of leadership, quite fairly acknowledges the danger of leadership that is too strong. "Italy's Benito Mussolini and Soviet Russia's Nicolai Lenin," wrote McCoy, "towered over all other chiefs of state, but it must be said of Coolidge that if he did not have their flair for leadership, neither did he possess their megalomania or their instinct for terror." (42, p 419) The most dangerous politicians are those who want to save a country and have the "leadership" to do so.

Coolidge was aware of the tyranny of the majority as well as the tyranny of dictators and minorities. "It was to establish a free government," said Coolidge in his address at the Sesquicentennial Exposition in Philadelphia, "which must not be permitted to degenerate into the unrestrained authority of a mere majority or the unbridled weight of a mere influential few . . ." that the founding fathers acted.

William Allen White, no great admirer of Coolidge, nevertheless concluded that the ex-president had been "a competent, intelligent, hard-working politician; honest as his times would permit, courageous as the prod of circumstances and a political habit of mind could make him, endowed with such common sense and such high purpose as were the people whom he represented." (45, p 419)

At one of his last press conferences, just before Hoover's inauguration, Coolidge humorously summed up his own character, philosophy, and record. "Perhaps," he said, "one of the most important accomplishments of my administration has been minding my own business."

Amen.

CHAPTER 10

THE UNPOLITICIAN

Horatio Alger, compared to Herbert Hoover, was a master of mediocrity. Had Hoover lived only thirty years instead of ninety, the comparison would have suffered no damage. Fatherless at six, a poor orphan at eight, shunted between two uncles for the next eight years, and on his own after that, Herbert Hoover was one of the more disadvantaged of the disadvantaged youths of West Branch, Iowa. Since there were no do-gooders in West Branch (everyone was so busy trying to scratch out a living that there was no time left over for them to mind other people's business), young Herbert never found out that there was no hope for fellows living in rural ghettoes and he had no inhibitions about improving himself.

A mile and a half walk through mud or snow got him to school. He performed chores and worked for his board and keep, and he became his uncle's office boy when he moved to Oregon. On the side, Hoover worked in the onion fields and also repaired sewing machines which he then sold. A chance talk with a mining engineer fired his interest in mining and geology, and Hoover decided to apply to newly founded Leland Stanford University. His uncle gave him fifty dollars, which brought his total assets to $410, and with this he set off for California.

Hoover, deficient in English and composition even after some special tutoring, entered with the new university's first class. He was no star in the classroom—he didn't earn a single A in four years. He was no star athlete—he tried for baseball but couldn't make it. Instead he managed baseball and football, ran a laundry service, delivered newspapers, had secretarial jobs in both the school and the geology department, and worked during his summer vacations on geological surveys. He was also elected manager of all student activities. No wonder he wasn't an A student! But he paid his own way and when he graduated he had forty dollars left over. And he met Lou Henry, a geology student, who would one day become Mrs. Hoover.

The best job to be had near Lou Henry, who still had three years to go at Stanford, was as a laborer in a gold mine. For a seventy hour week the pay was fourteen dollars, but Hoover learned a lot about practical mining, and about religion too.

"In two or three months," wrote Hoover, "the Cornish foreman appointed me a helper on a drill and I became an acknowledged and real miner. In the meantime I had learned some Cornish dialect and listened to an enormous amount of religious doctrinal debate. The Cornishmen were very determined in their religious views but capable of suspending religious discussion for a period of profanity when something went wrong in the mine." (18, v I, p 26) Writing later about Cornish miners at a turquoise mine at Mt. Sinai, he stated that "the venture had its romantic aspect; for one thing, it brought the miners closer to the Ten Commandments than usual . . ." (18, v I, p 96)

The job in the gold mine, which kept him near Lou, gave out. In desperation Hoover took a job as a typist with Louis Janin, who was described by Hoover as "the outstanding mining engineer on the Pacific Coast." Janin's new employee was too good an engineer to be kept in an office. He was soon sent to a project in Colorado and then he became an assistant manager of a mine at Steeple Rock, New Mexico. Here he survived wild encounters with some untamed Mexican miners. Then Janin, who remained a lifelong friend, recommended Hoover to Bewick, Moreing and Co., a British mining firm, even though it meant loosing a valuable employee.

In his new job Hoover would make more than ten times what he earned as a mine laborer two years earlier, but he worked for it. His first assignment took him to Australia. In the barren, dry area where the mines were located the temperature never went below 100°F. Transportation was by obnoxious camels, and for companions there were swarms of flies and drunken, gambling miners. The outback mining towns were raw centers of petty crime and general looseness. But again Hoover was successful.

Bewick, Moreing and Co. next sent him to China at $20,000 a

year plus expenses. After returning to London for instructions on his new job, Hoover travelled westward, stopping in California in order to marry his beloved Lou, who would accompany him to Peking. When he reached China, in addition to battling the bitterest cold, Hoover had to contend with baffling political intrigues, warlords, and bandits. Like an oriental potentate, he travelled with a retinue of 100 Chinese cavalrymen plus hordes of bearers and beasts of burden. The Boxer Rebellion, aimed at eliminating foreigners from China, caught Lou and Herbert Hoover in Tientsien where they were besieged for a month in the foreign quarter of the city along with a few hundred Chinese Christians and foreigners of various nationalities.

By 1902, with operations in China proceeding successfully, Hoover became a partner in Bewick, Moreing and Co. He held a 20 per cent interest until 1908.

One of the partners taken in at the same time as Hoover was an accountant at the home office in London. A year after joining the partnership, Hoover, who had been in the field most of the time, returned temporarily to London to act as senior partner. After Hoover had been there for a time, the firm's accountant, a man named Rowe, disclosed that he had violated the partnership agreement, which forbade stock speculation, and that he had embezzled nearly a million dollars of the firm's and its customers' money. Hoover and the other partners, though under no legal obligation, personally made good the loss. Rowe fled to Canada where he was captured, convicted, and sentenced to a prison term. In the meantime Mrs. Hoover saw to it that Rowe's wife and four children were cared for until they could re-establish themselves.

During his six years with the partnership Hoover was sent to France, Italy, England, Australia, New Zealand, Canada, the United States, India, Hawaii, Germany, Egypt, the Malay States, and Burma. He usually spent no more than three months in any location and the places to which he travelled often were so rough and primitive that he could not bring his family along. So, when his term of partnership was up, he decided against a renewal and instead went into business for himself, locating his home office in the United States.

As a free-lancer Hoover opened offices in New York, San Francisco, London, Petrograd, and Paris. It was still necessary to travel, but far less so than when he was with Bewick, Moreing and Co. He found that he could spent more time at home in the United States where he could be with his family. In business for himself, Hoover was fantastically successful. In fact, so successful was he that in 1914, nineteen years after he left college with forty dollars, he had earned $10,000,000. He had also written a useful book, *Principles of Mining*, and translated with his wife's help, Georgius Agricola's 1550 Latin classic *De Re Metallica*, a book which had defied modern translation. Hoover now decided to retire and devote himself to public service. He was only forty years old.

His first public service was helping 150,000 stranded Americans return home from Europe after war broke out. To do this Hoover and a group of friends personally cashed checks and advanced money for the purchase of accomodations and transportation home. Next he headed the Belgian Relief Commission which fed and cared for 10,000,000 Belgians and Frenchmen in territory occupied by the Germans. When the United States entered the war Hoover became Food Administrator under President Wilson, responsible for seeing to it that adequate food was available at home and for American allies. Following the war, this work was continued and expanded to assist millions of former enemies in prostrated Europe. A private charitable organization was formed by Hoover and his friends to carry on after the American Relief Administration was discontinued by the government.

When Herbert Hoover returned home from Europe in late 1919 he was a figure of international importance. "A New York *Times* poll on the ten most important living Americans placed him high on the list." (46, p 139) As the 1920 nominations approached he was boomed for president by both Democrats and Republicans.

The Democrats could claim him as their own for he had served Wilson's Democrat administration. He and his wife were socially friendly with Franklin D. Roosevelt from Washington days, (47, pp 85-86) and none other than Roosevelt wrote a note to Josephus Daniels (Secretary of the Navy under Wilson, and Roosevelt's boss) that "Herbert Hoover is certainly a wonder, and I wish we could make him President of the United States.

There could not be a better one." (46, p 143) Later Roosevelt was told by Henry Cabot Lodge's daughter (47, pp 85-86) that Hoover was a Republican and this ended FDR's efforts. Other Democrats were not so easily dissuaded and Hoover won more votes in the Michigan primary as a Democrat than any other candidate. (46, p 143) (According to Gene Smith, when Roosevelt was nominated for the vice-presidency by the Democrats in 1920 "Hoover sent him a warm letter saying that although they were not of the same 'political tribe' he wished 'an old friend' and 'great public servant' the best.")

Gene Smith, in his story of Hoover and the depression years, made the statement that "Hoover had never been involved in any political activity and was not sure if he was a Democrat or a Republican." (47, p 86) This was probably the view of many Democrats in 1920. They, like the Republicans, were primarily interested in a winner, and secondarily in the winner's political philosophy. Political philosophy, unless it is beyond the fringe of acceptability, does not usually figure heavily in the selection of candidates. Smith's statement, however, was not accurate, as shown above by Hoover's 1920 letter to Roosevelt. Hoover was a Republican and he knew it. In 1909 he joined the National Republican Club and in 1912 he, in his own words, "rooted for Theodore Roosevelt and supported him by financing others to root." (18, v I, p 120)

Hoover, then, was a progressive Republican. The chapter of Eugene Lyons' book entitled "An Old-Style Liberal" (46, chap XIII) confirms Hoover's progressivism, but hardly convinces one that he was a mid-nineteenth century liberal, as might be expected from the term "old-style liberal." In fact, in an earlier chapter of the same book, Lyons wrote "As an Iowa Quaker he had been, one might say, born a Republican. And it was the Republicanism of Iowa Quakers—at bottom populist, liberal, grass-roots in quality—that meant anything to him." (46, p 73) Populists, their progressive children, and liberal grandchildren, are not even fifth cousins to "old-style liberals." His philosophy called for more government intervention in private affairs than existed at the time, in spite of his frequent and sincere incantations re individualism and initiative. Only if the presidents from Teddy Roosevelt through Coolidge could be considered as "old-style liberals," which they couldn't, could Hoover be considered as an "old-style liberal." Hoover was a progressive, new-style liberal who nudged the country toward more Federal statism more firmly than most of his predecessors, Teddy Roosevelt and Wilson included.

To the Senate Soviet, which arranged Harding's nomination, Hoover was not a certified party wheelhorse. His public service in this country had been under a Democrat president as a food administrator, relief worker, and coordinator of a conference on labor and industry. It was this service to the opposition, as much as Hoover's progressive inclinations which disqualified him, in the minds of the king makers, for a cabinet post. In addition, Senator Lodge, a more or less progressive member of the Senate Soviet, and therefore one who might have been expected to approve of Hoover, had a run-in with the Head of the Belgian Relief Commission in 1915 from which he emerged second best. (18, v I, pp 199-202) Lodge was not known for a gentle, forgiving nature.

Harding, a senator and the Senate Soviet's ultimate choice, had this to say about Hoover as a presidential possibility. ". . . in its deliberate moments the country does not want a dictatorial and autocratic personality like that we know our friend, Hoover, to possess." But Harding added, "There is no doubt about his marked ability." (40, p 125) It was because of ability that Harding, as president-elect, insisted upon Hoover as his Secretary of Commerce or Secretary of Interior. The king makers were equally insistent upon Andrew Mellon, who was unknown to Harding, for Secretary of the Treasury. Harding agreed to Mellon only when the reluctant king makers agreed to Hoover, who became Harding's Secretary of Commerce.

When President-elect Harding approached Mr. Hoover and asked him to serve in his cabinet as Secretary of Commerce, Hoover outlined some conditions which would have to be met before he would agree to take the job.

"I told him," wrote Hoover in his memoirs, "there were some ideas in my mind that he should consider before the matter was finally settled . . . that for the Department to be of real service, I must have a voice on all important economic policies of the administration. I stated this would involve business, agriculture, labor, finance and foreign affairs so far as they related to these

problems . . . I stated that, if I accepted, I wanted it made clear
to the other departments from the very beginning." (18, v II, p 36)

A predecessor, Oscar Straus, had told the new Secretary of
Commerce that his job would take no more than two hours a
day. In 1921, when Hoover took over, the department was made
up of the Bureaus of Foreign and Domestic Commerce, Light-
houses, Navigation, Coast and Geodetic Survey, Census, Standards, Fisheries, and Steamboat Inspection. Hoover stated that
"in the Washington social scale (the Department) was next to the
bottom at the dinner table . . . Putting the fish to bed at night
and turning the lights on around the coast were possibly the major
concepts of office." (18, v II, p 40-42)

By 1925, Hoover had managed to wrest the Bureau of Mines
(a special interest of his) and the Patent Office from the Department of Interior. These moves reflect his strong sense of organization. In 1922 he persuaded Congress to add a Housing Division,
in 1926 an Aeronautics Division, and in 1927 a Radio Division.
He added two secretaries and three assistants to his personal staff,
paying their salaries himself. The number of employees increased
during Hoover's eight years as secretary by about 2800, an increase
of 21 per cent. The department budget increased 54 per cent or
about $13,000,000. Hoover obviously spent more than two hours
a day on the job. The energy expended in organizing and expanding the department were well publicized and the publicity was a
source of criticism.

Hoover's efforts earned him the title of "Secretary of Commerce and Under-Secretary of Everything Else." Calvin Coolidge,
by this time president, was piqued at being upstaged by his
cabinet member, and referred to him sarcastically as "the wonder
boy" and "the miracle worker" after moves got underway to
nominate Hoover for president. (46, p 51) Villard, the liberal
New York editor, wrote that "Mr. Hoover has become a marvel-
lous self-advertiser and publicity expert. His speeches are endless;
his Department's press releases come like flakes of snow in a
heavy storm, and they do not forget Mr. Hoover. A small-town
California editor declares he has received a daily piece of Hoover
publicity, a picture, or a cut for several years. Situations like the
Mississippi flood have played into his hands precisely as did the
Belgian relief, and justly so, for he deserved the credit, and being

the head and forefront of the undertaking he naturally took the spotlight. But even in periods when he was not doing one of his magnificent pieces of relief organization, Mr. Hoover won the front page of the newspapers so often that Mr. Coolidge was known to be distinctly nettled." (34, pp 25-26)

Hoover's method as Secretary of Commerce involved convening of committees to study problems and make recommendations. The members generally served voluntarily and at no expense to the government. Villard described the technique.

"When dealing with problems affecting a given industry, he wisely gathers around him a group of its leaders," wrote Villard. "In this way he has initiated great reforms—he is said to have saved $200,000,000 for the consumer by changes in the lumber industry initiated by him, and it is asserted he has won better wages for millions of Americans . . . Colonel Roosevelt got pure food by legislation; Mr. Hoover set about 'giving us pure lumber without law.' " (34, p 28)

According to Villard ". . . his (*Hoover's*) slogan is 'self government in industry.' He prefers conferences and cooperation to legislative compulsion—the government, he thinks, too often becomes the 'persecutor instead of regulator . . . We are passing from a period of extremely individualistic action into a period of associational activities.' " Hoover made these statements on May 7, 1924, long before the codes of the National Recovery Administration were set up. ". . . committees, his critics say, are often his convenient smoke screens." (34, pp 28-30) And Hoover didn't always agree with his committees' recommendations.

Secretary Hoover thought that the twelve-hour day in the steel mills was uneconomic and barbaric. At Hoover's suggestion, President Harding appointed a steel maker's committee to look into the matter and Judge Elbert H. Gary, chief executive of the U. S. Steel Corporation, served as its chairman. Gary's committee pointed out that only 14 per cent of the steel workers were working a twelve-hour day and recommended against its abolishment at that time. Hoover disagreed with this recommendation and drafted a public statement for Harding's signature opposing the twelve-hour day. (40, p 255) The ensuing public outcry against the steel companies achieved Hoover's purpose and the twelve-hour day was abandoned. Hoover was not such an old-time liberal that he was above using the Federal government to force changes *he* decided were needed. Regardless of the merits of the case, this step represented application of Federal pressure to the resolution of a conflict between two separate private parties—management and labor. This sets a dangerous precedent for demagogues. Fortunately, Hoover was no demagogue, but in other hands the tactic might become dangerous.

The temptations of massive Federal intervention as a way of solving economic problems attracted Hoover in 1926, two years before he became president. The McNary-Haugen proposals to buy farm surpluses and dump them overseas at losses to be made up by the taxpayers were gaining popularity. Hoover worked out a counter proposal, with Secretary of Agriculture William M. Jardine, which eventually became known as the Curtis-Crisp bill. (42, p 310) Although never passed, it featured low-interest loans to farm cooperatives, creation of a Federal Farm Board with authority to loan $250 million to the cooperatives for supporting prices, and the imposition of production controls. As always, loans made by the government below the going rate at which the Federal government could raise the money by sale of its bonds, would require the taxpayers to carry the burden. Furthermore, operations of this type, in effect, place the government in the banking business. And since price supports were involved, it meant either surpluses or ruthless controls, or both, for many years to come.

In 1922, the Secretary of Commerce commenced agitation for the development of the Colorado River with the stated aim of providing hydroelectric power, irrigation, water supply, and flood control. The aims are similar to those of the New Deal's TVA a decade later. Hoover attempted unsuccessfully to have land reclamation and hydroelectric power projects undertaken in California and the Columbia River Basin in 1925. These, too, were later New Deal accomplishments. It is true that Hoover, while favoring government construction of the dams and power plants, favored private distribution of the power produced by them. The proposals were therefore only partly socialistic. Villard later wrote that Hoover "has never been really against the Power Trust though he has breached his own rule against the government's going into business by arguing that it should build and equip and operate Boulder Dam and its power plant." (34, p 30)

By the 1930's most conservatives were busy damning FDR's proposals for hydroelectric power and flood control as socialism, having forgotten that almost ten years before Herbert Hoover had made similar suggestions. To anti-statists the differences between the proposals were insignificant; socialism is socialism regardless of its sponsors.

Hoover is to depression as damn is to Yankee. It is a permanent marriage which no man can put asunder. For the Democrats, associating Hoover's name with the depression was a stroke of political genius and good fortune. Like most political gimmicks, it lacked a rational basis, which in no way detracted from its usefulness to the Democrats.

"We in America are nearer to the final triumph over poverty than ever before in the history of any land . . . ," said Herbert Hoover when he accepted the Republican presidential nomination of 1928. "We shall soon, with the help of God, be in sight of the day when poverty will be banished from this nation."

It was fate's bitter reward that for most of the Hoover years, the ones that are remembered at least, the dominant theme was poverty rather than plenty. Yet almost thirty years after the New Deal claimed to have restored prosperity, Lyndon Johnson, the New Deal's heir, would discover that there was enough poverty around to declare war on it. Progress seems hard to come by.

The depression in the United States was far from a provincial achievement of Herbert Hoover. A backward look at world economic conditions proves this. The American depression was, in fact, part of a general collapse and financial upheaval which started in Europe before it did in the United States. A disastrous bottom was reached here between April 1931 and July 1932, with perfect timing to serve the political purposes of the Democrats.

Mismanagement of money was an important contributing cause of the Hoover depression. It is ironic that Hoover was the sole member of Coolidge's cabinet who spoke out strongly and repeatedly against the laxity of the money managers. In 1925 the governors of the Federal Reserve Bank of New York and the

Bank of England agreed upon the need for easy money policies, i.e. inflation, in order to prevent a European economic collapse. In November of 1925 Hoover, who was then Secretary of Commerce, sent a warning to Governor Daniel R. Crissinger of the Federal Reserve Board.

"As to the effects of these Reserve policies upon the United States," wrote Hoover, "it means inflation with inevitable collapse which will bring the greatest calamities upon our farmers, our workers and legitimate business." (48, p 10)

By July 1927, the Federal Reserve Board had agreed to act in concert with the Reichsbank, Bank of Finance, and Bank of England in pursuing inflationary policies. In their documentary, *The Hoover Administration*, Myers and Newton correctly wrote "The United States was not in need of credit expansion. Our industry and commerce were amply supplied . . . The Board gave assurance that if . . . unhealthy speculation resulted they would reverse the process. The trouble with every inflation is that there is a long interval between the injection of the stimulant and its result in speculation and, likewise there is a long interval between the injection of the sedative and the lowering of the speculative fever." (48, pp 10-11)

Federal Reserve policies increased bank deposits held by individuals from 53.6 to 83.2 billion dollars within a year and a half. Stockbrokers' loans doubled from 3.5 to 7.0 billion dollars between June 1927 and June 1929. The effect was to double the prices of stocks in the two years preceding the crash. During most of this period Hoover was without authority in the Commerce Department. His private warnings to the Federal Reserve Board went unheeded. It was Coolidge's worst failure that he did not express similar views publicly and exert the pressure that Hoover was unable to bring about.

A severe drought in the summer of 1930 also contributed to the severity of the depression. Some of the country's most productive farm land was affected. The most devastating losses occurred in the Mississippi, Ohio, and Potomac river valleys. Charley Michelson who headed the "Hate Hoover" efforts of the Democratic National Committee, should have blamed Mother Nature for the farmer's troubles, but it was more useful to blame Hoover.

At first Hoover resisted a centralized Federal attack on the depression. Instead he worked through the governors of the states, through the Red Cross and other voluntary charitable groups, and through bankers, industrial and labor leaders. Later he trod unmarked paths as he urged massive loans for farmers and large-scale Federal construction programs for unemployment relief. He consistently maintained that local, city, county, and state governments should not seek Federal assistance until their own resources were exhausted.

"At once when the government is centralized," he warned in a 1931 Lincoln's Birthday address, "there arises a limitation upon the liberty of the individual and restriction of individual opportunity . . . (*which only*) . . . can lead to the superstate where every man becomes the servant of the state and real liberty is lost." Forty years later liberty has been limited, individual opportunity and action are hedged in by restraints, and the superstate is at the door.

Herbert Hoover was more of an economist than any other twentieth century president. His speeches, written by himself, show this to be so. While his successor admitted he was bored by economics and confined his reading largely to detective stories, Hoover, the young graduate, was interested enough to read Adam Smith, Bagehot, and Mill on his own after he realized that his undergraduate economics instruction was deficient. In addition, Hoover's world-wide activities gave him a practical grasp of affairs that no other modern president has had. Intellect, interest, imagination, and knowledge were the basis of his policies and recommendations. This is shown by his comments on advice he had received regarding the depression.

"Some talked of vast issues of paper money. Some talked of suspending payments of government issues . . . Some talked foolishly of dictatorship—any of which would have produced a panic," he said at Des Moines, Iowa on October 4, 1932. "Some assured me that no man could propose increased taxes in the United States to balance the budget in the midst of a depression and survive an election."

Hoover's detractors will smile and say that heeding this last bit of advice might have been just what was needed to save him from defeat. Perhaps so. It is more likely that defeat would have come anyway. He had to contend with the smears of Charley Michelson and he had to pit a serious, earnest personality against Roosevelt's casual charm, happy smile, and political skill. And Hoover was as short on political skill as he was long on integrity.

"The set of values to which Hoover adhered must have seemed quixotic to men acclimated to ward politics. To put duty above personal interests and rectitude above tactics must have seemed to some of them even a bit pretentious," (46, p 201) wrote Eugene Lyons, who went on to quote Mark L. Requa, who said, "I have seen Hoover at close quarters, in trying circumstances, and I have never known him to waver for a moment between right and wrong." (Mark L. Requa was a petroleum engineer who was associated in public service with Hoover from the days of the Food Administration and remained one of his many lifelong friends.)

The alternative to raising taxes in order to balance the budget was, as Mr. Hoover suggested, either printing-press money or bonds. It took courage for the president to ask for higher taxes in order to avoid inflation, and it showed his economic wisdom and sound judgement. Hoover was not defeated by economic errors.

"All human experience has demonstrated," said Hoover at Des Moines, referring to the use of printing presses to balance the budget, "that the path once taken can not be stopped, and that the moral integrity of the government would be sacrificed, because ultimately both currency and bonds would become valueless." In spite of President Hoover's efforts, the budget was unbalanced in fiscal years 1930-31, 1931-32, and 1932-33, all years for which his administration was responsible.

More common-sense economics was displayed when Hoover spoke to the American Federation of Labor in 1930. ". . . reduced costs (*from labor-saving devices and mass production*) shall be shared between labor, employer and consumer . . . labor gains either through increase of wage or reduction of cost of living or shortened hours . . . Indeed mass production must be accompanied by mass consumption through increased standards of living . . . A conception of this sort does not at once find universal application."

Forty years later, the message has still to be gotten across. It is hard to imagine Franklin Roosevelt making a similar speech so full of economic sense and so free of the demagogue's rhetoric to a meeting of labor leaders. The same is true of Harry Truman. Eisenhower might have made such a speech, but he couldn't have written it on his own and probably wouldn't have understood it. As for Nixon, he is certainly capable of both writing and speaking the words, but he has yet to do so.

Some business leaders, no less than some labor leaders, look to Federal intervention to solve their problems and provide special advantages. It is by government intervention that every group seeks to live at the expense of other groups. This reflects human frailty rather than conscious evil design. Thus, Gerald Swope, who was president of General Electric Company in 1931, came up with a plan that eventually was embodied in the National Recovery Act. Swope's plan provided for a structure similar to the Italian Fascist organization of industry. Hoover rejected Swope's ideas for sound economic reasons.

"This plan," Hoover wrote, "provides for the consolidation of all industries into trade associations which are legalized by the government and authorized to 'stabilize prices.' There is no stabilization of prices without price fixing, and this feature at once becomes the organization of giant trusts such as have never been dreamed of in the history of the world. This is the creation of a series of complete monopolies over the American people . . . if such a thing were ever done, it means the decay of American industry . . . because one can not stabilize prices without protecting obsolete plants and inferior managements . . ." (48, p 119)

The members of the Chamber of Commerce showed economic ignorance as abyssmal as that of Mr. Swope. A referendum, the results of which were reported on December 19, 1931, supported modification of antitrust laws to permit combinations which would keep "production related to consumption," with government enforcement and supervision of the rules voted by trade associations. The free market and freely determined prices are the best means of relating production to consumption. President Hoover recognized this and stated that the scheme was a step toward fascism or socialism, again demonstrating superior economic wisdom and judgement. The plan again emerged under FDR and became known as the NRA. It was a failure and was eventually rendered completely ineffective by decisions of the Supreme Court.

Mr. Hoover a liberal? Until about 1960 few would have answered this question with a *yes*. Toward the end of his life
Hoover's career was re-examined and he began to receive praise
from liberal writers. The most surprising feature of this is its
belated nature. If the public, liberal and conservative alike, had
heeded that sometime liberal of liberals, Walter Lippmann, instead
of Charley Michelson, the Democrats' axe-man, Hoover's liberal
laurels would not have been so long delayed.

"The partisans . . . would have us believe," wrote Walter Lippmann in 1935, "that Mr. Hoover was the faithful defender of
established traditions and that Mr. Roosevelt is the revolutionary
pioneer of the New Deal. Though it will outrage supporters of
both men, I must argue that this is not history, but partisan
mythology . . . the nature of a sharp break with the past . . .
was inaugurated in 1929 when . . . President Hoover assumed
the responsibility for recovery . . . President Hoover, let us remember, did not merely seek to create an atmosphere of confidence in which private initiative could act; he intervened at
every point in the national economy where he felt that something needed to be done . . . It was Mr. Hoover who abandoned
the principle of *laissez-faire* in relation to the business cycle,
established the conviction that prosperity and depression can be
publicly controlled by political action and drove out . . . the old
idea that depression must be overcome by private adjustment."
(3, pp 11-13)

It is not certain that Mr. Hoover, capable as he was, personally
accomplished all that Mr. Lippmann claimed for him. Hoover's
accomplishments were made possible in part by the depression
and, in a larger measure, by the liberal opinion makers who had
been in ascendancy for at least forty years prior to Mr. Hoover's
arrival in the White House. Nevertheless, Mr. Lippmann's statements seem to qualify Mr. Hoover as a member in good standing
of the liberal club, and not the old-time liberal club as claimed by
Lyons.

As president, Mr. Hoover was criticized by the opposition for
his bureaucracy, committees, commissions, and conferences. In
actual fact, the number of Federal employees at the end of Mr.
Hoover's term of office was about 4500 less than when he took
over. (Hoover claimed there were 8500 fewer employees, 18, v

II, p 280.) Less astonishing is the fact that Franklin Roosevelt added 150,000 Federal employees within two and a half years after taking office. (48, pp 530-531) This, in spite of Roosevelt's constant campaign criticism of the size of the Federal bureaucracy! As for commissions, 62 commissions were established during the Hoover years, 63 under Taft, 75 for each four year term of Wilson, and an average of 81 for each four years of the Harding-Coolidge eras. If the number of bureaucrats employed and the number of commissions established are taken as an indication of liberal, statist trends, Hoover's record seems contrary to Lippmann's evaluation. Alas, numbers alone do not tell the story. How does a charge of increasing interventionism square with a reduction in the Federal body count? Mr. Hoover managed more statism with fewer bodies because he was a better manager than his predecessors or successors! He was an organizer who outorganized any president we have ever had, before or since, and are ever likely to have in the future. He organized the Federal government the way he organized the Commerce Department before he got his hands on bigger things. Not only did he organize, he also publicized. A few examples will illustrate.

Four months after he became president, Hoover announced the Child Health and Protection Conference. Herbert Hoover, perhaps because of his own hard-pressed childhood, reinforced by his relief experiences in Europe, had strong feelings for children and child welfare. In 1920, while Secretary of Commerce, Mr. Hoover, who was President of the Child Health Association, undertook an expansion of this activity which continued until 1935. Originally this was a non-governmental, voluntary organization.

On May 1, 1930, the Child Health and Protection Conference had progressed to the point that President Hoover proclaimed Child Health Day.

". . . Our children," he stated in his proclamation, "have the right to be born in health, to be well throughout boyhood and the pre-school years; . . ."

What is significant here is the definition and official identification of a new *right* by the most powerful Federal spokesman. No one can argue that children do not deserve to be born in health and that they deserve healthy young lives and the other *rights* enumerated in the proclamation. But when the president proclaims a *right*, there is at once an implied governmental responsibility to guaranty the right. In this instance the central government is committed to provide for the welfare of children. Parents are correspondingly relieved of responsibility to the same extent that government assumes it. The government is guaranteeing to promote the welfare of a specific group, which is not the same as promoting the general welfare as provided by the Constitution.

President Hoover drafted the original Children's charter which was put in final form and adopted by the White House Conference.

"THE CHILDREN'S CHARTER

President Hoover's White House Conference on Child Health and Protection, recognizing the rights of the child as the first rights of citizenship, pledges itself to these aims in America . . ."

The charter then listed 19 aims *including spiritual and moral training*, understanding, love, security, prenatal and postnatal care, good schools, good dwellings, harmonious home environment, an adequate family standard of living, and so on. (48, pp 458-461) It was a masterpiece of rhetoric, the preamble for cradle to the grave security.

The Children's Conference outlined laudable aims. Considering, however, President Hoover's reputation for tightness of organization and methodical planning, it is out of character that the conferees failed to detail how the aims were to be achieved. Since the parents were not assigned the responsibility it must be inferred that an outside agency was expected to do the job. Furthermore, since the conference was sponsored by the Federal government, the logical choice for the outside agency would be the Federal government itself. Tender loving bureaucrats in Washington would then satisfy parental obligations, provide pre- and post-natal care, provide good dwellings and an adequate standard of living, and supervise the moral and spiritual atmosphere in which children were to be raised.

Right XV of the Charter demanded: "For every child the right to grow up in a family with an adequate standard of living and security of a stable income as the surest safeguard against social handicaps." This, being merely a declaration, is not socialism, but it is certainly propaganda for the socialism that we now know as Aid for Dependent Children, Family Assistance Plans, Child Day Care Centers, and the general concept of the welfare state.

Even Hoover recognized the effects of his efforts. "The Roosevelt administration," he wrote in his memoirs, "having a majority of its own party in both houses, was able to get legislation for Federal aid for the health and protection of children. No one will say that our years of public agitation for these policies did not greatly contribute to bring this about. I rejoiced at their action." (18, v II, p 266) This hardly qualifies Mr. Hoover as an old-time liberal.

The Child Health and Protection Conference was announced in July of 1929. In December of the same year, President Hoover announced appointment of a Research Committee on Social Trends which was to study the effects of the increasing life span and the increasing numbers of aged on "government obligations." There was, as might be expected from a government-sponsored conference, a notable lack of interest in "individual obligations." The study was also to examine the effects of technology on employment and to determine the "facts of unemployment, of housing, of recreation, . . . and problems raised by changes in rural life and by migration to the cities, slums, and other conditions of city life . . ." While Mr. Hoover's intentions may have been high-minded and, on the surface, innocuous, there is no doubt that the report, released in January 1933, was ready-made propaganda for the incoming New Deal administration. The government was granted a license for more intervention in private affairs. Individual and personal problems were to become increasingly solved by government-sponsored collective social action. Myers and Newton wrote that the report of the Research Committee on Social Trends "forms the first foundation for national social fact ever presented as a guide to public action. It has had a profound effect upon the thinking of the nation." (48, p 420)

While Hoover's committees, conferences, and commissions were preparing the propaganda which would, along with the depression, put Roosevelt in a position to accelerate socialization, Hoover continued to oppose government intervention in private affairs. He did this by word and deed. For instance, the president was the force behind the vast voluntary relief organizations set up in cooperation with local Community Chests during the hard depression winters of 1930, 1931, and 1932. "Federal activity," he said during his state of the nation address in December 1929, "in these directions (*Hoover was referring to Federal social services in education, home building, protection of women and children, public health, and recreation*) has been confined to research and dissemination of information and experience, and at most temporary subsidies to the States . . . Any other attitude by the Federal government will undermine one of the most precious possessions of the American people; that is, local and individual responsibility." Hoover was fighting a rear guard action against change. At the same time his bureaucrats, committees, and commissions, both government and voluntary, were promoting change. Hoover was a transition president, and his attitude soon reflected the transition.

As the depression deepened, President Hoover addressed the annual governor's conference in June 1930. He "urged further action by the states and municipalities in public works" to help those who were out of work. He noted, significantly, that for the first time the Federal government was concerned with such problems. Within a short time his concern was translated into direct government intervention.

The seeds for social security and Federal old-age assistance were also planted during Hoover's presidency. Shortly before the stock market crash in 1929, the president asked leading insurance men to work out a plan for old-age pensions to be paid for either by lump sum or by annual payments. So far, so good. However, it was Mr. Hoover's intention, after the private plans were developed, "to determine what steps might be necessary for the government to supplement it or to assist the companies to care for certain groups . . . It was the President's thought . . . ," that, "if desirable, the state and Federal governments could work out some form of contribution to assist." (48, p 406) The Federal government was about to assume responsibility for the care of persons claiming inability to care for themselves. The stock market crash, the drought and farm problems, and the depression forced abandonment of government-backed *private* old-age pensions.

In regard to Federal relief measures, Hoover claimed that such steps would destroy "local responsibility, and introduce graft, politics, waste, and mismanagement . . . The help being daily extended by neighbors, by local and national agencies, by municipalities, by industry and a great multitude of organizations throughout the country today is many times any appropriation yet proposed. The opening of the doors of the Federal treasury is likely to stifle this giving and thus destroy far more resources than the proposed charity from the Federal government."

In spite of President Hoover's warning, the doors to the Federal treasury were opened by Hoover's successor, and the ratio of private charity to government aid spending has decreased to an almost insignificant figure. Since government aid requires tax dollars (or inflation, which is another form of taxation) fewer personal funds remain for private charity. In truth, charity can not be equated to the efforts of the tax collector. When it is, it ceases to be charity. Government intervention diminishes the impulse to give because individuals tend to feel that personal obligations have been relieved by the state.

In early 1931, there was agitation in the Senate for Federal distribution of 25 million dollars for "human relief" in the drought areas. The Chairman of the American Red Cross stated that his organization could handle the task if the Federal government would maintain a "hands off" policy and restrict its activity to a loan fund for feed and seed. (A government loan fund is, of course, an intervention, even if it is only for feed and seed.) President Hoover supported the Red Cross plan and issued an appeal for 10 million dollars in contributions. After the Chairman of the American Red Cross testified again that a Federal appropriation was unnecessary, the House rejected the Senate proposal. (48, p 62)

President Hoover had a philosophy on relief which was stated often and clearly. That his administration did not always follow it rigidly can be blamed on the fact that our government and politicians are responsive to pressures exerted by the public. In September 1932, Hoover addressed the Mobilization of Private Charities. He said that the tasks were to see that no one went hungry, and that voluntary agencies for character building, child care, and help for the poor are maintained at full strength. It was necessary, he said, "to maintain the bedrock principle of our liberties by the full mobilization of individual and local resources and responsibilities . . . that we may maintain the spiritual impulses in our people for generous giving and generous service . . . A cold and distant charity which puts out its sympathy only through the tax collector, yields a very meager dole of unloving and perfunctory relief." In spite of this often-stated philosophy, direct Federal relief spending was over 200 million dollars in the last eight months of Hoover's presidency. All of which tends to show that the philosophy of the politician can be bent by the pressure of widely held views. Influencing the popular view may be very slow, but is a more certain way of shaping policy than is getting elected to office.

Peacetime Federal intervention in economic activities got under way on a large scale during the Hoover administration. In 1929, about 11 per cent of Federal expenditures were for "emergency" use. By 1930, about 17 per cent of Federal spending was for the same purposes. In 1930, for the first time, large loans were made to farm cooperatives through the Farm Board. Thus, the Federal government entered the realm of finance. Farm production was subsidized on a large scale. The perpetuation of farm surpluses and the farm problem can be attributed partly, if not entirely to these programs and extensions of them.

To be sure some of the interventions of Hoover did not require the use of public money and hence did not depend upon coercion via the tax power. For instance, the president succeeded in getting the railroads to haul feed for drought-stricken farmers at half-rates. This was a form of voluntary cooperation—as voluntary as it could be considering the power of the Interstate Commerce Commission and the fact that farmers' cash had been sharply curtailed by the drought.

Hoover, often considered by conservatives to be the champion of *laissez-faire* and defender of business against state interventions, did not restrict his administration to "helping" farmers. "The intervention," wrote Kimmel, "by the Hoover administration—the lending operations of the Reconstruction Finance Corporation and the like—was equivalent to recognition that reliance could not be placed solely on 'natural' economic forces." (4, p 205) Hoover was, of course, under terrible political pressure to "do something." Doing nothing would have been the most positive way of doing something. By doing something, Hoover unlocked the door for his interventionist successor, who had no inhibitions about intervening in economic affairs.

There is something of the split personality in Herbert Hoover as president. This conclusion is supported by the general public acceptance of him as a conservative, while more careful and less partisan observers have recognized him as a modern liberal, less rash and at the same time more thoughtful and deliberate than his successor. As president he promoted statism and socialism while he spoke against them.

"I used up much breath," wrote Hoover in his memoirs, "in expounding the follies of socialism. I strongly advocated the return of the railways to private ownership and the liquidation of the government ownership and operation of shipping and the ending of war controls of prices and wages." (18, v I, pp 29-30) He was serious in these protestations, but he failed to recognize the socialist direction of many of the steps he took: the establishment of the Reconstruction Finance Corporation, the expansion of the Farm Loan Banks, and founding of the Home Loan Banks. These agencies financed what ordinary banks would not dare to finance, and in effect the Federal government used its tax power to bestow benefits on the recipients of its cheap loans and easy credit. The businessmen, homeowners, and farmers who took out loans were subsidized by all taxpayers who did not take out loans. There were, in addition, many more Hoover activities which were either interventionist or laid the groundwork for intervention by his successor.

For instance, Hoover proposed an old-age assistance plan even before he became president. This called for a state-operated system by which the Federal government would only act as tax collector and distributor of grants. Employees and employers were to share equally in bearing its cost. The similarity to the New Deal proposal is obvious.

In the traditionally accepted areas of Federal intervention, such as in the roadbuilding program, President Hoover channeled additional funds into drought areas and away from areas not affected by the drought. Although the motives were admirable as well as political, it is likely that these policies resulted in an uneconomic expenditure of effort. Areas in greatest need of roads did not necessarily receive them unless they also happened to be drought areas. Such is the result of political interference with economics.

Hoover's reluctance to rely upon the government to stimulate the economy did not prevent him from proudly reporting that Federal spending for public works had increased "from a rate of about $275,000,000 a year prior to the depression to a rate of over $750,000,000 a year" in February of 1931. He was also proud of the "large appropriations to rehabilitate agriculture . . ." (48, p 63)

Federal spending for public works curtails non-Federal spending for construction in the same way that government spending for "charity" curtails private spending for charity. The funds spent by the Federal government for public works are funds that are not available for private or local spending. The same total of funds might be spent in both cases, i.e. the same effort might be expended in both cases. But through the intervention of the Federal tax collector, decisions about *how* the funds are to be used and *where* the effort is to be directed are no longer made by individuals or by local governments. Bureaucrats, some miles from the scene, are the new decision makers, and under these conditions, real needs are met less effectively.

When Federal funds are not derived by taxation they can be raised by issuing bonds. Bonds will either deplete funds otherwise available for local spending in the same way that taxes do, or they will cause inflation by monetization of the debt. Monetization of the debt, and the inflation it causes, indirectly dilutes and depletes private savings so that the result is similar to taxation. Inflation is a subtle tax on savings rather than a blatant tax on income.

Statist interventions sometimes yield unexpected ironies. The development of aviation under Federal sponsorship is an example. President Wilson established the National Advisory Committee on Aeronautics "to study . . . the problems of flight with a view to their solution." Hoover, as Secretary of Commerce, and later acting as his own man, expanded NACA and the growing socialist development of the air transport industry. When he forwarded NACA's annual report to the 71st Congress, Hoover wrote that ". . . progress on the two outstanding problems of increased

safety and decreased costs necessitates continuous scientific research on the fundamental problems of flight. To this end
enlarged facilities are being provided . . ." How the National Advisory Committee on Aeronautics became the National Lobbying
Committee for Aeronautics has been documented. (17) It has
become the focus for pressure groups lobbying for promotion,
control, and subsidy of air transportation. The proposals of the
late 1960's and early 1970's to develop a supersonic transport
(SST) called for additional socialization, by which all taxpayers
would have paid for a project whose benefits would be enjoyed
by only a few. Ironically, the fight against the SST found the
anti-statist libertarians in the same army with hysterical environ-
mentalists, who are statist liberals. It also separated anti-statist
conservatives, who oppose *all* subsidies, period, from the statist
conservatives, who oppose all subsidies excepting those from
which they stand to gain.

Neither law nor conscience restrain the statists upon their
self-appointed rounds. Encroachment upon private activities can
be either all-encompassing economic edicts or trivial and annoy-
ing attempts to intimidate creativity and legislate standards of
taste. For instance, consider President Hoover's first message to
the 71st Congress.

". . . the (National Capital) Fine Arts Commission should be
required," said Hoover at one point in his message, "to pass upon
private buildings proposed for sites facing on public buildings
and parks." A first response to this is likely to be favorable. What
could be finer than a commission assigned the job of insuring
that only attractive buildings would be erected adjacent to public
sites? The difficulty comes in trying to define what is attractive—
a very subjective task. What assurance is there that the designs
approved by the commission would be superior to those rejected
by the commission, and if so, superior in whose eyes? If it is
granted that a commission has some occult powers to divine
what is universally beautiful, then why limit its authority to sites
facing public property? Why not apply its judgement to the
entire capital city, in fact, why should the country beyond the
city limits be denied this godlike wisdom? What is to prevent
stifling of creativity and dreary standardization? Beauty by edict
has been a peculiar goal of those ultimate statists, the Nazis and

the Communists, in art, in literature, in thought, and in politics, as well as in the humble field of architectural design.

Herbert Hoover was an active and energetic man. He was an executive of great talents. He was quiet, forceful, intelligent, aggressive and strong willed. Men with these qualities influence and, in some cases, control much of what comes within their reach. In public life such men, if they lack integrity, are very dangerous indeed. It was America's good fortune that Herbert Hoover was a man of integrity.

Strong men, like Hoover, regardless of their integrity or lack of it, are restrained by external forces, by their backgrounds, and by their personalities. They are not free agents. President Hoover found himself thwarted by the 72nd Congress, which was controlled by the Democrats and which was at times almost frivolous and capricious in its opposition. Members of his own party were suspicious of his background. Never a registered Democrat, he served well a Democrat in the White House and urged election of congressmen in 1918 who would support Wilson. He was thwarted by his Quaker background and his training as an engineer, both of which tended to suppress ordinary political approaches and maneuverings. Hoover was not an exciting writer or speaker. His speeches were often over the heads of his listeners. After fifteen minutes of talk about gold drain, foreign exchange restrictions, foreign dumping of American securities, strangulation of credit, and gold reserves, an audience at a mass rally was likely to be either asleep or wishing they were somewhere else. Of course, what Mr. Hoover was saying was important, but it was not likely to capture many voters. The successful politician cannot afford to get too far ahead of the troops. And finally, contrasting Hoover's serious appearance and personality with Roosevelt's gayety and charm (which, incidentally, Wendell Wilkie said was exaggerated), appealing voice, and emotional ghost-written rhetoric, it is obvious that, even as an incumbent president, Hoover was at a disadvantage.

The presidential career of Herbert Hoover was wrecked almost before it began. The foreman of the wrecking crew was Charley Michelson, formerly Chief of the Washington Bureau of the New York *World*. Shortly after Al Smith's defeat in 1928, the Democrat National Committee hired Michelson for the express purpose of destroying Hoover. This was a bit of historical burlesque, for in 1920 Michelson had said Hoover was "the best qualified possibility that had approached the presidency in modern times." (47, p 50)

Michelson was paid $25,000 a year (46, pp 231-243) to convince a majority of the people that Hoover was a heartless, cold, cruel man who was responsible for the Hoover depression, for Hoover breadlines, and Hooverville shanty towns.[1] That Michelson achieved his goals is all the more remarkable in view of Hoover's public acclaim only a decade before as the director of war and post war relief in Europe and Russia, and his part in relief of flood victims only a year earlier. Michelson also tried to convince the public that the administration was corrupt as well as cruel, but in this he failed. Rumored scandals of oil shale leases and shady deals with sugar lobbyists proved unfounded.

Lies and rumors spread by others helped Michelson along. Hoover was accused of being a gambler and promoter rather than an engineer, he was blamed for mine failures which occurred even though he was not connected with them, he was said to have become a British citizen because, by local law, his name automatically appeared on a voter's list where he lived, he was accused of being a slave driver and exploiter of human beings, he was said to be guilty of murdering two veterans in connection with the Veterans' Bonus March, a lie for which John T. Pace, an ex-Communist, later took responsibility in Congressional hearings. (46, p 242) And of course, none of his genuine accomplishments were ever mentioned. Hoover's demise was as complete and cruel as it was unjustified.

Regardless of whether one agrees or disagrees with Hoover's many statist proposals regarding child welfare, old-age pensions, unemployment insurance, and Federal subsidies for business, farming, and transportation, there is no basis for his being pictured as cold-hearted and insensitive. In spite of the fact that many of his policies were liberal, not in the classical, but in the modern, sense

[1] According to Eugene Lyons, John J. Raskob financed this effort to the extent of $462,000. Other contributors included the DuPonts, Thomas Fortune Ryan, Vincent Astor, Herbert Lehman. The initial motivation for the assault on Hoover may have been Catholic revenge for Smith's defeat, even though all of the backers were not Catholic. Raskob was a prominent Catholic layman and leader of the backers. Many of the men who financed the effort against Hoover later supported the Liberty League, which was formed in opposition to Franklin Roosevelt and the New Deal!

of the word, he was damned at every turn by the liberals of his time, probably because most liberals were hostages of the Democrat Party. Most people accepted his damnation as gospel. Here again is evidence that the politician is the captive of the public and the public is the captive of the opinion makers.

Herbert Hoover presided over the end of an era which commenced during the term of Woodrow Wilson. It was an era of transition rooted in the XVIth and XVIIth amendments to the Constitution by which, respectively, Federal income taxes were legalized and the direct election of senators was made mandatory.

The XVIth amendment, by giving the central government dominant tax power, insured that the dominant political power would reside in the capital city. Political power, following tax money, drained away from the states for its grand rendezvous in Washington. As federal power waxed, state and local power waned. There are, after all, only limited resources which the tax collector can seize, and as Washington took more and more, the localities were left with less and less. The XVIth amendment made possible American entry into World War I, for without it the war effort could not have been financed, just as during the Civil War it was necessary to collect an illegal income tax. By the 1960's and 1970's the states and cities would become so impoverished that they would beg the Federal government to share its tax revenue.

If the states were laid to rest in a coffin made of the XVIth amendment, the XVIIth amendment furnished the nails to hold down the top. It was this amendment which destroyed the concept of the United States as a union of individual and autonomous states. The amendment stopped the "purchase" of senate seats by bribery of state legislators, a moral defect of the people rather than a defect in the system. By weakening the power of the state legislatures and the significance of the states as political units, the amendment shifted the balance of power further toward Washington. At the same time, the direct election of senators made the United States Senate more sensitive to organized pressure groups by the removal of an intermediate barrier formerly provided by the state legislatures. In a government strictly limited to protection of citizens against fraud, predation, and violence, direct election vs indirect election and insulation from pressure groups is of little or no importance. But in a system where providing for the general welfare has been corrupted to providing for specific welfare, direct exposure to pressure groups has great significance and danger.

The Republican Party at, and for a long time after, its founding had favored the ascendancy of Federal power over state power. This, of course, was the central political, if not moral or economic, issue of the Civil War. Reduced to basics it was a question of whether or not a state could withdraw from the union. The Republican tradition of Federalism was maintained and strengthened by Teddy Roosevelt and his progressive reformers. They were limited in their political power, however, because they were limited in their tax power.

When Wilson came to power as a minority president, the Democrat Party power base rested upon a loose coalition of Northern immigrants (most of whom were Catholic), Western populists, Southern conservatives (most of whom were Protestant), and big city machines. It was from the Southern Democrats, the largest and most powerful group in the party, that the party inherited its states' rights tradition. Wilson, under whom the era of transition began, had a Southern boyhood and background. Wilson's part in the transition was, however, by accident rather than by design.

Wilson was the first Democrat to become president in sixteen years, and was only the second Democrat to serve in the half century since the Republican Party was founded. Under Wilson the Democrats became the party of a strong Federalism, and the individualists and state's righters began their retreat to Republicanism. The World War and the XVIth and XVIIth amendments were factors in this shift of positions. Harding and Coolidge represented a desire for a return to "normalcy" and a rebellion against Federalism. They were the first anti-Federalist Republicans. Hoover, although by natural inclination an individualist, was tainted by war time service as a Wilsonian Federalist. He spoke like a Harding or Coolidge anti-Federalist, but acted more in the tradition of a modern liberal statist.

With Hoover's demise, the bank panic, the resurging, persistent depression, and the war, there came a long series of Democrat victories. During this new era the Southern conservative states' righters and the old-time city bosses slowly lost influence in the party and were replaced by liberal left intellectuals, labor leaders, and various ethnic and pressure groups. The twin disasters of the depression and World War II gave Roosevelt the excuse to use the vast tax powers of the XVIth amendment. The local machine politicians and ward heelers, whose power had been based on bussing babies, baskets of food for the poor, and small favors for friends, were gradually replaced by armies of Federal bureaucrats distributing, no trivial goodies, but billions in tax dollars. Labor unions through the contributions of their political arms purchased more influence in the directly elected United States Senate than had ever been wielded by buying the senate seats of indirectly elected senators. The distinction between labor contributions and business bribes is, after all, not large. The traditional roles of the parties with respect to Federalism, states' rights, and individual freedom were switched. The Democrats became the new Federalists, ignoring more and more their Southern bloc, collecting more and more in Federal taxes, and forcing more and more dependence upon Washington. The Democrats, whose New Deal platform damned Federal expansion, bureaucracy, and spending, went much further down the statist road than any of their Republican predecessors, progressives included. Hoover served at the end of a transition period which began with Wilson; when he left the White House the Republican monopoly on Federalism was broken. Hoover, who was much less a Federalist than his successor, was to be the last Republican president for a long time.

CHAPTER 11

THE PATRICIAN

Youthful adversity, at one time, seemed almost a constitutional qualification for men who wished to occupy the White House. Birth in a log cabin and a paucity of childhood pleasures, if not required by law, were certainly political assets for many of the more colorful presidents of the nineteenth century. As we moved into the twentieth century, presidents and party leaders have less frequently been able to claim log cabin rearing and lantern light learning. Al Smith, who settled for a tenement and Fulton Street in lieu of a log cabin and the forest, and Coolidge and Hoover were among the last who lived truly lean youths. Progress and prosperity sent this American tradition westward. Franklin Roosevelt was, in the new tradition, hardly born in a log cabin. In this, and in other respects, his life and career paralleled that of his fifth cousin Theodore, the first of the twentieth century presidents.

Both Roosevelts were well born New Yorkers who headed north to Harvard for their undergraduate days. Both attended Columbia Law School, but neither followed law as a profession. FDR did pass the bar in 1907 and was an unenthusiastic practitioner for several years, but he was hardly known for any success in the field. What really fired Franklin was his cousin's record of political success. Both Roosevelts were political mavericks: FDR was an insurgent Democrat and Theodore was an insurgent Republican. Both served in the New York state legislature, both became assistant secretaries of the navy, both served as governor of New York, and both were nominated for the vice presidency by their respective parties. And both were strongly motivated to win in politics, other considerations being secondary. Both, too, were troubled by physical problems. Theodore seemed to have inherited physical weakness, but he overcame this by fierce personal determination, just as Franklin Roosevelt overcame the crippling effects of his infantile paralysis.

The term *economic royalist* was one of those derogatory, divisive terms made popular by Franklin Roosevelt. He may not have coined it, but by usage he endorsed it. Determining exactly who qualifies as an economic royalist is just as difficult as deciding where the poverty level lies and who qualifies as poor. In spite of this, FDR's family background and his inherited wealth would seem to qualify him as at least a duke, if not a baron, in the court of economic royalty.

Some of Roosevelt's biographers were reluctant to admit, it seems, that Roosevelt was born, as his enemies claimed, with the proverbial silver spoon in his mouth. Emil Ludwig portrayed Roosevelt as a sort of kid from the family down the street. William S. White conceded that he was better off than most of us, but shyed away from picturing his family as wealthy, describing it as essentially mercantile and upper-middle class.

James MacGregor Burns' description was both honest and more specific.

"Parents and child," wrote Burns of FDR's boyhood, "formed the focal point of a large establishment. House and grounds were peopled with nurse, cook, gardener, coachman, stable boys, and farm hands. The estate spread over several hundred acres, embracing fields and forests, gardens, green house, grapery, ice houses, barns, and stables . . . When the Roosevelts went by rail, they travelled in a private car . . . Tall, gracious, beautiful, Sara (*FDR's mother*) was the product of an upper class of international scope. As a girl she had sailed to Hong Kong on a square-rigger; she had been educated abroad; she had moved in society in New York, Boston, London, and Paris."

At Groton, the boys in Franklin's form were, according to Burns, "those of wealthy, socially established families from a few centers on or near the eastern seaboard . . . over 90 per cent of the boys were from families listed in social registers." (2, pp 9-12)

When Roosevelt was assistant secretary of the navy the family spent time at Campobello and Hyde Park. Burns claimed that as many as ten servants attended the family. Roosevelt's salary and investments brought him about $27,000 a year, but he and his wife lived so well that occasionally his mother's help was needed. Gene Smith was not delicate in describing Mama Sara's role. "Tammany politicians dismissed him as a mama's boy which he was," wrote Smith, adding parenthetically that "his widowed mother controlled all his money, dictated the furnishings in his homes, and decreed the manner in which his children should be raised." (47, p 91) Emil Ludwig, who interviewed the president, confirmed that young Roosevelt and his wife spent about $25,000 a year, (28, p 116) which, considering the effect of inflation would certainly be the equivalent of $100,000 a year in the 1970's, and would require a correspondingly larger gross income before taxes. The facts would seem to place Franklin Roosevelt squarely in the camp of those whom he sarcastically referred to as "economic royalists." Perhaps this accounts for the frequent bitter charge made by other courtiers that the duke "was a traitor to his own class."

Franklin Roosevelt's unlimited self-confidence and his belief that the end justified the means were demonstrated during his service as assistant secretary of the navy. When World War I started, and for at least two years afterward, America was officially neutral. Roosevelt's immediate superior, Josephus Daniels, the secretary of the navy, supported the president's official stand. Roosevelt was from the start a zealous supporter of the Allies and, obviously convinced of the rightness of his position, he did not hesitate undercutting the people he worked for. "His zeal led him onto dubious grounds," according to Burns, "he maintained contacts with Theodore Roosevelt, Henry Cabot Lodge, and other critics of Wilson's policies, and even passed on naval intelligence information to Republicans who used it in attacking Daniels for naval unpreparedness." (2, p 61) He was sort of an early day Daniel Ellsberg, the "author" of the *Pentagon Papers*.

More of Roosevelt's character was revealed by the view he held of his war time service as a civilian in the Navy Department. He claimed to have repeatedly sought a commission, without success, presumably because even at this early date he had already achieved indispensable status, a role he later assumed unblushingly as president. Burns told the whole story.

"The next best thing was to go near the fighting, if only as a civilian," wrote Burns. "He finally induced the Secretary to send him on an unofficial mission to inspect naval bases . . . Eager for adventure, Roosevelt departed early in July 1918 on a destroyer bound for Europe.

"It was an exciting and satisfying trip. Zigzagging across the Atlantic Roosevelt's destroyer experienced nothing more than a few false alarms, but even these furnished the basis for future yarns . . ."

"And finally he saw war . . . He toured a sector where Marines had fought (*not where they were fighting*), describing the war-torn area . . . He saw fighting at a distance. Most exciting of all, he came under sporadic artillery fire.

"Roosevelt was keenly disappointed but he tried to make the best of it. 'Though I did not wear a uniform,' he wrote later to a Grotonian who was preparing a World War tablet at the school, 'I believe that my name should go in the first division of those who were "in the service," especially as I saw service on the other side, was missed by torpedoes and shells . . .' " (2, pp 65-66) (He was also missed by an *American* torpedo fired from a U.S. destroyer at the ship taking him to a World War II conference. Contrary to rumor, this was accidental.)

"Following the war," Burns reported, "Franklin Roosevelt applied for membership in the American Legion. As the years passed his stories of his military experiences and risks overseas became more and more expansive—to the point where he was claiming that he had probably seen more of the war than anyone else." (2, p 80) Before it was discovered that wars are immoral, a war record was a political asset.

In the summer of 1921, Roosevelt was crippled by infantile paralysis. With a great deal of persistence and buoyancy of spirit he finally was able to get back into the political arena. In 1928 he ran for governor of New York and was elected in spite of Hoover's huge victory over Al Smith. Roosevelt became governor of New York in January 1929, and his inaugural address is revealing. In it he expressed ideas that were very different from the reputation he earned in Washington a few years later. Apart from its style, the Albany inaugural address might have been ghosted by Herbert Hoover.

". . . this is an illustration of the present dangerous tendency," Roosevelt warned his audience, "to forget a fundamental of American democracy, which rests on the right of a locality to manage its local affairs—the tendency to encourage concentration of power at the top of a government structure, alien to our system and more closely akin to a dictatorship or the central committee of a communistic regime."

"The doctrine of regulation and legislation by 'master minds,' in whose judgement and will all the people may gladly and quietly acquiesce, has been too glaringly apparent during these last ten years," continued Roosevelt sounding now more like Goldwater of the 60's than Hoover of the 30's. "Were it possible to find 'master minds' so unselfish, so willing to decide unhesitatingly against their own personal interest or private prejudices, men almost godlike in their ability to hold the scales of justice with an even hand—such a government might be to the interests of the country, but there are none such on our political horizon, and we can not expect a complete reversal of all the teachings of history."

In the 1932 campaign Roosevelt wavered from side to side, from right to left and back again, like the local drunk staggering uncertainly homeward after a bout at the bar. He was for low tariffs when the campaign began, but before it ended he was in basic agreement with the Republican stand; he was for government interference in economic affairs at the Commonwealth Club in San Francisco, but the closer he got to Washington the more severely he criticized Hoover's bureaucracy, spending, and unbalanced budget. It was very difficult for persons who were knowledgeable about foreign affairs to have confidence in a man who had backed Wilson on the League of Nations in 1920 and who now attacked the idea of American participation.

"What was Roosevelt up to?" asked Professor Burns in *The Lion and the Fox*. "He was trying to win an election, not lay out a coherent philosophy of government. He had no such philosophy; but he knew how to pick up votes, how to capture group support, how to change pace and policy. 'Weave the two together,' he said to an astonished Raymond Moley when the academic man presented Roosevelt with two entirely different drafts on tariff policy. 'I think you'll agree,' he wrote . . . about . . . a farm speech, 'that it is sufficiently far to the left to prevent any further suggestion that I am leaning to the right.' " (2, p 144)

Oswald Garrison Villard, the liberal reform editor and journalist, predicted in 1910 that Franklin Roosevelt would some day be president. In 1928 he supported FDR's quest for the governorship of New York, but by the time Roosevelt became a leading contender for the Democrat presidential nomination Villard had cooled off. He thought Roosevelt played along with Tammany Hall and lacked leadership. In a January 1932 editorial in *The Nation*, Villard wrote that the governor was ". . . a charming person, an increasingly astute politician able to pull with reformers, the Republican party, Tammany Hall, and a man who does not advance the cause of reform one whit."

Michael Wreszin, Villard's biographer, wrote that ". . . Villard felt that Roosevelt toward the end of the (*1932*) campaign had become even more evasive: 'His sickening wobblings on the tariff . . . his pathetic belief that he had outlined a big constructive program . . . only reveals his ignorance, callousness, yes the juvenility of his mind.' The editors of *The New Republic* echoed his sentiments: 'This is an election in which we can find more satisfaction in rejoicing at defeats than at victories.' " (50, p 219)

Roosevelt's 1932 campaign resembled John F. Kennedy's campaign twenty-eight years later. In both cases, neither man had a definite goal other than to win the election and acquire power. Neither man had as firm a grip on current problems as the man he opposed. The elections were decided not so much by what the challengers said as by the sounds of their voices, by their personalities, and by their appearance. On all three counts Roosevelt and Kennedy towered over their respective opponents.

Events following the 1932 election also paralleled the events following the 1960 Kennedy victory. In both cases, the acquisition of power was consolidated by a crisis: for Roosevelt it was a banking panic; for Kennedy, the Cuban crisis. The result was a disaster in both cases. Roosevelt's policies did not get rid of the depression; it persisted until domestic crises were replaced by foreign ones. Under Kennedy, the problems of the cold war grew steadily hotter as the Bay of Pigs fiasco was followed by the Cuban missile crisis, Berlin wall, and crescive floundering in Vietnam.

After the 1932 election President Hoover tried to get the president-elect's cooperation on economic problems. By early 1933 there was a run on gold as signs increased that the incoming administration planned inflation. Roosevelt's continuing consultations with men who favored currency manipulation were reported in the newspapers.

"President-elect Roosevelt," stated the Washington *Herald* on January 30, 1933, "has assured advisers he will sign a measure for controlled currency inflation . . .

". . . he was said to be prepared to accept some form of currency inflation in order to raise commodity prices and ease the financial stringency of the nation.

"As a consequence of this commitment, Senator Carter Glass, of Virginia, according to his friends, is hesitating about accepting the post of secretary of the treasury . . ."

Carter Glass, who favored sound currency, refused the job when Roosevelt's monetary plans unfolded.

By this time the situation was desperate. Gold was leaving the country in a wild flight. During the first two weeks of February, gold exports were almost triple what they had been during the last two weeks of January. President Hoover repeatedly urged Mr. Roosevelt to issue assurances that there would be no "reflation," a word coined by the inflaters to mask their true intentions. Hoover's efforts produced no results. All the while banks were failing and closing their doors as people withdrew their savings in a growing panic.

President Hoover's last plea to FDR was delivered in person by a Secret Service messenger on February 17th. It was only after a second urgent letter, written on February 28th, that Roosevelt even replied to the earlier letter. FDR apologized for the delay in replying, claiming his secretary had assumed the reply Roosevelt had given him was "only a draft of a letter." This was typical of Roosevelt's cavalier negligence in time of crisis. It is, of course, unthinkable that the President-elect could have failed to follow up such an important matter to insure that a reply had actually gone out.

The gay, jaunty president-to-be arrived in Washington on March 2nd, two days before the inauguration. After conferring with congressional and political leaders of his party, he called on President Hoover. Roosevelt steadfastly refused to give any assurances or take any action on the monetary crisis. By March 4th the financial machinery of the country was coming to a screeching halt, with wholesale runs on banks and statewide bank closings. Not until March 6th, two days *after* the inauguration did Roosevelt take action, declaring a banking holiday. In the meantime thousands of additional banks failed which need not have failed had action been taken two weeks earlier.

Hoover's suspicions of Roosevelt's motives were well put in his letter of February 20th to Senator David Reed of Pennsylvania.

"I realize," wrote the president, "that if these declarations (*namely, pledges not to inflate and pledges to follow a policy of sound money*) be made by the president-elect . . . it means the abandonment of 90% of the so-called new deal. But unless this is done, they run a grave danger of precipitating a complete financial debacle. If it is precipitated, the responsibility lies squarely with them for they have had ample warning—unless, of course, such a debacle is part of the 'new deal.' "

"That Roosevelt viewed a pressing problem 'as not my baby,' " wrote Gene Smith, "encouraged the concept of him that most people had always held—charming, human, but irresponsible in the end." (47, p 222)

Less generous critics, such as John T. Flynn, accused Roosevelt of willfully attempting to sabotage Hoover's efforts in order to add glory to the remedies applied *after* he became president. (49, pp 16-22) Even James MacGregor Burns, admiring critic and biographer of Roosevelt, wrote that FDR was "so sure of the rightness of his aims that he was willing to use Machiavellian means." (2, p 477)

Emil Ludwig, popular historical biographer of the 1920's and 1930's helped create the Roosevelt myth, one aspect of which was that FDR was a great orator and thinker. Justice Oliver Wendell Holmes thought Roosevelt was "a second-class intellectual, but a first-class temperament." (2, p 157)

"He writes his speeches himself . . ." wrote Ludwig admiringly, (28, p 285) who then went on to describe the process, citing Roosevelt's claim that he dictated his Chicago October 1937 speech in one hour. " 'Under other circumstances' " Ludwig quotes Roosevelt as having said, " 'I ask two or three friends what they would say in my place, and use some of their thoughts; but I could never have a speech written for me by some department.'

". . . his speeches," wrote Ludwig, "the one definite and fixed expression of his personality . . . emerge from decade to decade as masterpieces." By this statement, Ludwig confirms his own innocence more than he establishes Roosevelt's oratorical ability.

Roosevelt wrote his own speeches before 1928 and they were not known for any special brilliance. Certainly, they were not known as masterpieces. His "Happy Warrior" speech gained him his first national fame (with the help of radio) as an orator, and this speech was said to have been written by a New York judge. (49, p 283) As governor, and later as president, he assembled a corps of ghost writers among whom were Louis Howe, Judge Samuel Rosenman, and Raymond Moley. The most famous phrase in Roosevelt's first inaugural address was "the only thing we have to fear is fear itself." This was probably inserted by Judge Rosenman who heard the same phrase as a student in a Columbia University English class. Thoreau used the identical words. (49, p 284) Later Roosevelt replaced Raymond Moley with Tommy Corcoran. Stanley High, Harry Hopkins, Robert Sherwood, and Archibald MacLeish all ghosted for Roosevelt at various times during his tenure. FDR thus relied upon others for the thought and the well-turned phrase, limiting his contribution to a cultivated voice and artful delivery. The character of FDR *is* shown by his speeches, just as Ludwig claimed, not because his speeches were masterpieces, but because they were ghosted by others and passed off as his own. Meanwhile he was acclaimed as a master thinker and great orator. He was neither of these.

"Hiss'[1] contempt for Franklin Roosevelt," wrote Whitaker Chambers in his book *Witness,* "as a dabbler in revolution who understood neither revolution nor history was profound. It was the common view of Roosevelt among Communists, which I shared with the rest." This appraisal is not too different from that shared by many conservatives and a few objective liberals. Roosevelt was a political butterfly, a man whose thin intellectual capacity was hidden by an abundance of charm.

Emil Ludwig disparagingly compared Theodore to his fifth

[1] Alger Hiss held various government jobs, his most important being a high post in the State Department. He was accused by Whitaker Chambers (an admitted ex-Communist) of being a Communist. As an outgrowth of the charge and subsequent denial, Hiss was convicted and jailed as a perjurer in 1950.

cousin Franklin, and in doing so he inadvertently supports a charge frequently made by FDR's foes. Ludwig wrote "that all the rubbish of the new (*1933*) German Führer-idea was anticipated ideologically by Theodore thirty years ago, down to the very slogans." Yet Ludwig recognized that Franklin too had dictatorial inclinations when he wrote that ". . . Theodore's character had much stronger leanings toward dictatorship than Franklin's." Ludwig was also conscious of the dictatorial threat in FDR's 1933 inaugural address:

> "But in the event that Congress shall fail . . . , and in the event that the national emergency is still critical, I shall not evade the clear course of duty that will confront me. I shall ask Congress for the one remaining instrument to meet the crisis—broad executive power that would be given me if we were in fact invaded by a foreign foe. . . ."

This, Ludwig admitted, was "a clear call for dictatorial power, to be entrusted to him (*FDR*) by constitutional methods." Roosevelt was not known to have spent sleepless nights worrying about such trifles as constitutionality.

James MacGregor Burns, the liberal Williams' College professor would be expected to approve of Roosevelt and his New Deal. However, Roosevelt's first term is shown by Burns to be a basically shallow performance. Some quotes from Burns' *Roosevelt, the Lion and the Fox* demonstrate the point.

"Roosevelt had no rounded program" when he assumed the presidency, wrote Burns. (2, p 150) "Roosevelt was following no master plan . . . He not only admitted to, he boasted of, playing by ear." He admitted to making "snap judgments . . . Partly by design, partly by chance, Roosevelt had gathered around him a group of advisers as diverse in philosophy as the New Deal itself . . . (2, pp 171-172) Roosevelt was no theorist. It is doubtful that he chose this course (*as a mediator or concilliator between opposing groups*) as a result of a well-defined political philosophy. It simply emerged . . . (2, p 198) The supreme test of Roosevelt's leadership in this area (*labor legislation*) was his handling of the Wagner Act . . . (2, p 218) Roosevelt's sudden reversal on the Wagner Act was symptomatic of his policy making during 1935 . . . (2, p 220) Nothing better showed Roosevelt's sudden change of direction (*in response to Huey Long's and Dr. Townsend's wealth-sharing plans*) than the tax bill . . . (2, p 224) Gliding with the current of opinion favoring the probe, Roosevelt . . ." (2, p 254) wrote Burns in regard to the Nye Committee investigations of involvement in World War I. "At this crucial juncture Roosevelt offered little leadership . . . (2, p 255) The record is clear. As a foreign policy maker, Roosevelt during his first term was more pussy-footing politician than political leader." (2, p 262)

Roosevelt was so intent on following public whims and so devoid of leadership, that one must conclude that the country would have done just as well had the Gallup Poll taken the oath of office on the Capitol steps on March 4, 1933.

The Communists of the USSR have been known to re-write history to suit the political taste of whoever happens to be in power at the time of the revision. Thus, Stalin transformed Trotsky into the arch villain and, in turn, Stalin has been pictured as hero, villain, and semi-hero. Roosevelt did not match the Communists as a revisionist, but he didn't shy away from a little helpful editing. Burns relates an episode that occurred as the elections of 1936 approached.

"When the National Emergency Council early in 1936 submitted to Roosevelt some statistical tables and statements implying that recovery began in 1932," wrote Burns, "(*Stephen*) Early (*Roosevelt's assistant and press secretary*) indicated that this would not do at all. Changes must be made in the report.

" 'The President is insistent,' he wrote to the NEC, 'that the low point in the depression be fixed as March, 1933, or early in the year 1933—this for obvious reasons.' " (2, pp 268-269)

Both Emil Ludwig and James MacGregor Burns appraise Roosevelt's efforts as socialistic, but his opponents who said this in the 1930's were not taken seriously by a majority of the voters. Since Socialist Norman Thomas received only a little more than two per cent of the popular vote in 1932, it is obvious that there was little open support for a socialist approach to national problems. How did Roosevelt manage to promote socialism with such little public support for the socialist package?

Ludwig admired Roosevelt's skill in "transforming a conservative state into a semi-socialist state, all via popular elections and Congress, and in the most complete freedom of speech and opposition . . ." (28, p XI) He also claimed that ". . . Roosevelt had taken over all the socialist slogans of his opponent (*Norman*) Thomas . . ." (28, p 258)

Ludwig is incorrect in asserting that Roosevelt took over "all of the socialist slogans." He could not afford to do so in the face of a two per cent vote for socialism. Therefore, his 1932 election campaign was oriented toward conservatism, as previously pointed out. However, his words and his actions were contradictory. In fact, some of his actions were themselves contradictory.

"There was nothing but contradiction," Burns wrote, "between the spending for public works and the economy act, between the humanitarianism of direct relief and the miserliness of veteran's cuts, between the tariff-raising provisions of the AAA and the new interventionism of the State Department, between Roosevelt's emphasis on strengthening of government as a tool for social betterment and his reducing the cost of government, including the salaries of government workers." (2, p 179)

The socialism of Roosevelt, to which many voters later acquiesced (even though tradition had prevented them from breaking with the two party system in 1932), had been gradually popularized since the turn of the century by increasing numbers of teachers, ministers, writers, speakers, philosophers, and politicians. Roosevelt was shaped by the same influences as the general public, and Burns suggests that Roosevelt's socialist indoctrination may have occurred at Groton. "Peabody (the headmaster) was a Christian Socialist," wrote Burns. (2, p 15) He was both a minister and a teacher, and therefore he was influential.

Did Roosevelt's deceitfulness also originate at Groton? If it did, the source was not the headmaster. According to Burns: "Never lie, the Rector said—without taking up the further question whether in politics lies are sometimes necessary to reach 'good' ends. Never compromise with evil, the Rector said— without arguing whether politicians must work with corrupt forces to carry out popular mandates." (2, p 15)

Frank R. Kent was a part owner of the Baltimore *Sun* papers, a Washington columnist and a Democrat. In 1932 he voted for

Roosevelt, but his admiration lasted less than a year. "We thought he was one kind of a man when we voted for him," wrote Kent. "He has turned out to be quite another kind of man." These were very strong words from a man of Kent's mild, gentlemanly style. By 1936 Kent was thoroughly disillusioned.

Roosevelt was the first president to realize the full potential of radio and the press conference. His voice and personality were ideal for the new techniques. Hoover laid down a barrage of press releases and Harding capitalized on his photogenic face and working knowledge of the press, but their efforts pale when compared with Roosevelt's. After 1932, Roosevelt's election victories were one-man popularity contests. Both Burns and William S. White agree on this point.

". . . Roosevelt had fought the campaign (*of 1936*)," according to Burns, "on a highly personal basis. And he had built a winning coalition around himself . . ." (2, p 314) William S. White in appraising Roosevelt concluded that "he had habituated the people to voting not for parties but for men—in his case, for one man—" (5, p 163)

So effective was Roosevelt the showman, that his inconsistencies and waverings, his irresponsibility and deceit, and his fuzziness and opportunism were overlooked by the voters and he won resounding victories in 1936, 1940, and even in 1944. However the price paid by the country was high. Part of the price was the superstate apparatus which was an essential corollary to "tax and spend, spend and elect" politics. And part of the price was the development of a class cleavage hitherto virtually nonexistent in American life. Just as Hitler drew strength from attacking the Jews, Roosevelt drew strength from flailing the rich.

"Such simple and tangible language . . . ," wrote Emil Ludwig regarding Roosevelt's polemics, "was bound to split people into two groups, just as in the days of Lincoln, except that now the split was stronger, being, indeed, exclusively between rich and poor." (28, p 137) A Detroit auto unionist told Sam Lubell shortly after the 1940 election, "I'll say it even though it doesn't sound nice. We've grown class conscious." (2, p 254)

At the 1912 Democrat convention Champ Clark and Woodrow Wilson were the leading contenders for the presidential nomination. FDR bucked Tammany Hall and the New York state party machine, both of which supported Champ Clark. Roosevelt got together an unofficial group of 150 Wilson supporters, gave them buttons for Clark, and sneaked them into the Baltimore convention hall.

". . . suddenly they began to chant in chorus: 'We want Wilson!' " wrote Emil Ludwig in his unctuous biography. "It was a lark after his own heart, for what he thoroughly liked then, and still likes today, was to carry out by a mean trick what he earnestly believes to be the right thing." (28, p 63)

The 1912 production was sort of an off-Broadway trial run for the wild 1940 comic opera convention which, in spite of widespread rank and file reluctance to break the tradition against a third term, re-nominated the president. The plot was conceived by Harry Hopkins, Roosevelt's confidante in residence, and the lyrics were written by Postmaster-General Frank Walker. Boss Ed Kelly, mayor of Chicago, was the stage manager. The leading *basso profundo*, ensconced in the bowels of the Chicago stadium was Kelly's commissioner of sewers. The chorus was a mob of Chicago's finest political thugs, sneaked in by Boss Kelly and provided with fake state standards.

When Senator Alben Barkley, permanent chairman of the convention, finished reading the president's mock denial of an interest in the nomination there was a hesitant moment of silence. Then the sewer commissioner, described by James MacGregor Burns as a "leather-lunged, pot-bellied little man," (2, p 428) went into action. Provided with a microphone connected to loud speakers throughout the hall, he boomed over and over the chant, "We want Roosevelt! New York wants Roosevelt! Pennsylvania wants Roosevelt!" (49, pp 213-215) And then the fake delegates, jiggling their fake state standards up and down, burst screaming onto the floor in a fake demonstration which neutralized and overwhelmed the opposition. Fakery was triumphant.

In 1940, the Gallup Polls showed that 83 per cent of the American people were opposed to American participation in the war in Europe. Right up to December 7, 1941 the overwhelming majority of Americans remained opposed to our going to war. During the 1940 campaign Roosevelt made his famous Boston speech in which he said, "I say to you fathers and mothers and I will say it again and again and again. Your boys will not be sent into foreign wars." This statement represents fairly Roosevelt's public position on the war. The steps he publicly took were ostensibly taken to keep the country at peace by strengthening it and, after Dunkirk (May 1940) and the collapse of British-French-Belgian resistance on the mainland, by aiding in the defense of England. Thus, in September of 1940 he traded 50 World War I destroyers in return for American bases on British territory. He signed the Draft Act and took part in the first drawing on October 29, 1940. In early 1941 he proposed the Lend-Lease Act which, after two months of savage debate, became law and destroyed most of what remained of the American neutrality which Roosevelt had been publicly supporting.

"The 1940 campaign," wrote William S. White, "had been notable for his (FDR's) promises 'again and again' that the sons of this country would not be sent to fight 'in foreign wars'. This was of course, a pledge of highly debatable integrity; it was in fact, a false promise. No informed and compassionate person in this country in the autumn of 1940 doubted that Hitler's defeat must be brought about and that an American participation to this end was inevitable." (5, p 41)

There was no doubt that Roosevelt was well informed, and if one is willing to grant that he was compassionate, then we are forced to the conclusion that he deliberately lied to the people of this country. White came to the same conclusion but shied away from strong language, confining himself to the phrases "debatable integrity" and "false promise."

By 1941 Roosevelt was secretly moving to provoke an incident which would commit us to war. The British government released hitherto secret papers on January 1, 1972 which indirectly quote Churchill reporting to his war cabinet on August 19, 1941:

> "The President had said *he would wage war but not declare it* and that he would become more and more provocative. If the Germans did not like it, they could attack American forces."

In September the U.S.S. *Greer* dropped depth charges on a submarine and was the target of German torpedoes. In mid-October the U.S.S. *Kearney* was torpedoed and eleven sailors were killed.

On October 31, 1941 the U.S.S. *Reuben James* was sunk by torpedoes and 115 men were lost.

The British papers quoted Churchill further: "The President's orders to these escorts (*U.S. ships convoying lend-lease supplies to England*) were to attack any (*German*) U-boat which showed itself even if it were 200 or 300 miles away from the convoy. Everything was to be done to force an incident."

Thus, the loss of the U.S.S. *Reuben James*, and the attacks on the U.S.S. *Kearney* and the U.S.S. *Greer* could not have surprised Roosevelt. What did surprise him was that Germans, as well as Americans, could and would shoot without bothering to declare war. A more provocative strategy was required.

It was in the Pacific that Roosevelt's strategy to get us into the war, while publicly committing himself to noninvolvement, was successful. There was more than a decade of growing Japanese-American friction to aid him in his secret designs. In early 1940 the U.S. Fleet was moved to Pearl Harbor under instructions from the president. (51, pp 54-59, 65) This was contrary to the competent advice given by the fleet commander, Admiral J. O. Richardson. Richardson opposed basing the fleet in Hawaii because there it was unable either to defend itself adequately (52, pp 64-73) or prepare, provision, and train for war. In *October 1940* (more than a year before Pearl Harbor) Richardson disagreed with a plan of Roosevelt's to blockade Japan because it would have meant war and because it would have involved a disastrous dispersal of a fleet unprepared for war at the time. The Roosevelt blockade proposal was made a few weeks before the President's Boston campaign speech where he promised "again and again and again" not to send Americans to fight in a foreign war.

Four months after Richardson's disagreement with Roosevelt, and ten months before his normal tour of duty was ended, Richardson was summarily removed from command. The hapless Admiral Husband Kimmel replaced him.

Captain Russell Grenfell, R.N., told in 1952 in his book *Main Fleet to Singapore* (pp 107-108) how the United States under Roosevelt maneuvered and pressured Japan to launch the attack at Pearl Harbor. Grenfell quotes Mr. Oliver Lyttleton, who was British Minister of Production as saying in 1944 that "Japan was provoked into attacking America at Pearl Harbor. It is a travesty of history to say that America was forced into war." The various pressures to which Grenfell refers are detailed in reporter George Morgenstern's book *Pearl Harbor, The Story of the Secret War.* (51)

Franklin Roosevelt's duplicity in the pursuit of an incident was matched by his irresponsibility in failing to prepare his field commanders to meet it. Captain Grenfell wrote (p 107) ". . . What seems never to have crossed their minds was that the attack would come at Pearl Harbor. But a miscalculation of this kind was hardly the fault of the Japanese; especially as the American Ambassador in Japan had previously warned Washington that this very attack was being freely rumored in Tokyo." In Washington, at least five persons in positions of authority could have supplied vital intelligence to the field that the Japanese were about to attack. Incredibly, *all five* withheld this information from General Short, Army Commander at Pearl Harbor, and Admiral Kimmel, Commander of the Pacific Fleet. These five people included the president, his secretaries of War and the Navy, General Marshall, Army Chief of Staff, and General Marshall's Navy counterpart, Admiral Stark, Chief of Naval Operations. Orders from Washington were to take precautions against sabotage only. Strangely, more than a full year before, in June 1940 General Marshall had ordered Hawaii placed on a full war time alert against the possibility of a trans-Pacific raid. This was at a time when the situation was far less threatening than in November and December of 1941. Was Marshall's failure again to alert Hawaii a deliberate omission on orders from his superiors? Was the failure intended as an added incentive to a Japanese attack? Or was this and the failure to supply vital and complete intelligence a weird coincidence and collosal blunder?

Without judging the rightness or wrongness of American participation in the war and without judging the rightness or wrongness of how we got into the war, a gross crime was committed in connection with Pearl Harbor. The crime was the failure to provide all the intelligence available and necessary for the field commanders to discharge properly their duties. The basing of the fleet at Pearl Harbor can be dismissed as an error in judgement, and the pressure to provoke an incident while proclaiming peaceful intentions can be charged as an exercise in chicanery, but the failure to prepare the men in the field for the blow, resulting in unnecessary death and destruction, was nothing short of a crime. But this crime was alone not enough—it was compounded by publicly disgracing the field commanders without even a hearing of all the evidence. (See references 51 and 52)

The primary job of the politician is to get elected. Therefore most successful American politicians have found it impossible to stride off boldly in directions divergent from the wishes of the voting majority—unless a particular politician is willing to crawl below the loosely defined levels of acceptable political knavery. Was Roosevelt such as politician?

"So sure was he of the rightness of his aims," wrote Burns of his political idol, "that he was willing to use Machiavellian means; and his moral certainties made him all the more effective in his struggle. To the idealists who cautioned him he responded that gaining power—winning elections—was the first indispensable task. He would use the tricks of the fox to serve the purposes of the lion." (2, p 477)

Thus it was that Americans, overwhelmingly opposed to involvement on the morning of December 7, 1941, found themselves at war in the afternoon of the same day.

You need not teach an old fox new tricks, specially if he has a good stock of old tricks from his younger days. Presidential candidates, including incumbents, have been known to offer, confidentially, of course, the number two spot to several hopefuls. Even though this is an old trick, it never fails to gain support for number one. It is the official presidential con game; how the old pros fall for it is hard to fathom.

Before the 1944 convention Roosevelt led Henry Wallace and Jimmie Byrnes to believe that he would support them for the vice-presidential nomination. Roosevelt really wanted unpopular Associate Justice William O. Douglas. However, at a meeting of party leaders, Roosevelt was finally convinced that Harry Truman, a rather quiet and obscure senator from Missouri was his best bet. Ed Flynn, the Bronx Democrat said that "it was agreed that Truman was the man who would hurt him least," which doesn't seem like much of a compliment. (54, p 209) Even after the decision was made, the fox continued to string along Wallace and Byrnes. If the two gudgeons had been on speaking terms they might have swapped stories and discovered the deception. As usual, Roosevelt's luck held out until it was too late for Wallace and Byrnes to take effective revenge.

During 1944 Roosevelt tried to achieve a realignment of voters into two parties.

"We ought to have two real parties," Roosevelt is said to have told Judge Rosenman, "one liberal and the other conservative." (2, p 466)

Roosevelt made indirect approaches to Wendell Wilkie, his opponent of the previous campaign, seeking his support for the idea. Wilkie was in general agreement but was unwilling to act until after the election, for obvious reasons.

"Roosevelt," wrote Burns, "wanted to pursue the matter before election, and it was here that his reputation for cunning and indirectness tripped him up. The more the President pressed for an early meeting the more Wilkie was convinced that he was engaged in an election tactic . . . A series of leaks to the press . . . served only to heighten the latter's (*Wilkie's*) suspicion." (2, p 467) The idea of a realignment of voters into two parties has merit. Jefferson, Jackson, and Lincoln might agree.

The Jeffersonians, from whom the present day Democrats claim descent, were called Republicans in their day. They were, in fact, more like today's Republicans than they are like today's Democrats.

"There was a fundamental difference of opinion between the two parties (Federalist and Republican) with respect to centralization of functions," as Kimmel has pointed out. "The Jeffersonians or Republicans looked askance at almost any expansion of Federal activity in new directions; the philosophy of Hamilton and other leading Federalists permitted a broader outlook." (4, p 14)

It would seem that the Democrats had the wrong hero in Jefferson and the Republicans had the wrong hero in Hamilton!

President Thomas Jefferson, champion of today's Democrats, did not exactly sound like a New Frontiersman when he spoke proudly in his second annual message to congress of "large and effectual payments toward discharge of our public debt and the emancipation of that mortal canker . . . The earth," thought

Jefferson, "always belonged to the living generation," and hence public debts should be discharged in twenty or so years. (4, p 14) In a letter to Governor Plumer of New Hampshire, Jefferson wrote, "I place economy among the first and foremost of republican virtues, and public debt as the greatest of the dangers to be feared." (4, p 14)

Andrew Jackson, a founding father of the Democrat Party, was no New Dealer. His first annual message to congress in 1829 reads as though it were ghosted by an ancestor of Barry Goldwater or the late Senator Robert Taft. After the Federal debt was retired, Jackson said "our population will be relieved from a considerable portion of its present burthens, and will find not only new motives to patriotic affection, but additional means for the display of individual enterprise." (4, p 19)

Jackson and the then developing Democrat party opposed Federal spending for roads and canals. Opposition was based on constitutional grounds and fear of extravagance and corruption. Jackson proposed that the Federal surpluses, expected to result after the national debt was paid, be distributed to the states which could use them as they saw fit. Revenue sharing, it seems, is neither new nor Republican.

Democrat opposition to federalism and large Federal government expenditures was firm through the nineteenth century. Republicans and their predecessors, the Federalists and Whigs, stood for an expanding central government, high tariffs and more Federal activity in areas originally reserved to the states and for which there was no constitutional authority. For instance, Democrat President James Buchanan (1857-1861) did not believe that Federal powers should extend to cover internal improvements for "the jarring and collision which would occur from the exercise by two separate governments of jurisdiction over the same subjects could not fail to produce disastrous consequences." A "General Government in carrying into effect a system of internal improvements" was sure to be a corrupting and seducing influence. (4, p 35)

Most of today's Republicans and all conservatives shuddered when they first heard the cliché that the national debt is nothing to worry about because "it is something we owe to ourselves." Few modern Republicans, if any at all, know that the founding

father of their party said the same thing and perhaps even originated the idea.

". . . The great advantage," said Abraham Lincoln, "of citizens
being creditors as well as debtors with relation to the public debt
is obvious. Men readily perceive that they can not be much oppressed by a debt which they owe themselves." (4, p 65)

Lincoln, like the modern economists who have purveyed this
sophistry, failed to acknowledge that the debtors and creditors
are not identical, that there are more debtors than there are
creditors, and hence the debt is not something we owe ourselves,
but is essentially something many persons owe to a smaller number of persons.

If the monetary system is not juggled by the politician the
creditor is likely to be content. But if the monetary system is
manipulated to produce inflation, the creditor on fixed income,
facing rising expenses, is likely to become more and more un-
happy in the same proportion as debtors become happier at being
able to pay off their debts in cheap dollars. Since there are more
voting debtors than there are voting creditors, it doesn't strain
one's mental abilities to recognize a political bias favoring inflation. Inflation is the cheap, and dishonest, way of paying off both
interest and principal. Not only is government a miserable accounting agency, it has also become a dishonest financial manager
—a fact which may be related to the political discovery that there
are more debtors on the voting rolls than there are creditors.
Somewhere, between Abraham Lincoln and the New Deal, the
Democrats and the liberals appropriated the originally Republican
line: "Why worry about the debt, it's just something we owe ourselves." About the same time, with the help of a Britisher named
Keynes, it became obvious that there was little intention of ever
repaying the debt.

Andrew Johnson, who was Lincoln's vice-president and successor, was, unlike his boss, a Democrat. While Republican Lincoln was telling us that the debt was a great boon and was taking
steps to increase Federal power, Democrat Johnson pressed for
fiscal conservatism. Johnson was alarmed by the fact that Federal
expenditures which were $2.00 per person in 1860 would grow to
$9.78 per person in 1869. Johnson would have dropped dead on
the spot had someone been able to convince him that his name-

sake in office, also a Democrat, would, a century later, supervise federal spending of over $1000 per person.

The dramatic concentration of power in Washington under Roosevelt was accompanied by an erosion of the power of local authority from the state level down to the smallest town council. At the same time, individual, family, and the voluntary, nongovernment social organizations were weakened. The bossism of the Federal government replaced the bossism of local Tammany Halls; the dole of Federal politicians, and of Franklin Roosevelt in particular,[2] replaced the largess of the Jimmie Walkers, Boss Hagues and Big Bill Thompsons (respectively former mayors of New York, Jersey City, and Chicago). Federal grants-in-aid took the place of ward heelers' cigars, Thanksgiving turkeys, and Christmas food baskets. Federal aid to the poor, which started under Hoover, grew and grew, until thirty years later a large number of individuals feel little or no need to save, many persons feel little or no obligation to care for members of their own families, and churches have largely abandoned help for the poor, the ill, and the aged in favor of funding political agitators and propagandists.

History does not start with one man or one event. So it was with the federalization of America. Although the seeds planted when the XVIth amendment was adopted took root and grew during the administrations of Wilson, Harding, Coolidge and Hoover, it was not until Roosevelt arrived in Washington that the first bumper crop of Federal tax money was harvested. The power to tax not only confers the power to destroy, it also bestows the power to bestow—and get elected.

"On the day he (*FDR*) died," wrote William S. White in 1961, "every state still had the constitutional obligation to sustain its own internal order, to educate its children, to make provision

---

[2] This was made possible by "blank-check appropriations." Previously, in ordinary times, specific appropriations for specific purposes were made in congress at the request of congressmen or the president. The National Recovery Act made available $3.3 billion dollars which could be spent by the president, as he saw fit, for relief and recovery, without specific congressional approval. Thus, local politicians, and congressmen themselves, were forced to go, hat in hand, to the president if local relief or recovery expenditures were needed. The political leverage of the president was enormously increased. The amount of money appropriated for one year was equal to the amount spent for similar purposes in the preceding ten years.

against such common dangers and problems as were not national in scope or external in origin.

"But no state had any longer either the will to do so or, in terms of reality as distinguished from theory, even the political power to do so . . ." (5, p 110) (Italics added.)

What was true in 1945 was even more so twenty-five years later, if it is possible for degrees of truth to exist. The states and cities clamor for more and more grants-in-aid to finance housing, hospitals, schools, urban renewal, recreation, welfare and a thousand and one other needs which can not be financed locally—because local money has gone to Washington to pay for the grants-in-aid.

William S. White focused on Roosevelt's demagoguery and divisiveness by which there was an illegal centralization of power in Washington. White concluded that the "true contest . . . had not been, as Roosevelt so often pictured it, a contest simply between the greedy rich and the misused poor . . . the true contest had been over the central issue whether the federal government for 'good' purposes . . . could amend the Constitution to reduce . . . *(the states')* . . . heretofore unchallengeable basic position as assigned repositories of all such powers as had not been specifically granted to the Federal authority." (5, pp 107-108)

Starting with the second quarter of the twentieth century, the political popularity of American presidents has varied directly with their economic ignorance. This conclusion is supported by Herbert Hoover's political failure and Franklin Roosevelt's astounding success.

Republican bias accounts for the fact that Republicans generally consider Franklin Roosevelt as the greatest economic ignoramus ever to sit in the White House. This, from Republicans, is not surprising. Nor would it surprise one to hear the same opinion expressed by conservatives. It is, however, surprising to find that many far out and not so far out liberals hold the same opinion.

"Any effort," wrote James MacGregor Burns, certified liberal, "to shape long-term economic programs ran up against *(Roosevelt's)* limited understanding of economic problems." As the economic picture continued dark and gloomy, Roosevelt was, according to Burns "still groping . . . Pressed to act but not know-

ing what to do, Roosevelt turned from one scheme to another
. . . Roosevelt's fumbling and indecisiveness during the recession
(*1937*) showed his failings as an economist and thinker . . . Keynes
was disappointed that the President was not more literate in economics." (2, pp 321-322)

Walter Lippmann, one-time Socialist and a man of impeccable
liberal credentials (most of the time), recognized as early as
1935 that Roosevelt's New Deal economics had not won a victory over the depression. "The Great Depression," wrote Lippmann, "has run nearly six years. During the first half of this
period Mr. Hoover and the Republicans were in power; during
the second half, Mr. Roosevelt and the Democrats." (3, pp 10-11)
Lippmann was not entirely correct in his statement, for the Republicans lost control of congress midway through Hoover's term
so that only during the first sixth of Lippmann's six years of depression were the Republicans solidly in power. And, of course,
the depression continued, not for just five more years, but for at
least another eight years until the war in Europe rescued Roosevelt.

Frederick Lewis Allen, a less liberal observer than either Lippmann or Burns wrote that neither Theodore nor Franklin Roosevelt "had a systematic economic philosophy; both in devising
their policies and programs played by ear; and both thought of
economic problems as essentially moral problems." (9, p 151)

Politicians who think of economics in terms of subjective
morals end up attempting to force human behavior to conform
to their subjective standards of what is right, fair, decent, etc.
The subjective standards adopted, it may be suspected, will be
influenced by their voter appeal. All this leads to a Robin Hood
philosophy of lawlessness and a tyranny of the state, and the end
result is likely to be an attempt to legislate price controls, wage
controls, minimum wages, rent controls, interest rates and so
forth, in the futile pursuit of fairness. Fair prices, fair wages, fair
rents, and fair interest rates can exist only in a free market
economy. A fair price for anything: product, money, housing,
food or service, is only, always, and forever what the buyer and
seller can agree upon for a voluntary exchange. There is no other
definition. Fair prices may exist in a controlled economy as well as
in a free economy. When they do, there is no need for controls.

But if the price the seller is permitted to charge is legislated to a figure below what he is willing to accept, the supply of what is being offered drys up and no exchange will occur at the legislated price. Black markets will then arise and in these, exchanges at fair prices will result. These prices will be higher than would have been the case had price controls been avoided. When labor unions, through bargaining advantages granted by legislation, push wages, i.e. the prices paid for labor, beyond what buyers are willing to pay, there is unemployment. Some unemployed union workers may accept nonunion jobs offered by other employers at wages below the union scale. The number of such jobs is limited and some unemployment persists. If the unemployment is serious enough, political pressure will force inflation of the currency so that real wage rates are lowered and again become acceptable to buyers of labor.

Local determination of minimum wage rates by fiat was first attempted by individual states and by congress acting for the District of Columbia. The National Recovery Act attempted the same thing on a national scale. Minimum wage determination by law is either harmful or redundant. If the legal minimum wage is above that determined by free market conditions, that is, if the cost of performing the task is set above its real value, unemployment results. If the legal minimum is below the free market wage, the law is redundant.

Attempts to establish maximum hours of work are equally fruitless. If a man is willing and able to work for a given employer for more hours than permitted by law, he merely takes another job with a different employer. He becomes a moonlighter. Around the turn of the century the United States Supreme Court overruled a New York law limiting the hours of work in bakeries. Justice Rufus W. Peckham wrote that "limiting the hours in which grown and intelligent men may labor were meddlesome interference with the rights of the individual." [3]

At about the same time the Supreme Court declared Section

---

[3] Later the court became snarled in its own inconsistencies, ruling that legal maximum hours for *women* were permissible. It obliquely referred to the XIXth amendment which states that: "The rights of citizens of the United States *to vote* shall not be denied or abridged by the United States or by any State on account of sex . . ." How this can be applied to working hours for women stretches the imagination of all excepting members of the court!

7a (dealing with labor relations) of the National Recovery Act unconstitutional, the Wagner Act became law. Somewhat typically, Roosevelt did not support it until it had been passed by better than a 5 to 1 majority in the Senate, and it appeared it would be passed by a similar large majority in the House. As usual, Roosevelt wanted to be on the winning side.

The Wagner Act was, wrote Burns, "the most radical legislation passed during the New Deal, in the sense that it altered fundamentally the nation's politics by vesting massive economic and political power in organized labor . . . It had an essential part in building powerful unions that in turn would furnish votes, money, and organization to future liberal coalitions." (2, pp 218-219) The effects of the Wagner Act, and the power it gave to labor unions, were far more than merely political.

Frederick Lewis Allen in *The Big Change* comments on the rising wage scale of the 1940's. He bemoans, however, the fact that the rise did not affect intellectuals: "One might have wished that intellectual workers—teachers for example—had been among the beneficiaries of the new order." (9, p 213) Later he wrote about "one like myself who has worked for a great many years for a magazine which nowadays (*1952*) can pay its authors no more than it did a decade ago, because it has to pay its typographers and shipping men so much more . . ." (9, p 271) Allen stated that it was the industrial workers who fared best, but he did not offer an explanation. The reason is *not* that industrial workers have through their own efforts increased their productivity more than nonindustrial workers. Had this been the case it would have been a valid reason for raising their wages. (Their productivity has increased, but mainly as a result of additional mechanization, improved engineering, and better management.) The reason for their preferred status is that unionized industrial workers have been able to demand a disproportionate share of the benefits of greater productivity. Had industrial unions not been so favored by the Wagner Act and the National Labor Relations Board, the intellectuals, writers, and teachers might have received a larger share of the national product. How? Not by increased wages as much as by reduced prices brought about by lower labor costs and competition. All segments of society would then have shared in the improved efficiency of production.

The situation with regard to nurses and the nurse shortage demonstrates the point. An editorial on the problem appeared in *Journal of the American Medical Association* (January 15, 1949) which stated that "many of the nurses themselves insist that it is simply a question of adequate remuneration in comparison with what other employees, particularly those affiliated with unions, are paid for their services." (19, p 119)

There is some irony in all this, for the intellectuals, writers, teachers, and preachers are among the leading opinion makers. In increasing numbers it is they who have been in the forefront of liberal efforts to grant special power to unions. Intellectuals like to consider themselves as individualists and might therefore be expected to put self-unionization in the Index Expurgatorius. Yet unionization by the 1960's had caught up with the teachers and professors. It had also forced retail clerks, engineers, and government workers to unionize as the only way to protect themselves against higher prices forced by industrial unionization. But what happens to garage mechanics, gas station attendants, domestics, clerks in small stores and millions of others whose occupations do not lend themselves to union organization? They end up at the bottom of the wage scale, dependent upon ineffective minimum wage laws.

Allen also mentions that under the New Deal "at the top of the scale there has likewise been a striking change. The enormous lead of the well-to-do in the economic race has been considerably reduced." (9, p 213) This trend of the forties has continued. It may offer a partial explanation for some of the problems of the seventies and it may forecast additional distortions and problems if the trend is not reversed.

For instance, if the lead of the well-to-do in the economic race is reduced there is a shift of emphasis toward consumer goods and away from capital goods. Some will argue that since industry was operating, say, at 70-80 per cent of capacity during 1970, there is no need for more capital, i.e. we are over-capitalized. That is not so, considering the unsatisfied needs of the millions who are not working and who are on relief. To put all these people to work so that they could be self-supporting will require billions more of capital. In addition, the spreading blight in the cities represents worn out capital that is not being replaced: we are consuming capital faster than it is being replaced. If the standards of living are to be raised we must not only replace obsolete capital, we must add new capital. It is capital, the mechanical means and tools of production, buildings and facilities, wisely used, which has made our standard of living possible. One has only to compare the capital wealth per capita in the various countries of the world to realize this truism. The solution for the poverty in underdeveloped nations is not socialism and sharing the non-wealth, it is not to be found in handouts of consumable food and fibre, and it is not to be found in distribution of TV sets, cars and luxuries to the local politicians. The solution to poverty in these countries is free enterprise and stability and a political atmosphere which will attract capital investment. The capital will be invested most wisely and be most productive if free markets rather than international politics dictate where it is used. In the developed countries, including the United States, it is entirely possible that too much wealth is being channeled by political means, rather than by economic forces, into the hands of persons who will spend it for consumer goods rather than save it for capital goods.

Franklin D. Roosevelt, in addition to being known for his charm and gaiety, was also known as a big spender—of other people's money. No previous president had larger peacetime and wartime budgets (and deficits).

Burns, who didn't think much of Roosevelt's economic acumen (but for the wrong reasons), faults FDR for not institutionalizing deficit spending as the means of creating permanent prosperity. ". . . this idea," wrote Burns, "in its full dimensions seemed but another fanciful economic theory . . . Pump priming as a temporary emergency measure he could understand—but not deficit spending as the central, long-term approach to a full-scale economic theory." (2, p 335) For a man who, according to Burns (and also Keynes), failed to understand the value of a long-term deficit policy, Roosevelt did pretty well. During his twelve years in office he managed to eke out twelve years of deficits.

Six days after his inauguration in 1933, President Roosevelt sent a message to Congress asking for Federal payroll cuts and reduced veterans' benefits. But he was not long in office before he forgot his campaign criticisms of Hoover as a wastrel who unbalanced the budget. His new spending policy was formulated by a group of professors, including Paul H. Douglas (a modern economist and later a liberal Democrat senator).

"The balancing of budgets," stated the policy, "should be regarded as a series of long-term operations in which deficits will be incurred and debts increased during years of economic adversity while Treasury surpluses and the rapid retirement of the public debt will be planned for during years of prosperity." (4, p 159)

The first portion of the policy was adopted, but the second portion was forgotten—not only by Roosevelt, but also by his successors. Only one feeble attempt at cutting Federal deficits was made during the Roosevelt years. This was in 1937-1938 and it was followed by a hasty retreat. During the post-war Truman and Eisenhower terms balanced budgets were rare, and even in those years Federal debt retirement was minimal. If one can believe the politicians at election times, more than a few of those years were prosperous—but even so prosperity never managed to justify the debt retirement which the ivory tower budget policy called for.

Budget deficits, still unpopular in 1972 after more than forty years in which the balanced budget has been an oddity, were even less popular in the 1930's. Then, as now, there were all sorts of tricks to make it seem that the budget was balanced.

In spite of what his admirers claimed, FDR could not walk on the water, but he could and did accomplish an almost equally difficult task: he ran off in two directions at once. In one breath he stated that his budget was approaching a balance (in general expenses) while in the next he achieved the largest peacetime deficit to date (in emergency expenses). He said his 1934 budget would show only a $120 million deficit as he casually ignored eight billion dollars in emergency spending! His only balanced budget was via press release. We have had budgets based on normal expenses and cash budgets which ignore trust fund obligations, and now we have, under the auspices of Mr. Nixon, a balanced full employment budget, which, translated, means we wouldn't have a deficit if business was good, but it isn't. Nixon may yet walk on the water and surpass the old master.

Large-scale subsidized public housing was another of Roosevelt's New Deal innovations. A conversation between Roosevelt and a realtor friend is recorded in *The Lion and the Fox.*

". . . could private builders take care of families earning less than a thousand dollars a year. 'Housing is particularly and always has been a private matter and absolutely local,' the realtor replied. 'There is nothing whatever in the Constitution or our scheme of government authorizing or indicating any Federal interest in the housing question.' He feared that the government was starting on a voyage which 'I frankly must call communistic or socialistic.'

" 'What are we going to do with them?' Roosevelt answered. 'Are we going to compel them to live under slum conditions? . . . Has society as a whole no obligation to these people? . . .' "
(2, p 245)

Time has proved that the realtor sensed the situation correctly. Thirty-five years later the subsidized housing program was still growing, and it was not only for "poor" people. It was for middle income people who were so heavily taxed that they were left without enough money to finance their own housing. A good portion of the Federal subsidized "low-cost" housing is operated at a loss, even above subsidies, paid for by taxpayers, and wrecked by tenants. Newly constructed subsidized housing is turned into new subsidized slums, and local government landlords have been no more successful in preventing this than private landlords.

Roosevelt's slippery rhetorical questions "Has society as a whole no obligation to these people? Are we going to compel them to live under slum conditions?" deserve some questions in reply. What obligations do the people in the slums have to help themselves? What have they done to help themselves in the past? (Millions of slum dwellers who had extricated themselves from the slums by the time Roosevelt asked his questions would be called on to help pay the subsidies.) What is the basis for concluding that *we* compelled them to live under slum conditions? Who, specifically, does *we* include?

The Wagner Housing Act subsidized low-cost housing and gave selected beneficiaries a prior claim, by virtue of the Federal government's tax power, on the earnings of others who by thrift, diligence, or just good fortune, had managed to acquire and pay for their own homes.

Nor were the farmers forgotten. The 1934 Congress extended the statist measures passed by the 1933 Congress. Cotton and tobacco were added to the farm products subsidized by price supports. An additional $2 billion dollars in government bonds were authorized to refinance farm mortgages, taxpayers and inflation making up the difference between interest paid on the bonds and interest received for the mortgage loans. In 1937, the Guffey-Vinson bill was passed which put the Federal government in control of marketing, pricing, and trade practices. The Farm Tenancy bill was passed, making government loans available to tenant farmers for purchase of farms. Again taxpayers paid the interest differential and assumed the risks private lenders would otherwise have been expected to assume. In 1938 the Agricultural Adjustment Act decreed a quota system for farm production in return for supporting prices of cotton, rice, corn, wheat and tobacco. At the same time farmers who observed acreage allotments, retired acreage, and practiced soil conservation were paid for their nonefforts. While the Federal government was encouraging restriction of farm production, Federally-supported experiment stations were promoting better farming methods and research to improve production! The AAA also provided for Federal control of prices and marketing within given areas where two-thirds of the farmers voted approval. Government loans on commodities were also made available in order to support prices. Thus, farm surpluses were assured for the years ahead.

Like the farmers, taxpayers were not neglected by the New Deal. Most of them wished they had been. Graduated personal income tax rates soared as did corporate taxes, and in a flush of wartime enthusiasm and patriotism the withholding tax was approved. This pay as you go scheme sped the collection of taxes in a sort of one-shot windfall, and at the same time obscured the depth of the tax bite. Hence, it was popular with the politicians. It was unpopular with the employer who was stuck with added accounting and tax-collecting expenses. The withholding method of tax collection has encouraged government extravagance at all levels, because the taxpayer, who sees only his net pay, does not realize how much he is being taxed.

When it came to negroes, Roosevelt did not get out of character. Jack Bell, in *The Johnson Treatment,* wrote that Southern segregationists knew that "Franklin Roosevelt . . . talked a good civil rights case but . . . never sent a message to Congress on the subject." (53, p 163)

Had Roosevelt fought to insure full rights for negroes under existing laws and the Constitution he would have lost Southern Democrat support. At the same time this would not have gained him support from Northern negroes who were not numerous, who were largely Republican, and who already enjoyed most political rights. But by means of welfare and relief programs, he acquired an increasing number of Northern black votes and at the same time avoided risking loss of Southern support.

Bernstein and Matusow, liberal historians, recognized Roosevelt's record on discrimination. "Though Roosevelt," they wrote, "had successfully wooed the Negro vote away from its traditional Republicanism with his welfare and recovery programs, the New Deal had done virtually nothing to fight discrimination." (19, p 95)

Roosevelt's performance in foreign affairs was no less shoddy than his domestic performance. He was criticized not only by isolationists, conservatives, and Republicans, but also by liberal Democrats, like Burns, (2, pp 400-403, 421) for expediency, opportunism, and lack of leadership. He had no basic philosophy to guide his foreign policy and so, improvising always, he operated from day to day.

A government which is merely despotic and tyrannous is not automatically qualified as a potential enemy nor is it automatically disqualified as a possible ally. Even if a cruel and tyrannous foreign government is aggressive and expansionist it is necessarily neither a foe nor disqualified as an ally. But if the foreign state operates from a strong power base and is at the same time expansionist and aggressive as well as oppressive and domineering, then it is a serious threat to our security and is barred from being a true ally.

In Europe, prior to World War II, both the Germans and Russians were clearly threats to our national security. The failure of Roosevelt's foreign policy between September 1939 and June of 1941 was a failure to evaluate and act on the potential danger from both Communist Russia and Nazi Germany. Between these two dates there was ample opportunity to recognize the aggressive nature of both countries and the systems under which they operated. And between these dates Roosevelt, particularly during 1941, moved toward bringing the United States into the war.

The alternative would have been to have remained out of the war while providing enough military assistance to the Russians to assure mutual extermination of Communism and Nazism. Roosevelt's error lay in his naive trust of "good old Uncle Joe" and the Communists. Because of Roosevelt's death, the results of his errors did not materialize until Truman assumed office. Harry Truman shares no blame for the loss of Eastern Europe.

Roosevelt "as always," wrote Burns of the Yalta performance, "was acting pragmatically, opportunistically, tactically. As usual he was almost wholly concerned about the immediate job ahead—winning the war." (2, p 469) Stalin was thinking, and had been thinking long before Yalta, of the realities of the post-war world. Stalin, an effective Communist, was a strategist; Roosevelt was a tactician, and not necessarily a brilliant one.

Roosevelt laid open large areas of Europe, Asia, and Africa to Communist assault and conquest. Of the European nations gobbled up by the Communists with Roosevelt's approval, Poland and Yugoslavia were the most inexcusable losses. In China and Africa the disasters were longer in coming and probably, for the long run, even more serious.

The fumbling in China contributed to the Communist domination of 700 million people and three million square miles. The basic mistake was an unrealistic approval of Mao-Tse-Tung as a harmless agrarian reformer, a myth that was fostered by the Communists, fellow travellers, and cocktail party intellectuals. American policy at first called for the formation of a Nationalist-Communist coalition. This was resisted by the Nationalists, who had dealt first-hand with the Communists. Roosevelt sitting safely five thousand miles away could think kindly of Mao and his agrarian reformers and how cozy it would be if the lion and the lamb would just sit down to dinner together.

The Chinese Communists fled to Yennan and allowed the Nationalists to bear the brunt of fighting the Japanese on the mainland. After the defeat of the Japanese, and having failed to bring off a working coalition, the Communists resumed full-scale revolutionary activities, while their propagandists hammered away at the idea that Chiang's government was corrupt. On this basis, American aid and military assistance eventually was stopped and the Nationalists collapsed during Truman's term.

At Cairo Roosevelt secretly agreed with Chiang Kai-shek to keep the British out of Hong Kong, Shanghai, and Canton. At Teheran he and Stalin agreed to act against the British in China. The general anti-British, anti-colonial bias of our foreign policy ignored the possibility that the withdrawal of European colonial powers would leave behind unstable independent nations susceptible to Communist influence and intrigue.

"Even during the war then ending," wrote William S. White of Roosevelt at the end of World War II, "he had over and over insisted upon policies and actions which would strip the exhausted and bloodied British of those very foreign possessions and quasi possessions through which alone they could even hope to draw economic revivification to a shattered homeland economy.

"It is true of course that in the long movement of history— and no doubt all the considerations of abstract justice—would in any event have meant the end, in time, of colonialism. But Roosevelt had persisted in demanding much too much, much too soon, driven as he was by a suspicion of the clever, the tricky British that was almost a schoolboy's stereotype; by an almost incredibly naive belief that since they voted in Massachusetts they must vote *at once* in Sudan." (5, p 153)

Roosevelt lived from day to day and showed little interest in the long view. This conclusion is shown in his improvisation and use of stop-gap measures to achieve prosperity during his first two terms, his selection of Henry Wallace as his running mate in 1940, his failure to indoctrinate Truman as his successor in 1945, and his dismal failure at Yalta and in dealing with Stalin. Why was this so? Was it merely typical of the man or was it a requirement of the system under which he operated?

In a nation where the government is both democratically chosen as well as interventionist in nature, the successful politician is forced to seek quick solutions. As statism and interventionism grow he must respond to an ever-widening network of pressure groups, in which each group seeks benefits paid by persons outside the group. Since group memberships overlap it is a political asset if one is able to build a winning coalition and at the same time minimize antagonizing groups outside the coalition. The poltical horizon is the next election, which is usually less than two years away and thus tactics rather than strategies are usually emphasized. Thus, while Roosevelt's short-sighted temporizing, improvising, and opportunism were typical of the man, they were also, to some extent, at least, requirements of the system.

Within four months of his first inauguration, President Roosevelt asked for and got the legislation which produced the greatest centralization of power in Washington since the founding of the nation. Legislation passed and signed into law included the Agricultural Adjustment Act, establishment of the Civilian Conservation Corps, the Federal Emergency Relief Act, establishment of the Tennessee Valley Authority, and the National Industrial Recovery Act. In 1935, under pressure to match the programs of Dr. Frances E. Townsend ($200 a month for everyone over sixty) and Father Coughlin and Huey Long (social justice and share-the-wealth), Roosevelt proposed unemployment insurance and old-age insurance, and called for an additional $5 billion relief program. In September of 1942 Roosevelt ordered Congress to produce, within three weeks, legislation to control the prices of farm commodities and to control the cost of living. In 1942, shortly after our entry into World War II, Roosevelt approved a round-up of thousands of Americans of Japanese descent. These citizens, without a hearing, were indiscriminately uprooted from their homes and businesses and incarcerated in concentration camps.

Some of these moves leaned toward fascism, others were more Marxist, but all were statist. The differences between fascism, socialism, and communism are less important than the areas of agreement. Centralization of authority and planning, usurpation of power by persons claiming superior wisdom, and mistrust of individual judgment and of the free market for goods, services and capital, are all common characteristics of fascism, socialism, and communism. The systems are distinguished by the fact that title to property remains to a greater extent in private hands under fascism as compared to socialism or communism. But the controls under fascism are such that the title to property becomes more nominal than actual. It is true also, that under democratic socialism, the policies of the government are slightly more sensitive to the citizenry, but the leverage of pressure groups eventually requires dictatorial power to resolve conflicts.

The TVA enterprise was the most openly socialistic and the National Industrial Recovery Act was the most openly fascist step. The NIRA permitted agreements to limit competition and fix prices in an imitation of Mussolini's fascist corporations. One should keep in mind that fascism was admired by many intellectuals in the early 30's. Ezra Pound, for instance, thought well of Il Duce and moved to Italy. After all, Mussolini built roads and public buildings and managed to make the trains run on time, the price for which was putting the opposition on a castor oil diet.

William S. White, writing of the Roosevelt era, concluded that "it was not at all pro-Communist. In the deepest sense it was only profoundly anti-Fascist." (5, p 48) This verdict is questionable. Roosevelt was no card-carrying Communist, to be sure. On the other hand he was not wise enough to keep Communists out of important positions in the bureaucracy. The tales of the accusers come to mind: Elizabeth Bentley, Louis Budenz, Whittaker Chambers, all admitted Communists, told what they knew, and so did J. B. Matthews, the fellow traveller. The names of the accused, some of whom were never legally proved to have been Communists, bring to mind murky memories of espionage, intrigue and influence: Owen D. Lattimore (State Department consultant on China and the Far East), William Remington (sentenced to five years imprisonment), Lauchlin Currie (Roosevelt's administrative assistant), Harry Dexter White (Secretary of Treasury Morgenthau's assistant), Alger Hiss (instrumental in organizing the United Nation's charter), John Stewart Service, Frederick Vanderbilt Field, Haldore Hansen, and many others. White's claim that the Roosevelt administration was anti-fascist is open to question if one takes into account such efforts as the concentration camps for Americans of Japanese descent, the NRA, and controls on farm production. Even if one considers the New Deal to have been anti-fascist, this alone is of no merit, for Stalin's administration was also anti-fascist.

Even though William S. White seems to have been on balance an admirer of FDR and the changes that had come about during his terms of office, White had some reservations. Writing in 1961 of the changes wrought in the people by the New Deal, White noted ". . . the lean and devoted and hungry labor philosophers of the Thirties were to become the obesely arrogant and over-privileged labor bosses of two decades later. The distracted farmers of the Thirties . . . in so many instances, were to become

the greedily distended and flabby swallowers of endlessly overdone Federal subsidies, elderly cry-babies . . . They were to join
that vast American phalanx . . . which, as the saying was to go,
'didn't give a damn.' The store clerks who didn't give a damn,
either for the boss or the customer. The carpenters who didn't
give a damn whether the plank was truly or crookedly nailed up.
The 'relief clients' so ready to accept a status . . . which had
once been regarded as acceptable only in utter personal extrem-
ity . . .

". . . All of us could remember, and most of us could remember with resentment, the litany of warning and protest with which
for endless years the anti-Rooseveltians had bored to distraction
the very air itself . . . he was ruining the United States; he was
killing free enterprise; he was regimenting and cheapening the
whole American society; he was ending the power of management to manage and the willingness of the worker to work; he
was sapping the vital strength of capitalism; and so on, and so on.

"It was mostly nonsense when it had been said . . . But . . . it
could be fairly said that there was a chemical trace of truth in
these long caveats. For, in plain fact, the man who had taken so
very much responsibility to himself alone *had* reduced the power
of his people to accept and to face their own private and group
responsibilities.

". . . this has been, but would be no more, a country of *man-
ners* as well as of mines and manufacturers. Somehow as we had
become more secure economically . . . we had become in some
deep and largely inexplicable way more crude, more selfish and
less truly compassionate than we had been before. Everybody,
everywhere, had begun wildly to overstate his own rights and
privileges, and profoundly to understate his own obligations and
responsibilities." (5, pp 116-119)

Now, a decade after White expressed this opinion, he would
probably have to admit that there was much more than a "chemical trace of truth" in the warnings of Roosevelt's critics. What
seemed partly true in the early 'sixties seems much more so in
the early 'seventies.

Albert Jay Nock was no doubt one of the Rooseveltian critics
that William S. White disparages in his tribute to FDR, *Majesty
and Mischief*. Nock published in 1937, when criticism of Roose-

velt was still lively, a collection of essays under the title *Free Speech and Plain Language*. (21) In an essay entitled "The Value of Useless Knowledge," Nock concludes that "Bolshevism, Fascism, and Hitlerism, are all essentially identical, all branches off the same tree planted by the German idealist philosophers in the early years of the last century. They all mean, in essence, that the state is everything, the individual nothing. Fichte put it that 'the state is the superior power, ultimate and beyond appeal, absolutely independent,' and Hegel said that 'the State is the general substance, whereof individuals are but accidents.' "

Nock quotes, in a footnote, Mussolini's claim that "the State embraces everything, and nothing outside the State has value. The State creates right," and Hitler's "the State dominates the nation because it alone represents it," and Lenin's frank admission that "it is nonsense to make any pretense of reconciling the State and liberty." (21, p 204)

Nock wonders what will happen to the character of Americans under the New Deal variant of Statism, which had, at the time his essay was published, managed to see that "thirty million persons, nearly one-fourth of our population, are being subsidized by the Federal Government; . . . a vote-controlling bureaucracy has been prodigously expanded; . . . executive control over legislation has been made almost absolute through distribution of money in Congressional districts; . . . centralization has been made almost absolute by Federal grants to the states, or, as one writer puts it very well, these subsidies have set up a carpet-bag government in every state." (21, p 205) Since 1937, the situation has gotten worse; some call it progress.

Nock's magnificent essay "Thoughts on Utopia" naturally did not ignore the New Deal, which he threw into the pot along with Lycurgus, Sparta, and a few Marxists. He cooked and stirred well. The stew was delightful.

"Lycurgus," wrote Nock, "established the New Deal in Sparta on the right idea; he believed in keeping his people poor, and his success seems to have been without precedent. He was the greatest leveler on record. Other rulers have managed to keep most of their people broke, most of the time, but in Sparta everybody was broke all the time. Lycurgus did not need any Brain Trust to help him further this excellent enterprise; he was all the Brain Trust there was, and he was enough. He did not fiddle around at nicking partial values off the basic currency-unit; he devalued the whole currency right down to zero at one stroke, and substituted iron money so heavy that if by some miracle a Spartan accumulated a bank roll of $165, he had to have a two-ox team to carry it around. Hence, obviously, Lycurgus had no trouble with predatory bankers; also he had no trouble with foreign exchange, for foreigners would not handle his money on any terms whatever . . .

"As an exponent of collectivism, Lycurgus must have made Marx, Engels, Lenin, et al, look like bush leaguers. With him the state was collectivist to a degree that made the individual's status determinable only by algebra. He had the prescription down to what one might really call a fine point; and as for 'social legislation,' it seems to have been his specialty. Nobody could have any ornaments or even clothes to speak of. Lycurgus believed in nudism on moral and social grounds as well as on hygienic grounds; Plutarch's observations on this point are worth the attention of those who are interested in such matters nowadays, as are also his observations on the arrangements instituted by Lycurgus for a sort of quasi-companionate or tandem marriage. Sumptuary laws extended even to haircutting; everyone had to have the same style of haircut. One could not wriggle out of compliance with Lycurgus' regulations by the aid of resourceful shysters; nor on the other hand, did Lycurgus need a pliant contortionist judiciary to validate his incursions upon the liberties of the subject. The subject had no liberties, and there were neither lawyers nor lawsuits in Sparta—though prescription would seem to have been unnecessary on this latter point, for with everybody hopelessly busted, there was really nothing on which to found a lawsuit. Plutarch sums this situation up by saying that: 'no man was allowed to live as he pleased, the city being like one great camp, where all had their fixed allowance and knew their public duty.' " (21, pp 154-155)

Some say history doesn't repeat itself. But unfortunately it comes pretty close.

CHAPTER 12

MISSOURI MULE

"Sam Rayburn [1] once told me," wrote William S. White, "from all the remembered experience of nearly fifty years of high places in Washington, that the least partisan President he ever knew in foreign affairs—and one of the most partisan in home affairs—was Harry S. Truman. This remark consciously included both Roosevelt and Woodrow Wilson." (5, p 56)

At times the partisanship, of which Sam Rayburn spoke, coupled with a pugnacious character when aroused, led Harry Truman to renegade rhetoric and divisiveness. Nowhere is this better demonstrated than in his 1948 campaign speeches.

In Detroit on September 8, 1948 for the traditional Labor Day speech, Truman said that the Republican-controlled 80th Congress "promptly fell into the familiar Republican pattern of aid for big business and attack on labor. The Republicans promptly voted themselves a cut in taxes, and voted you a cut in freedom . . . you men of labor can expect to be hit by a steady barrage of body blows . . . Not only the labor unions, but all men and women who work are in danger . . . If you place this Government under the contral of those who hate labor . . ."

A few days later, on September 18, as the campaign warmed up, Truman's appeal was based on tired old prejudices, and on envy, hate, and fear.

"The Wall Street reactionaries," said Truman, "are not satisfied with being rich. They want to increase their power, regardless of what happens to the other fellow. They are gluttons of privilege.

"These gluttons of privilege are now putting up fabulous sums

[1] Sam Rayburn was a Congressman from Texas and was for many years Speaker of the House of Representatives.

of money to elect a Republican administration . . . I think that Wall Street expects its money this year to elect a Republican administration that will listen to the gluttons of privilege first, and to the people not at all . . .

"The Democratic party puts human rights and human welfare first . . .

"But the attitude of the Republican gluttons of privilege is very different . . .

"The Republican gluttons of privilege are cold men . . . They want a return of the Wall Street dictatorship . . .

". . . The Republican congress (*80th*) has already stuck a pitchfork in the farmer's back . . .

". . . farmers can thank this same Republican 80th Congress that gave the speculative grain trade a rake-off at your expense . . .

"Now you are faced with another kind of disaster—a man-made disaster bearing the Republican trade mark."

Truman's style is evident in these speeches, but there is no certainty that he wrote them. He was still using some of FDR's speech writers, including Sam Rosenman who wrote Truman's 1948 acceptance speech, the last half of the 1949 inaugural address and the 1949 state of the union message. If Truman did not write the speeches, did the ideas accurately reflect his private views as well as his wrangling street politic's style?

Liberal Washington political observers and columnists of the Truman era, Robert S. Allen and William V. Shannon concluded that Harry Truman's "private political views were not liberal. They were the stock agglomeration of opinions and prejudices of the moderately well-to-do, rural, border-state Democrat. He stood for economy, was suspicious of both organized labor and Wall Street, believed in legal rights for Negroes but not in social equality, and favored as little government action as possible. As a consequence, Truman often felt rather uneasy in the Democratic Party as Franklin Roosevelt was running it." (55, p 10)

In 1936 the newly elected Senator Truman received a letter from a student asking him why he was a Democrat. Allen and Shannon printed Truman's reply. (55, p 10)

" 'This is a matter,' Truman replied, 'of history and policy more than anything else . . . The Republican Party has always stood for a strong centralized government, and the Democratic Party has always stood for strong state and local governments. However, under the present administration, that situation seems to be somewhat reversed, because the Republicans are now asking for strong state government and the Democrats have been working for strong centralized government under the emergency.' "

Truman did not mention, perhaps because he hadn't been in Washington long enough to recognize it, that the Democrats were succeeding because their leadership was more alert to the possibilities of exploiting the Federal income tax, authorized almost a quarter of a century before. The first major increase in Federal income tax rates came during FDR's term, and power followed the tax collector to Washington. From this time onward, local and state governments would suffer, as wampum, favors, and "solutions to problems" spewed from the teepee of the Great White Father in the capitol city.

"However," Truman's letter continued, "the *general principles of the Democratic Party are for as little government as possible* (italics added) and for that government to be as close to the people as it is possible to put it. That is the principal reason I am a Democrat."

Not a good reason, for under the circumstances of FDR's leadership, the principles of Jeffersonian democracy had been abandoned. If one can believe the pronouncements of Coolidge, Hoover, Taft, Eisenhower, Goldwater and pre-1969 Nixon, the Republican party appropriated the discarded Democrat dogma of "as little government as possible." Nevertheless, both parties remain a heterogenous hodgepodge of persons holding divergent basic political philosophies.

Both Democrats and Republicans are reluctant to switch parties. This partisan inertia has been the major obstacle to the formation of two parties of distinctly different views, say liberal versus conservative, statist versus anti-statist, federalist versus states-rightist, etc. In his letter to the student, giving his *best reason* for being a Democrat, Truman reflects this reluctance of party members to change parties.

"Another good reason (*for being a Democrat*)," wrote Truman, "is that I was raised one. My mother and my grandmother and all the rest of my family have all been good Democrats. That is about the best reason, I think."

Harry Truman was a loyal party man and party loyalty was a factor in his selection as FDR's running mate. There were only two notable occasions in the Senate when Truman deserted his party and its New Deal leadership, a remarkable record in view of the divergence between his own beliefs and those of the New Dealers. In 1936 he voted against Senator Wagner's bill to set up a subsidized low-cost housing program. Three years later he voted to cut the relief appropriation bill, and it was by only one vote that the President was repudiated in this case. Other than these departures from the party line Truman was a good Democrat plodding along in the footsteps of his mother, grandmother, Boss Pendergast, and the New Deal leadership.

Although Truman was both suspicious and critical of labor unions when he came to the Senate, and even though as president in 1946 he threatened to draft railroad workers if they struck, he grew gradually aware of the value of labor support. The reason is found in a senatorial speech criticizing labor unions and cooperatives but in which he also stated that "there is no difference between a labor leader with too much money to spend and Marc Hanna with too much money to spend on an election." Obviously, if labor money was available to win elections to what better purpose could it be applied than to help win elections for Democrats? The alliance was about to be born.

Clark Clifford, President Truman's special counsel, had the reputation of being one of the sharpest and most shrewd men on the Washington scene. It was Clifford, serving as Lyndon Johnson's Secretary of Defense, who got the Vietnamization policy under way some months before Nixon became president and claimed credit for it.[2] Allen and Shannon credit Clifford with playing a major part in turning Truman leftward away from his natural conservative inclinations.

[2] Under Clifford, the administration finally began to supply modern weapons in large quantities to the Vietnamese. Prior to this time the South Vietnamese had been equipped with obsolete World War II models for the most part, and they were supplied only in very meagre quantities. Clark Clifford, who succeeded Robert McNamara in 1968, altered this policy. For unexplained reasons the Democrats never claimed credit for the concept of Vietnamization of the Indo-China war.

"Simply because he did not talk or look like a doctrinaire liberal, Clifford gradually won the Chief Executive's full confidence," wrote Allen and Shannon, "and became his chief speech writer and administrative coordinator." (55, p 26) Clifford won his first decisive liberal victory when he convinced Truman to veto the Taft-Hartley labor relations bill. It was Clifford who wrote the veto message for Truman and this sealed the Truman-labor union alliance.

Probably one of the best estimates of Harry Truman's character came from Roy Roberts, a Republican, managing editor of the Kansas City Star, friend of Truman, and political foe of Tom Pendergast, the Kansas City boss who was Truman's early idol.

"Humility," wrote Roberts right after Truman became president, "probably would be the first characterization. Then loyalty, perhaps excessive loyalty that sometimes gets high officials in trouble; common sense; deep patriotism; and above all an abiding faith in his country and its democratic system . . . he understands the average man . . ." (54, p 238)

It is to Roberts' credit as a judge of men that he correctly predicted the new president's proneness to getting into trouble via excessive loyalty. Truman displayed much common sense during his term, again bearing out Roberts' opinion. Although it can be argued that he was dangerously soft on domestic Communist influences, this was probably the result of poor advice and certainly not because of any lack of patriotism.

If guilt could be proved by association, not only Warren Harding, but Harry Truman as well, would have been impeached and convicted. In both cases personal loyalty and cronyism served to blind these presidents to the dishonesty of their associates. Yet neither man came to the top job innocent of the darker side of machine politics. Truman was a protege of Tom Pendergast, who had an unsavory reputation in Kansas City politics.

After Truman became president he decided to purge Missouri Congressman Roger Slaughter, chairman of the House Rules Committee. Slaughter, who had blocked much of Truman's legislative program, was defeated, but there were charges of vote fraud. The Justice Department conducted a half-hearted investigation, but the scandal would not die. A local grand jury investigated and indicted some 71 persons, but somehow the impounded ballots were stolen from the election commissioner's office in Kansas City.

Then came the scandal of William B. Boyle, a long-time Kansas City friend of Truman and Pendergast, who got Reconstruction Finance Corporation loans of $645,000 for one of his clients. Donald Dawson, Truman's man in charge of patronage, accepted a free stay at a luxury resort hotel after the RFC approved a $1,500,000 loan. Dawson's wife was a secretary at the RFC. There were other RFC dealings involving Merle Young, whose wife was a White House stenographer. Young claimed he was a cousin of the president and soon advanced from a $4500 a year job with RFC to a $46,000 a year job with a company that had been granted an RFC loan.

Finally, there were the tax collection scandals involving ridiculously low settlements of tax claims. One claim for $800,000 was settled for one-eighth of a cent on the dollar! A dozen tax collectors in various cities were finally removed along with almost 200 other Internal Revenue Service employees. Even the Commissioner of Internal Revenue was accused of failing to pay taxes and the Assistant Commissioner was indicted for income tax evasion.

When Harry Truman was thrust into the presidency by Roosevelt's death in 1945, he inherited the coterie of liberals, statists, socialists, and communists who dominated the New Deal leadership. It was inevitable that Truman's home-grown conservative tendencies would be bent leftward. Nevertheless, the new helmsman altered course from due west to northwest and although he came right a little, the ship of state remained on the port tack. The change of course was most noticeable in foreign affairs where Roosevelt's frothy faith that he could get along with the Russians by charming "good old Uncle Joe" was replaced by a more realistic view. In domestic affairs, particularly in economic matters, interventions proceeded, but at a less vigorous pace than in the preceding twelve years.

As the Second World War drew to a close, Truman was burdened with some of the worst predictions ever made by economists. Economics is a hindsight science, much more able to explain the past than to predict the short-term future. This is so because economic performance depends upon human behavior which does not always lend itself to predictability. Thus, while the administration was trying to plan for postwar unemployment of 8 to 10 million, it was surprised by an unprecedented boom and labor shortages.

President Truman's message to congress on September 6, 1945, soon after he assumed office, called for an extension of the statist trend.

"The goal of 40 cents per hour," he stated in regard to the Fair Labor Standards Act of 1938, "which . . . was to be made effective by 1945, was actually made fully effective more than a year ago by the voluntary action of industry committees.

"I believed that the goal of a 40 cent minimum was inadequate when established. It has now become obsolete."

What Truman was really saying was that the minimum wage was no longer able to cause unemployment since inflation had reduced the real minimum wage to the point where it had again become economic to hire the least productive workers at the minimum wage. By pushing for an adequate, nonobsolete minimum wage Truman meant to establish one that would be above that which would be accepted by "the voluntary action of industry committees." (If it were not *above* what would be *voluntarily* accepted, there would be no point in *legally requiring* it.) Being above what was acceptable on a voluntary basis, Truman's new minimum wage would create unemployment. If a fair wage at 40 cents an hour is good, why not set it at 80 cents an hour? Or 80 dollars an hour? What makes a fair wage fair is not legally determined by congress but by whatever the buyer and seller of labor can voluntarily agree on.

"We must consider," continued Truman's September 6th message, "the redevelopment of large areas of the blighted and slum sections of our cities so that in the truly American way they may be made to accomodate families not only of low-income groups as heretofore, but of every income group . . ."

Slum areas accommodate low-income groups. If they are to be rebuilt to accommodate other than low-income groups it is obvious that some of the people from these groups will have to be displaced by the incoming higher-income residents. The houses formerly occupied by the higher-income families will stand vacant unless their rents are lowered to meet what displaced low-income tenants can afford. This will lead to deterioration of the property and new slums will be created. The net result is a displacement of slums from one area to another. Nevertheless such a program has political appeal for it creates the illusion of progress. The undiscerning public notes new buildings replacing slum areas, but it overlooks gradual deterioration of diffuse areas which become new slums.

". . . we must make it possible," continued the president, "for private enterprise to do the major part of this job. In most cases, it is now impossible for private enterprise to contemplate rebuilding slum areas without public assistance . . . the land cost is generally too high . . .

"The time has come to begin to undertake a program of Federal aid to stimulate and promote . . . redevelopment . . . Such Federal aid should be extended only to those communities which are willing to bear a fair (*there's that word again!*) part of the cost of cleaning their blighted city areas and preparing them for redevelopment and rebuilding."

This general philosophy partly explains the rising cost of local government and rising property taxes. As the Federal octopus offers more and more subsidy programs which require local participation and more local taxes, the localities are trapped by the lure of "getting back our share of Federal taxes."

In order to stimulate redevelopment, localities frequently offer tax concessions to the developers, such as in the case of the Prudential Center in Boston. When this is done the other parts of the city must pick up an extra tax burden equivalent to the concession granted. Furthermore, the money raised for the local share of the cost of the program must come from all the taxpayers in the community. Thus, property owners end up paying a significant part of the loss realized by the purchase of condemned land at a high price and its subsequent sale at a lower price to the developers. Such a scheme benefiting a favored few is politically feasible if the cost is distributed over a large enough number of unorganized and unsuspecting taxpayers. The net effect is to drive marginally profitable properties to full slum status. More prosperous areas also suffer. Eventually there is a clamor to redevelop the new slums so created and the cycle repeats itself. Truman's (and other) housing and redevelopment programs have not provided a solution to the slum problem. This can be verified by anyone who remembers and compares Boston, New York, Chicago or Philadelphia of 1945 with today. (It is interesting that Senator Robert Taft, a conservative, supported publicly subsidized housing in a major defection from his generally anti-statist stance. Steinberg (54, p 342) quotes a lobbyist against the housing bill who asked "How did President Truman get a Republican floor leader?")

At the beginning of the twentieth century, Henry George, the single tax reformer, made some harsh observations about slums and slum dwellers.

"It is obvious and easy to say," commented George, "that the people who make city slums possible do not want to own houses and would not live upon the land and improve it if they could.

"The worst about this statement is that it is true. They are so sunken in fear, superstition, and indifference that they lack the squirrel's thrift in providing a home and laying in a stock of provisions; they are without the ground hog's ambition to burrow. They are too sodden to know what they are missing and are lacking in the imagination which pictures a better condition."

While George's words are a blanket condemnation of slum dwellers and should therefore be taken with reservations, there is truth in his conclusions. An examination of "low-cost," subsidized housing bears this out.

Perhaps recalling his days as an unsuccessful haberdasher, President Truman called for aid to small business. "It is very important," he wrote in his message to congress on September 6, 1945, "to the economy of the United States that these small businesses and many more of them be given an opportunity to become a part of American trade and industry. To do this, assistance should be given to small businesses to enable them to obtain adequate materials, private financing, technological improvements, and surplus property."

The notorious Small Business Administration emerged as the vehicle for helping small businesses, and the principal form of help was high-risk loan money. Some businessmen whose credit was so risky that they could not borrow from the banks found, if their politics were right, they could borrow from the government. It must be remembered that government money comes from three major sources: taxpayers, bonds, and printing presses. Money to aid business which comes from taxpayers is a burden placed on successful enterprises to subsidize risky or unsuccessful enterprises. Money to aid business which comes from the sale of government bonds represents a high-risk use of "depositors" money at a rate of interest far below the going rate for high-risk investments. Thus, the taxpayers, who pay for the difference in interest rates, subsidize the risky businesses using this type of financing. Money raised by inflation to aid business, or for any other purpose, is money stolen from every person with a bank deposit, with bonds in his safe deposit box, with a life insurance policy, and even with a few dollars in his pocket or under his mattress. Federal funds to aid business, regardless of their source, represent a diversion of capital from more efficient enterprises to less efficient enterprises, and this increases the cost of goods and services to the general public. Politicians, who are not known for business or economic prowess, should not be expected to realize this, but unfortunately even people who should know better do not seem to realize what is happening.

After the war ended, President Truman attempted to maintain price and wage controls as a means of avoiding the inevitable rise in prices resulting from the World War II expansion of the money supply. Truman's initial policies called for permitting wage increases which would not require price increases. This was a case of the politician wanting his cake and eating it, too. Yet Truman's deeds did not match his words and common sense.

"What happens to wages," the President stated on October 30, 1945, "is important to all of us . . . It is important to business . . . not only because wages represent an essential item in the cost of producing goods, but because people can not buy the products of industry unless they earn enough wages generally . . . I am convinced that we must get away as quickly as possible from government controls, and that we must get back to the free operation of our competitive system."

Then the President's political instincts sent his common sense scurrying and he summarized his policy as one which "allows management to make wage increases without government approval, but requires government approval before the wage increases can be reflected in higher price ceilings."

There were attempts to rally public opinion, appointments of fact-finding boards, and charges and countercharges by union and industry spokesmen. But the situation continued to deteriorate and by January of 1946, one and a half million men were on strike in the steel, auto, meatpacking, and electrical industries. In February the administration permitted the steel and auto makers to raise prices.

"I am now modifying our wage-price policy," President Truman stated lamely as he tried to wriggle out of the economic trap he had built for himself, "to permit wage increases within certain limits and to permit any industry placed in a hardship position by an approved increase to seek price adjustments without waiting until the end of a six months' test period . . ."

In May 1946 price-wage stabilization and labor problems still plagued Harry Truman. A coal strike in April had been followed by a brief return to work and a second breakdown in bargaining. At this point the president seized the coal mines. Within a week the government granted union wage demands and another hole was punched in the stabilization program. At about the same time the rail workers struck against the government, which had previously seized the railroads. Truman's response was an address to congress, threatening to draft the strikers and asking for severely restrictive labor legislation. While the president was speaking he was handed a note stating that the unions had accepted the government's offer and were calling off the strike.

These two incidents should have been expected considering the combined effects of inflation and breakdown of the free market for labor. Curtailment of competition by means of labor legislation had done away with some of the restraint that would otherwise act on union demands. In the absence of these, the government had to resort to seizure and threats of forced labor in order that the country would not lack coal and transportation. One intervention requires another intervention; the web of statism grows.

By the end of June 1946, the President was ready to do away with the Office of Price Administration, allowing wages and prices to seek their own level. Congress passed HR 6042, a bill continuing controls, but with amendments allowing for additional relaxation. Truman vetoed the bill, claiming that it continued the government's responsibility without continuing its authority, i.e. the controls were weaker than he thought they should be. The experiences of the first eleven months with peace-time controls should have demonstrated (and perhaps did demonstrate) the futility of controls—strong or weak. It is possible that he was glad to be done with controls. Although his veto was in keeping with his statement of the previous October, he yielded to politics and placed the blame on his Republican opponents, Taft and Wherry, for a bad bill, anticipating that the Republicans would surely be blamed for the upward adjustment of prices that were certain to follow decontrol.

In his veto message Truman used some ridiculous figures to cast scorn on the Taft-Wherry amendments. "Ceilings for steel," said the President, "will have to be raised $4 to $8 a ton. These increases will in turn be reflected in the ceiling of everything made of steel." So far so good, but in the next paragraph Truman continued, saying that "the average price of low-priced automobiles would be increased $225 to $250 on top of the substantial increases already granted." The implication is that a $4 to $8 increase in a ton of steel would cause an increase in the cost of the finished product of $225, which would mean that 30 tons of steel are consumed either directly or indirectly in the production of a low-priced car. This is utter nonsense.

At another point in his veto message, President Truman wrote that "the Taft amendment puts into prices the profit per unit of sales which the industry received for the particular product in 1941. That was a year in which manufacturers and processors received a much greater profit out of each dollar of sales than in any one of the five peacetime years which preceded 1941 . . ." Truman must certainly have been aware that at least three of those five years were depression-recession years and that only toward the end of 1939 did the war in Europe bring about stimulation of the economy. It would certainly be expected that average profits for 1936-1940 would be far lower than for 1941. Truman was bogged down in the sands of trying to determine what was fair and normal in the way of profits, an impossible task. It can also be claimed that Taft was in the same quagmire. It is more likely, however, that Taft was merely seeking to weaken controls. He was successful in this end, in fact, got more than he bargained for when Truman vetoed the bill.

After the veto of the stabilization bill at the end of June, congress, under pressure, passed a revised price-control bill which the President signed at the end of July. Under this bill meat prices were permitted to rise only 15 per cent above June prices and meat virtually disappeared from the market. Three weeks before the 1946 election Truman gave up trying to control the price of meat, and meat again returned to the market. This was supposed to pacify outraged housewives and produce enough votes to elect a Democrat congress. It was too little and too late, and short as is the memory of the voter, it is longer than three weeks. After the election President Truman admitted defeat on the wage-price control issue and ended all controls. "There is no virtue in controls for control's sake," said the President, improving thereby his reputation as an economist.

Under the pressure of wartime budget deficits and more inflation during the Korean War, price and wage controls were again restored in September of 1950. President Eisenhower discontinued controls when he took office in January of 1953.

The Full Employment Act of 1946 bestowed respectability upon inflation. Coupled with the Wagner Act, and later laws and rulings of the National Labor Relations Board, it guarantees continuing inflation. President Truman gave his whole-hearted support to the measure's passage and signed it on February 20, 1946, amid ruffles and flourishes from assembled liberals, leftists, and statists. The law establishes as the policy of the Federal government the creation of conditions under which there will be employment opportunities for all who are willing and able to work. The rhetoric is at times inspirational and at times innocuous, as below. The Act establishes an Economic Council of three advisers to the president who are directed to "analyze and interpret economic developments," and the Act requires the president to submit an annual economic report to Congress. In practice, the inspirational rhetoric is far from innocuous.

The Full Employment Act of 1946 has been perverted into an excuse for deficit financing and subsequent inflation resulting from monetization of the debt.

In his 1949 State of the Union Message, President Truman said that the Full Employment Act of 1946 "pledges the Government to use all its resources to promote maximum employment, production, and purchasing power. This means that the Government is firmly committed to protect business and the people against the dangers of recession and against the evils of inflation." (19, p 155)

Since 1949 most politicians, influenced by the "modern" economics they learned in colleges in the 40's and 50's, have come to the conclusion that there is a mutually exclusive choice of recession or inflation. Whenever a choice has been made, inflation has always won out. There is, of course, no need to make such a choice, for inflation is necessary for full employment and avoidance of a depression *only* if free market forces are prevented from determining wage rates. This is the situation which exists as a result of the near monopoly powers granted to organized labor under current legislation and rulings of the National Labor Relations Board. When wage rates are coercively forced above free-market wage rates, unemployment results. The only way the real wage rates can be brought down to economically sound levels is to inflate the currency. Nominal wages remain high, real wages drop, and employment picks up, but anyone who has accumulated savings in the form of cash, bank deposits, insurance, etc., suffers from higher prices.

President Truman never realized the full potential of the Act for there was no prolonged period of serious unemployment during his years in office. Just about the time the bloom of the postwar boom began to wilt in 1950, along came the Korean War and a wild race to re-arm. It was unnecessary to rely upon the Full Employment Act as an excuse for deficit financing and inflation.

The economists, opinion makers, and politicians who have promoted deficit financing, and its corollary, inflation, as a means of stimulating the economy, have ignored the historical truths that inflation will stimulate only if continued at an accelerating pace; that the first results are a disaster for savers; and that the final results are a disaster for all. The blame for the financial Gotterdamerung will descend upon the thrifty, upon speculators, upon businessmen, upon greedy union leaders, upon bankers, and upon foreign intrigue. It will be laid at every door, excepting the doors of the politicians who made inflation both respectable and possible, and the doors of the voters who elected the politicians.

Probably at no time did Harry Truman score lower as an economist than in his budget message for the fiscal year ending June 30, 1947.

"Considering the whole Nation," declared the president, "total expenditures must equal the total receipts, because what any individual or group spends becomes the receipts of other individuals or groups."

Expenditures need not equal receipts when the Federal government enters the picture, and this can produce inflation. If an individual wants to spend in excess of his income he must borrow the difference from a saver. But when he borrows from a saver, that person's purchasing power is correspondingly reduced and the total quantity of money competing for available goods is unchanged. If the government sells bonds to individuals (who put the bonds in their safe-deposit boxes) to cover its deficits there is likewise no increase in the money supply. But if the government trades bonds for checking account credit at the bank, new money is created. This is the equivalent of printing money, it is inflationary, and it upsets the balance between expenditures and receipts. The Federal Octopus can get away with manufacturing money. A few individuals try it every so often, but it is frowned upon. This is a little surprising because the government has printed excess dollars since the 1930's whenever the going got a little tough. One would think the government would appreciate a little help from the counterfeiters, but that has not been the case.

The Committee for Economic Development, the accuracy of whose predictions is on a par with those of many stockbrokers,[3] stated with much self-assurance that setting 1947 tax rates to produce a $3 billion surplus would result in a "normal" (their word) unemployment rate of 4%. In 1971, Secretary of Treasury

[3] And thus, far worse than the weatherman, ground hog, or brown woolly capterpillar.

Connally, a Texas Republicrat, concluded that a normal unemployment rate of 4% was a myth and that the only times it had been attained was in war time.

In 1950, the Committee claimed that their stabilizing budget policy "would produce surpluses in good years to retire debt created in bad years." Unfortunately we seem to have had, if we can judge from the years of Federal surpluses, only about four good years out of the last twenty-two years. Yet in November of every election year the party which happens to hold power claims unprecedented prosperity. (On occasion they have also been known to claim simultaneous unprecedented poverty!)

By 1954, the Committee for Economic Development "did not stress the desirability of achieving a surplus and aimed merely at a balanced cash budget at high levels of unemployment." The Committee seemed to be losing confidence in the accuracy of its predictions which were no longer as specific as they had been seven years earlier.

Harry Truman handled domestic social problems better than he handled economic problems. He took major steps in the area of race relations which were well within the jurisdictional province of the Federal government. On July 26, 1948, the president issued two executive orders. "All personnel actions," stated the first order, "taken by Federal appointing officers shall be based solely on merit and fitness; and such officers are authorized and directed to take appropriate steps to insure that in all such actions there shall be no discrimination because of race, color, religion, or national origin." His second order, #9981, directed that "there shall be equality of treatment and opportunity for all persons in the armed services without regard to race, color, religion, or national origin." This was followed by instructions implementing this policy.

In so far as any government collects taxes from all of its citizens without regard to race, color, or religion, it should therefore, in all its dealings with them, disregard differences in race, color, or religion that may exist. Its services should be provided without favoritism. President Truman recognized this and was the first president to take steps to make this a reality.

But Truman and the statists went far beyond seeing that the government should dispense services with an impartiality matching its collection of taxes. The road was laid out in the 1947 report of the President's Committee on Civil Rights.

There are aspects of American life which, to many people, are both unreasonable and without moral justification. But it is not the government's task to see that such absurdities are eliminated from the scene. Rather this is a job for family and church. When a government becomes an instrument of personal morality and attempts to take the place of the church or family, tyranny is on the doorstep. If the state becomes the church, separation of church and state is but a fiction.

Herbert Hoover's 1930 Child Health Day proclamation became the nineteen points of the Children's Charter, i.e. nineteen "rights" of children. By FDR's time Hoover's children had become adults, and Roosevelt spoke of their "rights": to a job, to earn enough for adequate food, clothing and recreation, to a decent home, to adequate medical care, to good health, to protection from the hardships of old age, accident, sickness, and unemployment, and to a good education. President Truman's Committee on Civil Rights covered the same ground again: the right to education, the right to housing, the right to equal opportunity, etc. But according to Jack Bell, the Southern segregationists recognized the President's duplicity when he "demanded passage of FEPC (*Fair Employment Practices Commission*) and other legislation at a time when he knew he couldn't get it." (53, p 163)

Harry Truman's fondness for history was exceeded only by his affection for politics, yet his fancies certainly failed him in his speech to farmers at Dexter, Iowa on September 18, 1948. Here the campaigning president claimed, with obvious pride, that "the Democratic Party originated the farm support program. We built the price support plan out of hard experience . . ." Prudence and politics would seem to demand silence on the issue of credit for such a dismal and consistently ineffective program. His sense of history also seems to have either lapsed or have been overwhelmed by his partisan zeal. Although it is of no credit to them, the farm subsidy idea was originated by the Republicans to solve a problem that first appeared when they chanced to be in power.

Harding's proposals for easier farm credit, a form of subsidy, was the first big step toward Federal intervention in agriculture.

The National Agricultural Conference, convened by President Harding, declared that the Federal Government had an obligation "to subsidize farm prices in order to give the farmer a fair return for his labor." Harding did not agree with this principle, but the idea was catching on.

Under Coolidge, Republicans in congress passed the McNary-Haugen Bill in 1927. This would have paid farmers subsidies for farm products which would then have been dumped at a loss overseas. Coolidge to his credit, vetoed the bill. And so far, Truman, the historian, seems correct since the Republicans who controlled congress were not firmly enough united behind price supports to override the presidential veto.

Herbert Hoover, as Secretary of Commerce, in cooperation with Secretary of Agriculture Jardine, proposed the first farm aid legislation directly supporting prices and restricting the farmer's freedom to plant as much as he wished. The proposals, embodied in the Curtis-Crisp Bill, called for establishment of a Federal Farm Board with authority to loan $250,000,000 to farmer's cooperatives for price supports. This proposal was never passed by congress, but soon after he became president, Hoover was more successful. Congress established the Farm Board and authorized a half-billion dollar credit for price support loans. Since this was done by a Republican president with a congress controlled by Republicans, Truman was wrong when he claimed for the Democrats the dubious honor of "originating the farm support program."

Yet censure of Mr. Truman's historical prowess must be tempered, for, in truth there was no clear cleavage along party lines in support of or in opposition to Federal control of agriculture. Partly because of this lack of cleavage and partly because of log-rolling politics in an unlimited representative democracy, the voters have never had a clear choice on the question of intervention versus nonintervention in general, or the question of specific interventions in agriculture, housing subsidies, old-age assistance, et cetera, which are among the many arms of the Federal octopus. This is an inherent shortcoming of unlimited government by representative democracy. If the functions and authority and responsibility of government could be restrained and limited, log rolling for favors and to advance special interests would find no place in the scheme of things. Under these circumstances questioning whether or not voters were ever given a choice on the issue of statism versus freedom would be a meaningless abstraction.

Professors Bernstein and Matusow, who would have to be classed as liberals, assessed Harry Truman's domestic performance in a chapter of their book (*The Truman Administration*) headed "The Fair Deal 1945-1953."

"From one point of view," they wrote, "Truman's domestic program, known as the Fair Deal, can be judged as a failure. After nearly eight years in office Truman could point to only a few tangible accomplishments: his executive orders ending discrimination in the armed services and in the Federal government, the public housing act of 1949, a rise in minimum wages passed that same year, and a social security measure in 1950 that increased benefits and extended coverage to ten million more Americans. But his boldest proposals were ignored or defeated by congress: civil rights legislation, national health insurance, the Brannan Plan for agriculture, rational and humane immigration laws, Federal aid to education. His achievements, then, seem mainly negative. In a conservative era he helped prevent repeal of the New Deal and preserved its vision of mild welfare capitalism.

"The judgment, while true, is also incomplete. Truman's best proposals proved to be a form of public education that prepared the way for enactment of similar programs in more favorable times." (19, p 86)

No doubt, education was necessary. Leonard Read in his *Outlook for Freedom* (Foundation for Economic Education, Irvington-on-Hudson, N. Y., 1951) mentions the study made in 1949 by Link and Freiberg "which showed that 75 per cent of the American people believed themselves to be against socialism, yet 66 per cent of them favored governmental measures that fell within their own definitions of socialism."

All of which tends to support the theory that the president, the party in power, and politicians in general, tend to be followers rather than leaders. The education of the people to a particular viewpoint is more important than which party or which politicians happen to be in power. If majority opinion can be altered, or even given the appearance of having been altered, the politicians will respond.

As director of the nation's foreign affairs, Harry Truman, compared to Franklin D. Roosevelt, looks good, even brilliant. This is not to say that the record is without blemishes or that mistakes were not made. But given the world situation that the vice president suddenly inherited in 1945, considering the serious Communist infiltration and penetration of our government (which Truman for political reasons could not admit), and in view of the ineptness and errors of some of his subordinates, the record of Harry Truman is all the more remarkable and admirable.

In June of 1941, just after the Nazis invaded the Soviet Union, Harry Truman, who was then serving in the Senate, made a comment to reporters which shows that he had a far better understanding of the situation than most Americans. It also showed that he had a better strategy for guaranteeing American security than any leader then or afterwards proposed.

"Asked about this turn of events (*the German invasion of June 23, 1941*)," wrote Alfred Steinberg in *The Man from Missouri* ". . . he gave an off-the-cuff opinion that is the complete reverse of President Roosevelt's reaction and policy. 'If we see Germany is winning we ought to help Russia,' he said, 'and if Russia is winning we ought to help Germany, and that way let them kill as many as posisble (*of each other*), although I don't want to see Hitler victorious under any circumstances. *Neither of them think anything of their pledged word.*'" (54, p. 186) (Italics added.)

Now this was an off-the-cuff comment, unrefined, and open to nitpicking criticism. For instance, first helping one side and then the other would have been awkward, if not impossible, but it would have been possible to have helped the weaker side, the Communists in this case, to the extent that an equilibrium would have been established by which both sides would have exterminated each other as threats to our security. It would also have beaten the Communists at their favorite game of supplying the arms to others who then do the fighting for them (as in Korea, Vietnam, and Egypt).

The most awesome decision facing the new president concerned the atomic bomb, about which he was kept in total ignorance while vice president. The perspective of years and
additional information have given us a vantage from which it is
tempting to criticize the use of the second and third atom bombs
on Hiroshima and Nagasaki.

The decision to use the bomb on actual targets was based on
several assumptions: unless the bombs were used an invasion
would be necessary to defeat the Japanese, an invasion would
involve casualties far in excess of those produced by the bombs,
and with only two untried aerial bombs available, the alternative
of demonstrating them in an uninhabited area was too risky to
attempt. (The test bomb was detonated from a fixed position on a
tower.) Likewise it was decided not to warn the Japanese of the
specifics of the new weapon because it was feared a dud was possible which would weaken the psychological impact of the device.

A study group, known as the Interim Committee, made a
unanimous recommendation to use the bomb and on June 1, 1945
the president gave his approval. This did not end the agitation
and debate.

In the ranks of the scientists who had developed the bomb
there was division on the question of whether and how it should
be used. Twelve days after the Interim Committee's recommendations were made, Dr. James Franck, one of a committee of seven
atomic scientists, recommended a demonstration on desert land or
an uninhabited island. Four days later four atomic scientists of
the Scientific Advisory Committee considered the possibilities of
a demonstration and concluded it would be a poor substitute for
actual use of the bomb as a means of ending the war. Dr. Leo
Szilard submitted a petition on July 17th containing the signatures of sixty-nine Chicago scientists urging against use of the
bomb "at least not unless the terms which will be imposed after
the war on Japan were made public in detail and Japan were
given an opportunity to surrender." (This was done by the Potsdam Ultimatum of July 26, 1945.) Other scientists presented
petitions and submitted the results of a poll of 150 scientists on
July 12th. The poll favored, by about 3 to 1, a limited use, such

as a demonstration, over other possibilities. Finally, the actual order to use the bomb was issued on July 24th calling for a drop on August 3rd.

While the use of the bomb was being debated and final assembly completed in preparation for its testing and use, the Japanese were sending peace feelers. The first of these were delivered to the Soviets on May 30, 1945 and were known to the United States government by virtue of breaking the Japanese code used for their transmission. Peace feelers continued to be sent during the Potsdam meeting in July. On July 26 a joint U.S., U.K., Chinese proclamation was issued, calling for unconditional surrender and ending with "the alternative for Japan is prompt and utter destruction."

On July 28th the Japanese rejected the ultimatum. They erroneously believed that the basis for the Potsdam declaration was American knowledge of Japanese peace efforts. While it is true that the United States did have this knowledge, the real basis for the ultimatum was the development of the new weapon. Had the Japanese not gone astray in judging the basis of the call for their surrender, it is likely that they would have acceded to the surrender terms. In this event, President Truman's July 24th order could have been remanded before execution.

As early as April 7, the peace party in Japan was able to install Admiral Baron Kantaro Suzuki as Prime Minister. His mission was to make peace. By May 1945 the Emperor, Lord Privy Seal, Foreign Minister, and Navy Minister, as well as the Premier, all favored peace. They were opposed by the War Minister, the two Chiefs of Staffs and the war party. Suzuki was unable to accept unconditional surrender because of strong war party opposition, although instructions had been sent to Ambassador Konoye in Moscow that he was to "secure peace at any price, notwithstanding its severity."

"Based on a detailed investigation of all the facts," concluded the U.S. Strategic Bombing Survey, "and supported by the testimony of the surviving Japanese leaders involved, it is the Survey's opinion that certainly prior to December 1945, and in all probability prior to 1 November 1945, Japan would have surrendered even if the atomic bombs had not been dropped, even if Russia had not entered the war, and even if no invasion had been planned or contemplated." (*Japan's Struggle to End the War*, U.S. Strategic Bombing Survey)

It should be pointed out that this conclusion is based partly on the hindsight of the Japanese leaders interviewed. It was also reached by an organization which had a special interest in establishing the effectiveness of strategic bombing. In any event, use of the atom bomb, tragedy though it was, can at worst be blamed on fallible human judgments and lack of information. The president did not know the realities of Japan's weakness; the Japanese did not know about the reality of American strength and the ability to bring about their "prompt and utter destruction."

"The end of the war," wrote Truman in his message to congress of September 6, 1945, "came more swiftly than most of us anticipated." Truman expected that a costly invasion would have to be mounted and that Russian help would be needed to immobilize the 2,000,000 Japanese troops in Manchuria and prevent them from joining the 2,000,000 man home army in the islands. The Russians knew, as a result of Ambassador Konoye's efforts, that the Japanese were near collapse and that for a small, safe investment they would guarantee large returns to themselves. Two days after the bomb was dropped on Hiroshima and the defeat of Japan was sealed, the Russians entered the war. Two days later the Japanese sued for peace.

Franklin D. Roosevelt died on April 12, 1945. Less than two weeks later, on April 23, 1945, President Truman dressed down Soviet Foreign Minister Molotov because of Russian aggressiveness as the USSR advanced through and occupied Eastern European countries. Molotov lamented to the new president: "I have never been talked to like that in my life." Dauntless Harry Truman, at his pugnacious best, flared back: "Carry out your agreements and you won't get talked to like that." (Quoted by C. L. Sulzberger in *History of World War II*, © American Heritage Publishing Co., Inc., 1966, p 623)

Truman hadn't been president long before he recognized that the Communists in the Soviet Union respected power more than talk. Steinberg relates that after the President informed Tito he would be driven from Trieste by force, if necessary, he told Cabell Phillips of the *New York Times* that "I drove Tito out of Trieste, or rather I scared him off from moving in, which he was planning to do with Stalin's backing. I did the same with Stalin when he was settling his forces down for good in Iran. I ordered the Mediterranean Fleet into the Persian Gulf and told Stalin he had better get out before they got there. And he did, too." (54, p 276) Yet it remains a mystery why Truman did not order the Berlin blockade broken by force. It was not until almost two years after the end of the blockade that the Soviet Union detonated its first atomic bomb.

The Truman Doctrine was proclaimed on March 12, 1947 in an address to congress. The president urged "support for free peoples who are resisting attempted subjugation by armed minorities or by outside pressures." This was, of course, a reference to resisting Communist aggression. The Greeks were fighting Communist terrorists and were under pressure from neighboring Communist troops in Albania, Yugoslavia and Bulgaria. The Turks were under pressure from neighboring Soviet troops. The Truman Doctrine saved both Greece and Turkey from Communist domination, but in Greece the cost was high before success was achieved. One wonders if Greek lives could have been saved by threatening to use our own armed forces, including the atom bomb. The atomic bomb monopoly was not broken until two years after proclamation of the Truman Doctrine.

The Marshall Plan was a natural outgrowth of the Truman Doctrine. It was announced by Under Secretary of State Dean Acheson in May 1947, but did not achieve real prominence until Secretary Marshall's Harvard Commencement address on June 5th. It called for aid to rebuild and restore Europe. Almost unbelievably, the original plan offered help to the Soviet Union and its satellites as well as to non-communist countries of Europe. The USSR, in one of the stupedest foreign policy blunders of all time, walked out of the Paris meeting which had been convened to consider the aid plan. Had they remained in contention for aid, the plan would almost certainly have been defeated in congress, and the strength of Western Europe relative to Eastern Europe would have been weaker if neither side had been aided.

The Brussels Alliance followed the Marshall Plan in 1948 and the North Atlantic Treaty Organization, NATO, which expanded the Brussels Alliance, was formed in 1949. The NATO Treaty, signed on October 4th, was a mutual defense pact promising military support by the signatories if any one of them was attacked. Useful in the 1950's and 1960's, the importance of NATO has diminished with the spread of nuclear weapons and improvements in delivery systems.

Truman's Far East policies were disasters compared to his efforts in Europe. The initial source of the trouble was an almost pathetic innocence of Chinese Communist intentions. At first, policy called for cessation of hostilities and the formation of a Nationalist-Communist coalition government. Once established, the coalition was to be supplied with American aid for the rebuilding of China. According to the theory, after China was rebuilt, communism was supposed to lose its appeal and be rejected by the people.

"Of course," said Truman, "the struggle for power would continue, but there was no reason why the Nationalist Government could not be successful in this struggle, as non-Communist governments had been in Europe, if it attended to the fundamental needs of the people."

No reason, that is, excepting that there was not a single non-Communist government in Europe which had successfully resisted communism via a coalition. Truman's common sense, of which he had an abundance, was overwhelmed by bad advice, for, after a coalition there would soon be no Nationalist government to attend to anyone's needs. There does not exist anywhere in the world a non-Communist government which has accepted Communists in a coalition government.

Although Truman can not receive all the blame for the loss of China he can not avoid being assigned a major share. "The Administration (*Truman's*)," according to Bernstein and Matusow's documentary, "regarded Wedermeyer's suggestions (*for aid to Nationalist China*) and others like them as mere palliatives. But in February 1948, to secure support of the China bloc in Congress for the Marshall Plan for Europe, Truman found it necessary to request a large appropriation for China." (19, p 342) In other words, aid to China was based on a political log-rolling effort to secure aid for Europe. Under such circumstances it is not surprising that the 1948-49 appropriation of $463,000,000 for nonmilitary aid voted by Congress remained largely undelivered.

Acheson objected to further aid for fiscal 1949-50. By December 1949, midway through the fiscal year, the Nationalists had been forced off the mainland.

Even if it could be proved that the Nationalist government was as corrupt as claimed by its American critics, withholding American aid was frightful stupidity. The Nationalist government was neither aggressive nor did it represent a power-based despotism able to threaten American security. On the other hand, the Chinese Communists are part of an aggressive, powerful international despotism, and this is so regardless of whether they are allies or competitors of the Russians. Additionally there is no government or system more basically corrupt, immoral, evil, and degenerate than communism, but this fact *alone* does not make Communist countries our enemies.

The effect of withholding aid from the Nationalists resulted in the replacement of one regime, alleged to be corrupt, by another regime known to be corrupt, and corrupt in the most base way. But corruption is not a major foreign policy issue. It is futile for Americans to attempt to stamp out corruption throughout the world. The foreign policy failure was in encouraging replacement of a friendly, inoffensive regime with one that is violently unfriendly, aggressive, and a threat to our security, charges of corruption aside. A telling criticism of our China policy is quoted in Walter S. Robertson's letter to Philip C. Jessup, dated October 8, 1949. (19, pp 310-314)

One of President Truman's major blunders was his reliance on General George C. Marshall as Secretary of State. Nowhere does this show up more clearly than in the circumstances leading up to and the handling of the Berlin Blockade.

The Russians got hold of the plates for printing Allied occupation currency in Germany through the efforts of Harry Dexter White. (White was the author of the Morgenthau Plan to reduce Germany to a pastoral state. He was later identified as a Communist and took his own life.) As a result of uncontrolled Russian printing of currency the situation had gotten so out of hand that the Western Allies decided currency reform was necessary. The Russians retaliated against this by harassing ground traffic passing through their zone to and from Berlin. After new currency was exchanged for the old currency in the French, British, and

American sectors of the city, the Russians stepped up their harassment and blockaded all ground traffic from the Western zones of occupation. This violated previous agreements. Although earlier Russian harassment was an indication of what might be expected, the Department of State was not ready with a countermove. Not until two weeks after the blockade started did Secretary Marshall finally send a formal protest to the Communists.

Marshall's note to the Soviet Union on the blockade was not only late, it was weak as well. It restated Allied rights to free access and declared that the United States would "not be induced by threats, pressures, or other actions to abandon these rights . . . There can be no question of delay in the restoration of these essential services, since the needs of the civilian population in the Berlin area are imperative." But there *was* a delay in restoration of these essential services—and it was very costly to us in lives and material. The blockade was not lifted by the Russians until almost one year had passed. (The blockade lasted from June 23, 1948 to May 12, 1949.) Perhaps the delay can be explained by Marshall's final paragraph in his note of protest. His proposal merely called upon the Russians to meet us at the negotiation table!

Ambassador George Kennan [4] sent a long cablegram from Moscow on February 26, 1946. Soviet power ". . . is highly sensitive to logic of force. For this reason it can easily withdraw—and usually does—when strong resistance is encountered at any point. Thus if the adversary has sufficient force and makes clear his readiness to use it, he rarely has to do so." Unfortunately, neither Marshall nor Truman acted on this advice when faced with the Berlin Blockade.

The Korean War was born of a miscalculation of what would be required to defeat the Japanese, namely, Russian participation in the war. It was compounded by the fact that the Secretary of State was led to believe by lower echelons in the State Department that dealing with Russian Communists was basically no different than dealing with nations of the West. Byrnes was more

---

[4] Ambassador Kennan is generally criticized as the author of the policy of containment which, in effect, acquiesced to the Russian oppression of Eastern Europe. Nevertheless, containment was an improvement over FDR's policy of retreat.

directly exposed to these views than was Truman. In December 1945 he agreed to a coalition provisional government for Korea, consisting of democratic political and social organizations. When it came time to set up the provisional government in 1946, Byrnes was surprised to find that for the Russians to recognize any organization as democratic or social it also had to be certified as Communist! In Newspeak, war is peace, love is hate, and communism is democracy.

After two years of stalemate, Secretary of State George Marshall, who was just as naive as Byrnes, asked the United Nations to supervise elections in Korea. The Russians, genial and accommodating as usual, would not allow the United Nations Temporary Commission north of the 38th parallel. So free elections were held under supervision of the UN in South Korea, while the Communists held their own "free" elections in the North. Having failed to learn the lesson in Eastern Europe, one would have thought that surely the Korean experience would have demonstrated for all time the impossibility of dealing with Communists on any rational basis—other than as international gangsters. But the Korean experience had not yet matured.

The Communists of North Korea were invited to attack South Korea on January 12, 1950, by Secretary of State Dean Acheson. The Secretary stated in a speech that our "defensive perimeter runs along the Aleutians to Japan and then goes to the Ryukyus . . . from the Ryukyus to the Philippine Islands." This line excluded South Korea and Formosa. In 1947 General MacArthur and the Joint Chiefs of Staff also excluded Korea as being of strategic interest to the United States. (19, p 430) However, at the time of the Joint Chiefs' decision, mainland China had not fallen to the Communists and there was still a sizeable American occupation force in Korea. When Acheson made his statement in 1950, all American troops had been withdrawn and Chinese Communist troops controlled mainland China and were at the Manchurian-Korean border.

Five months after Acheson's declaration, the Communist North Koreans invaded the South. Truman's response to the attack was a bold and courageous attempt to rectify Acheson's error. His statement on June 24, 1950 additionally recognized the threat to Formosa and he announced that the United States Seventh Fleet would "prevent any attack on Formosa," thus extending Acheson's defense perimeter westward to include a staunch anti-communist ally. Amazingly, at the same time Truman weakened the American position by also declaring that the Seventh Fleet would not permit the Nationalists on Formosa to attack the Communists on the mainland. The United States guaranteed the safety of an enemy! Public proclamation of this policy put the Chinese Communists on notice that they could devote their total effort to consolidation of their mainland conquest!

Almost a year to the day after the North Korean invasion of South Korea the Soviet Ambassador to the United Nations, Jacob Malik, proposed a negotiated settlement to the Korean War. The armistice team met two weeks later on July 7, 1951, but negotiations, and fighting, continued for two more years. In 1952 the North Koreans demanded forced repatriation of prisoners, and Truman stubbornly rejected this saying that "we will not buy an armistice by turning over human beings for slaughter or safety." After Stalin died in 1953 the Communists agreed to permit voluntary repatriation. Over 27,000 anti-Communist North Koreans held captive by the South Koreans were freed just before the cease fire was signed. During the time the armistice talks were being held 80,000 American casualties were suffered. These losses were more than those which occurred during the years of fighting *before* "peace" was being negotiated.

The Korean War, which started as a courageous move by President Truman, deteriorated into a disgraceful mess. The sad results were eloquently summed up in a letter which appeared in *Life* magazine, August 20, 1953.

"The display of moral weakness which we have made in Korea," wrote Katherine Tabor, whose husband was killed in Korea, "can only encourage the Communists to try again, can only assure them that they have nothing to lose and everything to gain by aggression, that next time they may hope for at least a similar compromise.

". . . What reason is there to expect the enemy to be warned that any future aggression will be punished or defeated when we do not punish or defeat the present aggression?

". . . We have not prevented the (Chinese) Communists . . . from retaining power in North Korea, and from demonstrating our weakness and their strength, from humiliating us, demoralizing the anti-communists, and enhancing their own prestige throughout Asia.

". . . So much good has been nobly spent to expulse the evil, and still the evil is not expulsed, but remains prosperous . . ."

On July 8, 1959 the first United States soldiers were killed in combat in Vietnam. They would be followed by many more. The evil had not been expulsed.

CHAPTER 13

GENTLEMAN, GENERAL, AND GOLFER

Many Republicans, most conservatives, and all authentic liberals omit Dwight D. Eisenhower from their list of favorite presidents. And yet among the liberals, even those in the frenzied fringe who might be expected to allow their political tastes to temper their personal views, Ike comes through as a very personable man. Richard Rovere, Eric Goldman, Emmet Hughes, Norman Graebner, and others describe Eisenhower as comfortable, happy, genial, gregarious, selfless, sensitive, humble, dignified, decent, and conciliatory. After all, could anyone dislike a man whose nickname was Ike?

Dean Albertson was the liberal editor of *Eisenhower as President*. Albertson's book reprints articles reflecting on Eisenhower's performance: the authors are left of center. A final chapter reprints Eisenhower's Farewell Address. Albertson in his preface wrote that ". . . neither could the critic overlook his apparent humanitarianism, his genuine decency, and above all the high sense of moral purpose which underlay his undoubted concern for the welfare of the nation . . ." (56, p XV)

In May 1950, Richard Rovere made a liberal's appraisal of the would be nominee.

"Eisenhower," stated Rovere, "is forthright, pragmatic, gregarious, alert, even-tempered, calmly energetic, more shrewd than wise, generous, courteous, but neither courtly nor grand, modest but never humble. He is unintellectual and probably anti-intellectual, but he is enormously respectful of learning and knowledge . . ." (57, p 8)

Rovere's claim that Eisenhower was unintellectual explains how, coming from a conservative background, Eisenhower ended up in the liberal interventionist camp. Being unintellectual Ike would have been bored by what is required for a critical evaluation of the ideas thrust upon him by the articulate authorities around him. And further, since he was impressed by and "respectful of learning and knowledge," he probably felt incompetent to challenge them. He therefore accepted what was laid before him. So Ike, raised as a conservative, slipped into liberalism, not perhaps, liberal enough to please the liberals, but liberal enough to dismay the conservatives, and interventionist enough to disturb the anti-statists.

Rovere concluded that Harry Truman was in many ways similar to Dwight Eisenhower. "Both operate at low pressures," Rovere wrote. "Both are moderate, middling, median figures in character and doctrine . . . Both were brought up in a stern, semi-fundamentalist Protestant morality. Both are men of simple integrity and personal honor . . . Simplicity, frankness, and openness of manner commended each to his own following." (57, p 247)

Emmet John Hughes, former editor of *Life*, was a speech writer for Eisenhower. He recorded his impressions of the man he worked for in *The Ordeal of Power*. Of himself, Hughes claimed to have been "of the Generation of the New Deal . . . I would have voted without exception, until that date (*1952*), for all Democratic candidates for the presidency . . . I worked on his staff, shaping ideas and words toward speeches and pronouncements through the climax of that (*1952*) National Election." (12, p 10)

Hughes stayed on at the White House, presumably as a chief idea shaper. Why was Hughes, the leftish liberal Democrat, attracted to Eisenhower? For the same reasons other Democrats wanted Ike to run as *their* candidate—he looked like a winner. Hughes and many other liberals probably sensed that even without Ike the Democrats were due for a defeat in 1952. If this was to be the case, the liberals could not allow Taft, a conservative with convictions, to have the Republican nomination. As president, Taft would have been much tougher on liberals than Ike, who was somewhat of a political zero. Harry Truman gave his estimate of the General's political savvy just before the 1953 inauguration. "Why this fellow," said Truman in the colorful language reserved for people who crossed him, "don't know any more about politics than a pig knows about Sunday." (57, p 72)

A fellow like Ike could be shaped by the ideas of a chief idea shaper such as Hughes.

In spite of Ike's likeable qualities, he was humanly imperfect. Hughes reported that "an unwelcome report of some baseless criticism or some unfinished labor or some blemished performance could ignite an explosion of temper almost fiercely physical. His voice would shout, his cheeks would flame with rage, his arms wave threateningly." (12, p 149)

Eisenhower's personality, which was such an asset in his Army staff assignments, served him well as president. Rovere comments on the 1955 Geneva Conference, quoting first from *Le Monde*, the influential Parisian newspaper, which stated that "Eisenhower whose personality has long been misunderstood has emerged as the type of leader humanity needs today." "The President," Rovere continued in his own words, "drew bouquets of this sort not by doing anything in the least uncharacteristic but simply by showing to the conferees the same amenable countenance, the same yearning for conciliation and 'tranquility' . . ." (57, p 289)

Politics, domestic as well as international, is one of the emotional human arts which is dominated by personality more than by intellect. Political conventions testify to this as did the mobs who chanted their *Sieg Heils* for Hitler and *Il Duces* for Mussolini. Not only does the personality of the politician affect the crowd, the crowd's enthusiasm affects the politician. This feedback tends to dispel personal self-doubts and uncertainties which would otherwise act as restraints. Hitler, as an extreme example, was so deceived by cheering mobs that he led Germany to disaster and having done so he proclaimed, while surrounded by the debris of burning, bombed-out Berlin, that if Germany was to go down to defeat it was because the Germans were unworthy of his greatness! Eisenhower's response came nowhere near Hitler's, of course, but it was there nevertheless. It showed up in the fact that he planned in detail the mammoth public funeral for himself.

"His warm surge of pleasure," wrote Hughes, "in great gatherings and before shouting rallies, was open and genuine: the excitement still deepened the ruddy glow of his cheeks and widened the famous smile . . ." According to Hughes, Eisenhower would say "We need a few more 'cheer lines' in this speech, 'cause a

mob like this doesn't want to think—they just want to yowl."
(12, p 193) (Hughes apparently forgot that he had written on
p 25 about Ike that ". . . his greatest aversion was the calculated
rhetorical device . . . it extended to a distrust of eloquence."
But it didn't exclude "cheer" lines.)

Hughes pictures Eisenhower as a gentleman of great integrity
with an aversion to personal attacks in politics. In refusing to
counter Harry Truman's "give 'em hell" techniques, Eisenhower,
according to Hughes, said "I'm sure they would like to get me
down to *their* level. Well that's *one* satisfaction they will *never*
have." (12, p 26) Eisenhower brought to the presidency a dignity which had been missing for some time. Nor were he and
his family gaudy and flashy as were the Kennedy clan. There is
no doubt, that Ike was a gentleman whose reserve was the product of instinct and training.

In spite of Ike's gentlemanly qualities and private aversion to
personal attacks in politics, he did not stop his supporters' mean
personal campaign against Senator Robert Taft, Sr., his chief
rival for the Republican nomination. And after having engaged
in black tactics, his cronies were never repudiated nor did
Eisenhower publicly apologize for them. The culmination of the
attacks against Taft was the repeated convention chant of the
Lodge-Dewey-Eisenhower forces "Thou shalt not steal!" The
implication and charge was that Taft was dishonestly stealing the
election with illegally chosen delegates. There was irony in this,
probably calculated, for the same words were used by Teddy
Roosevelt against the Senator's father in 1912. Teddy, having
bolted the party and been nominated as a Bull Moose, opened
his acceptance speech with the words "Thou shalt not steal."

The gentleman General's view of a miliatry man in the presidency was different in 1952 than it had been on January 23, 1948
when he wrote to the Manchester, New Hampshire, *Union Leader*
that he "could not accept the nomination even under the remote
circumstances that it would be tendered me . . . The necessary
and wise subordination of the military to civil power will be best
sustained when life-long professional soldiers abstain from seeking
high political office."

The nomination of Dwight D. Eisenhower was a bitter blow

to conservatives and anti-statists. He was the nominee of the politically bankrupt Lodge-Dewey northeastern wing of the Republican party. Republicans and most of his countrymen did not know what he stood for, excepting perhaps in regard to military affairs. How could they? He had no personal political philosophy and poor Ike himself may not have known what he stood for, either.

For experience, Eisenhower had only military staff adventures to offer. He was ignorant of civilian life in general, and of economics in particular. He didn't know what a reporter was talking about when asked how he felt about open and closed shops. Politically, according to Truman, a qualified political expert if ever there was one, he was as ignorant as a pig is about Sunday. But he was a glamorous personality compared to the dry, intellectual politician, Robert Taft, the bald headed senator with a slight pot belly and high-pitched Ohio twang. Since it appeared that the Republican nominee would have to battle urbane, witty, articulate Adlai Stevenson, the "Taft-can't-win" refrain finally overwhelmed the Senator's supporters at the convention.

It is of no credit to those delegates at the convention who called themselves conservatives, but who backed away from Taft and gave the nomination to the General, for the Senator came closest to representing their ideals. As Rovere put it, the conservatives, who outnumbered the Lodge-Dewey-Eisenhower coalition "grumbled publicly over a fate which forced them to reward a man they regarded as a parvenu, an amateur, a boob, and a heretic of sorts and to destroy a man whose leadership they both acknowledged and enjoyed . . . Even in the New York delegation, where enthusiasm for Eisenhower was higher than in most, a good forty per cent of the vote, in the view of well-informed members, would have gone to Taft if Dewey had not cracked down hard . . . For all that, they accepted the hateful argument. Twenty years is a long time to be out of office. Loyalty to the organization was in the end more powerful than loyalty to the individual . . ." (57, pp 27-31) Or to an ideal, Rovere might have added.

Therein lies the weakness of the nation's conservative majority, split between the Republican and Democrat Parties, it has more loyalty to an organization than to an ideal. Eisenhower became the Republican nominee because parties usually pick the man thought most likely to be a winner rather than the man who is thought most nearly to reflect party philosophy.

Ike was a man who almost instinctively sensed how others felt about him. After he was nominated he addressed a group of traditional Republicans who originally had supported Taft but who were, out of party loyalty, attending an Eisenhower rally. The nominee told them he was aware of their feeling and then he "delivered a stirring impromptu discourse on the value and nature of loyalty. He urged them to keep faith with their lost causes and defeated leaders as long as they continued to believe their lost causes and defeated leaders were honorable, and explained to them . . . that enduring human agreements can be made only by those who do not indulge in self-deception." (57, p 40) Here his sensitivity and his ideals of loyalty, the latter so important in the armed services, produced a powerful speech. Loyalty had an overriding appeal to Eisenhower who also abhorred corruption and dereliction of duty. These are essential qualities in a good president, but they alone are not enough.

Eric Goldman, the ultra-liberal, would-be intellectual-in-waiting to Lyndon Johnson recognized that Eisenhower was less "Republican" than many Republicans hoped he would be.

"The President's (*Ike's*) attitude," wrote the author of *The Crucial Decade—and After: 1954-1960,* "toward specific domestic and foreign problems also had its varying aspects. He was, as is frequently remarked 'basically conservative.' But it was just as true to say that he was—and more so than any President in recent history—generally non-ideological." (58, p 254) That Eisenhower had no real economic philosophy is not unexpected from a man whose background, like Truman's, tended toward midwestern conservatism, but whose greatest rewards came from the New Deal administration, and who had never been required or inclined to think about economic problems. He made remarks which sounded conservative, he even acted the part on occasions, but he also encouraged extension of social security, widening of unemployment benefits, more subsidized housing, and expansion of Federal activities in health, education, and welfare. He was probably more conservative when he entered the White House than when he left, but it was an inherited conservatism, not rooted in any intellectual conviction.

Ike was at first very determined to balance the budget, but his determination was not persistent enough to accomplish his goal. He was in office from 1953 to 1961, and he can fairly be assigned responsibility for the fiscal years 1954 to 1961 inclusive. This is the result of the time lag between budgeting and spending and the fact that the fiscal year runs from July 1 of one year to June 30 of the next year. For instance, fiscal 1955 includes the last half of 1954 and the first half of 1955. During Ike's tenure he had two surplus years totaling $2.9 billion and six deficit years totaling $27.6 billion. He managed to add $24.7 billion to the national debt.

Eisenhower's most notable and solid conservative and anti-statist accomplishment was the elimination of price and wage controls. Even here, Eisenhower's policy directive showed inter-ventionist bias. ". . . As you know," Eisenhower wrote to Sinclair Weeks, his Secretary of Commerce-designate on December 2, 1952, "we hope to discontinue such controls as this becomes possible in favor of indirect controls, which under a sound fiscal program, are much more effective." (*Fortune,* Feb. 1956, "The Eisenhower Shift" by Charles J. V. Murphy.) In spite of favoring "indirect controls" and a failure to achieve a sound fiscal program, the last price control was lifted after Eisenhower had been in office less than two months.

Eisenhower can also be credited by anti-statists for attempting to move the government out of the electric power business. He had some successes and some failures. He recognized the subterfuge by which Roosevelt II had extended the original Federal intervention (Muscle Shoals, 1907-1925) in the power industry.

"Although," wrote Ike in *Mandate for Change,* "the government established TVA in 1933 principally to control floods, preserve farmland, and improve navigation—with power production as a side-effect—by 1957 the operating expense of its power program totalled nearly $178 million, against the expenses of all other functions of about $9 million. Although in 1939 TVA produced nearly all of its power in hydroelectric plants, by 1956 its steam plants were producing 70 per cent of the total." Thus, when late in 1953 pressure was brought to have TVA build a steam generating station to take care of the power needs of the city of Memphis, Eisenhower balked.

"I told the group," Eisenhower related, "that I could see no justification in building a steam plant for Memphis, to be paid for by the nation's taxpayers, any more than for any other city in the United States." (59, p 377)

Because of this refusal, the city fathers of Memphis decided to sell bonds in the public market to finance their power plant. But the victory was a skirmish and not a major battle, for Eisenhower goes on to say that ". . . during my eight years in office the TVA prospered. Between 1953 and June 1960 it took on . . . nearly 100,000 new customers. It boosted its kilowatt-hour output nearly two and a half times, adding 38 million kilowatts compared to the 25 million added in a similar period prior to my inauguration." (59, p 385) Eisenhower didn't explain why he felt it was right for all the taxpayers to pay for this expansion of services to the residents near the Tennessee River Valley yet he felt it was unjustified to expect all the taxpayers to pay for Memphis' power plant.

Under Eisenhower, the proposed Federal Snake River power development was turned over to the Idaho Power Company. During the twenty years of the New and Fair Deals, the Federal Power Commission licensed about 1.8 million kilowatts of private generating capacity in the Northwest. During Eisenhower's eight years, 5 million kilowatts of private capacity was licensed. Eisenhower also attempted, unsuccessfully, to have the Rural Electrification Administration charge 4 per cent rather than 2 per cent interest for the Federal money it loaned. This would have at least partially eliminated taxpayer subsidization of REA activities. Congress, however, was uncooperative.

Professor Norman A. Graebner, writing in *Current History*, made the comment that "whatever the composition and interest of the new (*Eisenhower*) leadership, it could not ignore the twin legacies of the past—the New Deal and the cold war. Republican leaders might speak the rhetoric of free enterprise, but in the essential areas of national action they deviated scarcely from the Truman tradition. Secretary Humphrey (*of the Treasury Department*) could neither dismantle the budget nor halt the continuing inflation.[1] Nor could Secretary Benson return the American farmer to free enterprise. Eventually he would hand out more in agricultural subsidies than any of his Democratic predecessors."

Albertson evaluated Eisenhower's alleged conservatism by quoting from a speech by Gabriel Hauge, economic aide to the president. Eisenhower "was 'cognizant of the thievery and worse that price inflation visits on the citizenry . . .' Nevertheless, the Eisenhower conservative sought 'to conserve the market mechanism when the government must act to avert depression or inflation.' "

"There was little here," Albertson then stated, "with which free enterprise might quarrel unless one wished to take issue with the 'moderative' character of the Eisenhower government. The words, meant to rally the conservative Republican faithful to the crusade, belied an internal policy which maintained and occasionally improved upon the welfare aims of the New Deal." (56, pp xv-xvi)

Albertson is dead wrong in concluding that advocates of free enterprise would assent to government intervention to avoid a depression. Government intervention in the form of deficit spending, inflation, and pump priming would be opposed by anyone understanding the nature of free enterprise for these are the antithesis of and incompatible with the free market and free enterprise. They are incongruous.

Dean Albertson has, on the other hand, focussed sharply on the mismatch between the Eisenhower administration's words

[1] The Cost of Living Index of the Bureau of Labor Statistics, although subject to political manipulation, is the best readily available index of the *results* of inflation. Using 1947–1949 as a base of 100, the percentage rise in the C.O.L. each year, compared to the preceding year has been as follows:

| 1952 | +0.7 | 1954 | −0.8 | 1956 | +3.2 | 1958 | +1.3 |
| 1953 | +1.14 | 1955 | +0.3 | 1957 | +3.6 | 1959 | +1.3 |

The base was changed to 1957–1959 equal to 100 in 1960. The rise in the C.O.L. for subsequent years was

1960	+1.6	1963	+1.7	1966	+3.3	1969	+6.0
1961	+0.6	1964	+1.1	1967	+3.1	1970	+5.6
1962	+1.2	1965	+2.0	1968	+4.7	1971	+3.9 (est)

Because of the lag between deficits and the results of deficits and the lag between inflation (i.e. increase in money supply) and results of inflation (i.e. rise of prices) Eisenhower should be held responsible for the years 1955 to 1962 inclusive, Kennedy for the years 1963 to 1965, and Johnson 1966 to 1970.

and deeds. While claiming for itself moderate-conservative leanings it drove the country further down the New Deal free-
way, it expanded compulsory social security, it enlarged Federal
interventions in housing, slum clearance, education, the TVA,
farmers affairs, and in public health, it intervened in the economy
via Federal deficit spending, and it permitted inflation to continue
(See cost of living figures previously quoted. During Eisenhower's eight years, the cost of living rose 13.1 per cent, an improvement over the Truman years, but not a great one, considering
that Truman's term reflected the effects of World War II spending.)

Rovere concluded that Eisenhower "can treat a problem like
finance rather casually." For instance he reported that Eisenhower had said he believed that we could get "a sound money"
by proper use of "the Federal Reserve Bank and all that stuff." (57,
p 41)

Credit for whatever fiscal sanity Eisenhower showed should
go to George M. Humphrey, his Secretary of the Treasury, and
Joseph M. Dodge, his first Director of the Budget. Humphrey is
credited by Emmet John Hughes as saying in 1957 that "there
are a lot of places in this budget that can be cut." (12, p 236)
Hughes claimed that Humphrey's attack on the budget inflicted
"deep and irreparable damage upon the political repute and power
of his friend, the President of the United States." (12, p 241)
The budget for fiscal 1958 was finally cut by $4 billion, and
Sherman Adams, according to Hughes, wrote that "it was a
serious and disturbing personal defeat" (12, p 239) for Eisenhower. Humphrey resigned in 1957. The 1958 budget from which
he had succeeded in chopping $4 billion ran a $2.8 billion deficit.
The next year, without Humphrey, the deficit jumped to $12.4
billion. Depending upon whether or not social security and other
trust fund receipts are included as income, the total gross deficit
for the Eisenhower years was either $27.6 (*The 1971 World
Almanac*, p 82) or $23.4 (*U. S. News and World Report*, v
LXXI, no. 7, Aug. 16, 1971, pp 24-25) billion. After subtracting
the two or three years of surplus, as reported in the respective
sources, the total net deficits were either $24.7 or $15.8 billion.

After a year in office President Eisenhower delivered the 1954
State of the Union Message. He called for a public housing

program to construct 35,000 units a year, liberalization of social security, and movement into health insurance by guaranteeing private insurance companies against loss. Even though the size of the public housing program was miniscule, (the camel has only to get his nose under *one tent*) compared to total housing construction and although the social security proposals are an expansion of a socialist system already operating they are no less statist interventions than government guarantees against health insurance losses.

All three proposals are similar in that they offer benefits to certain groups at the expense of persons who are not members of the groups; the proposals differ with respect to which groups are special beneficiaries. Public housing proposals would reward contractors, construction workers and tenants; the expanded social security program would benefit those who receive immediate or increased coverage even though they have not contributed proportionately to the system; health insurance guarantees would favor the insurance industry. In each case, the cost is spread thinly over a large number of persons so diverse in character that they cannot organize to resist. In addition, these same persons are members of other special benefit groups, and on the basis of mutual back scratching would hesitate to resist even if organized.

The assumption may be made that if government "assistance" is widely enough distributed each person will receive enough to offset what he pays in taxes. If true, this would be a self-defeating admission of the failure of the welfare state, which is aimed at taking from those who allegedly don't need and giving to those who allegedly do need.

There are at least four important overlooked features of systems by which, with government as the friendly Federal middlemen, everyone seeks to live at the expense of everyone else. First, the accounting gets horribly complicated and one can never be sure he is getting back what he contributed. Putting it another way, the government is not bound to the practice of fair labeling and honest advertising, so the consumer is neither sure of the price nor the quality and quantity of the contents of the package he has been forced, by taxation, to purchase. The second overlooked feature of the system is its cost, above value received. This is brought about by the essentially nonproductive efforts of the cumbersome government apparatus which first collects and then disburses what is left over after the collection, handling, and disbursement costs have been deducted. Third, the system reduces the options open to the taxpayer to use his property (i.e. dollar earnings which are claims to goods and services) as he sees fit. He is instead forced, by taxation, to buy what he may, or may not, want. Fourth, the system has a self-expansionary bias, for as the consumer is forced to buy more and more from the government (through taxes) he becomes less able to buy in the free market what he really needs (such as housing, education, and medical care) and less and less able to save (for old age, unemployment, and those rainy days). He ends up being forced to beg the government to provide more and more "free" or "low-cost" services, which it can only do by more and more taxation, which results in fewer consumer options, more nonproductive government efforts, and even more obscure accounting.

President Eisenhower's message also urged federal "assistance" for school construction in the form of loans and grants which would "stimulate a total investment . . . of more than $7 billion in new school construction."

Learning is said to be the search for the truth, and yet there are no worse liars than some educators who make up the more-sacred-than-mother education lobby.

In 1955, according to Eisenhower's *The White House Years: Mandate for Change*, "as a result of the burgeoning population, there existed an estimated deficit of more than 300,000 classrooms in our country. The current building rate, then 60,000 a year, was doing little more than keeping up with increasing student numbers." (59, pp 499-500) In 1957, Eisenhower wrote in *The White House Years: Waging Peace* "the United States, according to calculations of the Department of Health, Education, and Welfare, had a shortage of 159,000 classrooms. The states were building sixty-nine thousand classrooms a year, enough to stay one jump ahead of the increase needed every year but not to cut materially into the shortage." (20, p 138)

Congress did nothing in 1955 on the president's request, and yet, miraculously, the shortage dwindled in two years from 300,-000 to 159,000! This, in spite of a building rate that was barely "keeping up with increasing student numbers." Congress, sensing that since doing nothing had solved the 1955 problem, decided to do nothing again in 1957!

Eisenhower's statism was not always on a multibillion dollar scale. For instance, he ordered the Secretary of Health, Education, and Welfare to arrange for distribution of the Salk polio vaccine in 1955, as he put it "to make certain that no child in the United States would be denied this emergency protection for want of ability to pay." The government appropriated $28 million for purchasing vaccine, and it was indiscriminately given to the nonneedy as well as the needy, and not only to children. No libertarian would deny the goal, but to achieve it by government action reflects the abandonment of faith in voluntary charity efforts. The "easy" solution is always for the government to use its tax power. Of course, anyone opposing such government activities is likely to be accused of being hard, selfish, insensitive, and mean, a hater of children, the poor, the old or the sick, as the case may be.

At the end of Eisenhower's first term, Richard Rovere wrote "The administration may still proclaim its hostility to 'creeping socialism,' but one hears little said in dispraise of the 'welfare state' . . . he has bent before the wind—indeed before the gentlest of breezes. He has not been hard enough to be called a true conservative." (57, p 346) The same statement could just as well have been made at the end of Ike's second term.

The Eisenhower appointments of Earl Warren and William J. Brennan, Jr. to the Supreme Court were, from a libertarian and anti-statist viewpont, probably the supreme domestic disasters of his presidency. Eisenhower had the opportunity to swing the court to a non-interventionist, limited government, anti-statist stance, and away from its position as an agency of social, rather than legal, justice. He failed and his failure was a legacy of long life. In addition, Warren had as qualifications no record of practice before the court, he had no scholarly reputation of brilliance, legal or otherwise, and, in fact, he was not even recognized as a practising attorney. To commend him he had only a bill for services rendered as the man who, at a crucial moment during the 1952 Republican national convention, insured Ike's nomination for the presidency. There is evidence that Eisenhower later regretted his appointment.

The Eisenhower Administration made real progress in the treatment of negroes in Federal jobs and the armed services. But Emmet Hughes reported that Eisenhower, referring to the school integration decisions said, "I am convinced that the Supreme Court decision set back progress in the South at least fifteen years . . . It's all very well to talk about school integration—if you remember you may also be talking about social disintegration. Feelings are deep on this . . . We can't demand perfection in these moral questions . . . And the fellow who tries to tell me that you can do these things by force is just plain nuts." (12, p 209)

The Republican Platform of 1952 contained a plank attributed to John Foster Dulles, who later became Eisenhower's Secretary of State. The Republicans proposed to "mark the end of the negative, futile, and immoral policy of 'containment' which abandons countless human beings to a despotism and godless terrorism . . ." Presidential candidate Eisenhower's campaign speech of August 25, 1952, expanded this theme.

After recounting Communist post-war conquests of the countries of Europe and Asia, Eisenhower said, "We can never rest—and we must so inform all the world, including the Kremlin—that until the enslaved nations of the world have in the fullness of freedom the right to chose their own path, that then, and only then, can we say there is a possible way of living peacefully and permanently with communism in the world.

"We must tell the Kremlin that never shall we desist in our aid to . . . any man who keeps burning among his people the flame of freedom or who is dedicated to the liberation of his fellows."

The intent of the platform planks and of Eisenhower's rhetorical elaboration may have been commendable, but the end results did not advance the American stand against international Communist aggression. These policies contributed to the premature and futile riots of June 1955 in East Berlin, the Polish riots a year later, and the Hungarian revolution of October 1956. The Hungarian revolt was the bloodiest and, in terms of human suffering, the costliest of these uprisings, all the more tragic because it was so ruthlessly put down by the USSR while the administration which had encouraged the revolt was unwilling to give military help because it feared that it might lead to war.

Adlai Stevenson, Eisenhower's Democrat opponent, foresaw the consequences. "The cruel grip of Soviet tyranny," said Stevenson in his Labor Day answer to Eisenhower a week later, ". . . can not be loosened by awakening false hopes which might stimulate intemperate action that would only lead . . . to the execution squads: we remember only too well how thousands went to their death in Warsaw but a few short years ago." Yet Stevenson had nothing better to offer than the continuing bankruptcy of negotiation. "I tell you now," said Stevenson, "that I will never fear to negotiate in good faith with the Soviet Union . . ."

The Korean War and associated problems pressed upon the new president who took office in early 1953. Eisenhower took a first sensible step to undo one of the mistakes of the Truman administration in his State of the Union message.

"In June 1950, following the aggressive attack on the Republic of Korea," said the president, "the United States Seventh Fleet was instructed both to prevent attack upon Formosa and also to insure that Formosa should not be used as a base of operations against the Chinese Communist mainland . . . but since the Chinese Communists have joined the North Koreans in attacking the South . . . consequently, there is no longer any logic or sense in a condition that required the United States Navy to assume defensive responsibilities on behalf of the Chinese Communists . . ."

Then falling back into the American habit of always trying to be nice guys, a futile gesture when dealing with Communists, the president flawed his performance by adding ". . . this order implies no aggressive intent on our part . . ." He then recovered enough to say that ". . . we certainly have no obligation to protect a nation fighting us in Korea."

The threat of stronger action, possibly coupled with Stalin's death on March 5, 1953, brought the Korean fighting to a halt on July 27, 1953, two years after talks with the North Koreans had begun. Eric Goldman, the liberal Princeton historian and no admirer of the president, described the Eisenhower tactics.

"Eisenhower," wrote Goldman in his book *The Crucial Decade and After—1945-1960*, "agreed with Dulles that the Communists should be told that the new American policy was: peace or else. The Administration would continue to negotiate sincerely. But if the stalemate went on, the United States would fight to win, and this meant air attacks beyond the Yalu and the tactical use of atomic arms. The Secretary of State undertook to see to it that the Chinese thoroughly understood the American position. He explained it personally to Prime Minister Nehru of India—a man with decidedly good communication lines to Peiping." (58, pp 243-257)

But the end of the war in Korea was "The Unmentionable Victory"—to liberals and anti-communists alike. Richard Rovere, former editor of the communist-oriented *New Masses* and later assistant editor of the radical left *Nation*, occasionally found himself on the same side as the conservatives. (For instance, he held Senator Robert A. Taft, Sr. in high regard.) Chapter 17 of his book *Affairs of State: The Eisenhower Years* is titled "The Unmentionable Victory." The gist of this chapter, which deals with the Korean War and the armistice, is that the end result was a victory for the Communists. In Washington, only Dulles and the State Department, according to Rovere, fail to recognize it as such. Katherine Tabor's letter to *Life*, previously mentioned and quoted in part, summarized the situation, ". . . They had no right to send men to die without intending to win. If they had wanted to they could have defeated the Chinese Communists. They have not used every means available to do so. It is not right. It is intolerably unjust." By 1959, under the same president who negotiated "The Unmentionable Victory" in Korea, the first Americans died in Vietnam. History was planning a replay.

Eisenhower's efforts were more successful in checking the Communists in Guatemala in June of 1954. Here, Colonel Jacobo Arbenz Guzmán, who had taken power in 1950, was by 1953 openly following the Communist line. Ambassador John E. Peurifoy testified on October 8, 1953 to the House Select Committee on Communist Aggression that the "Communist conspiracy centered in Guatemala represented a menace to the security of the United States." In March of 1954, the United States introduced a resolution at the tenth meeting of the Organization of American States which declared that "domination . . . of the political institutions of any American State by the International Communist movement" constituted a "threat to the sovereignty and political independence of the American States, and would call for appropriate action in accordance with existing treaties." This was approved 17 to 1, with two abstentions. Guatemala continued to move toward a Communist dictatorship and on June 18, 1954 was invaded by a force of 200 men from Honduras under the command of Colonel Carlos Castillo Armas. This force was given indirect United States support and an arms blockade was attempted to prevent shipment of arms to the Guatemalan Communists. Castillo Armas deposed Arbenz Guzmán who hastily left for Czechoslovakia.

Eisenhower's Middle East policies are not made easier to understand by a paragraph in his *Waging Peace* which described the 1955 situation, a year before the Suez Canal crisis.

"These Communist efforts to foment difficulties were of course completely consistent with their avowed and continuing design to cause global confusion. At the moment the Reds apparently believed that the Middle East provided an unusually bright opportunity to make inroads into the Free World and to disrupt the normally close cooperation among the nations of the West . . . We had to step in to counter the weight of Soviet power." (20, p 25)

If Eisenhower really believed in his words as a statement of policy, the condemnation by the United States, joined by the USSR, of its anti-Communist allies France, England, and Israel in late 1956 is a mystery. Retelling the story shows that the USSR acted with consistency, but not the United States.

The Suez Canal was an international waterway, 44 per cent of whose shares were owned by the British government, 50 per cent by French citizens, and 6 per cent by others. Additionally, the other nations of the world were vitally interested that it should remain open as a trade route. This was true not only of European nations who were *using* the oil shipped through it, but also of the Middle East nations who were *selling* the oil shipped through it. Lengthy negotiations between the British and Egyptians had failed to resolve the differences over its operation and defense.

On July 26, 1956 President Gamel Abdel Nasser seized and nationalized the canal, using as a pretext that Egypt needed the canal tolls to finance the Aswan irrigation and power dam. Nasser ordered that all employees of the Suez Canal Company, including non-Egyptians, remain at their jobs under threat of prison sentences for disobedience. Over the next few months Egyptians took over operation of the canal, including pilot duties. Meanwhile, Israeli and Egyptian troops had expanded their sporadic skirmishing, and on October 29, 1956, Israel invaded the Sinai Peninsula, which borders the canal. The French and British demanded a cease-fire which was rejected by Egypt. On October 31st the British and French jointly bombed Egypt and on November 5th put troops ashore. At this point the United States condemned the British and French and supported a UN move for a cease-fire. All four nations involved in the fighting accepted the UN call and fighting stopped on November 7th. The British and French withdrew their forces, but not before the Egyptians blocked the canal by sinking thirty ships in it. This closed the canal until March 1957 when the last of the obstacles was removed. It was closed again in 1967 during the Six Day War between Egypt and Israel and remains closed at this writing.

The net result of the action strengthened Nasser's position as the leader of anti-Western, pro-Soviet Arab nations. It also accelerated substitution of Soviet colonialism for European colonialism in Africa. Communist influence in the Eastern Mediterranean countries and in North Africa was extended, and Israel alone remained to block the Soviets southward thrust in this area.

". . . it was to be in Eisenhower's administration," wrote William S. White, with regret, if not amazement, "that we would support the Russians in denouncing as aggressive invasion this convulsive leap of our friends into Egypt to meet the peril demonstrably gathering about their (*and our*) vitals in the Middle East." (5, p 153)

A year and a half after the Suez flap, Eisenhower got a second chance to do something about Russian expansion in the Middle East. He did a better job this time around.

The countries around the Eastern end of the Mediterranean are predominantly Arab countries ruled by dictators or tribal kings. Intrigue and instability have been heightened by the presence of Israel and the varying degrees of hostility shown by Israel's Arab neighbors. Communist penetration into the area, exploiting this hostility, led in 1958 to the formation of the United Arab Republic, consisting of Syria and Egypt. The UAR was oriented toward communism but was not completely dominated by Communists. In July of 1958, Iraq and Jordan formed a loose federation, known as the Arab Union, to counter the threat of being gobbled up by the UAR. Excepting for the small country of Yemen, most Arab nations leaned toward the west rather than toward the UAR and the Soviet Union, but all were bound by hostility toward Israel. This was true of Lebanon, an Arab country whose population is equally divided between Moslem Arabs and Christian Arabs. Palestinian refugees in Lebanon became useful tools of leftists and UAR agitators.

Eisenhower recognized the source of the trouble, but unlike his reaction to Suez, he did not botch the job.

"Behind everything," wrote Eisenhower in *Waging Peace*, "was our deep-seated conviction that the Communists were principally responsible . . .

"Although temporarily pursuing a 'soft' propaganda line, the Communists were pushing everywhere, stirring up trouble in Venezuela, Indonesia, and Burma, not to mention the Middle East. Radio Cairo, which was blasting forth its encouragement to the Lebanese rebels, was an additional annoyance . . . The Lebanon-Syrian border was open to a steady influx of Syrians who meant no good to Chamoun's (*pro-Western Lebanese*) government.

"On the 22nd of May President Chamoun requested an urgent meeting of the Security Council (*of the UN*) to consider his complaint that Egypt and Syria had been instigating the revolt and arming the rebels . . .

"The situation in Lebanon, which had seemed to be quieting, was now made critical by events in another land—Iraq. On Monday morning, July 14, 1958, I was shocked to receive news of a coup in Baghdad . . . This was the country we were counting on . . . as a bulwark of stability and progress in the region." (20, pp 266-269)

Pro-Nasser UAR rebels in Iraq, supported by neighboring Syrians on Iraq's western boundary, engineered the assassination of King Faisal and his prime minister, overthrowing Iraq's pro-Western government. This increased the threat to already-threatened Lebanon, Syria's western neighbor. The stability of Jordan, the other member of the Arab Union, was also put under stress.

The United States, for once, was ready. American forces landed in Lebanon on July 15, 1958 and stimultaneously British forces occupied Jordan with United States logistic support. In both cases the established governments of Lebanon and Jordan requested outside help. The Lebanese rebels were routed and a strong pro-Western government succeeded President Chamoun when his term expired. Stability was maintained in Jordan and Communist expansion was stopped. It is possible that an error was made by not entering Iraq and toppling the government of General Kassim. King Saud of Saudi Arabia suggested this, but nothing was done and Iraq fell into the UAR-Communist orbit.

Chapter 21 of Dwight Eisenhower's *Waging Peace* begins with a quote from brother Milton's book *The Wine is Bitter:* "We can not afford the luxury of ignorance; it costs too much." A more appropriate introduction to the story of the most costly foreign policy blunder of Eisenhower's presidency could not have been penned, for ignorance of the true nature of Castro and Castroism permitted the establishment of the first Communist regime in the Western Hemisphere.

President Eisenhower wrote that "a bearded young man named Fidel Castro had succeeded in gathering together a band of about a thousand guerrillas in the Escambray Mountains, a force promising to throw out the self-enriching and corrupt dictator Fulgencio Batista and end the suppressions and brutality of his police state." (20, p 520) The appeal to Ike's American sense of justice coupled with the luxury of ignorance ultimately led the president to proclaim a policy of non-intervention.

"We repeatedly," continued Eisenhower, "seized cargoes of arms headed for Castro and in March suspended the delivery of arms to Batista . . .

"During . . . the final days of 1958, the Central Intelligence Agency suggested for the first time that a Castro victory might not be in the best interests of the United States. (Earlier reports I had received of Castro's possible Communism were suspect because they originated with people who favored Batista.)

"One of my advisers recommended that the United States should now back Batista as the lesser of two evils. I rejected that, of course . . . our only hope, if any, lay with some kind of non-dictatorial 'third force', neither Castroite nor Batistiano." (20, p 521)

Eisenhower was so pathetically naive and indecisive about Castro, that as late as the middle of April 1959 he did not disapprove a State Department visa for the new dictator. Castro came to Washington in triumph to address the American Society of Newspaper Editors.

The worst that Eisenhower could say at this time, after Castro had embarked on a mass execution of his opponents and had announced a two year postponement of promised elections was, "Having personally become highly suspicious that Castro was a Communist . . ."

The President's statement that anti-Castro reports were suspect because they came from supporters of Batista was more than matched by Ike's abysmal failure to recognize that the information he chose to believe was filtered through and evaluated by the State Department Caribbean Desk, occupied by the notorious pro-communist William Wieland.

Evelyn Lincoln, John F. Kennedy's secretary, relates an incident in her book *Kennedy and Johnson* which bears on why Ike was so easily misled.

"One day Senator Dirksen called on Mr. Kennedy," wrote Mrs. Lincoln. "After he left, Mr. Kennedy came out to my desk and said, 'Do you know what the Senator told me today? Dirksen told me, *"Let's face it, Eisenhower did not know much about what was going on during his administration. He would call a group in—let others do most of the talking—he used to sit and doodle for about two hours and then he would say, 'okay, boys, who is going to carry the ball?'* " The Senator said that it was frightening—Eisenhower's lack of knowledge of what was taking place and the things he didn't know about the United States Government.' " (60, pp 190-191)

Wieland, to get back to the Castro fiasco, was appointed to his post in 1957 over the protests of Ambassador William Pawley, who warned both the State Department and the President of Wieland's strange background. Wieland was responsible for the policy of withholding arms shipments from Batista, and less than a year later Castro's forces were victorious. While Wieland was managing the Caribbean Desk in the State Department Ambassador Arthur Gardner, and later Ambassador Earl T. Smith, both of whom opposed Castro, were replaced.

Truly, "we can not afford the luxury of innocence; it costs too much."

The parallels between the loss of Cuba and the loss of China to the Communists are so obvious that even a nitwit would be expected to recognize them. In both cases the revolutionists were portrayed as "mere agrarian reformers." In both cases, distorted reporting by the press aided the revolutionists. The Chinese Communists had Owen D. Lattimore as an advocate in *The New York Times*, *The Saturday Evening Post*, *Colliers* and in publications of The Institute of Pacific Relations. Castro had on his side Herbert Matthews of *The New York Times*. In 1972 Matthews was still offering the lame excuse that Castro, at the start, was not a Communist. (Did he mean as a new born babe?) In both cases arms shipments to the anti-Communists were stopped by the State Department. In both cases friendly governments were replaced by unfriendly, threatening governments. Regimes which were said to be corrupt and known to be brutal were replaced by regimes equally or more corrupt and in which brutality was an efficient large scale public service rather than a small scale private hobby. The bill for the China policy was partly paid in Korea, with later installments still being rendered for service in Indo-China. The bill for Cuba has not yet been tallied.

In view of the China debacle it is almost incomprehensible that Eisenhower could have repeated the experience in Cuba. His only claim to redemption rests on planning and preparing for the Bay of Pigs invasion. Even here there was such a delay that the program could not be executed until after he left office, and this led to another failure. Eisenhower started too late; Kennedy arrived with too little.

CHAPTER 14

PRINCE CHARMING

The winter wind had swept away the clouds and snow and now the towers of Camelot sparkled brightly in the sky. The old bard, shielding his eyes from the sun's bright glare, wisps of his white locks rippling in the breeze, proclaimed that "the land was ours long before we were the land's." Then Boston's beloved lantern-jawed prelate, intoned a long, long, very long prayer, strident voice rising and falling to the cadence of his phrases, until smoke swirled from the lectern as if protesting the length of the benediction or perhaps as an evil omen of the sad fate that was to befall the gallant prince.[1]

What manner of man was this prince? His courtiers had made fun of old King Ike's syntactical struggles, they had made sure that throughout the realm it was known that speechwriters and actors coached the old king when he had appeared before the all-seeing eye, and they had even whispered that the brave Republican Knights were mere Madison Avenue Mercenaries. The prince was, by comparison, at least, pure; the prince was charming, and there was no dragon the prince could not slay. But weren't there Merlins in Prince Charming's court, too? Was the prince real or just a myth? A little of both perhaps, for the miracles of the twentieth century created the prince and hid the man.

Before the age of press photography most voters had only a vague idea of what presidential candidates looked like, so looks counted for little. And before the XIXth amendment many ladies couldn't vote and even among those who could, many didn't, so that manly virility counted for even less. But in 1920 the news

---

[1] The prayer of Cardinal Cushing seemed almost as long as the inaugural address itself. The smoke from the lectern was caused by an electrical fire. It was neither a protest nor prophecy.

photographers had a cooperative and photogenic candidate, the girls trooped to the polls in unprecedented numbers, and a handsome Senator from Ohio was sent to the White House. This is not to say that looks and sex appeal decided all, for they didn't, and they wouldn't in the next two elections. Cal Coolidge in 1924 was no matinee idol and could hardly be expected to arouse female instincts, but he was an incumbent and the country had never before been more prosperous. Under the circumstances, any incumbent, even an Australian aborigine, could have won in 1924. Four years later, choosing Hoover and Smith as the candidates of their respective parties, the politicians once again neglected the possibilities of capturing the women's vote and ignored the power of the photographic image. The lesson of Harding had not been learned. Nor was the political power of radio, another twentieth century miracle yet appreciated.

By 1932 prosperity had deserted Hoover and incumbency's dividend was censure rather than acclaim. The Great Engineer no longer was so great. The race was a contest between the Glumest Man in Town and a Gay Blade. It was as if radio had been invented for Franklin Roosevelt's voice, photography for his face, and the female franchise for his virility. Thus, was insured the demise of the dour Mr. Hoover. Four times the golden-voiced charmer with the jaunty jaw would be victorious.

In 1948, Dewey's honeyed baritone competence should have overwhelmed Harry Truman, and would have, but for the scrappy determination of the incumbent and the challenger's rash presumptuousness. After all, polish and a good voice can't do it all alone.

But by 1952 glamor, abetted now by television, once again was decisive. The Republicans, blinded by the hero's glitter, chose the hale and hearty general over the able, experienced, and intelligent Ohio senator. Unfortunately for Taft, he was not exactly a photographer's model, nor a hale fellow well met and, to boot, his voice was hardly soothing. Republicans, however, after thirty years on the outside looking in, wanted an *attractive* candidate, and they were not about to be sidetracked by trivial considerations such as ability—or lack thereof—in their choice. Eisenhower's grin and glamor came across on television as strong as Roosevelt's voice and charm had come across on radio thirty years before, and in the end Ike's heroic luster, matched against Stevenson's urbane wit, won out.

But the 1960 election demonstrated, more than any previous election, the potential of the XIXth Amendment, the miracles of the twentieth century, photography, radio, and television, and the political advantage of a well-spoken handsome male candidate—as well as the advantage of having the make-up men, lighting technicians, and camera men on your side. After the election, the marvels of the modern world were not retired and forgotten.

Jacques Lowe was the Kennedy campaign photographer who followed Prince Charming to the White House as a semi-official picture taker. He performed well with the help of an able and cooperative subject, and he recognized the importance of the candidate's (to use an overworked word) image. Victor Lasky, who wrote *JFK, the Man and the Myth,* quoted from an article by Lowe which appeared in *Editor and Publisher.*

"Let's face it," Lowe wrote, sounding for all the world like Marshall McLuhan, "We're in an age when the visual means more than the word to the great mass of the people who decide an election one way or another. They looked at the debates (*between Kennedy and Nixon*) but many didn't listen to what was said but they studied how the candidates looked."

Kennedy's increasing popularity in the face of dismal defeats and failures as a president testify to the value of a hearty public relations effort. He was continuously featured in the popular general circulation magazines and his wife provided endless copy for the true romance-movie-television journals devoured by women at their beauty bars. Live and taped television programs were produced to show how the president lived and made, or didn't make, decisions.

"The Kennedy build-up goes on," wrote James MacGregor Burns in the *New Republic.* "The adjectives tumble over one another. He is not only the handsomest, the best-dressed, the most articulate, and graceful as a gazelle. He is omniscient; he swallows and digests whole books in minutes; he confounds experts with his superior knowledge of their field. He is omnipotent." Even the courtiers began to worry about overdoing it; *overexposure* was their word.

Eric Goldman, one of liberalism's gifts to the Johnson adminis-

tration recorded what he admitted was a generally truthful, although somewhat inaccurate, appraisal of President Kennedy.

"One pastime of a particular group of Johnsonians was to
take apart President Kennedy's reputation for interest in the
cultivated life. It was like his claim for being a connoisseur of
food, they said; when not putting on a display in the White
House, his choice was clam chowder and hamburger. They told
of the celebrated Cassals evening that, as soon as politeness
permitted, he made his way to a corner to talk politics with a
Boston henchman. In all of this there is some general truth, in-
accuracy in details and a crashing irrelevancy; the point is not
what a President himself likes and dislikes but what he encourages
and holds up before a country as good." (10, p 141)[2]

If many Americans are disillusioned with presidents who want
to seem to be what they aren't, and if there is a gap between
claims and reality, behavior of the type described is hardly irrelevant.

The shallowness of the Kennedy affection for artistic refinements should not have been unexpected. The Prince never showed
any interest in art, music, or literature until it became a political
asset to do so. He and his family's abiding interests were in
making money, their church, politics and power. And Jackie
Kennedy's professed interest in the refinements, so exploited by
the public relations experts, was the thin interest acquired in the
right finishing schools. Jackie had a hard time convincing anyone
she was an intellectual or serious about beauty, excepting her own.

The frivolous nature of the Kennedy culture cult is shown up
by comparison with another American political family, the Tafts.
The Taft's were intellectuals. William Howard Taft, finished
second at Yale, whereas Kennedy was a mediocre student at Harvard. Pringle, Taft's biographer, stated that "ordinarily," Taft
was not quickly stimulated by the aesthetic things of life. Music
bored although it sometimes soothed him. He cared almost as

---

[2] It is interesting to note that this passage in Professor Goldman's book follows two and a half pages of quotes taken from letters written to Goldman
by an assortment of liberals. These letters repeatedly stress the low quality
of American morality and a general revival of interest in the non-material
aspects of living, themes in which Goldman, liberal that he is, professes
interest. It is incredible that Goldman ignores the Kennedy guile and dis-
misses criticism of it as irrelevant. Sham and chicanery become immoral in
the liberal view only when used for selling deodorant or Republicans.

little for art." (29, p 172) However Ishbel Ross wrote that "Taft's own tastes and sophistication led him instinctively to cultivate men of letters during his term of office and he was in his element at a dinner given for William Dean Howells, celebrating the writer's seventy-fifth birthday." (27, p 238)

Taft was quite unlike Kennedy who put Robert Frost on display at his televised inaugural ceremonies and then proceeded to ignore him as he lay dying in 1963. (This cost Amherst College the private papers of Robert Frost, who was long connected with the school. When Frost's family learned that President Kennedy had been chosen to dedicate the Frost Library on the campus, they decided that the papers would be deposited elsewhere. Loss of an invaluable collection was the price the college paid for a fleeting flirtation with Prince Charming.)

The contrast between the two presidents extends to their immediate families. A Taft brother and a Taft nephew were Cincinnati patrons of the arts. Another brother founded the Taft School, and Taft's daughter became a Dean of Bryn Mawr. Of the vast Kennedy clan, only Jack Kennedy's brother Ted made an academic reputation for himself and this was for being expelled from Harvard for cheating on a language examination. His later behavior at Chappaquidick hardly qualifies him as a lover of the arts.

There is a contrast between the two president's wives, as well. "A succession of gifted artists, musicians, and writers performed at the White House . . . Mrs. Taft . . . made a point of staging Shakespearian productions . . . ," according to Ishbel Ross. (27, p 238) In Pringle's frank, and sometimes uncomplimentary, book he gave this description of the future Mrs. Taft: "On the surface, Miss Herron must have been just a little formidable; she had a firm way of taking charge at literary discussions. She maintained a salon where culture permeated the atmosphere. She was very musical." (29, p 70) On the other hand, Jackie Kennedy was a society photographer for a Washington newspaper, and the Kennedy's intimates included the so-called Rat Pack, whose members were not known for their addiction to the finer side of life.

The Democrat Convention of 1968 will long be remembered for the blue name calling that went on. Beside the hapless police and Mayor Daley, Gore Vidal and William Buckley got in the act by verbally assaulting each other on live television. Vidal, resorting to a four-letter epithet, called Buckley a Nazi. Buckley, who ordinarily can't express himself in words of less than five syllables, responded magnificently by calling Vidal a "damned queer." Neither charge has ever been legally established, but that is beside the point. All this is mentioned only to prove that if Buckley is a conservative, as generally acknowledged, then Vidal, his opposite, must be a liberal. And as a liberal, Vidal's view of his liberal kissing cousins, (by marriage) the Kennedy's, must be given some weight by detached and impartial observers.

Vidal has described the Prince as mediocre and claimed that Kennedy reached the top by virtue of imperious family wealth and connections. The worldwide myths surrounding the dead Prince are stronger than were the accomplishments of the living president in Vidal's eyes. All the work of a slick, high-powered public relations effort.

That erstwhile dean of the liberals, Walter Lippmann, was also unkind to the late president. "Kennedy was out of his depth," Lippmann is reported to have concluded, in agreement with Dean Acheson, Truman's liberal Secretary of State. "The result is that we had that very dangerously inflated inaugural speech, and then we had the Bay of Pigs and a lot of other things, and the mess he made during his meeting with Khrushchev in Vienna. Only in the last few months of his life did he begin to see things more or less in their true proportion." (Quoted in *Human Events*, v XXXII, no. 6, Feb. 5, 1972, p 2.)

Kennedy, a liberal as president, was not always a liberal. When he was a senator he managed to wangle a job for his brother Bobby as special counsel to Senator Joseph R. McCarthy, who it turned out, was not liberalism's favorite. When Joe McCarthy was in the process of being censured by the Senate, Kennedy ducked the vote giving illness as his excuse. He wasn't, however, so ill that he was prevented from taking a stand, which he failed to do. This was probably the origin of Mrs. Roosevelt's well-known wrath and displeasure.

He was solidly conservative in the true sense of the word when, in 1954, he opposed in the Senate a proposed amendment to the Constitution which would have lowered the voting age to

18. All opponents of the amendment were either Republican or Southern states' righters—excepting for Senator John F. Kennedy. Rovere reported Kennedy as saying that "reluctance to amend the Constitution is one of our most valuable safeguards and bulwarks of stability."

Senator John F. Kennedy and eight other Democrats who are generally classed as liberals (including Lyndon Johnson, Fulbright, and Kefauver) unsuccessfully voted to send Eisenhower's 1957 civil rights proposals back to the Senate Judiciary Committee where it faced certain death. Later in the session Kennedy supported a jury-trial amendment which civil rights leaders vigorously opposed as weakening the legislation. (20)

The Nixon and Kennedy of 1960 were compared by Emmet John Hughes in *Ordeal of Power*. "Yet the difference in *substance*," wrote Hughes, "between these two young veterans of the Senate—whether measured by their views on national defense, their precepts of foreign policy, or their passion for civil liberties—were so small as almost to elude expression." (12, p 313)

The Prince was as strong on rhetoric as he was on charm. Kennedy, campaigning for the presidency early in 1960, said that "in the challenging, revolutionary Sixties, the American Presidency will demand more than ringing manifestoes issued from the rear of the battle. It will demand that the President place himself in the very thick of the fight . . .

"He must above all be the Chief Executive in every sense of the word. He must be prepared to exercise the fullest powers of his office . . . He must master complex problems as well as receive one-page memoranda.

"No president . . . can escape politics . . ."

All this, including the comments about one-page memoranda and escaping politics, was a not too veiled slap at Eisenhower.

The Kennedy rhetoric not only conjured up problems, it solved them too. During the 1960 campaign one of the frequent Kennedy charges was that the Republicans had allowed American missile development and production to lag dangerously behind that of the USSR. Did Kennedy as president take speedy action to end the so-called missile gap? He certainly did. In fact he ended it within eighteen days of taking office—by rhetoric. He had his Secretary of Defense, Robert McNamara, announce on

February 7, 1961 at the background briefing that there was no missile gap. (11, p 510) The missile gap disappeared in the same way it had materialized: via words.

The new 1961 Kennedy was a low-slung, snappy-looking, high-powered sports car. The lines were sporty, the interior could be described as chic, there was just the right amount of chrome in the right places, and the engine made the right noises. There was only one thing wrong with it—it wouldn't run. Someone forgot to supply the transmission and without a transmission you couldn't get all that zip and power to the wheels. However, parked in the driveway for show it impressed all the neighbors—excepting the ones in the house on the left, the house with the red clapboards. They were smart enough to know that car would never get anywhere unless it was pushed and they were happy to do the pushing. They pushed it into the Bay of Pigs, they pulled it out and pushed it around the Berlin Wall, through Vienna, back to Cuba for a missile crisis, and right on to the Congo and Vietnam.

The attempt at the Bay of Pigs to destroy the communist base in the west was not as successful as the elimination of the missile gap. Communists are not impressed by rhetoric.

Planning and training for the invasion commenced belatedly under the Eisenhower administration. It called for U.S. air support of the beachhead. Prince Charming decided against this and restricted air support to B-26 bombers to be flown from Guatemala (which was too far away) by Cuban defectors. This was bad enough, but to make matters worse, Secretary of State Dean Rusk, in a statement which matches Acheson's blunder of 1950,[3] issued a public statement that "there will not under any conditions be an intervention in Cuba by United States Armed Forces." Nothing could have added more to Castro's peace of mind.

Then, as if to insure failure, the president, under pressure from Adlai Stevenson (our UN Ambassador) and Dean Rusk, cancelled the second of the planned B-26 attacks from Guatemala.

When the invasion proceeded poorly, permission was restored to make attacks against Cuban air bases at will, but it was too late. By the first night the invaders were in desperate straits. In yet another panicky reversal, Kennedy authorized one hour of

[3] On January 12, 1950 Secretary of State Acheson announced that Korea was beyond our sphere of interest.

U. S. air support on the beachhead to cover landing of supplies the next morning. This did not occur as scheduled, which may have saved Dean Rusk's reputation as a truthful man, and the invasion collapsed. Indecision, errors resulting from inexperience, ignorance, political interference, and timidity made disaster a certainty. Kennedy, however, was honest enough to admit responsibility for the fiasco.

The Bay of Pigs fumble hardly put the Prince in a strong position to deal with the communists, specially on a face to face basis. This did not stop Jack and Jackie from journeying to Vienna to meet with Nikita and Nina. Presumably the American aim was to see if the Kennedy charm would yield a solution to problems like the division of Germany, restrictions on nuclear testing, and the growing aggression of North Vietnam. For Khrushchev the goal was much simpler—he wanted to size up his opponent. Khrushchev's preliminary estimate, formed as a result of the Bay of Pigs outing, that Kennedy was a pushover, was confirmed. (11, p 571) The Vienna tea party took place in June and before the summer was over, Khrushchev would confirm his preliminary evaluation.

The pressure point was Berlin, and as the weeks went by the tension mounted, ending in Khrushchev's ultimatum that Western forces be out of Berlin by Fall, that East Germany be recognized, and that a peace treaty with East Germany be concluded. After a month and a half of silence, the president finally appeared on television to reject Khrushchev's demands. Khrushchev's answer came three weeks later on August 13-14 when the Wall was built separating the East and West Sectors of the city. Lasky described Kennedy's reaction.

". . . once again Kennedy was caught off balance. As usual, on a weekend he was elsewhere than in Washington. This time he was sailing off Hyannisport . . ." This from the man who nineteen days earlier had warned that his rejection of Khrushchev's demands might mean nuclear war! ". . . the United States did nothing. In fact, it took days before the Allies could agree on a statement of protest. By that time, it was too late. The sealing off of East Berlin found the United States without a policy. The President and his advisers had assumed the Reds would return to the 1948 strategy of blockade." (11, p 573)

So the Berlin Wall stands as a monument to American failure to resist the aggressive encroachments of the communists. If, as the president said in his television address, we were prepared to risk nuclear war by rejecting Khrushchev's ultimatum, why did we not bulldoze the Wall and show a willinginess to use force, if necessary, to prevent its reconstruction? Was Kennedy's "Ich bin ein Berliner" speech another example of rhetoric without action?

The Berlin Wall stands not only as a monument to American timidity, it also is a monument to the failure of communism, for the traffic it stopped was the traffic of escape from tyranny, one-way traffic moving from East to West. The administration had been handed a magnificent opportunity for propaganda, but even this opportunity was largely wasted.

By late 1961 the trouble in the Congo resulted in a strange shift in American policy. The Communist-dominated regime of Patrice Lumumba, who had been killed early in the year, was fighting the anti-communist Katangese seccessionists under Moishe Tshombe. Kennedy, who had ruled against American intervention in Cuba, permitted American military planes to transport United Nations troops supporting the successors of Lumumba. Thus, within his first year in office, Kennedy withheld support from anti-communists close at hand and gave support to pro-communists at a distance!

All through the spring and summer of 1962, Kennedy repeatedly denied reports that the Russians were arming Cuba. In the fall, after continual prodding, the president finally confirmed the rumors. Lasky told the story in *JFK: The Man and The Myth.*

"President Kennedy's inability to convince the American people that his administration knew what it was doing in Cuba had alarmed even his supporters. In fact, Walter Lippmann began speaking of a 'crisis of confidence.' In February 1963, Lippmann pointed out that JFK had stated categorically on September 13, 1962, that Soviet shipments to Cuba 'do not constitute a serious threat to any other part of the hemisphere.'

"Two weeks later, Undersecretary of State George Ball told a Congressional committee there were no offensive weapons in Cuba.

"'But in fact there were,' commented Lippman. 'A week

later on October 10, Senator Keating *(liberal anti-communist New York Republican)* insisted that there were intermediate-range missiles in Cuba, and five days later the President received the photographs that confirmed the charge. This is how Senator Keating won the right to be listened to . . .' " (11, pp 550-551)

Kennedy ordered a naval blockade to stop Soviet missile shipments to Cuba. On October 28 an agreement was reached to end the crisis by which Russia agreed to dismantle the missile bases and remove the missiles from Cuba. The Soviets permitted American destroyers to "inspect" the homeward bound missiles by uncovering the missile cases lashed to the decks of their freighters. There were no assurances that the cases contained anything but air and there was no way of making sure that the missiles in Cuba were actually removed. There were, however, assurances from the administration that no deal had been made with the USSR. This proved to be untrue when Khrushchev announced on January 17, 1964 from Moscow that "we got a pledge that there will be no invasion of Cuba." The Kennedy campaign call of October 20, 1960 for U.S. intervention and aid to rebel forces in Cuba was forgotten.

The Cuban missile crisis was played for all it was worth in the 1962 off-year elections. In his column of November 11, 1962, three days after the election, Joe Alsop wrote that "until only a fortnight ago, the atmosphere of the Democratic campaign was downright dank, to put it mildly. The President's barnstorming on domestic issues had lighted no bonfires among the voters. There was no enthusiasm, no spark to ignite the faithful with excitement.

"Then came the Cuban crisis . . ."

The results showed up in the election returns which were generally favorable to the Democrats. Kennedy was a hero for establishing the blockade of Cuba, which he had said on September 30th his Republican opponents were promoting in order "deliberately to arouse public opinion."

The American role in Vietnam, which commenced under Eisenhower, was expanded under Kennedy. On June 2, 1962 the Majority Report of the International Control Commission (India, Canada, and Poland) stated that evidence showed North Vietnam to be supporting, organizing and carrying out hostile acts in

South Vietnam. By December of 1962, the American force had been increased about fourfold by Kennedy to a total of 4,000 men. A year later, when the president was assassinated there were 15,000 Americans in Vietnam and the country was in turmoil as a result of the assassination of President Ngo Dinh Diem (a little more than a month before Kennedy's death) and the ensuing coups. The death of Diem was one of the major foreign policy blunders for which the Kennedy administration must bear responsibility.

The *Pentagon Report,* based on stolen Pentagon documents, was summarized by the *New York Times* News Service. Here the blame for Diem's downfall was placed squarely on the Kennedy administration. The report charged the administration "with moves that encouraged and abetted the overthrow of President Ngo Dinh Diem of South Vietnam in 1963." (As published in the Boston *Sunday Herald Traveler,* June 13, 1971, Sec 1, pp 1, 27.)

Diem was a patriotic South Vietnamese anti-Communist with a record of effective civil service dating back to 1933. Both Diem and his brother Nhu were assassinated on November 1, 1963. It is not surprising that the Prince and Knights of Camelot would not greet Madame Nhu during her late October visit to Washington since at that very time they were plotting the downfall of her brother and brother-in-law. (The assassination may not have been a part of the original plot.) Following Diem's death, instability and turmoil crippled South Vietnamese resistance to the North Vietnamese communists and unnecessarily cost American lives.

Senator Mike Mansfield, Democrat majority leader, interviewed in late 1971, expressed his high regard for Diem and confirmed the serious nature of his loss.

Kennedy's favorite campaign pitches included promises to "get America moving again" and to "move America forward." After all, according to the Prince, we suffered from a missile gap, our prestige had never been lower, and the Republicans couldn't get the country off center because they couldn't control both congress and the presidency. We have seen what happened to the missile gap and American prestige after we crossed the New Frontier and arrived at the Berlin Wall and the Bay of Pigs. How did a Democrat-controlled congress and a Democrat president work out?

President Kennedy was rated generally as ineffective in his dealings with congress. That there is some truth in this view is supported by figures published by the *Congressional Quarterly*. These show that for his three years in office Kennedy managed to win approval for only 40 per cent of the proposals he sent to congress. Lyndon Johnson managed to win approval for 57 per cent of his proposals, and Eisenhower won approval for 45 per cent of his proposals during his last seven years of office (figures were not published for his first year), and in six of these he faced a Democrat-controlled house and senate. Since most of the Kennedy proposals were interventionist, anti-statists might wish to acclaim Kennedy as the best of these three presidents because his batting average was the lowest of all. However, batting averages don't mean much unless you know how many times the batter stands at the plate. Ike submitted an average of 216 proposals for each of his seven years and an average of 98 were approved each year. Johnson submitted an average of 380 and 218 were adopted, on average. For Kennedy the corresponding figures were 351 and 138. So Eisenhower should be the least unpopular with anti-statists, Johnson the most unpopular, and Kennedy somewhere in between. Kennedy was certainly less successful in handling congress than was Johnson. His proposals were rejected either because congress thought little of them or because he didn't have the ability to get them approved.

Evelyn Lincoln, President Kennedy's secretary and a Kennedy partisan, wrote admiringly of her former boss in *Kennedy and Johnson*. She blamed Johnson for the Kennedy failures with congress, at the same time claiming that "Mr. Kennedy felt that through the efforts of his staff members and leaders like Senator Kerr (*Democrat Majority Leader from Oklahoma*), he had ended the legislative stalemate that prevailed during much of the Eisenhower administration." (60, p 160)

The Kennedy proposals which Mrs. Lincoln mentioned included an increase in the minimum wage (which tends to price the least skilled workers out of jobs), area redevelopment (which is effective, and also harmful, only when it directs capital to uses which are uneconomic, otherwise it is redundant), housing (by which is meant subsidized housing for some at the expense of all who do not live in subsidized housing), water-pollution control (with which anti-statists can't argue in principle), and a continuation of long-term foreign aid. None of these proposals are startling or new. They are in fact mostly dreary extensions of the patchwork remedies by which Federal money is supposed to solve everything.

Kennedy's liberal admirers like to point to him as the paragon of civil rights leaders. In actual fact John Kennedy was not greatly interested in civil rights until after he became president. As a senator he supported some measures, opposed one, and did nothing on many more. In 1960 he was so busy campaigning that he missed most of the votes on the 1960 Civil Rights Bill. After he became president in 1961 he asked Senator Joseph Clark of Pennsylvania to draft a program for civil rights but he gave it no support until 1963. This was about the time he began to recognize the leverage of negro voters in the large Northern cities which would be needed in 1964. It was also after the turmoil and riots of 1963.

This interest in civil rights did not demonstrate Kennedy's sincerity, but it did demonstrate the power of any group that can be organized for agitation. The cause can be important or trivial, just or unjust, sensible or idiotic as long as it can convulse the group and scare the politicians. The group can be made up of negroes, Jews, Wasps, workers, old folks, young folks, or even taxpayers. John Kennedy may not have been sincere, but as a politician he was responsive. At the same time he was ineffective, being long on talk and short on action. In the three years of his presidency he could not get a single piece of civil rights legislation passed.

The Eisenhower administration began to push the space program seriously in 1957 after the first Soviet satellite was placed in orbit. Yet Evelyn Lincoln wrote that "shortly after his (Kennedy's) innauguration the space race began," and she cites as evidence the first suborbital flight of Alan Shepard on May 5, 1961. This is rather weak evidence since Shepard's fight was the end result of several years' intensive effort rather than the product of Kennedy charm applied between January 20th and May 5,

1961. It is true that later under Kennedy and Johnson the space program was flooded with tax dollars and used as an excuse to expand government support of research and scientific education. The surplus of teachers and space-oriented scientists which became evident in 1970 and 1971 was typical of the distortion of normal supply and demand arising from government stimulation and cutbacks.

In one area, Kennedy was far ahead of his predecessor. He was a great spender. In his three years in office he was responsible for deficits of $6.4, $6.2, and $8.2 billion dollars, for a total $20.8 billion dollars. The average annual deficit was about $6.9 billion dollars, whereas for Eisenhower's eight years the average annual deficit was about $3.1 billion. (*The 1971 World Almanac*, p 82)

In spite of all the money spent to win friends and influence votes, in spite of all the high-flying rhetoric, in spite of a glamorous wife and glittering parties, Kennedy did not, with the exception of those like Sorensen and Junior Schlesinger of the inner circle, appeal to the hard core-liberals.

Ben B. Seligman, leftist liberal that he is, might have been expected to look upon Kennedy with kindly eyes. Writing in the winter 1962 issue of *Dissent* he had this to say: "And New Frontier these days is comprised of one part thought, two parts hope, three parts rhetoric, and four parts political buck passing."

In early March of 1963, Tom Wicker, who is no half-way liberal, made a speech (i.e. asked a question) at the presidential press conference.

"Your policies in Europe seem to be encountering great difficulties," said Mr. Wicker to Mr. Kennedy. "Cuba continues to be a problem. At home unemployment is high. There seems to be more concern in the country over a budget deficit than for a tax cut. In view of all these things, there is some impression and talk in the town and country that your administration seems to have lost its momentum and to be slowing down and moving on the defensive."

William Shannon, described Kennedy in the liberal *New York Post* on February 12, 1961 as "the stylish young man at the end of the high diving board whose sole actions consisted of impressing upon the audience that the water down below is hellishly cold . . . he has read all the books on diving, . . . he knows

how important it is to dive, . . . diving is the key to the whole
show, etc., etc.

"All that remains for him to do is dive."

Kennedy, of course, never did dive. In foreign affairs he was
pushed, and if a big splash wet the audience it masked a magnificent belly flop. In domestic affairs he never got off the board,
and this was a blessing, for had he been more effective we would
have crossed the New Frontier and reached the happy, riot-torn
land of the Great Society three years sooner. In that case, there
would have been nothing left for Lyndon Johnson to do.

CHAPTER 15

BIG DADDY

Once upon a time there was a governor of Texas known, by friend and foe alike, as Pa Ferguson. Pa was an unsavory character whose wheeling and dealing went so far beyond the limits of propriety that the Texas legislature impeached him in 1917 and barred him forever from state office. This was a mere nuisance which Pa circumvented by getting Ma Ferguson elected to the governorship. Sam Johnson, a Texas-type local politician, state legislator, and part-time real estate dealer rode the Ferguson train, which was powered by populism and greased with corruption. Sam Johnson had a son, Lyndon, and Fergusonianism was the background of Lyndon's youth.

It was natural for Lyndon Johnson, long suffering and ever working to squeeze the last teardrop of sympathy from his listeners, to claim a poverty stricken boyhood. This existed only in his overworked political imagination. His penury was license, political, not poetic. Robert Sherrill, liberal author and Washington correspondent for the leftish *Nation* had no trouble raising LBJ above the poverty level.

"His father was so well-to-do," wrote Sherrill, "that he moved from Johnson City to San Marcos for no reason but to indulge himself in supervising the college careers of five children . . . at a time when a college education was considered something of a luxury . . . they were one of the few rural families in the area that could afford an automobile before World War I." (37, p 26) Sherrill also told a story about a Johnson tour for newsmen.

"On one of those pilgrimages-to-the-family shrine . . . ," wrote Sherrill, "They stopped in front of a shanty . . . and Johnson, stretching forth his hand and speaking in hushed and revered tones, identified it as the place in which he was reared to manhood. His mother, who tagged along a lot with him in those days, piped up: "Why, Lyndon, you *know* we had a nice house over on the other side of the farm.' " (61, p 24)

People who look carefully at the numerous photographs Johnson had taken of himself while in the White House will notice a miniature lapel service ribbon. This is for the Silver Star, the second highest award of the United States Navy, ranking just below the Congressional Medal of Honor. Johnson, who was a congressman at the time of Pearl Harbor, got himself a commission as a Lieutenant Commander and went on active duty on December 14, 1941. He arrived in the combat zone in the Pacific on May 14, 1942. While there he went on a combat mission as an observer and personal emissary of President Roosevelt (Big Daddy's big daddy). Members of the crew on this flight reported they were attacked by Japanese planes, but no one was hurt and the plane returned safely to base. For this act of conspicuous courage above and beyond the call of duty Lyndon B. Johnson, President Roosevelt's personal emissary, got the Silver Star. General Douglas MacArthur, who was known to be somewhat of a politician himself, made the award. On July 16, 1942, after two months in the Pacific, Johnson was out of uniform. He had had enough of war—and furthermore it was discovered that he was indispensable in congress.

In his years as a congressman, and later as a senator, Johnson was a typical Southern New Dealer. He voted for most tax and spend and elect legislation, for social security, for federal power projects and rural electrification, and for farm subsidies. He also voted against civil rights legislation and insisted on a jury trial amendment to the 1957 Civil Rights act.

Johnson's most notable displays of conservatism were his support of the Taft-Hartley Act and later the Landrum-Griffin Act, which attempted to protect labor against union abuses.

The Taft-Hartley Act was passed over President Truman's veto in 1947 during a four year period when Johnson was not in Congress. The act figured in the 1948 elections, during which Truman and the liberals scathingly attacked it. Sam Houston Johnson in *My Brother Lyndon* told about disagreeing with his brother's support of the act. After Sam admitted that he had not read the act, Lyndon reproved his brother.

"Well you had better read it," the Senator-to-be stormed, "before you go off half-cocked and call it anti-labor. I've read every word of that bill—several times—and it isn't what labor says it is. It's a good law and I'm voting for it." (7, p 74)

According to Sam, this stand caused his brother the support of organized labor. Instead of winning the primary, Lyndon was forced into a run-off from which he emerged the winner. Johnson's stand on Taft-Hartley shows a conservative bias in spite of the fact that he was a protege of Franklin D. Roosevelt. In Texas in 1948, even New Dealers were conservative on labor and civil rights.

Jack Bell, chief Washington political writer for the Associated Press, wrote a partial biography of Big Daddy in 1965, called *The Johnson Treatment*. Bell wrote that the liberal Americans for Democratic Action complained in 1960 that Johnson was a "conservative, anti-civil rights, gas-and-oil senator. He has supported all of the anti-labor legislation enacted during the past two decades—and bragged about it." (53, p 225) This was substantially true of Johnson the senator. It accounts for the Southern support the Kennedy-Johnson ticket received in 1960. The stance of Johnson changed after 1963, but the memory of him as a Southern conservative did not fade fast enough to cost him a significant loss of Southern support in 1964.

Regardless of what one thinks of Johnson personally, he set goals and achieved them in the senate. In this he was remarkably successful. By comparison Kennedy was an ineffective senator, long on talk and style but short on delivering the goods.

"There is no gainsaying the record," wrote Bell, "Johnson was effective in the senate. What Lyndon wanted, Lyndon nearly always got . . . Johnson's accomplishments did not come easy in the senate . . ." (53, p 35)

"There were those," Bell continued, "who remained in congress who said that as a Democratic leader Johnson had been bombastic, overbearing, boastful, vain, and corny. But in the same breath they acknowledged that this extraordinary man was shrewd forceful, knowledgeable, and competently able to dominate them despite the resentment they sometimes felt at what they characterized as his high-handed methods." (53, p 37)

As a congressman and senator Lyndon Johnson was a bona fide

New Dealer who supported Franklin Roosevelt, his idol, as long as Roosevelt lived. He was rated as a 10 per cent conservative and 90 per cent liberal senator by the Americans for Constitutional Action. In Texas, too, he was considered liberal but not in the leftist camp of Senator Yarborough.

Up until 1957, when he began to glance longingly toward the White House, Johnson voted consistently against civil rights measures. (53, pp 159-175) This qualified him for contemptuous treatment by the Northern Democrat liberals who controlled the party.

"I don't know where you could have gotten the idea that I am supporting the so-called bill for civil rights legislation now before Congress . . . ," wrote L.B.J. in a 1957 letter. "The bill that has been introduced is one to which I am very much opposed, as I do not believe it would advance any legitimate cause." (53, p 160) A few months later Johnson cast his vote for the 1957 Civil Rights Act. How could he do this?

On his shift in positions, Gettlemen and Mermelstein, the ultra-leftist professors, wrote that "one reason why he could accomplish the required transformation was a singular lack of commitment to any fixed ideology . . . A cool calculating pragmatist, he could take on the particular coloration that succeeded his growing ambitions." (13, p 6) His only fixed ideological commitment was to win elections, but in this he was no different than many other successful politicians.

Bell explained the Johnson shift this way. ". . . there was one 'legitimate cause' he believed could stand some advancing in this period and that was the nationalization of the Lyndon Johnson appeal to the voters. The time had come to turn away from Southern provincialism, and the man from Texas executed an about face that seldom has been paralleled." (53, p 169)[1]

---

[1] John F. Kennedy's shift from conservative to liberal was no less remarkable. Since Bell made his statement there have been two equally startling shifts. First, there was the Goodell shuffle. John Goodell was conservative when, as a congressman, he represented up-state New Yorkers. As a senator, whose constituency included the liberal voters of New York City, Goodell shifted himself leftward—and out of a job. Second, there was the Nixon shuffle, which commenced in 1971. On January 4, 1971 he commented to ABC interviewer Howard K. Smith, "I am now a Keynesian in economics." Smith is said to have commented that this compares to a Christian crusader saying "All things considered, I think Mohammed was right." (As quoted in *Human Events*, VXXX, no. 4, Jan. 23, 1971, p 8.)

The gradual Johnson shift, which began when he was still a senator, accelerated after he became vice-president. By the time he was president and was campaigning for election in his own right he was no longer a Southern conservative Democrat. Perhaps this is why he sent his wife to campaign for him in the South. The credibility gap was growing.

If Lyndon Johnson ever had any clear-cut basic political philosophy—other than to get elected—he successfully hid it. Otherwise Robert Sherrill could never have concluded that President Johnson "was elected with the approval of both *The Kansas City Star* and *The New York Post*, both the U.S. Chamber of Commerce and the AFL-CIO." (61, p 4)

The political leverage granted politicians by the XVIth (income tax) amendment was not lost on Lyndon Johnson. Campaigning as a vice-presidential candidate in 1960, Johnson showed that he recognized the shrinkage of local power and the growth of Federal power. This was a political fact of life, and Johnson was nothing if not frank in exploiting it. In arguing for support of the ticket, he told the local party officials who visited his campaign train, "And don't antagonize the Democratic men of power who can make or break your districts by decisions on Federal spending." (60, p 128) This is a later version of Roosevelt's "tax and tax, spend and spend, elect and elect" principle. Without the giant tax source of the XVIth amendment this political principle would be unworkable.

Johnson's record as president was certainly that of a liberal. He pressed for and got a civil rights program, farm subsidies, aid to education, and the anti-poverty program. At the same time he courted businessmen, spoke of fiscal responsibility, turned out the lights at the White House, and he refrained from using the caustic descriptions of businessmen that were so much a part of Roosevelt, Truman, and Kennedy.

"There were . . . newsmen who knew Johnson well, and all accepted him for what he was," wrote Jack Bell after Johnson succeeded to the presidency, "a man who could be alternately aggravating and soothing, imperious and humble, demanding and understanding, petty and generous, humorous and solemn, fretful and calm, picayune and grandiose. He was, in a word about as human as men come, and then some." (53, pp 141-142)

Evelyn Lincoln agreed with Bell's description of Johnson as a "man of explosive energy and earthy, hot-tempered personality." (53, p 29) Apparently the new president's personality was unchanged from his days as senate majority leader when, according to Bell, he was "always prodding everyone in sight to get along with the business in hand. He was forever fidgeting, twisting, bobbing up and down. He busied himself collaring his colleagues, thrusting his face up within inches of his victims' as he argued and cajoled. He was then the Senate's man in motion, as he was later to become the nation's man in motion." (53, pp 34-35)

Politicians are, as has been pointed out before, often egotistical prima-donnas. They feel a strong need to be liked by people, they respond to public approval, and hence, they are thin-skinned when it comes to criticism. Jack Bell, who was himself a reporter, wrote that "as the Senate's Democratic leader, Johnson had been known among newsmen who covered his activities as a whiner. Any story which depicted his accomplishments as extraordinary—and many of them were—drew a smile and a comment . . . But a critical report could set him off for days. He could call the reporter to his office and tell him how disappointed he was that an old and trusted friend had written about him in that manner. Moreover, he would often harangue one newsman about what another newsman had written." (53, p 139) It is these human qualities of Johnson and of our other presidents, and of presidents yet to be, which should ever be kept in mind when there is a tendency to fawn over presidents and politicians as miraculous men with divine powers who can solve the everyday problems of all the people in the country.

Since the Hoover era, presidential character has been increasingly difficult to discern by reading presidential speeches and messages. Grover Cleveland meticulously wrote his own veto messages, not so Harry Truman. Abraham Lincoln wrote his Gettysburg address, but a hundred years later Horace Busby, a public relations man, wrote Lyndon Johnson's Gettysburg address. Johnson was the vice-president at the time of delivery. As such, he should have had ample time to write his own speeches.

Johnson's statements and speeches, like those of Eisenhower, Truman, and Roosevelt, are a synthetic product. The real Johnson, if he comes through, appears in diluted form. Richard Goodwin is credited with authorship of the Great Society speech Johnson gave at Ann Arbor in May of 1964. Ted Sorenson and Arthur Schlesinger, Jr. were writers who, like Goodwin, were inherited from Camelot. Jack Valenti was, like Busby, a public relations man pressed into service by LBJ. Other Johnson originals were Eric Goldman, Abe Fortas, and Bill Moyers. Even the forty-nine words Johnson read to newsmen upon arriving in Washington with his predecessor's body were written by an aide, Mrs. Elizabeth S. Carpenter. (10, p 26)

So much for trying to judge a modern president by what goes out under his by-line. Truth in advertising need not be practiced in politics, but it is required in selling breakfast cereal. Happily, there are other ways to determine the character of a president.

Something of Johnson's character is reflected in the key men with whom he surrounded himself. All of these men were effective. One had a spotless record, one was convicted, fined, and sentenced to jail, one was nominated to be Chief Justice of the Supreme Court, withdrawing from consideration after his background was investigated and publicized, and one was arrested for indecent public activities, not once but twice. The four were, respectively, Clark Clifford, Bobby Baker, Abe Fortas, and Walter Jenkins. Clifford and Fortas were among Johnson's most intimate advisors. Baker was Johnson's "good right arm" as the former Senate Majority Leader described him before the fall from grace. Jenkins was an unfortunate choice as a top presidential assistant. After his second arrest, this time in the men's room of the Washington YMCA, Jenkins left Big Daddy's employ. Both Clifford and Fortas have been described as brilliant. Fortas, like Baker, was thought of as an operator, but Baker was careless both in his operations and in reporting his income tax. Clifford, Baker, and Fortas were also known to be tough and shrewd, and all four were hard workers. Then, too, there was the case of Billie Sol Estes, not an associate but a fellow Texan, whose scandalous conduct touched the Department of Agriculture and won him a jail term and loss of his ill-gotten fortune. Apart from Clark Clifford, Johnson's most intimate associates do not enhance the Johnson reputation. Of course, it has never been established that LBJ ever broke any laws, but this does not bar impartial observers from coming to unpleasant conclusions. The fact is, Johnson was a human being, stronger in some ways and weaker in others than most of us. It is these weaknesses which should make people question the wisdom of surrendering the responsibility of managing their affairs to a strong central government which will always consist of human beings like Lyndon Johnson. The stronger the government and the more unlimited its powers, the greater are the dangers of error, dishonesty, and terror.

Johnson's first senatorial election victory does no more for his reputation than his choice of assistants and advisors. It was a triumph that would have been approved by Pa and Ma Ferguson—there was a lot of fast footwork between the election and the recount. The final tally gave Big Daddy an 87 vote margin.

The record of Johnson's success in business, like that of his political success, is equally cloudy and murky. Not dishonest, not provably illegal, but also not clear, not clean, and not bright.

In 1943, Lady Bird Johnson invested $17,500 in KTBC, a run down Austin radio station. By 1947 the station assets had grown to $213,140, its power quadrupled with FCC permission. By 1954 it had expanded into television, boosted its power one-thousand fold to 247 KW and its assets had grown to $2,569,503, according to *The Wall Street Journal* of March 23 and 24, 1964. Now all this would be admirable if one could only ignore the fact that in 1948 Johnson was elected to the senate and appointed to the Commerce Committee. The Senate Commerce Committee oversees the Federal Communications Commission, which in turn grants licenses and oversees radio and television broadcasting. Bell commented that ". . . inquiring reporters could find nowhere on the record any special plea for the Johnson stations. But as John Barron of the Washington *Star* said, the FCC always seemed to approach the Johnson applications with a benevolent attitude." (53, p 78)

"The situation seems unique!" reported the March 24, 1964 issue of the *Wall Street Journal,* "officials are unable to recall that any other presidential family has had its wealth concentrated in a government-regulated industry with the full knowledge of the regulators." One FCC commissioner is quoted as saying "he was 'amazed' that the family retained, after reaching the White House, its clearly visible interest in a business so heavily dependent upon Federal regulation . . . Says a Democrat member of the FCC: 'Of course, every commissioner and every member of the staff is aware' of the presidential family's interest in the Austin stations. He terms Mrs. Johnson's trusteeship of the stock 'a half-way measure that does not divorce the family from the stations.' "

Arthur Shenfield's perceptive essay "The Ugly Intellectual" (*Modern Age*, Winter, 1972, pp 9-14) was written too late to warn Lyndon Johnson about the intellectuals whose favor he worked so hard to gain.

"There is," wrote Shenfield, "in our midst a large and growing body of men whose trade is that of ideas, who command an immense and expanding market, and whose activities are calculated to undermine the distinctive features of the free society. Their stock in trade is social criticism, for which their rewards are fame, influence, and material wealth. The outstanding effect of their social criticism is social turmoil. The more turmoil there is, the more does their criticism appear to be apt and needed, and the more do their rewards grow."

Intellectuals filling Shenfield's specifications seem to be emotional rather than analytical types. They tend, also, to be more socially active and outgoing than they are reflective and retiring, and they are among the most articulate and most gifted manipulators of words. In the academic community they dominate such fields as literature, the fine arts, sociology, political science, history—and faculty senates. For them the ultimate in wisdom is found in *The New York Times*,[2] *The Nation, The New Republic, The Saturday Review* and *The New Yorker*. The ugly intellectuals see little, or nothing, to admire in the American past, they slavishly repeat whatever James Reston, Tom Wicker and the other oracles proclaim as the current truth. It is they who have goaded simple students to assail the ramparts and barricades of tradition.

Soon after President Kennedy's assassination, Ted Sorensen, an

[2] Goldman's description (10, p 438) of this select group: "They are generally more intelligent, better educated and more concerned than the cashier at the supermarket, and at least they have read their *New York Times*." Goldman should know. He is one of them.

old Kennedy hand, and part-time history professor Arthur Schlesinger, Jr. a man with a very low pH, left the White House service followed by their entourage of intellectual hangers-on. In the meantime Johnson recruited Eric Goldman, a Princeton professor of history, assigning him the task of assembling a new team. Johnson, in imitation of his idol's Brain Trust, directed Goldman to get together an advisory group which would include "the best minds in the country." Goldman's Brain Trust, however, would turn out to be much larger than FDR's. This should be expected in an age of inflation. Furthermore it was to be a Texan's Brain Trust and therefore it just had to be the biggest ever.

B.G. and A.S., Before Goldman and After Schlesinger, that is, the working staff at the White House consisted mainly of transplanted Texas opportunists, trusties, and politicians. What better than to have a few intellectuals on call who could bestow a little class on Johnson's brotherhood of Texas toilers? Goldman was willing and he had the contacts with that world of frustrated intellectuals who long to be at the seat of power, so he became a sort of marriage broker for the political opportunists inside and the ugly intellectuals outside the White House. The marriage was not a happy one.

The newlyweds had hardly recovered from a strenuous honeymoon when the Presidential Scholars program, a scheme credited to Goldman, generated the first family row. One hundred twenty-one scholars, selected from the senior classes of the nation's secondary schools, were to be honored by the president. Each state was to recommend its top boy scholar and top girl scholar. No matter that the top boy might rank below five girls, the ticket had to be balanced, as the politicians say. (Women's lib, not yet underway, would have protested.) There was also fear that negroes might not be among the scholars selected, and so fifteen additional scholars were to be selected at large to prevent such a horrendous political possibility. There were no published plans to take care of Eskimoes, Indians, Chicanos, or Republicans.

Unable to raise scholarship money to go with the awards, Goldman settled on a medal. The medal was to be sculpted by Jacques Lipchitz who, according to Goldman, had "begun his career as a cubist (*perhaps Goldman thought he could convince Johnson that a cubist was a sort of three-dimensional square*) and gone on to works which did not exactly express the taste of Johnson City." Goldman described Lipchitz' arrival at the White House with his rough designs.

"A gray little man in a disheveled suit, beret atop an unshaven face, socks drooping over his ankles," Goldman wrote. "At the appointed hour a White House guard telephoned, 'There's a funny-looking guy out here with a crate (an orange crate held by a piece of string). He says he has an appointment with the President and he won't let us look into the crate.' Finally clearance was arranged and Lipchitz left the orange crate and contents for Johnson's later inspection. When the President finally looked at Lipchitz's work he exclaimed 'It's the goddamnedest thing. I don't want it, I won't see Lipchitz, and the hell with it.' In a cooler moment Johnson relented and 121 medals were cast with Johnson on one side and Prometheus on the other. His final verdict was that the resemblance to himself looked as though he'd 'been dead for three weeks.' " (10, pp 146-150)

Goldman slipped up on one detail of scholar selection. He hadn't specified a check for political reliability or a loyalty oath. At the award ceremony the response of the presidential scholars, according to Goldman, was irritation "to the point of bitterness as they spoke of the 'cheap politics' behind the scheme. One youngster who went on to Yale said 'Being a political pawn at the age of 17 or 18 is kinda fun.' " He and most of his co-scholars were in college in 1968 when unrest peaked and played a part in the president's political dispatch.

If the Presidential Scholars program was a minor abortion, the White House Festival of the Arts, another Goldman production, was an adult fiasco. Nearly three months of haggling preceded presidential approval for the show. The announced objective was to stimulate interest in the arts, the unannounced aim was to win support for Big Daddy from an unlikely source. Participants, guests, and exhibitors were invited from among the painters, sculptors, poets, authors, musicians, dancers, photographers, and actors. Robert Lowell, the poet, first accepted and then publicly withdrew on the basis of political opposition to Johnson's Vietnam war policies. If, as suspected, the festival was politically motivated, Lowell was merely beating the president at his own game. Lowell's public refusal was followed by an open telegram addressed to Johnson signed by twenty prominent portside artists and writers. The telegram supported Lowell and inferred that the festival was contrived to create the impression that artists and intellectuals were supporting the administration in Vietnam. This telegram received wide publicity and weakened Johnson's already shakey support in the academic community where preparations were being made for the teach-ins, riots, strikes and demonstrations that would do-in Big Daddy. Four additional refusals followed Lowell's telegram. One of the signers of Lowell's message received an invitation which was sent out before the telegram was published. This fellow accepted the invitation, attended the festival and spent his time collecting signatures for a petition critical of Vietnam and other administration policies! John Hersey, the author, attended and made a critical statement as a preface to reading one of his works. Somewhere along the line, the arts were all but forgotten. Johnson was in a snit, and Ladybird was near tears. If proof was needed that the White House Festival of the Arts was a failure, it came when *The New York Times* praised the idea. "By tolerating dissent within its own precincts," the *Times* solemnly proclaimed, "the White House raised its own and the nation's stature." Praise from the *Times* is, to many, a sign of something amiss.

While Goldman was rallying the intellectuals, Johnson went to work on the common people. Shortly after becoming president LBJ sent his first major message to congress. He called for medical care for the aged, aid to education, subsidized housing, aid to libraries and aid to hospitals. Simultaneously he called for aid to taxpayers, asking for ". . . the most far-reaching tax cut of our time." The impossible holds no fear for an enterprising politician.

"I have pledged that the Executive Branch will be administered with utmost thrift and frugality," wrote the new president to the heads of government departments and agencies. "The Government will get a dollar's worth for a dollar spent." (10, p 28) And with much publicity he went around the White House turning out the lights to save money. In spite of the ridicule this earned him, Johnson's years were a big improvement over Kennedy's years. The JFK deficits averaged $6.9 billion for each of his three years in office, while LBJ averaged $3.8 billion in the red for his five years, including years of increased Vietnam expenditures.

President Johnson originally had two major goals for the 89th Congress. The first was Medicare and Aid to Education was the second.

On January 7, 1965, President Johnson sent his message to congress dealing with health and medical care. The Medicare program was not like a mushroom which grew overnight. It was the result of agitation which began during, and was encouraged by, the statist tendencies of the Hoover administration. Truman was the first president to propose formally a program similar to Medicare, but it took twenty more years to become law. Even so, Johnson's Medicare was not the end of a battle, it was more of a beginning. The future is foretold by British experience.

According to an article, which appeared in the magazine of the Boston *Sunday Herald Traveler* (June 13, 1971, pp 6-16), by Anthony Lejeune and Christine Pickard, "The founders of the Health Service (*in Great Britain*) thought that it's cost would diminish as the nation became healthier; instead of which, the cost has already risen by about 1200 per cent." Lejeune and Pickard quote a comment from the British medical journal *The Lancet*, which explains the poor quality of service resulting from the shortage of facilities and doctors. "If taxi fares were abolished and a free National Taxi Service established, financed by taxation, the shortage of taxis would be endemic and the 'taxi crisis' a subject of periodic public agitation." They might have added that a good part of the British shortage of doctors has resulted from a large emigration of British doctors to countries where socialized medicine is not practised.

Federal intervention in education, like Medicare, did not suddenly appear as a Johnsonian innovation. Land-grant colleges had been operating for almost a century. Howard University was Federally established in Washington as a college for negroes many years earlier. Likewise Washington's Gallaudet College for the deaf and mute had a long history of Federal financing. During and after World War II, Federal funds subsidized graduate students (originally through the Office of Research and Development). After the war, undergraduates, graduates, and students in various noncollegiate programs were subsidized under the G.I.

Bill of Rights. And Federal grants were made to localities whose school populations were increased by the presence of nearby Federal installations, such as military bases. Such localities were known as "Federally impacted areas."

The major barrier to passage of the 1965 Aid to Education Act was the religious restriction of the First Amendment to the Constitution. Catholics were the largest single denomination of the population and six million of forty million elementary and secondary school children were in parochial schools. Strict adherence to the Constitution would bar spending Federal funds to assist parochial schools, even though they were just as hard pressed for funds as public schools. Yet it did not seem right that Federal taxes, collected partly from Catholics whose children would not attend public schools, should be spent to support those same public schools. The Catholics, who sponsor the largest parochial school enrollment, would stand to suffer the most, but they would not be entirely alone.

Federal intervention in education was bound to increase, ultimately, the proportion of educational costs paid by taxes and reduce the proportion paid by voluntary private contributions. It would force abandonment of private schools, force conformity of public schools to standards set by Federal bureaucrats, and reduce variety and freedom of choice in regard to schooling opportunities. Like other Federal interventions, it would restrict the options open to the people and would coerce support from a minority. It would also strain the Constitution as attempts were made to dodge the requirements of the First Amendment.[3]

Had education been allowed to remain strictly a private endeavor of churches and voluntary charitable organizations, as it was before establishment of public schools, the problem would not have arisen. Nor would there have been any squabbling about whether

---

[3] The First Amendment reads in part: "Congress shall make no law respecting an establishment of religion, or prohibiting the free exercise thereof; . . ." The arguments opposing Federal spending for *parochial schools* are based on the fact that such support favors the establishment of whatever religion receives the support. On the other hand, Federal spending for *public schools* acts against the parochial schools as explained above, and therefore tends to "prohibit the free exercise" of religion. Under the Constitution it would seem, therefore, that *any* Federal intervention in education is prohibited.

prayers are permissible in public schools.[4] Parents would have
retained more control over whether the private schools they
sought to patronize would teach sex education, and if so, how it
was taught, whether they would teach socialism, revolution, or
what have you, and whether the pledge of allegiance would be
required, and so on. The proponents of public education, com-
prising at least 125 per cent of the population, recoil in horror
at the thought of abandonment of the system. How could private
education possibly succeed? A little thought will suggest some
answers. How have religious groups, notably the Catholics,
managed, in the face of intolerable tax burdens, to send such a
high proportion of their children to private schools? This was
achieved at a time when real wages and real income were far
lower than they are today, and when the costs of education were
a larger proportion of family income than they are today. How
did the Jews, through centuries of oppression, manage the education of their children? If the desire for learning exists it needs no
Federal subsidy.

Passage of the Aid to Education Act came by large majorities
in both the house and the senate, where the votes were 263 to
153 and 73 to 18 respectively. Southern Democrats, many of
whom are tagged as conservatives, might have been expected to
oppose this extension of the tenacles of the Federal Octopus. In
this case any states' rights idealism was unable to resist the appeal of a scheme which would provide more Federal dollars for
the Southern states than they would contribute in taxes. Republicans, allegedly conservative, too, contributed support. Representative Gerald Ford, the new Republican leader in the house,
called upon the party to create an "attractive new image," and
pledged a program of "constructive conservatism." What the
growing new breed of "constructive conservatives" failed to
recognize was that what might be called "destructive" conserva-

[4] Incidentally the First Amendment is cited as the prohibition against prayer
in public schools, but there is nothing in the First Amendment, or anywhere
else in the Constitution, which prohibits a state of the union from requiring
or prohibiting, as it wishes, prayers in schools, or from establishing or preventing establishment of a religion. The First Amendment merely prevents
Congress from acting and requires separation, not of states and religion, but
of the Federal government and religion.

tism was really being *for* freedom and *for* local and individual options in meeting needs, and that votes *against* so-called "progress" were votes *against* Federal statist interventions.

Big Daddy maneuvered his farm subsidy bill through Congress by offering to support food stamp subsidies in return for a billion dollars in cotton and wheat subsidies. The food stamps would be given to those the government certified as poor. The certified poor would then swap them for food at participating stores and the merchants would swap the stamps for money. (Some of the certified poor would swap their stamps for money which was then used for booze, etc.) The taxpayers would pay and the certified poor would be expected to, and did, support Big Daddy handsomely at the polls in 1964. The Johnson treatment preserved the shaky marriage of liberal Northern Democrats and not so liberal Southern partners. Six years later food stamps were providing food for hungry hippies in their communes, and the marriage between Northern and Southern Democrats was all but dissolved.

Practical politics dictated that Big Daddy would have to discover a sudden affection for the black man if he was ever to reach the White House. This arose from the fact that Johnson was a Southern Democrat. Paradoxically liberal Northern Democrats, like Kennedy and Roosevelt could afford to show little interest in the negro cause, whereas a Southern Democrat would have to demonstrate an interest in blacks if he ever hoped to win a national election. Johnson, as a Southerner knew he could count automatically on most of the Southern states. But he also knew that unless he carried the industrial Northern states he could not win. In many of these states the negroes hold the balance of power in the cities, and the city vote often determines how these states go. So Lyndon Johnson, a Southern segregationist, became the best Democrat friend the negroes ever had. Blacks discovered they can expect more from a Southern populist Democrat than they can from the Northern liberal types.

Clearly, negroes had been denied their constitutional right to vote in most parts of the South, but Congress, the executive branch, and the courts had done nothing effective to remedy the situation in the years since 1870 when the XVth Amendment was adopted. Denial of voting rights made possible other abuses sanctioned by local laws and by elections in which blacks could not vote. The Civil Rights Act of 1965 was intended to insure that negroes who wanted to vote could do so. The act achieved this by declaring that voting rights had been denied in any county where less than half of the citizens of voting age had registered and voted in the 1964 presidential election. In those areas the Attorney General of the United States would declare literacy tests and similar requirements void, and further, the Federal government would provide registrars to register voters who were qualified by virtue of age, citizenship, soundness of mind and absence of criminal records. The act excluded certain areas in the North and West which might have come under the 50 per cent standard, and thus it was criticized, and rightly so, as punitive toward the South.[5]

Early in 1965 President Johnson delivered his second State of the Union Message to Congress. In this he proposed establishment of a national foundation for the arts. The Eighty-ninth Congress responded with establishment of the National Foundation for the Arts and Humanities. If there was ever an unnecessary piece of legislation this was it.

In the 1965 hearings on the proposal, Thornton Wilder, who became a successful author in spite of the fact that he had no Federal subsidy, stated: "There are no Miltons dying here today . . . anyone who can play the scales is run off to Vienna on money raised by some local music appreciation club." He concluded the foundation was unnecessary. Russell Lynes of *Harpers* said at about the same time: "I am not worried about creeping socialism in the arts, but creeping mediocrity. The less the arts have to do with political processes, I believe the healthier they will be." Lynes should, however, have been worried about creeping socialism, because it has long been recognized that socialism tends to be the great leveller which produces the mediocrity he feared.

Starting with nothing in 1965, $40 million in support was voted in 1971, to be followed by $60 million and $80 million scheduled for 1972 and 1973 respectively. In the 1968 debate, Congressman William Scherle, reflecting on the performance of

[5] For anyone interested in pursuing the question of universal suffrage, see Frederic Bastiat's *The Law*, The Foundation for Economic Education, Irvington-on-Hudson, N.Y., 1968, pp 14–17.

the foundation to date, asked "Why the foundation should subsidize box-office flops to the tune of $20,000 a year? Why a Rhode Island road official should have been granted $10,000 to 'rethink' public road signs? Why a $10,000 grant was given for 'completion of a long poem'? Why a $10,000 grant was made so that a person could travel to California to research a novel about Hollywood?" Now perhaps you, dear reader, think one, or perhaps all, of the grants and projects are worthwhile. But if you happen to be one of the many who think they are nonsensical, why should you, under the penalty of fines, confiscation of your property, and possible imprisonment, be forced to contribute to their support via Federal taxation?

This is the eternal problem of statism, the embarrassing question the statists can not answer. Statism requires that every taxpayer must pay for goods or services he does not want and would not freely purchase. Consequently he is denied the opportunity to purchase goods or services he might want, and he is prevented from supporting projects or charities which he feels are worthwhile to the same extent that his wealth is taken from him by taxes. This is yet another reason for limited government and for avoidance of all interventions not aimed at protection of individuals and the nation from predatory acts of others.

Before Big Daddy's reign would end, the Great Society's achievements would also include a $900 million dollar anti-poverty program (only the beginning), a rent subsidy program for low-income families, establishment of a cabinet rank Department of Housing and Urban Development, passage of a High-Speed Ground Transportation Act in an attempt to revive what was left of rail passenger service after decades of Federal interference and strangulation, and an additional $2.4 billion in aid to education. Octopus Federalis Domesticus would grow more rapidly under Johnson than under any other president since Franklin Roosevelt. Big Daddy was no doubt proud of emulating his idol.

Johnson's introduction to foreign affairs came when he took a ten-day vice-presidential tour of Southeast Asia. Upon his return he summarized his conclusions for President Kennedy in a memo. As reported by Goldman, (10, pp 391-392) Johnson saw Southeast Asia as the battleground where Communist expansion must be stopped at the peril of losing Taiwan, the Philippines, and

Japan if we did not act. In this case, in Johnson's words, "the vast Pacific becomes a Red Sea" and we would have to "take up our defenses on our own shores."

Prophetically, the vice-president cautioned that the decision to assist the non-Communist nations of Southeast Asia "must be made in a full realization of the very heavy and continuing costs in terms of money, of effort and of United States prestige. It must be made with the knowledge that at some point we may be faced with the further decision of whether we commit major United States forces to the area or cut our losses and withdraw should our efforts fail."

When Johnson became president he took the risks he had anticipated and followed the recommendations he had made, as vice-president, to Kennedy.

Johnson's Vietnam policies were the result of a variety of influences: his real concern about the need for stopping Communist expansion; a possible subconscious desire to be a great wartime leader like his idol FDR, whom he had rivalled in domestic affairs; his political nature which led him to attempt to mollify both hawks and doves, which resulted in his doing less than needed to win and more than needed to lose, and which, in turn, resulted in a premature end to his political career; and his desire to win the 1964 election by the greatest majority ever.

There is no doubt that Johnson could have been re-elected in 1968 had he been successful in rallying the country behind the American effort in Vietnam. His failure in 1968 was born in the campaign of 1964, when he attacked Goldwater for urging a more vigorous proscution of the war. The cynical approach of gaining votes by promising peace, much as FDR did in 1941 and as Wilson did in 1916, backfired when it became evident in the years after 1964, that plans for war were being made at the same time. The credibility gap grew as the faith of millions was destroyed, giving Communist-inspired "peace" agitators the public support they needed for their campaigns. Johnson, having painted Goldwater as a trigger-happy menace, could not become the instant warrior once the election was over. The Communists did not oblige him by bombing Pearl Harbor as the Japanese had done in 1941. His reversal of roles had to come more slowly and gradually. During the snail-paced build-up of American forces the Communist invaders from the North came close to achieving total victory and subsequent American losses were much higher than they should have been. The peace movement, strengthened by public disillusionment, grew more vocal, and violent, encouraging the North Vietnamese to continue their aggression and terror in the South. This, too, contributed to American losses.

Johnson's timidity in Vietnam was his biggest mistake. It was a case of too little and too late. But his timidity did not come from a lack of courage. Rather it came from the politician's urge to compromise, from a reluctance to offend any groups and risk losing their votes, from a desire to be all things to all voters. He did not save for himself the votes of the intellectual liberals, and at the same time he lost the votes of others. He was too political in a situation beyond politics. In 1966 he still had the option of full-scale attack, including the enemy's homeland, or withdrawal. He did not follow either course.

Arthur Schlesinger, Jr., who served Kennedy and who is classified by many conservatives as a liberal extremist, recognized the problem. In an article published in *The New York Times* on September 18, 1966, although he did not personally advocate the widening of the war, Schlesinger mentioned the many options open to us for doing so. His suggestions might have been borrowed from Barry Goldwater's 1964 list of bombing targets. His crowning thought was that an invasion of the North might settle the war if bombing failed. Johnson, of course, paid little heed to all this free advice and restricted his air strikes to oil depots.

Johnson's task in setting Vietnam war policy was probably not made easier by the presence of intellectual holdovers from the Kennedy administration. Among these was McNamara, the man who ignored competent military advice and was responsible for the $9 billion F-111 fiasco. He was the man with the computer memory who was suspected of making up, on occasion, statistics and figures when required to prove a point. Sam Houston Johnson observed that "quite obviously there were two McNamaras—one a hawk and the other a dove . . . He wanted it both ways, he wanted to be an agonized liberal and a tough pragmatist at the same time." (7, p 200) Dean Rusk and McGeorge Bundy both seem to have realized the importance of preventing Communist expansion into Vietnam, but neither they nor Johnson seemed to know what to do about it. The escalation was too slow, too late, too restrained and too timid. Until Clark Clifford came along no one seemed to have thought of arming the South Vietnamese so that they could fight their own battles.

Shortly after Clark Clifford became Secretary of Defense the first trickle of modern arms went to the South Vietnamese Army and Vietnamization was under way. Although the Nixon administration is credited by the public with originating the program, it actually commenced in the Spring of 1968, nine months before Nixon took the oath. On April 11, 1968 Clifford announced the decision to equip the territorial militia, allowing them to assume the job of pacification and releasing South Vietnamese regulars for combat duties so that American troops could be withdrawn. (*U.S. News and World Report*, July 8, 1968, pp 41-42) In June 1968 Clifford claimed that by the end of 1970 South Vietnam would have a "well-trained, well-drilled, effective army" of 1,-000,000 men, all equipped, at last, with M-16 rifles. In 1968, under Clifford, the South Vietnamese received M-79 grenade launchers, M-60 machine guns, 81-, 105-, and 155-mm howitzers, armored personnel carriers, trucks, and helicopters—all the best and most up-to-date equipment. Once Johnson escaped the influence of McNamara and the whiz kids, some long overdue steps were taken to end this dreary war. Johnson's toughness, which enabled him to withstand the vilest abuse of the peaceniks, professors, and even members of his own party, was not matched by a grasp of the situation which would have led him to take, three or four years earlier, the steps he took during his last year in office, and for which the Nixon administration received credit.

Any mention of the Vietnam War would be lacking if the battles at the negotiating table were neglected. In Paris the war was carried on, not with bullets and bombs, but with insults and invective. Johnson, perhaps remembering the futility of negotiating with the North Korean Communists, was leery of repeating the performance with North Vietnamese Communists. Always he asked: with whom am I expected to negotiate? He recognized that his position would be weakened by premature overtures to negotiate. Nevertheless, only two months after the bombing of the North commenced, an American offer was made, on April 7, 1965, to start "unconditional negotiations" with the

North Vietnamese (but not with the Vietcong or so-called National Liberation Front). There was no response from the North. "Stop the bombing," was the cry. The bombing was temporarily suspended for six days starting on May 13, 1965, and again for 38 days starting on December 24, 1965, and finally halted over 90 per cent of the North on March 31, 1968. The first two suspensions produced no response from the North. Forty days after the 90 per cent halt, "peace" talks began in Paris. This was on May 10, 1968. Between the time aerial attacks began on the North in February 1965 and the actual start of negotiations, nine attempts were made by various persons to get the Communists to the "peace" table. Approaches were made by Johnson (April 7, 1965), U Thant (December 2, 1966), the British (December 30, 1966), Johnson (February 1967), Senator Robert Kennedy (March 22, 1967), U Thant (March 28, 1967), Johnson (September 29, 1967), U.N. Ambassador Arthur Goldberg (November 2, 1967), and finally again by Johnson when he announced the 90 per cent bombing halt on March 31, 1968. All but the last effort were rejected outright or ignored by the North Vietnamese. On October 31, 1968, in what was obviously a political move to bolster the Democrats' sagging presidential campaign, *all* bombing of the North was stopped by Johnson and plans were made to expand the talks in Paris to include the South Vietnamese and the Vietcong. The first meeting of the expanded group of conferees met on January 18, 1969. In all these moves, the president was subjected to effective, highly organized pressure tactics. These must have been directed by the Communists because they were worldwide in scope and there is no other organization able to operate on the same scale. (The Communists had previously demonstrated a world-wide capability to stage riots and protests in the 20's after the Sacco-Vanzetti trial and execution, in 1951 for the Rosenbergs, in 1959 by riots throughout South America on the occasion of Vice-president Nixon's visit, culminated by assassination attempts in Lima and Caracas, and by the Japanese riots which forced cancellation of President Eisenhower's visit.) In any event the protests, marches, riots, strikes and demonstrations were followed by repeated American peace overtures and calls for negotiations which immeasurably weakened our bargaining position. The United States has made concession after concession, first to get "peace" talks started, and later at the "peace" table itself. TheCommunists have merely sat tight. They are hardnosed antagonists, and our failure to be equally hardnosed would seem to guarantee aggression elsewhere at a future date.

It will be forever a memorial to the stupidity of American foreign policy, particularly to the Eisenhower-Kennedy efforts, why we decided to make a stand against Communist expansion half a world away while we aided the rape of Cuba on our doorstep.

Yet it is true that Johnson redeemed himself to a degree by forestalling a Communist takeover in the Dominican Republic in April of 1965. The same liberals and fellow travelers who claimed Castro was an agrarian reformer howled and gnashed their teeth about the Dominican intervention, but Johnson stood firm on May 2, 1965 when he said, "The American government cannot, must not, and will not permit the establishment of another Communist government in the Western Hemisphere."

Lyndon Johnson was a disciple of Franklin Roosevelt's political philosophy: tax and tax, spend and spend, elect and elect. Even so, the liberals could not stomach the shallowness of his Great Society.

"The Great Society," wrote Robert Sherrill, Washington correspondent for *The Nation,* in 1967, "is a revolution without change." Nothing indicates more clearly the bureaucratic staleness of its concepts than the fact that more than 1500 permanent Federal anti-poverty employees earn $10,600 or more. In the Washington regional office of the Office of Economic Opportunity (OEO) more than 500 employees earn more than $14,600. The New York City poverty director earns $35,000—as much as a cabinet member. Do not suppose that in this broad pyramid of pay-offs and goof-offs much of the money reaches the lowest level." (61, p 179) Since 1967 the situation has gotten worse, not better.

The Great Society Reader: the Failure of American Liberalism is essentially a collection of essays critical of the Great Society and American liberalism in general. The essence of the book, which was edited by the ultra-leftists Marvin Gettleman and David Mermelstein, is that liberalism has failed because it did not go far enough to the left. There is one essay, however, credited to the libertarian Professor, Murray Rothbard, which presents the anti-statist case against liberalism. Rarely has the Great Society been damned more eloquently.

"The cruelest myth fostered by the liberals," wrote Rothbard, "is that the Great Society functions as a great boon and benefit to the poor; in reality, when we cut through the frothy appearances to the cold reality underneath, the poor are the major victims of the welfare state . . . The poor are the ones who lose their homes to the bulldozer of urban renewal, that bulldozer that operates for the benefit of real estate and construction interests to pulverize available low-cost housing. . . . The poor (e.g. negroes in the South) are the ones disemployed by rising minimum wage floors . . . The poor are victimized too by a welfare state of which the cardinal macro-economic tenet is perpetual if controlled inflation . . . Liberals have often scoffed at the anti-inflationists stress on the 'widows and orphans' as the major victims of inflation, but these remain the major victims nevertheless . . . And the burgeoning compulsory mass public education forces millions of unwilling youths off the labor market for many years, and into schools that serve more as houses of detention than as genuine centers of education. Farm programs that supposedly aid poor farmers actually serve wealthy farmers . . . at the expense of (*the*) . . . consumer and commissions that regulate industry serve to cartellize it. The mass of workers is forced by governmental measures into trade unions . . . these to be subject to arbitrary wage 'guidelines' and ultimate compulsory arbitration.

". . . at the heart of the welfarist mentality is an enormous desire to 'do good to' the mass of other people, and since people don't usually wish to be done good to, since they have their own ideas of what they wish to do, the liberal welfarist inevitably ends by reaching for the big stick with which to push the ungrateful masses around. Hence the liberal ethos itself provides a powerful stimulant for the intellectuals to seek state power . . . or as Isabel Patterson put it a generation ago (in *The God of the Machine*):

'The humanitarian wishes to be a prime mover in the lives of others. He can not admit either the divine or the natural order, by which men have the power to help themselves. The humanitarian puts himself in the place of God.

'But he is confronted by two awkward facts; first, that the competent do not need his assistance; and second, that the majority of people . . . positively do not want to be "done good to" by the humanitarian . . . of course what the humanitarian actually proposes is that he shall do what he thinks is good for everybody. It is at this point that the humanitarian sets up the guillotine.' " (13, pp 508-510)

CHAPTER 16

M IS FOR MACHIAVELLI, ALSO FOR MILHOUS

"Everybody knows how laudable it is in a prince to keep his faith and to be an honest man and not a trickster. Nevertheless, the experience of our times shows that the princes who have done great things are the ones who have taken little account of their promises and who have known how to addle the brains of men with craft. In the end they have conquered those who put their reliance on good faith." (From Machiavelli, Niccolo, *The Prince*, by J. R. Hale, as quoted in *The Horizon Book of the Renaissance*, English language edition © 1961 by American Heritage Publishing Co., Inc. Reprinted by permission of The Macmillan Company.)

Niccolo Machiavelli was the outstanding and possibly the first political scientist of the renaissance. Although he was an observer, rather than a practitioner, of deceit, craftiness, and treachery, his name has come to stand for evil. Yet, judged among the men of his times and by their moral standards he was not an evil man. Nor was he an ascetic. He was a servant of princes and his political observations bestowed upon him a far greater fame in death than had his civil duties during life.

"He (*Machiavelli*) judged private virtue to be the basis of all healthy national existence; but in the realm of politics he subordinated morals to political expediency. He held that the (*ordinary*) people . . . were the pith and fibre of nations; yet this same people had to become wax in the hands of the politicians—their commerce and their comforts, the arts which give dignity to life and the pleasures which make life livable, neglected—their very liberty subordinated to the one tyrannical conception." (Reprinted by permission of Encyclopaedia Britannica, Chicago, from *Encyclopaedia Britannica*, 14th ed. v 14, p 577.)

Speak of Tricky Dick and the ghost of Machiavelli enshrouds the subject. But is Tricky Dick any trickier than the rest of the political breed? Or has his opposition succeeded in merely making him appear so because they surpass him in the art of applying Machiavellian science? What kind of a man is Richard M for Milhous Nixon? We shall see.

The Nixon line came from Ireland in 1753, The Milhouses, also from Ireland, were Quakers who arrived twenty-four years earlier. However, there are strains other than Irish in the family.

Richard Nixon's father was a streetcar motorman, lemon farmer, and owner of a store and gas station in Whittier, California.

". . . It has been said our family was poor," Nixon told Stewart Alsop during an interview, "and maybe it was, but we never thought of ourselves as poor. We always had enough to eat, and we never had to depend on anyone else. Sure, we had to be careful. I was dressed in hand-me-downs, mostly in grammar school. Once in a while we'd go to a movie, but that was a luxury . . ." (62, pp 185-186)

Nixon also said that occasionally they had a week at the beach. He managed, also, to get through college (with the help of Federal handouts from Franklin D. Roosevelt's National Youth Administration), and he was not so close to starving that he could not afford the luxury of a new tuxedo while at Whittier College. (He gave his old one to a friend.) A scholarship helped him through Duke University Law School, where life was frugal and serious. Nixon and his family were hardly wealthy, but he never found it necessary to create a poverty legend as Big Daddy did.

Stewart Alsop, in his book *Nixon and Rockefeller: A Double Portrait,* drew on comments from Nixon's classmates in high-school, college, and law school, as well as on the results of a personal interview with his subject.

Alsop described a serious, hard-working, intelligent, combative, ambitious, introverted, reserved, and honest man. Effort and natural ability produced results: Nixon graduated number one from high-school, number two from Whittier College, and number three from Duke University Law School. He admitted he was a "lousy" football player, but he stuck it out. If he was put in for a few minutes at the end of a game, a classmate recalled, he always got a resounding cheer from the crowd. In his other activities he was more competent, particularly in debating and campus politics.

Alsop outlined two political crises and one personal crisis in Nixon's life: the move to drop Nixon from the Republican ticket in 1952, the dump Nixon move which was intended to keep him off the ticket in 1956 as Ike's running mate, and the 1958 riot in Caracas when his life was threatened.

"Nixon, in short, has guts," Alsop concluded. "No sensible person, however hostile to Nixon in other ways, can deny him that quality. He has other qualities, some admirable, some not so admirable. But the quality of guts is the quality which mostly marks him." (62, p 76)

"It is not," wrote liberal political reporter Richard Rovere of Richard Nixon, the vice-president, "by the practice of good fellowship that Nixon applies his healing touch. He has no gift for bonhomie and wisely leaves it to others." (57, p 298) He certainly does not impress one as a whisky-drinking president who enjoys raw jokes, but he is known as a skillful poker player.

"As a person and personality," Rovere wrote in 1956, "he embodies much that is held to be precious by a large and growing number of Americans . . . He is young, he is enterprising, he is successful. He is loyal to his organization and to his boss. He lacks humor, but he exudes earnestness and frankness. He has a weakness for dogs but not too many other weaknesses." (57, p 306) All in all, not a bad personality for a president, although since 1956 what the middle class holds as virtuous has been assaulted severely.

Emmet Hughes, like Rovere a liberal, was an Eisenhower speech writer who observed Nixon at first hand. ". . . the evidence," wrote Hughes, "mounted overwhelmingly that this man did not neatly fit the acid caricature of his enemies. To them, he appeared either a lion of Republicanism and reaction or a fox of ambition and guile. To closer witnesses he seemed neither. His private discourse betrayed scarcely any of the partisan excess he reserved for public consumption . . . Indeed, the philosophy of any policy interested him . . . far less than its efficacy . . . At his intellectual best in offering tactical counsel, he came to appear more and more the kind of politician who, but for some accident of partisan affiliation, could have rendered such service just as heartily to the Democratic party." (12, p 317)

There have been conflicting views on Eisenhower's opinion of Nixon. Ike, true to the politician's creed of being ever ready to cut the throat of anyone standing in the way of his success, was ready to dump Nixon in 1952. Only after Nixon's defense of himself on television and it appeared that the public was rallying to his support did Ike throw his arms around Nixon and say, "You're my boy." In 1956, before the convention, Ike suggested to his vice-president that he might advance his career if he took a job as a cabinet officer. This had been interpreted as a move to get rid of Nixon in response to efforts of Harold Stassen and others, but it may just as well have been a sincere attempt by Ike to broaden Nixon's experience.

Sherman Adams, President Eisenhower's chief administrative assistant, did not have a very high opinion of Nixon and this has lent credence to the view that Eisenhower himself was not very enthusiastic about his vice-president. (See, for instance, Felix Belair's interview with Sherman Adams, syndicated by the *New York Times* News Service, which appeared in the Boston *Sunday Herald Traveler*, sec 2, p 17, Mar 5, 1972.)

On the other hand, Arthur Krock, for many years *The New York Times'* man in Washington, while admitting there will always be room for disagreement among historians regarding Ike's evaluation of Nixon, concluded that "in the long run the General has demonstrated the greatest admiration for Nixon. He very much wanted him to be elected President." (63, p 315)

Nixon's speeches, particularly his early ones, reveal more of his character and personality than do the speeches of most politicians. As vice-president, Nixon told Stewart Alsop that he wrote all of his own speeches and made up his own mind on what to say. (62, p 200) He personally wrote the speech he gave on television in the 1952 campaign when he defended himself against charges that he had a personal "slush fund." The ideas for the speech were written in flight on the free postcards provided by airlines. (62, p 194)

One-thousand two-hundred sixty-one pages set in that miserable type the Government Printing Office uses in pamphlets on termite control, how to avoid diaper rash, and the Congressional

Record, all publications of questionable literary value, represents more words than an easy writer could set down in ten years. By conservative estimate 600,000 words would be needed to fill those 1261 pages. Part II of the *Final Report of the Committee on Commerce* of the U.S. Senate is 1261 pages long.[1] According to the title page, Part II is made up of "the speeches, remarks, press conferences, and study papers of Richard M. Nixon, August 1 through November 7, 1960." Even if he could claim to be an easy writer, Nixon in 1960 was obviously no longer writing his own material as he had done in 1952 and 1956.

In 1966, when Richard Nixon returned to the political wars, the first person he hired was a man who had caddied for him at Ike's Burning Tree Country Club. Patrick Buchanan, a Georgetown University graduate with conservative inclinations, was by then an editorial writer for the St. Louis *Globe-Democrat.* Buchanan was hired as a researcher, writer, and political aide for Nixon who was busy during 1966 rebuilding the party, electing Republicans to Congress, and regaining his leadership of the party. At this time, the ex-vice-president's speeches could be classed as conservative. Nixon also supplied a column for the North American Newspaper Alliance. According to Jules Witcover, who covered Nixon during the 1966 campaign, "most of the research and much of the writing were done by Buchanan." (66, p 126) Yet, Nixon was still doing a lot of his own writing.

On an eleven day trip in June of 1966, Witcover wrote that "on flights in small private planes, I would sit just behind him as he filled the dead minutes and hours by retooling his speech on his ever present yellow legal pad . . ." (66, p 133) Later, in a private interview with Witcover as the campaign trip drew to a close, Nixon said "I don't mean writing is easy for me, but writing phrases that move people, that to me is something. What memorable phrases have ever come from the Republican or Democratic national committee, or from speechwriters? My best efforts, my acceptance speech in 1960, my Moscow speech, my unity speech at the 1964 convention—all were dredged out by writing my head off." (66, p 149)

---

[1] *Final Report of the Committee on Commerce*, United States Senate, prepared by its Subcommittee of the Committee on Communications, Part II, November 28, 1961, Superintendent of Documents, Washington, $3.50.

Two years later, in 1968, Nixon told Witcover "I don't say I do all the writing. They do a lot, and I edit . . . *We've already* had more major speeches in 1968—breaking new ground—than in 1960 in the final. By the time we get to the convention, we'll have a good bank." (66, p 302) (Italics added.)

However, Nixon still saved the big ones for himself. According to Witcover, "Nixon . . . dictated three full tapes (*for his 1968 acceptance speech*) to Rose Woods (*his private secretary*), requiring forty-seven pages, then refined several drafts . . . to get exactly what he wanted. 'I write for a while on a yellow legal-sized pad,' Nixon himself told reporters one day, 'and then I talk what I have written into a machine, and if something doesn't sound right, I revise it.' " (66, p 337)

Is Nixon a liberal or conservative? His background, his speeches, his comments, his actions, and the opinions of others throw light on the question.

If there is any truth to the saying "like father, like son," Nixon's political behavior could have been predicted from his father's voting record. By Nixon's own account his father "was very strong for LaFollette" in 1924, in 1928 he was for Hoover, and "Hoover was then the liberal candidate." (62, p 186) Father Nixon supported Hoover again in 1932, but deserted the Republican fold for Roosevelt in 1936. Nixon has followed his father's erratic course, short of switching parties.

In the 1950 race against Helen Gahagan Douglas, Nixon proclaimed himself "a liberal in foreign policy and a conservative in domestic policy." But according to Ralph De Toledano, an admirer of Nixon in 1956, "the terms were an oversimplification. In neither foreign nor domestic policy did he vote with the extremists." (65, p 89)

In 1960, Stewart Alsop raised the question of whether Richard Nixon would be a liberal or conservative president.

"Nixon's record is not consistent," Alsop concluded. "In his first term in the House he voted like a down-the-line right-wing Republican. Thereafter he began a gentle movement toward the center, which has continued, with some zigs and zags, ever since." (62, p 176)

"The admiration among the Taft-worshipers is essentially irrational, since Nixon contributed to Taft's last defeat in 1952 and since he has none of Taft's hankering for a simpler past," wrote Alsop in 1960. (62, p 29)

". . . I'm not necessarily a respecter of the status quo in foreign affairs," Nixon told Alsop. "I am a chance taker in foreign affairs. I would take chances for peace—the Quakers have a passion for peace, you know." (62, p 198)

On domestic affairs, Nixon came through as a liberal.

"I've known unemployed people, . . . I know what their problems are," Nixon told Alsop in 1960. "I've always taken an advanced position on medical care . . . I feel very strongly about educational opportunities for people in the lower brackets. I would say that I was not especially conservative as regards civil rights . . . But in some other ways I suppose I am a conservative, yes." (62, pp 198-199) Nixon explained his liberal tendencies on the basis of his family background and youthful experiences.

As the conventions of 1960 approached, Alsop concluded that "it seems a fair guess that Nixon would be a less conservative President than Rockefeller—for he is at heart a less cautious man."

Earl Mazo, the reporter, in his generally friendly biography written in 1959, wrote that ". . . Nixon is not merely an 'Eisenhower-Republican'—he is a 'Nixon-Eisenhower-Republican'—and his innate tendencies are much less conservative." (64, p 289)

In August 1964 a Republican unity meeting was held at Hershey, Pennsylvania where an attempt was made to heal some of the wounds of the conservative-liberal fight which had ended with Barry Goldwater's choice as the party's presidential candidate. Nixon opened the meeting.

". . . In order to be a majority party, we must expand the base of our party rather than contract it . . . I want all Republicans to win; I am just as strong for a liberal Republican in New York as I am for a conservative Republican in Texas, and I can go and just as enthusiastically campaign for both, because we need both liberals and conservatives to have a majority. And it is a majority we want in the house, in the senate, among the governors, and for the presidency." (66, pp 100-101)

Nixon merely restated the politician's first principle—victory and power come first. Philosophy and ideology are secondary unless they contribute to victory.

During the summer of 1966, Nixon spoke in Birmingham, Alabama. He didn't sound like the Nixon who spoke in Hershey, Pennsylvania.

"If you have conservative friends," said the man who expressed a dislike for political labels, "who are looking where to go, tell them to come to the Republican Party, because the Republican Party is the party of conservatives. The Democratic Party on the national level hasn't been conservative for thirty years and never will be, so get out of it and join the Republican Party." (66, p 147)

"The standard speech" (*for the 1966 campaign*), according to Jules Witcover, "concluded with an old party refrain—the eroding effect of big centralized government on individual rights and local initiative. Nixon would warn of the day not too far off when a majority of Americans would have their rent subsidized, their medical bills paid, their income assured and their education determined by the federal government. Only the election of Republicans could prevent such a catastrophe." (66, p 138)

"Tell them," Nixon cried to a crowd of 2500 cheering Republicans in his final speech before the 1966 election, "a Republican congress will bring progress with peace and prosperity without inflation. Now go out and win. Make Tuesday National Price Protest Day. Kick the spenders out and send the savers in." (66, p 169)

By 1971, Nixon was outspending even Kennedy!

Soviet First Secretary Frol Kozlov was described by Nixon, and the description reveals as much about Nixon as it does about the First Secretary. Kozlov was said to be "extremely intelligent, capable, and equipped with a facility essential to the politician—that of appearing to answer a question emphatically when, in reality, the whole point of the question has been successfully evaded." (62, p 47)

The question of whether Nixon is a liberal or conservative is of little consequence. He is first and foremost a politician. Therefore, such political principles as he has are bent if they stand in the way of winning at the polls. Richard Rovere, who is in the ultra-liberal corner, made some interesting comments in 1955, based largely upon Nixon's earlier record in Congress.

"One of the unique things about him," wrote Rovere, "is that he has achieved his present eminence by concerning himself exclusively with strategy and ignoring the whole broad field of policy . . . Policy, it would seem, is something in which Nixon has only a mild spasmodic interest. He can take it or leave it alone. He does not fear it and avoid commitment . . . but there is no discernible pattern to his commitments . . .

"Indifferent to doctrine, he dwells somewhat apart from factionalism. He can not be classified as either a right-wing or left-wing Republican.

"On such matters as price controls, Federal funds for school construction, and the regulation of trusts, he often voted in a manner held to be correct and virtuous by the CIO and Americans for Democratic Action . . . On civil liberties bills issues he voted with the liberals and delivered himself of liberal platitudes.

"But what stands out in any consideration of the whole record is the flexibility that suggests an almost total indifference to policy." (57, pp 299-308)

Nixon, it appears, never felt the need to commit himself to any political principles beyond winning the next election. In this respect he may be Machiavellian, but he is no different than most victorious politicians. Arthur Krock, of *New York Times* fame, described one aspect of Nixon's character which helped make him president.

"One of the attributes," wrote Arthur Krock, "that makes Nixon unusual is his ability to appraise, with almost total objectivity, situations and political prospects in which he himself is deeply involved." (63, p 317) Nixon confirmed this appraisal of himself in his interview with Stewart Alsop (62, p 192) when he told of his decision not to withdraw, under fire, from the ticket in 1952.

By 1960 Nixon had both feet firmly planted in statist territory. He was still, in conservative Republican eyes, more of a conservative and more of a true Republican than was Ike, the usurper. But many conservatives, without realizing it, were by this time pretty adept statists themselves. It does not come as a surprise, then, that a Machiavellian would assess with total objectivity what was needed to buy him power. So Mr. Nixon, during the campaign, tried to match Mr. Kennedy's statism. He fell short only in eloquence of expression.

For instance his study paper of September 1960 euphemistically called for Federal aid (i.e. Federal intervention) to education. This catered to the popular view which had been shaped over the years by the education lobbyists and social propagandists. The first large-scale Federal interference with strictly local educational problems occurred in May 1949, when the Aid to Education Bill was passed. This provided for $270 million to be paid to the states for improvement of grade and high schools. This measure had as one of its sponsors none other than conservative Senator Robert A. Taft. (20, p 33) Nixon now called for Federal spending to help elementary and secondary schools and colleges, to improve the art of teaching, to provide scholarships and loans, to subsidize undergraduate and graduate study for prospective teachers, to subsidize medical education, to promote vocational education, to provide education for the handicapped and retarded, to expand adult education, and to provide funds for libraries. (67, pp 283-286) Was anything or anyone forgotten? Hardly.

By 1972, Federal aid to education was at the rate of $18 billion a year, almost seventy times the 1949 figure!

Nixon did not explain why it was necessary for the Federal government to do all this in the name of education, but the clear implication was that state and local governments and individuals were incapable of doing what should be done. If they were unable to do so, could it be because the Federal government, through the income tax and inflation, was siphoning off so much wealth that there wasn't enough left to do the job? Certainly it was not suggested that the Federal government was to engage in the actual production of the wealth needed to support these activities. The Federal government's part would be limited to collecting from the real producers of wealth the largess it would distribute. The amount distributed, that is the amount that would actually benefit education, would shrink in the process by virtue of politicking, bookkeeping and red tape.

The day before Nixon's staff released his proposals for mammoth Federal intervention in education, he spoke from the steps of the governor's mansion in Mississippi. It is hard to believe that he could face an audience and express a more diametrically opposed view. The Democrats, according to Nixon, said "the way to get the jobs and the schools and the housing and all the things that spell progress for America is to turn first to Washington and the Federal government and to work down to the people . . .

"We say," said the man whose position paper on Federal "aid" to education had just proposed transfer of additional responsibility from state and local governments to Washington, "that the way to progress in this country is not to weaken the power of our States and local governments, but to strengthen them.

"We say the way to progress is not through expanding the size of the Federal Government and its functions, except . . . where the job can not otherwise be done . . ." (67, p 568)

In Mississippi and the South, Octopus Federalis would not be one of the delicacies served at the Nixon smjorgasbord.

A week after Nixon pledged Federal aid and comfort for education, he repeated the promise for medical research. This was to be in the form of Federal medical fellowships, support of medical research, and a ten-year program of expanding medical research facilities and research laboratories. The Federal grant program for research facilities had, he claimed, "already resulted in attracting $4 additional for every Federal dollar allocated . . ." (67, p 393) He did not mention that $4 *less* in local funds (for each Federal dollar spent) was available for projects which would otherwise have received attention from states, localities, or individuals paying the tax bills.

The dessert table at the 1960 Nixon smjorgasbord held something for the aged. Having seen to it that youth was educated with the help of Uncle Sam, provided with the standard staples of peace and prosperity, and coaxed to old age by Federal banishment of disease and medical problems, what could be more logical than a table loaded with goodies for the elderly, who, by the time they reach the golden years, so-called, would be expected to need some Federal help after paying for government programs all their lives. Furthermore, the very nature of the welfare state had encouraged them to believe that saving, even if possible, was unnecessary, because the Federal Octopus would take care of their final struggles.

On October 30th, Nixon published his study paper entitled "Senior Citizen's Program." This sounded a call for guaranteed medical assistance, expansion of old-age insurance programs, provision of housing for the elderly, counselling and guidance programs for the aged, and assisting middle-aged groups to plan ahead. Most of this program would have been considered, a hundred years earlier, to have been an insult to self-respect, independence, and personal responsibility. About the only item Nixon forgot was a Federal safe conduct pass through the lines to the pearly gates.

Nixon, in his message for elderly eyes, did not forget the one area of concern to the elderly for which the Federal government had a legitimate responsibility.

"The Federal Government," stated the position paper, *"must do everything in its power to maintain the purchasing power of 'honest dollars.'"* The italics and the quotation marks appear in the original. Of course, had the Federal government, which has the unchallenged sole authority to control the number of dollars in circulation, and indirectly the dollar's value, discharged its duties, the problems of the aged could have been solved by the aged themselves and their families. Eleven years later Nixon would use Federal price and wage controls in an attempt to undo the damage to the dollar which he, and other politicians before him, had wrought. He would go after the symptoms of inflation, but not the disease itself.

Jules Witcover's *The Resurrection of Richard Nixon* is interesting, good reading, and full of information and first-hand observations. Witcover's standards of objectivity match those of most political reporters working the current scene, but he usually manages to keep his biases hidden. He does reveal himself, however, in his description of Bobby Kennedy at the "last round-up," a description illuminated by a flash of unembarrassed adulatory bias. Witcover is, alas, as liberal as most.

It is not surprising, then, that Witcover's Nixon is not dressed in shiney armor, replete with plumed helmet. Witcover creates the impression that the candidate's 1968 "two-track" campaign was sneakier than should be expected even of a Republican, so much so that Nixon qualifies for the Annual Tricky Dick Award. It could be, however, that Witcover, like the other liberal Democrat reporters who had earlier done in Nixon and were then being repaid in kind, was only showing the reaction of a reporter who has been shut out.

The "two-track" campaign called for privately screened TV appearances, from which reporters were generally excluded, and public personal appearances, to which reporters were admitted. The usual hordes of reporters followed Nixon's personal appearances and were free to report what they saw as they saw it. The effects of any bias were limited to the printed word. In the far more effective TV appearances, the candidate was bathed in biases of his own making, and since TV time was paid for by the Republican Party this should have been expected. Nixon was not overly generous with reporter interviews during the campaign and excluding reporters from his TV shows shielded him from their hostility. The TV shows consisted of selected questions, not all of them friendly, but generally not overtly hostile. The questioners represented a screened cross section of the voting public. Audiences were enthusiastic Republican supporters who insured an appropriate response to the right answers. Questions and answers were not rehearsed. However, the candidate and his staff worked hard preparing answers to anticipated questions, a technique which is no more contrived or tricky than what has been used ever since FDR's press conferences.

In brief, then, the TV shows were intended to provide a favorable forum for Nixon and a broader audience than could be obtained by personal appearances. The prejudices of reporters were neutralized; there would be no filters between the candidate and his viewers. The "two-track" campaign was Nixon's response to a press which had been hostile to him in 1960 and 1962 and which he had little reason to expect had changed. It was his way of nullifying press antagonism, and only after it was too late did most reporters realize what was going on. It is doubtful if the technique will be as successful the second time around.

But what is really important is what Nixon said and promised as he rode around his two campaign tracks. And how has his performance stood up to his promises? As Al Smith was fond of saying, "Let's look at the record."

Senator John Tower, conservative Republican from Texas, after conferring with Nixon at the outset of the campaign, said the candidate would concentrate on inflation, crime and violence, and Vietnam. (66, p 364) On Vietnam, in particular, there was little in the way of specifics, but of course this had to be. Neither of the candidates, as potential presidents, could afford to let the enemy know what was in store for them. On domestic issues there was the usual criticism of vagueness. Richard Whalen, biographer of Joseph P. Kennedy, who had signed on as a Nixon writer, left in despair. "What really does the man stand for," he asked. (66, p 366)

Nixon was probably no more or less vague than Frol Kozlov or Hubert Humphrey. Part of the art of the politician, as Nixon himself appreciated, is to appear to "answer a question emphatically when, in reality, the whole point of the question has been successfully evaded." (62, p 47)

On August 6, 1968, the day before he was nominated, Nixon met "privately" with Southern convention delegates. The next day, amid cries of "foul," *The Miami Herald* printed a transcript of the candidate's "private" remarks. Politics and politicians being what they are, it is impossible to determine whether this was a genuine scoop engineered by Nixon's rivals in an attempt to embarrass him, or whether it was a contrived plant by Nixon's friends to gain publicity for his views. In any event, Nixon's "private" views turned out to be about the same as his public ones.

For instance, in discussing the busing of school children, Nixon said, "I think that busing the child—a child that is two or three grades behind another child and into a strange community . . . I think that you destroy that child. The purpose of school is to educate. That is what we have got to do. We have got to educate them, and I don't believe in that manner of approach. . . ."

Following the Florida primary in early 1972, Nixon came out against busing as a means of improving the education of negroes. His critics claimed he waited until he saw how Governor Wallace's anti-busing stance was received by the voters before taking his own stand. However, not only in his "private" comments in Miami in 1968, but in later public comments, has Nixon opposed busing. On March 24, 1970, a year before the Florida primary, the president stated he was opposed to segregation where it existed by law. Where segregation occurred as a result of housing patterns, Nixon proposed a half-billion dollars in federal aid for 1971 and one billion dollars in 1972 to improve predominantly black schools. On the issue of busing Tricky Dick's trickery is the product of his foes' imaginations. He has been remarkably consistent on the issue.

Several times during his "private" Miami remarks to Southern delegates Nixon expressed himself on the Supreme Court. His first reference came in a reply to a question on busing.

". . . I think," said the candidate, "it is the job of the courts to interpret the law and not make the law."

"I don't know," he stated later replying to a question on Supreme Court appointments, "what the Senate is going to do. But if I have the chance to appoint Justices to the Supreme Court, they will be men . . . who are strict constitutionalists, men that interpret the law and don't try to make the law."

To conservatives, the most important accomplishments of Richard Nixon's presidency are his appointments to the Supreme Court. Here he has followed exactly his previously stated views. The court was never intended to be a super-legislative body beyond the reach of the electorate, but during the Warren years this is what it had become. Nixon's appointees, Burger, Blackman, Powell, and Rehnquist, are all known as strict constructionists. Hence, the court moves back toward legal rather than legislative functions. If he is supported for a second term by conservatives who are disillusioned by his economic and foreign policy decisions, it will be because of his Supreme Court appointments.

It is in the realm of economic and social activity that the Tricky Dick caricature has proved most accurate. But now the caricature is being used by some conservatives, who did not invent it, rather than by the liberals, who did. The reasons are easy to come by.

For instance, during the 1968 campaign, candidate Nixon called the Office of Emergency Opportunity a "failure," but President Nixon asked for and got authority to spend $400 million more for it during 1970 than when he took over. Promises of billions to rebuild cities, candidate Nixon claimed in Minneapolis on April 20, 1968, are "dishonest and a cruel delusion . . . I am not going to join those candidates who are promising more and more billions." In the last Johnson fiscal year $14 billion in aid went to the cities. In President Nixon's first two fiscal years the spending went from $16 billion to $21 billion, with $27 billion estimated for 1972 and $31.5 billion projected for 1973! (Source, U.S. Office of Management and Budget.)

The Family Assistance Plan and welfare reform are also touchy points with conservatives. In the 1968 campaign, candidate Nixon stated ". . . I do not accept . . . a guaranteed annual income or a negative income tax . . . because of my conviction that doing so, first, would not end poverty, and second . . . it would have a very detrimental effect on the productive capacity of the American people . . . I am against any system which would destroy or reduce that incentive, that determination, that self respect and that pride."

At the press conference on December 8, 1969, the recommendations of the White House Conference on Food and Nutrition were discussed. Nixon appeared to be standing firm when he said, "There is another recommendation by the White House Conference which I, unfortunately, can not give really sympathetic consideration to, and that is the one recommending a $5400 minimum for a family of four in America. That would cost approximately $70 to $80 billion in taxes, or $70 to $80 billion in increased prices . . ."

But shortly after this the administration came forth with its own Family Assistance Plan. According to congressional opponents, this would have guaranteed $2400 to each non-working family of four, cost between five and six billion dollars in Federal money in addition to the $72 billion current total spending, and add 15 to 20 million people to the welfare rolls.

About a month before the 1968 election, Nixon was interviewed by the staff of one of the leading weekly news magazines. In connection with his economic plans he emphasized the need to take steps that would stabilize the value of the dollar and stop the outflow of gold, while at the same time being careful to avoid a recession. He expressed the view that it was not necessary to have inflation in order to achieve prosperity.

Since expressing himself on these problems, the cost of living has continued to rise (for which the Johnson years are partly to blame; the results of Nixon's deficits are yet to be felt), the gold run has reached flood stage (it will eventually stop—when there is no more gold in Fort Knox), the dollar has been devalued once and continues to depreciate, and we have had (or are having) a recession.

In the same interview, candidate Nixon said he felt that the budget need not be balanced every year, but it should be balanced over a longer term such as, perhaps, a five year span. If Nixon serves a second term, he will have to aim for an $80 billion surplus in his *first* year to make up for his first four years of deficits. This may be a trifle difficult, since the largest surplus in the last twenty five years (which occurred under Truman in 1948) was only $8 billion.

In his interview, Nixon admitted to being an economic activist who would not hesitate to use tax and credit policies to stimulate the economy. He added he thought he could do this without inflation, but he did not explain how. In view of his tagging himself as an activist in economics, his later remark to Howard K. Smith about being a Keynesian should not have shocked so many.

Until the middle of August 1971, President Nixon repeatedly spoke against price and wage controls. In 1970 wages in the construction industry rose an average of 18.3 per cent. In 1971 construction unions demanded 25 per cent increases and Nixon's response was to set up (on March 29, 1971) a stabilization committee to oversee wages in the construction industry on a voluntary basis. The administration called for increases limited to 6 per cent, but the first union-industry agreement called for increases of double this amount.

Voluntary price and wage controls are not controls if they are *voluntary*. They either will not work, or if they do, they are unnecessary. Secretary of Treasury Connally, then recently appointed by Nixon, stated the official line once again: wage-price controls were not in favor "at the present (early April 1971) time." While Connally was making his statement, the steelworkers union flatly rejected any guidelines limiting *them* to a 6 per cent increase. They conceded that 30 per cent increases would be acceptable. Within a week the construction union leadership stated they would not be bound by any 6 per cent limitation. By summer it was obvious that jawboning was no substitute for economic law. Voluntary controls were a flop.

On August 15, 1971, President Nixon officially abandoned his former opposition to price and wage controls. He announced a 90-day freeze on prices and wages, but said he was going to rely on *voluntary cooperation* of employers, workers, and consumers. This is in contradiction to Section 5 of the Executive Order establishing the Cost of Living Council, which states that the Council "may require any person to maintain and produce for examination such records or other evidence, in such form as it shall require, concerning prices, rents, wages and salaries and all related matters." Section 7(a) states that *"Whoever willfully vio-*

lates this Order . . . shall be fined not more than $5000 for each violation." This is voluntary cooperation?

Not only does this tyrannous Executive Order appear to require accused persons to testify against themselves (as do the internal revenue acts), it also requires the violation of legal contracts such as those granting or promising specified wage, price, and rent increases. The government, which is the organized coercion permitted by citizens for purposes of enforcing the sanctity of contracts and agreements, has been perverted by the Executive Order to enforce the violation of contracts!

In 1966, the first syndicated column to go out under Nixon's signature stated that ". . . as prices and taxes rise, administration spokesmen will try to blame labor for demanding higher wages, they will try to blame businessmen for asking for higher prices, they will try to blame the war in Vietnam. There is only one place to put the blame—the budget-brinkmanship of the Johnson Administration." (66, pp 126-127)

"For a nation," said conservative candidate Nixon in New York on January 27, 1968, "with our wealth and growth over the past *five* years to spend 50 billion dollars more (*a Nixon exaggeration, political license*) than we take in—this is certainly economic insanity."

President Nixon would have total deficits estimated (in 1972) at 100 billion dollars for his first *four* year term.

". . . It isn't what Americans spend abroad," said conservative candidate Nixon on February 18, 1968 in Chicago, "but what the Administration is spending in Washington that is the reason for the weakness of the American dollar."

On April 20, 1968, the conservative candidate said in Minneapolis that we are facing "one of the greatest financial crises in our history."

By the middle of 1972, after three and one-half years of Nixon, the crisis was worse.

"Mr. Humphrey's public record," said conservative candidate Nixon when he reached Middletown, Ohio during the closing days of the 1968 campaign, "gives no indication that he believes there is a bottom to the well of the United States Treasury. He has built a public career out of buying the people's votes with the people's money." (66, p 424)

Has the unconservative President Nixon's record been any better?

In Saginaw, Michigan, the conservative candidate accused Humphrey of being one who would "rather spend than save." (66, p 426)

Was the pot calling the kettle black? Again, let's look at the record.

Nixon's years in office from 1969 to 1973 will have produced the worst deficits in "peacetime" history. The country, of course, has not been at peace. Nor has it been at war, in a full-scale sense. Nevertheless, even with the Vietnamese war expenditures diminishing, deficits, real and estimated, have increased. This is not unexpected from an administration which has boasted that it is spending more on welfare than on defense. In fiscal 1970 the deficit was $2.8 billion, in 1971 it was $23 billion, in 1972 it was $23 billion, and for 1973 the estimated deficit is $32.5 billion. The total, projected and reported, amounts to $81.3 billion. Keeping in mind that income is usually overestimated and expenditures are usually underestimated, the $81.3 billion figure is likely, but not certain, to be low. The lead editorial of *The New York Times* on January 31, 1972 stated that a total deficit approaching $100 billion was realistic. The editorial applauded Nixon's newly discovered fiscal unconservatism!

The gross national debt when the conservative candidate took over was figured at $354 billion dollars (at the end of fiscal 1969). The unconservative President, Richard Nixon, will have increased it by 28 per cent in four years if he adds $100 billion to it. This from the man who accused his 1968 opponent of favoring spending over saving.

Lewis H. Kimmel in his scholarly work *Federal Budget and Fiscal Policy, 1789-1958* summarizes the views of fiscally conservative thinkers of the 1930's.

"Unbalanced budgets lead to inflation," these men concluded, according to Kimmel, who then went on to quote Lewis W. Douglas, Franklin Roosevelt's first Director of the Budget.

"History demonstrates without exception that whenever a government continuously spends more than it takes in the social consequences are tragic," according to Douglas.

"The American colonies, it was pointed out (*by Douglas*) had destroyed their currency and impoverished their people, and France had experienced an extreme inflation about the same time. The Civil War inflation in the United States and the post-World War I inflation in France were other outstanding examples. The reason for the universal experience resides in two powers of government."

Then quoting Douglas directly, Kimmel wrote, "The first is the power to appropriate and expend money. The second is the power to manufacture money." (4, p 223)

Douglas might also have mentioned the most disastrous inflation of all time: the inflation in Germany in the 1920's which led to revolution, Hitler, and later, world tragedies.

Inflation is not a recent invention, here or abroad, as the terms "not worth a continental" and "coin clipping" attest. Henry Watterson, a Democrat and liberal in the original sense of the word, fought repeatedly "the greenback craze (*of the late 1800's*) and the free-silver craze against an overwhelming majority in the West and South . . . Both movements had their origin on economic fallacies and found their backing in dishonest purpose to escape honest indebtedness." (6, v II, pp 144-145)

In 1949 *Fortune* magazine polled 25,000 business executives regarding the steps the Federal government should take to prevent a recession from developing into a depression. (*Fortune*, v 40, no. 2, Aug 1949, p 48) The three options from which choices were to be made were even more illuminating than the results of the poll, for their limited nature as well as the responses to them show that the original concept of limited government has been largely cast aside. The executives were asked, assuming a moderate surplus at the start of a recession, whether they would (1) raise taxes and try to balance the budget, (2) leave taxes alone and let the deficit grow, or (3) cut taxes in order to strengthen business incentives and expand purchasing power. Fifty-three per cent chose the second option, twenty-six per cent chose the third, and only sixteen chose the first. Even more significant is the failure to include a fourth option: reduce *both* taxes *and* spending by the government. *Fortune's* editors stated that "a liberalizing process has been at work that increases the chances of fending off depressions in the future; or of preventing recessions from turning into depressions." The editors overlooked the possibility that the two most popular options could lead to continuing and eventual catastrophic inflation. In between the period of continued deficits and runaway inflation there will first be voluntary controls, then mandatory price, wage, and investment controls, and eventually rationing and black markets. All will fail. Will freedom then be a fiction?

Two ultra-leftists have concluded that Keynesian economics offers no hope of simultaneously reducing unemployment and stopping inflation. According to socialists Mermelstein and Gettleman "Under the Eisenhower administration higher unemployment rates and lower prices were favored. Kennedy and Johnson and their advisers seem to have a slight tendency in the other direction—lower unemployment and an increased measure of inflation." And they added in a footnote: "When all is said and done, this may be the major policy difference between the Republican and Democratic parties." (13, p 49) Nixon seems to have accepted this estimate of the difference between the parties and is doing his best, in an attempt to be all things to all men, not to eliminate the difference, but to maintain it by outdoing the Democrats.

The 1958 recession, so-called, was the first occasion in history when prices and the cost-of-living moved upward while unemployment increased and other indices showed that business was getting worse. By 1971, the power of unions to force higher wage demands had grown so great that contrary trends even more pronounced than in 1958 were observed.

U.S. News and World Report (July 12, 1971, p 63) compared figures for the low point of the 1970 recession with results six months following the low point, i.e. May 1971. Consumer prices had risen two per cent, "whereas in previous recoveries there was little change, with small declines in two cases. Cost of labor per unit of output in manufacturing, nearly two per cent above November, fell an average of 3.2 per cent in previous recoveries." Clearly labor power is great enough to prevent downward adjustment of wages. Wages above what the free market will permit causes unemployment. *Only by deficit financing and inflation of the money supply can real wages be brought down so that unemployment can be reduced.* We are locked into a cycle of rising wages and prices, increasing unemployment, and inflation by the political power of labor unions and by the ignorance of labor leaders, the politicians, and the people who support them.

A popular view in the middle 1930's (promoted by Alvin Hansen, a prominent and influential New Deal economist) was that the United States suffered from surpluses and overproduction. The fellows standing in the soup lines no doubt had different opinions. Nevertheless, economists concluded "that private demands for capital are unable to absorb all the savings generated by the economy. Government, it is said, must *permanently* take up the slack by spending in excess of its income." (4, p 199)

The question was never asked, and therefore not answered, why, if excess capital is accumulated it is necessary to dispose of it by deficit financing when it could just as easily have been disposed of by taxation. The answer is, of course, without condescending to agree that excess capital was the real problem, that taxation as a means of disposing of capital would have been political suicide for the party in power. Deficit financing inevitably results in printing more money and the resulting inflation is a less obvious and more acceptable form of taxation. However, taxes levied by inflation are discriminatory, being first levied upon the thrifty who hold bank deposits, bonds, insurance, and dollars tucked away in lumpy mattresses.

Regarding the effects of government intervention on savings and investment, some remarks of Lewis Kimmel in his book on federal fiscal policy are revealing.

"First," wrote Kimmel, "investigations of investment methods and practices, together with legislation enacted in 1933 and 1934, unsettled the investment climate. That reforms were necessary is recognized, but it was not so much the reforms as the zeal of the reformers that had an unsettling influence. Second, in formulating tax policy, little or no consideration was given to the impact of the tax structure on investment. Taxes on investment income became heavier than at any time after World War I. Sight was lost of the fact that high income taxes may act as a deterrent to investment—that 'taxation, especially taxation of income, shifts the odds against the risk taker'." (4, p 216) These statements seem to be at variance with conclusions that the problem was over-production and over-capitalization, and, in fact, suggest that the problem was one of under-capitalization and under-production. The men in the soup lines would have agreed to this.

Alvin Hansen, the "new economist" whose influence peaked

during the New Deal era, feared that no new inventions of significance would be made after the thirties. After all we had electricity, automobiles, airplanes, and the radio. All worlds had fallen before the conqueror and there was nothing left to do. Hansen gloomily felt that America had reached its last frontiers and that with a declining birth rate (his claim) and a "mature" economy "it would become," according to Lewis Kimmel's summary of Hansen's ideas, "increasingly necessary for government to take an active part in directing the flow of saving into investment channels." (4, p 200)

Kimmel stated that "some of the forces making for . . . stagnation, it was claimed, began to develop toward the end of the 19th century." (4, p 201) One wonders if the stagnation (in the form of business panics and depressions) could not have resulted from government action which disrupted private affairs: Civil War, Spanish-American War, World War I, and graduated income taxes which seized an ever higher percentage of production.

"Because of the paucity of outlets for savings," Kimmel continued in his summary of economic thought of the thirties, "and declining rate of population growth, it was asserted that the problem of . . . stagnation may well overshadow that of the business cycle." (4, p 201) Was Hansen wrong in assuming there was a paucity of outlets for savings? Did the high interest rates of the twenties suggest there was an excess of savings over demand for savings, or was it the other way around? Was Hansen overlooking the fact that increased capitalization (up to a point best determined by the free-market) is the most effective way of lowering unit cost (in terms of human effort), that increased capitalization was required to eliminate long hours of work and child labor, and that increased capitalization would be needed to raise the standard of living, to provide better housing, food, clothing and conveniences at a price people below the existing "poverty line" could afford to pay? Perhaps Hansen was wrong, and under-capitalization resulting from government diversion of income to consumer spending has helped to prevent the most economical and profitable use of resources, human and material, which could contribute to the elimination of poverty.

In the post World War II years, the Keynesian chorus, which

by then had moved to center stage from offstage left, wailed ever more loudly that budget surpluses cause depressions. Deficits, they sang, are the food of prosperity. Their theory has been repeated so often that it is now accepted by many as a maxim. It is true only so long as it is supported by unprecedented labor union power and a Federal commitment to full employment through inflation. Few economists any longer bother to note that the average annual surpluses for the *decade* of the twenties was about $800,000,000 (or about 20 per cent of federal tax receipts) and the decade of the twenties was a decade of almost uninterrupted prosperity.

Nixon, not Johnson nor Kennedy nor Truman nor Roosevelt, has turned out to be the biggest peacetime spender in our history. The *New York Times* estimate of a $100 billion dollar deficit for the first four Nixon years has already been mentioned. *U.S. News and World Report* estimated the total at $86.5 billion early in 1972. Taking the lower figure, Nixon's average annual deficit will be $21.4 billion. By way of comparison the figures for average annual deficits for the four preceding presidents are: Truman and Eisenhower, $3.2 billion, Kennedy $6.9 billion, and Johnson $3.8 billion.[2]

In 1968, the Nixon Campaign Committee quoted Nixon as having said that "in every year since 1961 the Federal government has spent more money than it has taken in." This is not so. In fiscal 1966, when Johnson was president, there was a surplus of $2.0 billion dollars. Although Nixon could not have foreseen it in 1968, Johnson's last budget year showed a surplus of almost $5.0 billion. (*The 1971 World Almanac,* p 82)

Since 1962 the national debt ceiling has risen, on the average, about $13 billion each year. In 1971 Congress raised the ceiling by $35 billion, nearly three times the average annual increase, and another huge increase was granted for 1972. In the thirty-four years since Congress first set a debt ceiling in an attempt to check FDR's spending, the limit has been increased twenty-four times and lowered five times. Richard Nixon, the biggest spender in peacetime history, unable to produce a balanced budget during

[2] *World Almanac,* 1971, p 82. Using figures from *U.S. News and World Report,* Aug. 16, 1971, supplied by U.S. Office of Management and Budget, the figures in billions of dollars are: Truman $0.2, Eisenhower $2.0, Kennedy $5.6, and Johnson $7.2.

his first term has hidden behind the fiction of a so-called "balanced full-employment budget." This means that spending is planned at a level which would match income *if* the economy was operating at capacity and generating what politicians define as "normal" revenues. This quite obviously leaves a lot of room for maneuver, something politicians like. A full employment balanced budget doesn't insure sensible fiscal policies. On the contrary it is a guarantee of continued inflation.

With prospects of an $80 to $100 billion deficit at the end of his four years, Nixon proposed that $5 billion be set aside in his 1973 budget for Federal revenue sharing with the states. Since the 1973 budget is planned to have a $25.5 billion deficit, it would seem that Mr. Nixon, who has acquired a reputation as a pragmatist, would do better to recommend Federal *deficit* sharing!

One plan for Federal revenue sharing would base a state's share entirely on the extent of the state's income tax take. States without any income tax (there are still in 1972, a few, very few) would receive a token share, but only for a two-year grace period. Then, if they failed to impose a state income tax they would be cut off! No real octopus is more terrifying than the Federal one.

Nixon has also revived the idea of a "value added" tax, which is supposed to return us to the land of balanced budgets at the same time it provides nourishment for the growing Federal animal. A value added tax is really a sales tax in disguise and it is not a new idea. Jouett Shouse, who was Chairman of the Democrat National Executive Committee called for a national sales tax in 1932. Hoover administration spokesmen opposed the tax, and sounding like today's liberals, opposed it because "it bears no relation to ability to pay and is regressive in character." Enough Democrats deserted their leadership when the issue came to a vote and a 2 ¾ per cent manufacturers sales tax was defeated in the Democrat-controlled House of Representatives on March 24, 1932. (4, p 149) Hoover later relented and proposed a 2 ¼ per cent manufacturers tax in early 1933 on all items excepting food. (4, p 167) It is difficult to estimate how much a one or two per cent value added tax will add to the cost of an item, but it borders on the astronomical. An eighteen per cent increase in retail prices has been suggested as a reasonable estimate.

The big issue in 1968 was the Vietnamese war, just as it had been for four years before. In early 1964, American participation was not large but it was growing. By mid-summer the war had grown to such an extent that Nixon was moved to write an article about it which appeared in the August issue of *Reader's Digest*.

"What we must do," wrote Nixon, "is to instill in our allies a determination to win this crucial war—and win it decisively. We must recognize that we are in a life and death struggle that has repercussions far beyond Vietnam and that victory is essential to the survival of freedom."

After he became president, Nixon continued support of South Vietnam through arms and economic aid, but his primary emphasis shifted from winning a decisive victory to achieving American disengagement.

When Nixon campaigned in the 1968 New Hampshire primary he pledged to "end the war and win the peace in the Pacific." Pressed for details, Nixon claimed that he had said many times that there were no "magic formulas or push-button solutions." Later he said that "if I had any way to end the war, I would pass it on to President Johnson." (66, pp 274-275)

Nixon planned a radio speech on Vietnam for March 31, but cancelled it when Johnson decided to give a speech the same night. This was the dramatic speech in which Johnson, after announcing a bombing halt, withdrew from the presidential race. It is doubtful that Nixon had any specific plan in early 1968 by which the war would be ended. Nor did he, in 1969 after he was inaugurated, unveil anything new or unique. Johnson's Vietnamization program was merely continued.

At his "private" conference with Southern delegates to the 1968 Republican convention in Miami, Nixon was asked again about the war in Vietnam. *The Miami Herald* reported his answers.

"How do you bring a war to a conclusion?" Nixon replied. "I'll tell you how Korea ended. We got in there and had this war on our hands. Eisenhower let the word go out—let the word go out diplomatically—to the Chinese and the North (*Koreans*) that he would not tolerate this continual ground war of attrition. And within a matter of months they negotiated . . .

"My point is that only by a strong position can you bring your enemy to negotiate. And that is the way we won the war. (*Did we win the war?*) You can't run away from the commitment. Tell the enemy you want to (*run away*), then negotiate a surrender that will bring home those 21-year-old boys and their brothers . . . and before long they'll be out fighting somewhere else, and I'm not going to have that happen."

One might have asked, if a future war is rendered any less likely by bringing the "boys" home in the absence of a negotiated settlement—as Nixon proceeded to do when he became president? The Korean war *was* brought to an end—but was the war won, as Nixon claimed, if it merely displaced communist aggression from the northern to the southern boundaries of China? When we ran away from a commitment to see that free elections were held throughout *all* of Korea did we not encourage a divided Vietnam and "before long . . . fighting somewhere else?"

"I think," said Nixon at another point in his Miami conference, "we've got to change our position in regard to training the South Vietnamese.

"We need," said Nixon, "a massive training program so that the South Vietnamese can take over the fighting."

By August 1968 the change that Nixon thought was necessary, the training of the South Vietnamese, was *already* underway. Vietnamization had been announced by Secretary of Defense Clark Clifford in the Spring of 1968.

Nixon repeatedly refused to reveal what he planned to do about Vietnam, although he recognized it as the major election issue. His grounds for maintaining silence were that he did not want to jeopardize the negotiations by indicating any of the various avenues he thought should be explored in order to get the talks off dead center. This led to the assumption by his supporters that he had a "secret plan" for ending the war. Simultaneously his foes charged that he had nothing to offer and his claim of not wanting to upset Johnson's efforts was the kind of fakery to be expected from Tricky Dick. The charge would have been disproved had Nixon, as president, come up with something new to achieve his pledge to end the war. Since he merely continued the Clark Clifford-Lyndon Johnson Vietnamization policy upon which ultimate American withdrawal would depend, if would seem that he did not, in truth, have any better or different ideas than the administration he succeeded. The eventual invasion of

Cambodia and the toppling of Prince Sihanouk did not come immediately as *new* innovations: they did not occur until *more than a year after* Mr. Nixon took office. It is possible that the new president would have liked to resume and expand the bombing of the North at once rather than to wait until 1972, as he did. It may be that the violent and riotous atmosphere of 1969 prevented action until American withdrawals and lowered draft calls had deflated the "peace" agitators. In so far as the Vietnam problem has subsided, it seems to have succumbed to a combination of old Johnson policies plus new Nixon improvisations rather than to any well thought out new plan.

American forces in South Vietnam which stood at 540,000 men when the new president was sworn in were well below 100,000 men by April 1972. Whether the South Vietnamese will be able to repel the communist invaders from the North remains to be seen. If the objective of Vietnamization was merely to disengage American troops it has been a success. Whether it can be done safely also remains to be seen. On the other hand, if the South Vietnamese can not expel the invaders, the original American objective of preventing armed Communist expansion will have been lost—as will also thousands of American and Asian lives, and rather pointlessly lost at that.

No tale of Nixon, Vietnam, China, and the Communists would be complete without at least a brief mention of Henry Kissinger. At one time the pre-Nixon Kissinger urged strengthening of NATO, military superiority for the West, and use of tactical nuclear weapons under certain conditions in limited wars. (Great shades of General Curtis Le May!) Kissinger also opposed a mere stalemate in fighting Communists and suggested that the North Korean Reds were not sufficiently chastised for what they did to the South Koreans. But then, playing the role of a crazy mixed-up kid, in the December 1968 issue of *Foreign Affairs*, Kissinger proposed that the South Vietnamese deal directly with the National Liberation Front. In the same article he proposed the folly to end all follies: a *coalition* commission to supervise elections in South Vietnam, not throughout the entire country, but just in the South, mind you! If a reason was needed to reject Mr. Kissinger as a National Security Advisor and send him to the isolation ward, this was it. (As a matter of fact, during his first term Mr. Nixon has suffered at least two contagious infections: first Moynahan on welfare problems and then Kissinger on foreign affairs. Both are suspected by most conservatives of being political typhoid Mary's, having been drafted from the professorial ranks of Harvard University.) Nixon certainly knew, even if Kissinger could claim he didn't know, the end result of a coalition effort with Communists. The female praying mantis always feasts on the male mantis after the honeymoon!

Richard Nixon has had lots of first-hand experience and contacts with Communists and this should be kept in mind when attempting to evaluate his China-Soviet Union policies. A recounting of some of Nixon's adventures is worthwhile.

When Nixon, as a newly elected representative from California, accepted an appointment to the House Un-American Activities Committee, he was introduced to International Communism. Gerhart Eisler, a German Communist refugee and functionary in the United States of the International, appeared before the committee which Nixon had just joined. Ralph de Toledano reported the opening of the hearing in his book, *Nixon*.

> "Chief Investigator Robert Stripling: Mr. Gerhart Eisler, take the stand.
> Eisler: I am not going to take the stand.
> The Chairman: Mr. Eisler, will you raise your right hand?
> Eisler: I am not going to take the stand.
> Stripling: Mr. Chairman—
> Eisler: I have the floor now . . .
> The Chairman: Just a minute. Will you please be sworn in?
> Eisler: You will not swear me in before you hear a few remarks.
> The Chairman: No, there will be no remarks.
> Eisler: Then there will be no hearing from me.

"The committee," according to de Toledano, "made several more attempts to persuade Eisler to follow orderly procedure, then voted to cite him for contempt. Before the guards had removed the arrogant witness, Richard Nixon took a long look at the small, balding man . . . Here was a professional Communist revolutionary—a man who had plotted in Germany and China and Spain, who had ordered murders and perhaps committed them, who had practised every form of deceit and participated in sabotage, and who yet had the temerity to act the injured party before a committee of congress and defy it." (65, p 55)

Eisler, released on bail, skipped the country and went to East Germany where he served as a Communist official until his death.

Nixon achieved his initial national fame by his dogged legal pursuit of Alger Hiss. This was done in the face of the overt or covert opposition of Eleanor Roosevelt, then Under-Secretary of State Dean Acheson, and a slippery liberal chorus, academic, bureaucratic, reportorial and otherwise. Hiss was never proved to be a Communist but was convicted of perjury, something many consider less offensive. Thirteen years later in 1960 Hiss, who by now had served his term, was paraded on TV and given an opportunity to pass judgment on presidential candidate Nixon, the man largely responsible for trapping Hiss in lies.

In 1955, Richard Rovere, who had in the late 1930's been an associate editor of the Communist-controlled *New Masses*, praised Nixon's action in the confrontation of Hiss by Whitaker Chambers.

"He (*Nixon*) also had the courage," wrote Rovere, "—and it does no particular violence to the word to use it in this connection, for the cards at the time were surely stacked the other way—to push ahead with what appeared to others to be an eccentric view of the case (*Hiss' trial for perjury*)." (57, p 305)

Rovere's belated acclaim may have been, in part, payment for Nixon's treatment of Joe McCarthy. The Eastern liberals who controlled the Republican Party during McCarthy's rise and fall accepted the senator and gathered voting strength in the 1952 election from his activities. Once in power their attitude changed, for the liberal chorus soon succeeded in equating any public support of McCarthy with moral leprosy. (The metamorphosis of the Kennedys from supporters to enemies of the Senator took a while longer because friendship and cronyism interfered, and because, as the liberals were happy to forget, Bobby Kennedy served on McCarthy's staff.) Rovere recognized Nixon's part in the destruction of McCarthy even though he felt the action should have been a little faster.

"The credit or discredit," wrote Rovere, "that attaches to the administration's handling of Senator McCarthy can mostly be put

on Nixon's account. He established and executed the strategy."
(57, p 297) In this light, Nixon appears to have been doing-in
McCarthy as a penance for his transgressions in the Hiss case.
Nixon had learned that the liberal opinion makers were very
powerful.

Richard Nixon's most frightening, and probably the most in-
structive, brush with International Communism came during his
1958 goodwill tour to South America. The Communists organized
demonstrations in all the countries visited. In Peru and Venezuela
the vice-president and his party were bombarded with spit,
rocks, garbage, and obscenities. They were threatened several
times with physical harm by ugly mobs out of control. In Caracas
the violence was the worst. Earl Mazo, the reporter, gave a full account.

" 'We just sat there in the car,' Mazo quotes the vice-president as
saying. 'I looked into the face of the guy who was smashing the
window on my side with a club. He smashed it and smashed it,
and finally busted it. He hit it about ten times before it cracked.
It's hard to hit (*sic*) a window like that. You have to hit it with a
good crack. It won't cave in with just a nudge.'

"Nixon said the man with the club looked to him like a combination of Gerhart Eisler, Eugene Dennis, and all the other Communists he had faced in various places.

" 'What went through my mind was the complete unreasoning
hate in their faces—hate, just hate. I'd never seen anything like
that before. Never. This was a killer mob . . .

" 'I thought, How are they able to stir the people up to this
pitch? Then I realized as I was going on that right here was the
ruthlessness and determination, the fanaticism of the enemy that
we face. That was what I saw in the faces of the mob. This is
really Communism as it is. Some people had been telling me . . .
that Latin American Communists were different, that they were
"theoretical Communists" and really nationalists. Well, I figured,
they should know better now.' " (64, p 233)

In August 1955, when the world was basking in the effusive
good will of Geneva and when, for no good reason at all, as
time has proved, a thin veneer of good feeling hid the gap between East and West, Vice-president Nixon remained a realist.

"Here are some steps," he said, "which the Communists can

take to prove that they honestly want to live in peace with the rest of the world:

Agree to free elections and the unification of Germany.

Withdraw Chinese Communist troops from North Korea and agree to free elections and unification.

Agree to the President's aerial inspection plan and thereby pave the way for disarmament.

Dismantle the barbed wire, the land mines, the watch towers, the machine guns of the Iron Curtain which divides the people of Europe.

"Give freedom to the satellite countries.

"Curtail the activities of Moscow-controlled Communist organizations in free nations.

"What they do on these basic issues will determine whether there is a real thaw in the cold war . . . Affability can be simulated and cordiality can be turned on and off like a faucet. Hard deeds are what the world wants to see." (65, pp 185-186)

Now, almost seventeen years later, the USSR and Red China having taken none of these steps, (excepting, perhaps, withdrawal of Chinese troops from North Korea) one wonders why the trips to Peking and Moscow.

". . . I say to you at this time," Nixon told a crowd in October 1960 when he stopped at Middletown, Ohio, "America can not afford in the White House a man who jumps from one position to another and who, if he did that as President, would lead to this very miscalculation, in my opinion, which we must avoid in dealing with Communist leaders." (67, p 764)

Now if Nixon had merely opposed seating Red China in the United Nations in 1960 and then decided eleven years later that a seat was appropriate because of changes that had occurred in China in the years between, he could hardly be accused of jumping from position to position. But Red China has not changed all that much and Nixon has gone far beyond simple support for their admission to the United Nations, as we shall see.

Nixon's farewell press conference after loss of the 1962 election in California is best remembered for the dressing down he gave the reporters. Less well-remembered, but in retrospect of greater significance in view of the 1972 Peking trip, were his remarks at the time about President Kennedy and the problems he faced.

". . . I am confident that if he has his own way he will face up to them," said the defeated candidate for governor, "if he can only get those . . . who want him to admit Red China to the UN, all the woollyheads around him—if he can just keep them away from him and stand strong and firm with that good Irish fight of his, America will be in good shape in foreign policy." (66, p 19)

Henry Kissinger, who happens to be woollyheaded in a literal sense, was kept away from Kennedy, but he was not, obviously, kept away from President Nixon. One wonders if the old Nixon would have included Kissinger, architect of ping-pong diplomacy and the Peking ploy, among the figurative woollyheads he feared would subvert John Kennedy.

When President Nixon hears his critics say his China trip was motivated by politics he must cringe a little at the memory of his comments about President Johnson's Manila meeting with Vietnam's President Ky in 1966. This was a mid-term election year and Johnson's trip took place just a month before the voting.

"From diplomats in Tokyo," wrote Nixon in his syndicated column, "to members of the President's own party in Washington the question is being posed: Is this a quest for votes?"

The same question was raised about Nixon's trip to China, but not by ex-columnist Nixon.

The first-hand evidence of a Nixon shift on China was observed in 1969 when the administration ordered a halt to navy patrols between Taiwan and the mainland. A year later the United States ceased pressuring its allies to withhold recognition of Red China. At this time the president said that we had "historic ties of friendship with the Chinese people," and he was critical of China's isolation.

On April 13, 1971, Premier Chou En-lai expressed to an American ping-pong team, which was being soundly trounced by the Chinese, the hope for more contacts with the United States. The very next day President Nixon fell over himself responding: he announced that controls over trade and travel to China would be eased. Chou was, of course, hoping that American credits and goods would help repair the wreckage caused by Mao's Red Guards and their "cultural" revolution. He hoped also to offset the withdrawal of Russian technical and economic aid which had been accompanied by strained relations with the USSR.

At his televised news conference on April 29, 1971, the president stressed that overtures to China were not intended to "irritate the Soviet Union . . . It would make no sense for the United States, interested in world peace, to try to get the two to get at each other's throats, because we would be embroiled in the controversy."

By June of 1971 the administration was agreeable to admission of Red China to the United Nations. "Red China" became the "People's Republic of China" in Washington officialese,[3] but that did not result in any reduction of military support for the North Vietnamese Reds!

Henry Kissinger, the presumably woollyheaded assistant to the president, made a secret trip to the Chinese mainland on July 9, 1971. After two days of talks he returned home and on July 15th Nixon announced he was accepting an invitation to visit China sometime before May of 1972. This change in Red Chinese official policy has been interpreted as a move to help them gain admission to the United Nations where they would be in a position to challenge the Soviet Union. It also gives Red China an opportunity to confront Red Russia in the battle for leadership of the Communist world. No doubt the mainland Chinese also hope for eventual American economic aid, just as did the Soviet Union in the twenties and thirties.

Nixon's reasons for cozying up to Red China are not likely to become clear for many years. It is impossible to believe that a man who has been spit at, insulted, and almost killed by Communists in Caracas, and who had personal experiences with Alger Hiss, Gerhart Eisler, Eugene Dennis, and others could have any wishful illusions about Communists in China, the USSR—or anywhere else. Given their record of encouraging aggression in Korea and Vietnam, and of interferring in Malaysia and Indonesia, the only justification for seeking better relations with Red China is to neutralize the Communist threat by encouraging Chinese-Russian competition, to get them "to get at each others throats," the very thing Mr. Nixon claimed he did not want to do, and, of course, the very thing he could not admit he wanted to do even if this is what he really wanted.

---

[3] President Nixon first referred to the "People's Republic of China" in Bucharest during a visit to Red Rumania in October 1970. A subsequent visit of the Rumanian Premier to China was believed to have played a part in the "thaw."

On August 2, 1971, the United States abandoned opposition to admission of Red China to the United Nations. This was a reversal of a policy which had been established more than twenty years earlier. In the intervening years China had grown neither more tractable nor respectable, more peaceful or less aggressive. But American acquiescence to Red Chinese membership in the United Nations was part of the price paid for Nixon's trip to Peking.

The sole cost of the Peking invitation was not merely admission of Red China to the United Nations. Loss of the Nationalist seat on the Security Council and the forced withdrawal of Taiwan from the General Assembly of the United Nations was also part of the price. These moves also damaged our claim to leadership of anti-Communist forces in Asia, raised doubts about our reliability in the event of a showdown with Communists in Europe and South America, strained our relations with Japan and embarrassed Prime Minister Eisaku Sato and our other allies who were not informed of our shifting policy and negotiations.

If it turns out that Nixon's Chinese romance was merely the act of a president who wants liberal support for his re-election, the price paid was disastrously high. But Nixon may be merely using the woollyheads to court liberal favor, at the same time setting the stage for a neutralization of International Communism by feeding Russo-Chinese conflicts.

In late October 1971 Henry Kissinger returned from his second visit to Mainland China in preparation for the president's forthcoming visit. He stated that the president and Red Chinese leaders did not plan to discuss the Soviet Union or the Vietnamese War. Instead, they would center their talks on issues between the two countries. This is either a diplomatic lie or nonsense. If Vietnam and the Soviet Union are not issues of interest to both the United States and Red China, what, in heaven's name, are?

A story on the president's Peking venture was carried in the *U.S. News and World Report* for February 28, 1972. The most interesting comments were found in a summary of the concessions and conciliatory gestures made by the United States under Nixon since 1969. It added ". . . in return for all this: China has freed two imprisoned Americans and commuted the life sentence of a third American to five more years. Peking has also opened its doors to cultural, scientific and journalistic visitors from the

U.S." This, in the diplomatic language of communism, is known as a fair trade practice.

There were two parts to the Nixon-Chou Communiqué on their meeting, one setting forth the American view, and the other the Red Chinese view. The American portion did not mention Taiwan. The Chinese repeated their claim to Taiwan and stated again that American failure to recognize the correctness of their position was the chief obstacle to friendly relations, which they quaintly called "normalization of relations." As usual, the American good guys step back, but the Communists don't budge a bit. They never do—unless forced to.

The Republican Platform of 1968 stated that "only when Communist nations prove by actual deeds that they genuinely seek world peace . . . will we support expansion of East-West trade."

How has Nixon performed on this pledge? Not very well. Trade has been expanded with most, if not all, Communist countries. Trade with Red China has been increased and trade restrictions relaxed in the wake of the Peking excursion. Secretary of Agriculture Butz busily negotiated a grain for oil deal with the USSR in advance of the president's Spring visit to Moscow in 1972. At the same time Russia and China were still providing the arms and oil for the Vietnamese invasion from the North.

"As we approach the day of nuclear parity," Mr. Nixon said in an NBC radio address on March 28, 1968, "between the U.S. and the Soviet Union, we approach the moment of truth in relations between East and West . . .

"We must restore at least a part of the strategic advantage that we once held . . . because in the world as it is, we need power if we are to be secure."

Since becoming president, in 1969, with the non-Communist world in 1972 still facing unrenounced Red goals of world conquest, Nixon has allowed America's strategic advantage virtually to vanish—and simultaneously has allowed the Russians through our failure to develop a matching ABM system to gain a defensive advantage.

Yet, according to Witcover, just before the 1968 election, Nixon criticized the Democrats for having adopted "a peculiar, unprecedented doctrine called 'parity' . . . America would no longer try to be first. We would only stay even. This concept has done us incalculable damage . . . by 1970 or 1971 we could find ourselves with a survival gap." (66, pp 427-428)

Critics of Nixon's presidential policies agree with his 1968 conclusion about the survival gap of 1970 or 1971.

When asked about his plans for national defense, candidate Nixon told a questioner in 1967 that he disagreed with the McNamara theory that parity with the Soviet Union is enough. Nixon went on to say that he planned to talk with the Soviets and, giving as his reason for rejecting parity, said that it is necessary always to negotiate from strength and never from weakness. He added that we had to deter adventurism on the part of the Soviet Union.

It took President Nixon only about four months to forget his criticism of parity. At his very first press conference after taking office, Nixon rejected the concept of superiority. In March 1969 he cut back the anti-ballistic missile program of the Johnson administration. In a statement reminiscent of pre-Pearl Harbor idiocy, when we refused to arm Pacific islands for fear of offending the Japanese, Nixon said that a full-fledged ABM system might look to an opponent like "the prelude to an offensive strategy threatening the Soviet deterrent . . ." Our reduced program, said the president, "is not provocative." In a strange jungle of twisted words and mangled logic our own purely defensive system is denounced as provocative and offensive while the same system in enemy hands is proclaimed as defensive. We seem to have arrived in the world of Newspeak twelve years ahead of schedule!

In the Fall of 1971 there was world-wide agitation against the Amchitka hydrogen bomb test. A world-wide uproar, as pointed out earlier, can be organized only by the unmatched international organization of the Communists. It is no wonder they protested Amchitka. The war-head to be tested was designed to produce a high yield of x-rays which would harmlessly destroy incoming ballistic missiles beyond the earth's atmosphere. The Soviets have been testing such ABM war-heads since 1961 and had already deployed ABM's around Moscow. The latest Russian tests were on September 27 and October 14, 1971, but there were no international protests against *these* tests. President Nixon, to his credit, rejected requests to cancel our Amchitka tests. San Francisco and

California did not slide into the sea, nor was Japan washed away by a tidal wave, as predicted. No, Nixon is not all bad, nor does he deserve the epithet Tricky Dick any more than any other twentieth century politician.

Richard M. Nixon has established himself as slightly less liberal, less statist, and less interventionist than his predecessor, and much less so than his opposition in the 1972 election. At the same time, he is more of a spender, inflater, and Keynesian who likes to tinker with the economy than was Mr. Johnson. He has helped feed the Federal Octopus; his 1972 opposition is likely, if elected, to resort to forced feeding. On domestic issues he is no conservative and certainly no libertarian, but he has restored the Supreme Court to a judicial function and this is no small accomplishment.

In foreign affairs, a niche is yet to be prepared for him. Machiavellian that he is, he may work the grand strategy of removing two major threats by playing them off against each other, and he may secure South Vietnam against the attack from the North while removing Americans from Indo-China. If he does these things he will be called a hero. But if he concedes and concedes again to Communist pressure from Peking, from Moscow, from Hanoi, and from homegrown Reds, if Hanoi becomes the capitol of a unified Vietnam, and if China and Russia cooperate to do us in, he will be classed as a wretched failure and menace. History will place him in his niche.

CHAPTER 17

AMEN

There are three striking examples which show the relationship between tax power and the strength of a central government. When Germany and Italy first became organized as nations in the last half of the 19th century they were weak coalitions of small states. The central governments were dependent for tax money on the generosity of the politicians and princes who controlled the member states. With establishment of a national system of taxes, the power of the member states diminished and the power of the Federal governments grew. The ultimate result in both cases was a despotism which had as one of its prerequisites a central taxing authority.

The close tie between a Federal tax power and the strength of a central government is also shown by early American history. Under the Articles of Confederation, the Continental Congress had to requisition money from the states to meet its expenses. During its first two years of existence it requisitioned $10.6 million and the states came forth with $1.6 million. Inability to meet interest on the debt led to collapse of the Federal government and a call for a Constitutional Convention.

The new Constitution permitted Congress to collect tariffs and levy excise taxes. Income from tariffs enabled the new Federal government to finance defense, pay off its debts and created the surpluses which were used for internal improvements.

In the early years of the Republic, the politicians were faithful to the idea that the public debt should be repaid. Two centuries later fidelity to this principle is gone and the debt remains— larger than ever. In those early times, debts, both public and private, were looked upon quite differently than today. Debtors' prisons testify to the fact that private debt was expected to be repaid and that failure to repay what was borrowed was almost the same as stealing. Debtors' prisons are long gone, but defaulting debtors are still with us, probably in larger numbers than ever before. Bankruptcy is even looked upon by some as being respectable, and by others as being a smart way to get ahead. Growing public acceptability of private default has been matched by a similar change in attitude toward public debt.

The only reason for public borrowing given by Adam Smith in 1776, when he published *Wealth of Nations*, was to meet the cost of a war. This, too, can be debated, but not here. Although Smith recognized that governments of free nations had a legitimate responsibility to administer justice, to defend the nation against foreign attack, and to construct and maintain, on a very limited scale, public works, public indebtedness, excepting for prosecution of a war, was strictly taboo. In general Adam Smith's ideas were endorsed by Jean-Baptiste Say, David Ricardo, and most economists of the early 19th century. Public borrowing, according to Ricardo, "is a system which tends to make us less thrifty—to blind us to the real situation." (4, p 42)

Ricardo's view supports the conclusion that governments are the poorest accounting agencies, and the more complex government activities become the more nearly impossible it is to tell what has and what has not been paid for and who and how much has been paid for it, whatever "it" is.

The basic charge to a limited government is the protection of life, liberty, and property, without which protection the pursuit of happiness is impossible. Citizens are enjoined from using force as a means of guaranteeing their own lives, liberty, and property, excepting in circumstances where the threat is immediate and the authorized force of government is not available on the spot. Apart from this circumstance, the government has a monopoly on the use of force, and the citizen surrenders his individual claim to use force in return for government guarantees of order and peace. For this guarantee the citizen pays taxes. Ideally, the citizen should pay taxes in direct proportion to the services he requires and receives. (In modern parlance this is sneeringly called regressive taxation!) Thus, one person who owns ten times as much property as another has ten times as much at stake and should be expected to pay ten times the taxes.

This is a concept basic to limited government, and as long as government in the United States did not greatly deviate from this principle the government remained limited. Adoption of a graduated scale of taxation represented acceptance of the first half of the basic socialist tenet: From each according to his ability, to each according to his need. This released the Federal government from the fiscal bonds which restrained it and kept it limited. The second half of the basic socialist tenet: to each according to his need, has been increasingly accepted in the last forty years. Thus, limited government has been replaced increasingly by unlimited government.

The leading citizens at the end of the 18th century were familiar with classical economics. In turn their influence determined public attitudes toward government borrowing and indebtedness.

"It is not meant to imply," wrote Kimmel in *Federal Budget and Fiscal Policy, 1789-1958,* "that a large majority of the people were seriously concerned about the size of the public debt or that they were capable of appraising budget policies. Rather . . . the more influential citizens generally took a rather narrow view of public finance; whatever opinions the general public held usually paralleled closely those of their better informed neighbors." (4, p 55)

Public debt was not advocated by any politician who had hopes of getting elected in the early 19th century, for politicians then, as now, reflected the views of voters more than they formed them.

During the last half of the 19th century American economic thought underwent major changes. Kimmel told about the effect of German beliefs upon American economists who studied in Europe. (4, pp 116-124) Among these was Henry Carter Adams who accepted the German view that a laissez-faire role for government was inadequate. Adams believed that the money supply would be contracted by government surpluses, and for this reason continuous surpluses should be avoided. It follows from Adams' theory that continuous deficits result in inflation or expansion of the money supply. It was this theme which was pounced upon by John Maynard Keynes nearly a half century after Adams.

Richard T. Ely was another American economist influenced by

European study. Ely went far beyond Adams in rejecting the laissez-faire position of William Graham Sumner. He took the dangerous German position that the "state exists as an organism in itself." It was this concept which led Germany from Bismarck's socialism to Hitler's national socialism.

Ely was dean, or at least associate dean, of the zealous moralist school of economics. He conned himself into believing that principles of economics could be shaped by religion. Thus, laissez-faire came under attack and was gradually abandoned. Abandonment of laissez-faire did not in itself disprove the principles of classical economics. Ely believed his "social Christianity" was incompatible with laissez-faire, which it was. The social Christians believe in a sort of compulsory group Christianity enforced by the coercive power of the government. Keeping in mind the barbarisms of the crusades one shudders at the possibilities of a fiat Christendom.

The essence of socialism, as of communism, fascism, national socialism, democratic socialism, Christian socialism, the welfare state, the planned economy, and state interventionism is, as put by Leonard Read in his *Outlook for Freedom,* (The Foundation for Economic Education, Irvington-on-Hudson, N.Y., 1951) "belief in the use of organized police force—government—as a means to attain social performance." The differences among these various systems are in the degree to which the police force is organized and administered.

Still another influential late nineteenth century American new economist was Simon N. Patten. America, according to Patten, had a "surplus economy," which sounds like the oft expressed view that the "Hoover" depression was caused by overproduction. Patten believed that improvements in productivity created an abiding surplus, which hardly squares with the Great Society's contention more than a half-century later that 25,000,000 Americans lived in poverty. Patten stated that the abiding surplus could "be reserved for public benefit or be permitted to pass into private hands." Patten would have been more accurate if he had said the surplus could have been "seized for public benefit or allowed to remain in private hands." Patten wrote this in an article brazenly called "Liquidation Taxes." (4, p 122) In 1902 he had proposed that citizens' rights include the right to be reimbursed for losses resulting from accidents, sickness, and bad weather. By 1919 Patten had progressed from liquidation taxes, and compulsory insurance via taxation, to writing articles such as "Making National Debts National Blessings."

The Federal indebtedness of the first World War was not intended to be permanent. As often happens, results do not match intentions, and the unpaid debts of the war became the first installment of the permanent national debt. The original wartime bond issue authorized $5 billion in bonds, supplemented by $2 billion in certificates of indebtedness. The authorized indebtedness was increased, and following the war during the Harding, Coolidge, and initial Hoover years it was reduced. But with the depression and the New Deal the debt increased again. In 1938 a single limitation, applicable to all forms of Federal debt, was established at $45 billion. (4, p 86) Since then the limit has been raised from time to time, and with greater frequency in recent years. Statutory limitations on the debt are meaningless. Senator Carter Glass lived to see the truth of his 1919 prediction that "there appears to be a grave danger that the extraordinary success of the Treasury in financing the stupendous war expenditures may lead to a riot of public expenditures after the war, the consequences of which could only be disastrous." (4, p 88)

Deficits, in the long run, as Henry Carter Adams concluded, can only be financed by inflation. Past inflations here and in other countries have shown the perils of continuing inflation. A given expansion of the money supply results in an initial stimulation of business, but to continue this stimulation the money supply must be continually expanded. Furthermore, it has been observed that a fixed percentage expansion of the money supply becomes less effective as a stimulant. In other words an accelerating inflation is required to maintain business activity, and the end result is a wild acceleration with inflation completely out of control as the politicians seek to retain power through creation of an artificial prosperity. Are we now entering this final stage which ends in disaster? While it might be difficult to establish the role that Communists are playing in current pressures for greater public spending, financed by higher taxes and inflationary deficits, it is worth noting that a graduated income tax and debauchery of the monetary system have been stated Communist goals for over half a century.

At the end of the Civil War the national debt was $3 billion and the annual interest on it was estimated at 3 per cent of the annual national income for the years 1865-1867. (4, p 136) Using 5 per cent as the annual interest rate, the national income can be estimated at about $5 billion. By 1970 the interest on the national debt was $19 billion, which is about 2.5 per cent of national income. It might be hastily concluded that we were not much worse off in 1970 than we were a century earlier. An examination of Federal expenditures and deficits leads to a different conclusion.

Following the Civil War, in the years 1866 to 1870, annual Federal receipts averaged $447 million and expenditures averaged $378 million for an average annual surplus of $69 million. The surplus was used to retire the debt. In the years 1966 to 1970, annual Federal receipts averaged $159 billion and expenditures averaged $162 billion. Thus, one hundred years after the Civil War the Federal debt, instead of being retired, was increasing at an average of $3 billion a year! And apparently any intention of ever repaying it had been abandoned.

A comparison of Federal expenditures and national income sheds further light on where we stand. At the end of the Civil War, Federal expenditures, including interest payments, were 8 per cent of national income. Total Federal expenditures, including interest, in 1970 were $194 billion against a national income of $770 billion, or about 25 per cent of national income. Admittedly these figures are inexact because there is no uniform way of calculating national income for both the Civil War period and the present, yet they demonstrate an obviously insatiable Federal appetite for tax money. They also demonstrate abandonment of the principle that borrowing without intending to pay is the equivalent of stealing. Not only is there no present intention to repay the national debt in its entirety, but as it is continuously refunded, the refunding is in dollars of far lower purchasing power than the dollars originally borrowed. The notorious Boston swindler Ponzi [1] was a piker and amateur when compared to the politicians who control our monetary and fiscal affairs.

---

[1] Promises to double your money in a month were kept by using newly borrowed money to repay old loans and gains. The first people to cash in (if they didn't "re-invest," which most did) found the scheme handsomely profitable, but those bringing up the rear were worse off than the fellow on the bottom of a chain letter. When you're ahead at the horse races, quit betting.

The people who were swindled by Ponzi were no less gullible than the people who support irresponsible politicians.

"When it comes to rising prices," said President Nixon on October 17, 1969, "it seems to most people there is no end in sight. Americans are upset and many are even angry about this, and they have a right to be, because the ever-rising cost of food and clothing robs them of their savings and cheats them of those vacations and necessary extras they thought they had been working for."

In 1970 and 1971, the annual losses from inflation were far higher than when Nixon spoke in 1969. The losses are born by every holder of life and other insurance, savings bank and demand deposits, cash, bonds, annuities, notes, and mortgages. The seriousness and reality of the losses are seen if one considers a savings account deposit of $1000. If the interest rate is 5 per cent, the interest will amount to $50. Assuming the depositor is in the 25 per cent income tax bracket, his after tax (disregarding state taxes) deposit totals $1000 plus $37.50 in interest. If the cost of living climbs at a rate of 5 per cent, the $1037.50 will purchase only about $980 worth of goods or services. The depositor has lost $20 of his principal and a total of $57.50 has disappeared as a result of inflation.

The most disastrous inflation of the century occurred in Germany in the 1920's. France and Italy suffered less serious disasters. More recently the inflation of Brazil, while not as serious as Germany's, has attracted world wide attention. From 1959 to 1966 the average *annual* rise in the cost of living was 60 per cent, for a total rise of 420 per cent in seven years. During one year the cost of living jumped 85 per cent! From 1967 to 1969, with inflation under "control," the rate was 25 per cent. During one two-week period in 1964, Brazilian food prices doubled in the capital city. Imagine the effect on anyone holding cash, bonds, or insurance.

The clearest sign of Federal intervention in private affairs is the amount the government spends, for it can not spend without intervening and, conversely, it can not intervene without spending. From 1830 to 1840 the Federal government spent less than two dollars per person per year. From 1871 to 1915 Federal spending was under eight dollars a year for each person. In the five years 1926 through 1930, which are usually thought of as years of conservatism and economy in government, Federal expenses rocketed to nearly thirty dollars per person. In 1955 the figure reached $398, in 1960 it was $425 and in 1970, $980. The table on the next page summarizes Federal spending in more detail.

The conservative Coolidge-Hoover era saw a fourfold increase over pre-World War I spending. The Roosevelt-Truman years brought a fifty-fold expansion of 1911-1915 spending—and a fiftyfold increase in Federal intervention. Expenditures during the Eisenhower administration in terms of dollars of constant value actually showed a slight decline, but rose sharply again under Kennedy and Johnson and are apparently going to continue to rise under Nixon. At his press conference on December 8, 1969, Nixon acknowledged that "between 35 and 37 per cent of the total income of the United States goes to taxes—that is in Federal, state, and local taxes." He added that he believed "that amount is high enough." Around April 15th most people might conclude that that was the understatement of the age.

The burden of government spending is carried by middle Americans, the factory worker, salesman, machine operator, real estate man, store owner, and town cop. It is the $12,000 a year-and-under wage earner who pays 90 per cent of the take. It will always be so since their income represents the largest pool of wealth available for the Federal drainage project. The poor, who represented some 25,000,000 people in 1968 (according to estimates of the liberals) have virtually nothing that can be seized. Additionally there are insufficient numbers of very wealthy persons to supply significant portions of what the government spends. For instance, it has been estimated that if every income of one million or more was confiscated by the Federal government, it would produce only enough revenue to operate the government for 39 hours.

The growth of statism since 1929 is shown by figures for Federal, state and local spending published in *The Wall Street Journal* (March 27, 1972, p 1). Government spending as a percentage of the Gross National Product [2] rose from 8.2 to 22.2 per cent from 1929 to 1971; during the same interval the GNP

[2] The Gross National Product is simply the sum of all spending in the United States. The two largest components of the GNP are public spending and private spending. Business capital spending is another component.

FEDERAL SPENDING OVER THE YEARS

Year(s)	Annual or average (as applicable) Federal spending in millions of dollars	Population for year reported or for middle year of term reported, millions of persons	Dollars spent per person	Dollars spent per person in terms of 1939 dollars	Value of 1939 dollar
1790	$ 4.4	3.9	$ 1.25	—	—
1830–1840	25	15	1.67	—	—
1871–1875	288	42	6.86	—	—
1901–1905	536	80	6.70	—	—
1911–1915	720	96	7.51	—	—
1926–1930	3,183	109	29.30	—	—
1955	64,570	162	398	$207	$0.52
1960	76,539	180	425	193	0.47
1970	194,968	200	980	353	0.36

Data for 1790 from (4, p 8); for years 1830–1970 from *The 1971 World Almanac*, Newspaper Enterprise Association. Inc., and for the value of the dollar from *Economic Education Bulletin* v XI, no. 4, May 1971, American Institute for Economic Research. War years have been excluded from the above excepting for the Vietnam War which shows up in the figures for 1970.

increased ten times but government spending rose *twenty-seven-fold*. Since 1929 private employment has grown from 28 million to 58 million, an increase of 104 per cent. In the same interval government employment has increased from three million to 13 million, an increase of 319 per cent.

Just how far the tenacles of Octopus Federalis can reach are shown by various government and private publications. For example, the *Catalogue of Federal Domestic Assistance* (compiled by the Office of Economic Opportunity, Washington, D.C., 1969) is a massive 610 pages. It's cover describes the contents as "a description of the Federal government's domestic programs to assist the American people in furthering their social and economic progress." There are 551 programs described in its pages. For each, eligibility requirements, the aim of the program, what the program will provide, and the addresses of Santa Claus' helpers are listed. The programs are divided among the various departments of the Federal government and among the various independent agencies, offices, and commissions. The spread among the departments is interesting and may, just may, bear some relation to the voting strength of the beneficiaries. For instance, as can be seen in the listing below, the Department of Health, Education, and Welfare and the Department of Housing and Urban Development are the longest and strongest tenacles of the Federal Octopus.

Department

	Number of Programs
Agriculture (Still lots of farm votes, but shrinking. It's hard to get rid of programs once established.)	60
Commerce (We have to buy a few businessmen.)	29
Defense (How many enlisted men's votes can you buy?)	10
Health, Education, and Welfare (Oodles of students, everyone has doctors bills, and there are 15,000,000 on welfare.)	179
Housing and Urban Development (We'll subsidize *middle-incomers* now, they're so broke subsidizing low-incomers; lots of votes here.)	57

Interior (Not many Indians, and trees can't vote.)   24
Justice (Mostly aid for local police training, not
      many votes here.)   16
Labor (Lots of votes here, but labor gets it else-
      where.)   38
Post Office (No comment.)   1
State (No votes here.)   4
Transportation (Watch us grow, car pollution,
      congestion, SST's and "free" transportation,
      everyone travels.)   13

A word of caution, the number of programs does not necessarily correlate exactly with the amount spent and the votes
bought. It does give an idea, however, of what one can expect.

A sampling of the goodies available shows how the Octopus'
tenacles ensnarl most of us. For example, the Department of
Agriculture has seven programs aimed at helping farmers sell
food, or making sure junior gets the "right" nourishment, or
helping people who can't (and in some cases who can, but claim
they can't) buy food for themselves, or a combination of these
aims. The first of these programs is known as the Plentiful Foods
Program. This is pretty much a marketing-surplus-economics
program. The second is the School Breakfast Program which
puts up as much as 80 per cent of the cost of the food. Closely
coupled with this are the School Lunch Program and the School
Milk Program. Just in case Big Brother has missed someone during
the school year, there is a Special Food Service for Children to
take care of kids during summer vacations. The Food Stamp
Program, which has found favor among hippies, permits "needy"
persons to swap money for food coupons which are worth more
toward the purchase of the food than the money given in exchange. The taxpayers make up the difference. (The *Catalogue*
states "the government" pays the difference, which is less likely
to stir up the peons.) And finally there's the Non-Food Assistance
Program which provides grants to schools in low-income areas
for purchase of equipment needed for the feeding of school children.

Stockholders, bond holders, executives, hard hats and long-
shoremen may gripe about ADC, food stamps and other give-
aways when they are not busy collecting their own benefits

which come to them from the taxpayer via the Department of Commerce's Maritime Commission. Payments known as operating differential subsidies and construction differential subsidies, and loan and mortgage insurance help to keep them prosperous and content at taxpayer expense.

The Department of Interior is really not interested in Indians and trees alone. It will help you develop an airport or assist you to build outdoor recreational facilities: parks, snow ski areas, golf courses, urban play grounds, swimming pools, marinas, and bicycle paths.

Among the 57 programs of the Department of Housing and Urban Development there are thirteen different ways of qualifying for mortgage insurance. There are separate mortgage insurance programs for (1) older declining neighborhoods, (2) experimental housing, (3) moderate income housing, (4) urban renewal housing, (5) veterans housing, (6) nonprofit hospitals, (7) nursing homes, (8) land development and new communities, (9) group practice facilities, (10) condominiums, (11) cooperative housing, (12) special credit risk families, and (13) armed services housing near military installations. But there's no way an eskimo can get igloo mortgage insurance south of the Mason-Dixon line!

There are always two sides to every coin, and if you have one left to look at when you have finished supporting the 551 "Federal domestic assistance programs" you can verify this for yourself. The other side of the coin is what the programs cost and who pays for them. Perhaps the *Catalogue of Federal Domestic Assistance Programs* should include the *Regulations of the Internal Revenue Service* as an appendix. It also should be issued as a companion volume of the *Budget of the United States!* It may be significant that no "domestic assistance programs" under the Treasury Department were noted in the *Catalogue.* The Internal Revenue Service has a program known as the Taxpayer's Assistance Program. Lest your hopes be unduly raised, this is limited to helping you fill out your Form 1040, 1040A, 1040ES, etc., etc. They don't assist you in figuring out how to get the cash you use to pay your taxes.

Toward the end of the decade of the 1960's, the Corporation for Public Broadcasting went on the air. The way CPB operates

and how it is financed illustrate why the ship of state is likely to
remain on the port tack for a long time to come. CPB owns no
stations, but it supports them with funds and acts as a network
agency which coordinates and promotes the system. Some public
agitation has been mounted against the slanting and bias of the
private broadcasters, (see, for instance, Edith Efron's *The News
Twisters*, and Joseph C. Keeley's *The Left-Leaning Antenna*)
but the public should be outraged by the efforts of the public
broadcasters. Not only are CPB's programs far more slanted and
biased than those of ABC, NBC, or even CBS, they are in addition partly supported by taxes and the donations of tax-free
foundations. In 1969 taxes took care of 33 per cent of the corporation's $60,000,000 expenses. At the end of 1969, John W.
Macy, president of CPB estimated that by 1974 about $110,000,-
000 would be needed and of this about 64 per cent would be
provided by taxpayers. Macy suggested a two per cent excise tax
on all new television sets to foot the bill. (*U.S. News and World
Report*, Dec 8, 1969, p 95) The capability of the mass media
monster to lobby for its own aims and other statist goals, with
the help of a subsidy paid for, in part by persons opposed to those
goals, carries us at least one month nearer to 1984.

Although the funds spent for CPB are miniscule compared to
other government programs it is a program of enormous leverage.
It has provided a tax-subsidized platform for professional revolutionaries, America haters, radicals, and agitators, as anyone who
heard its broadcasts of the National Welfare Rights convention
in 1971 can testify. The funds directly spent for CPB's support
will in turn accelerate growth of and support for the other government programs favored by liberals and statists, and worse.
Even without CPB these programs have expanded enormously.
Take for instance aid to urban areas and welfare programs, just
to mention two.

In 1961, $3.9 billion in Federal money was spent to aid urban
areas. These grants were exclusive of direct government-to-people
payments such as social security, veteran's benefits, and Federal
salaries. The funds were earmarked for housing, medical care,
food, welfare, education, police, highways, mass transit and
other public services. By 1969 payments were about three times
the 1961 figures, but by 1973 they are projected at $31.5 billion

annually, almost ten times what they were in 1961. By 1973, it is estimated that $160 billion will have been spent to solve the problems of the cities. (Source U.S. Office of Management and Budget, as reported in *U.S. News and World Report*, April 10, 1972, p 43.) Will the cities be any better off then than they were in 1961? "Progress" to date doesn't predict an improvement.

The magnitude of the welfare problem is, like the infinity of space, absolutely beyond comprehension. In New York City, one person in every six was on relief in 1971. In Newark, just across the Hudson River, almost one out of every three people was on relief. In seven of the twenty largest cities ten per cent of the people were on welfare. According to *The Wall Street Journal* (Mar 27, 1972, p 1) fourteen million people were receiving aid in 1971 and the figure increased to fifteen million by 1972. In the 1960's, the population increased by 13 per cent, but welfare rolls increased by 94 per cent, and welfare payments increased 240 per cent. (During this same period the cost of living has increased 20 per cent and so the actual increase in welfare costs is slightly under 200 per cent, or about fifteen times as great as the population growth.) In the years 1965-1970, welfare rolls grew from 7.7 to 13.2 million and welfare costs rose from $5.8 to $12.8 billion. These were years when the gross national product was reaching new peaks each year. Aid for Dependent Children and their mothers accounts for 54 per cent of all welfare costs.

Outrageous abuses of the welfare program receive continuous publicity. In New York City relief clients housed at $650 per month in hotels caused a stir. Legal aid lawyers have been used not only for divorce proceedings and settling family squabbles, but also for the defense of militants and rioters. Food stamps, which were intended to provide food discounts for the needy, have been traded in black markets. Some college students, dropouts and hippies have found they qualify for welfare payments and are taking advantage of the fact. There have been fraudulent payments to doctors, dentists, and druggists, which proves again that poverty is not a prerequisite for dishonesty. There also have been payments for fraudulent poverty claims, including multiple claims from the same persons, and from persons who are not legally qualified, which proves again that poverty, while not a prerequisite for dishonesty, is also no guarantee of sainthood.

It would seem that the biblical observation that the poor would always be with us is supported by experience. The United States is the richest nation in the world, both in an absolute sense as well as on a per capita basis. Yet official 1971 figures claim that 12.5 per cent, or one out of every eight Americans lives in poverty. Poverty is officially defined to exist when a nonfarm family of four lives on less than four thousand (in round figures) dollars annually. Even if we are unwilling to accept the creation of poverty by statistical fiat, it would seem that the billions spent for welfare, aid for children, education, slum clearance, and other social welfare schemes have not solved, or come close to solving, the problems of poverty. Perhaps a partial explanation is found in the political nature of all statism. This is suggested by an article appearing on page one of the February 28th, 1972 issue of the *Wall Street Journal:*

"One element . . . may be that much of what passes for Federal aid to the poor amounts mainly to income for middle-class bureaucrats. A poster-sized Senate Finance Committee list of more than 160 such programs shows, for instance, that of $450 million in model cities' money, only $144 million would aid people classed as poor. Similarly, it indicates the poor get only $2.7 billion of the $4 billion annual aid to families with dependent children, and that administrative costs are $241 million." One wonders what accounted for the difference between total aid and the $2.7 billion received.

The proportion of officially designated poor among the nation's population decreased in the twenty years from 1959 to 1970 from 28 per cent (which seems unbelievably high) to 12 per cent. (*U.S. News and World Report*, July 12, 1971, p 53) Since then the figure appears to have stabilized. In the 1960's, fifty poverty-stricken families of Chemung County, New York were given special attention by social workers for 31 months. This included special job training for working members of the families. At the end of this time there was "only slight, almost meaningless, improvement in family functioning." This leads one to conclude that climbing out of the poverty pit is not made easier by the helping hands of social workers, regardless of how well-intentioned the efforts may be. Long before welfare became a Federal folly there was much more poverty around because technology had not yet raised the standard of living to its present level. And the poverty was more grim than now. (For instance, welfare recipients didn't demand television sets.) Yet people escaped the poverty trap—and it was largely by their own efforts. The Chemung experiment seems to show that people have not changed much in this respect.

As pointed out earlier, many of the welfare state ideas were born in Sweden, raised in England, and emigrated to the United States. How fares the welfare state in Sweden? Unlike most countries in Western Europe, Sweden has not been at war since 1815 and hence has escaped the calamities which might be blamed for the sorry condition of the welfare state in England and elsewhere. Yet in 1971, according to the *United States News and World Report*, (May 1971, pp 91-93) housing shortages persist, rents are controlled in Stockholm, and people wait months or years for adequate housing. The homes of many old people are sadly run down. Doctors, nurses and medical facilities are in such short supply that it often takes months to get into a hospital. The country has been plagued by strikes since 1969. In both 1970 and 1971 the cost of living rose about 8 per cent a year. Income taxes take 32 per cent of a married couple's income at the $6500 level, 40 per cent at $10,000, and 52 per cent at $20,000. The value added tax, currently gaining favor at home, adds 17.6 per cent to the prices of all consumer goods!

The ultimate in the welfare state is the USSR, which, in April 1970 celebrated the 100th anniversary of Lenin's birth. At that time the Soviet Union ranked 21st in per capita production, exactly where it was 50 years earlier, shortly after the revolution was under way. The collective farm system has proved so inefficient that in recent years increasing concessions have been made to private farming efforts, which now grow over half the potatoes and vegetables produced in the country. In the winter of 1969-1970 there were acute meat and grain shortages and Russia continues to import millions of tons of meat.[3]

The czarists and royal ruling class and their bureaucratic hordes have been replaced by the Communists and *their* bureaucratic hordes, the *aparatchik*. The condition of the average citizen is little improved, excepting for those changes attributable to world-wide improvements in technology. Relative to the men in the other industrial nations of the world, the average man in the

[3] *U.S. News and World Report*, April 20, 1970, pp 66–70. See also May 15, 1972, pp 29–32.

Soviet Union is almost exactly where he was a half century ago. A new tyranny has replaced an old tyranny. The statism of the Communists has replaced the statism of the czars. In the meantime, millions have been slaughtered in the Ukraine, a quarter of a million Tatars have been exiled, the Jews have been harassed, intellectuals stifled, writers muzzled, and political dissenters are detained for psychiatric examination or imprisoned. (Before reacting to the idea of detaining political dissenters in mental institutions, keep in mind the famous case of General Edwin C. Walker during the Little Rock integration disorders of the Eisenhower years. It not only *can* happen here, it has!)

Barry Goldwater once expressed the thought that we should be just as worried about the people inside the house breaking up the furniture as we should be about the thugs outside trying to burn it down. If we ever reach that supreme socialist promised land, regardless of whether it is called the welfare state or something stronger, it may very well be because the fellows inside the house have been doing such a good job. They've been trying for a long time.

Way back in the late 1930's one of the governors was quoted as saying: "In these days we have to make promises that we know we can't carry out. We have to promise old people pensions that would bankrupt the state if we paid them. We have to promise higher salaries to school teachers, higher wages to working people, higher prices to the farmers, bigger allotments of public funds from the federal government. I am ashamed of what I have done. But I wanted to win." (From *The New Deal in Old Rome*, by H. J. Haskell, Alfred A. Knopf, N.Y., 1947, p 230.)

A quarter of a century later the situation has not changed. On page one of the *Wall Street Journal* for March 28, 1972 there was a feature article about Hubert Humphrey, the talkative druggist who would be president. It was headlined:

> "Promises, Promises
> Now the Front-Runner
> Sen. Humphrey Pledges
> Something for Everyone

"His emphasis shifts from area to area," the article stated. "In the dairy lands he proposes higher milk price supports. In labor halls he promises more jobs . . .

"Everywhere, an array of big-spending plans come tumbling forth . . . Yet Mr. Humphrey tells business audiences . . . that tax reforms and bank-type financing schemes will pay for it all without higher taxes . . .

". . . he promises attentive high-school groups that he'll set up a Cabinet-level department of youth affairs, if elected. He also advocates a department of the aging.

"Mr. Humphrey, in short, is promising something for everyone, and," in recognition that this is merely the stock of a politician's trade, the article added, "to a degree unmatched by any other candidate."

Of course, the coin, as always, has two sides and Mr. Humphrey's pitch is only one side of it. On the other side is the gullibility of enough Americans to elect people like Mr. Humphrey, or reject a Barry Goldwater for a Lyndon Johnson. Admittedly there is rarely much choice, but this is because a large enough body of Americans have been led so far astray by the opinion makers that they don't demand much in the way of a choice. Only because majorities of Americans have bought what the Humphreys, McGoverns, Muskies, and Nixons sell have we arrived where we are and will end up where we're going.

Stephen M. Young, until his retirement a few years ago served as United States Senator from Ohio. Young was a liberal last, a politician first, and no one's fool. He also had a sense of humor and was known to answer bellicose letters from constituents with brief letters reading "Dear Sir: Go to hell. Yours truly . . ." It would seem appropriate at this point to quote from one of Senator Young's more memorable newsletters to his constituents.

"A young man lived with his parents," wrote the senator, "in a low-cost public housing development in Hamilton County (Ohio). He attended public school, rode the free school bus, enjoyed the free-lunch program.

"Following graduation from high school, he entered the Army and upon discharge kept his National Service Life Insurance. He then enrolled in an Ohio university, receiving regularly his GI check. Upon graduation, he married a Public Health nurse, bought a farm in Southern Ohio with an FHA loan.

"Later going into the feed-and-hardware business in addition to farming, he secured help from the Small Business Administration when his business faltered. His first baby was born in the county hospital. This was built in part with Hill-Burton (Act) Federal funds.

"Then, he put part of his land under the Eisenhower soil-bank program and used the payments for not planting crops to help pay his debts. His parents, elderly by now, were living comfortably in the smaller of his two farm houses, using their Social Security and old-age assistance checks. Medicare covers most of their doctor and hospital bills.

"Lacking electricity at first, the Rural Electrification Administration supplied the lines, and a loan from the Farmers Home Loan Administration helped clear the land and secure the best from it. That agency suggested building a pond, and the government stocked it with fish.

"The government guaranteed him a sale for his farm products. The county public library delivered books to his farm door. He, of course, banked his money in an institution which a Federal agency had insured . . . As the community grew, he signed a petition seeking Federal assistance in developing an industrial project to help the economy in his area. About that time he purchased a business and real estate at the county seat, aided by an FHA loan.

"His children in college received financial assistance from the Federal government, his son under the National Defense Student Loan Program and his daughter under the Nurse Training Act. Both lived in dormitories and studied in classrooms paid for with Federal funds. He was elected to office in the local chamber of commerce.

"A little later it was rumored he joined . . . right-wing extremist groups. He wrote his Senators and Congressman denouncing excessive Government spending, medicare, big government, the United Nations, high taxes, etc., and enclosed . . . propaganda pamphlets, some containing outlandishly false statements. He wrote:

" 'I believe in rugged individualism. People should stand on their own two feet, not expect Government aid. I stand on my own two feet. I oppose all those socialistic trends you have been voting for and demand return to the free-enterprise system . . . I and my neighbors intend to vote against you this year.' "

Laissez-faire. No one has put it better than William Saroyan:

> "Nobody is able to do anybody any good. . . .
> After we make the small discovery that anybody can
> do anybody else a little *insignificant* good now and
> then, we make the large discovery that not only is it
> not possible for anybody to do anybody else any *real*
> good, it is almost impossible for everybody not to do
> everybody else a great deal of harm." (23, p 112)

Amen!

BIBLIOGRAPHY AND COPYRIGHT NOTICES

1. White, William Allen, *Masks in a Pageant*, The Macmillan Company, 1928. Excerpts reprinted by permission of Mr. W. L. White.
2. Burns, James MacGregor, *Roosevelt, the Lion and the Fox*, Harcourt, Brace and World, Inc., 1956, © 1956 by James MacGregor Burns. Excerpts reprinted by permission of Harcourt Brace Jovanovich, Inc.
3. Lippmann, Walter, *The New Imperative*. The Macmillan Company, 1935, copyright, 1935, by Walter Lippmann. Portions of *The New Imperative* appeared originally in the June 1935 issue of the *Yale Review*. Excerpts reprinted by permission of The Macmillan Company.
4. Kimmel, Lewis H., *Federal Budget and Fiscal Policy, 1789–1958*, copyright © 1959. The Brookings Institution, Washington, D. C. Excerpts reprinted by permission of The Brookings Institution.
5. White, William S., *Majesty and Mischief, A Mixed Tribute to FDR*, McGraw-Hill Book Company, 1961, copyright © 1961 by William Smith White. Quotations used with permission of McGraw-Hill Book Company.
6. Watterson, Henry, *Marse Henry, An Autobiography* in two volumes. George H. Doran Company, copyright, 1919, by George H. Doran Company.
7. Johnson, Sam Houston, *My Brother Lyndon*, Cowles Book Company, 1970, copyright 1969, 1970 by Sam Houston Johnson.
8. White, William Allen, *The Old Order Changeth*, The Macmillan Company, 1928. Excerpts reprinted by permission of Mr. W. L. White.
9. Allen, Frederick Lewis, *The Big Change, America Transforms Itself, 1900–1950*, Harper and Brothers, 1952, copyright, 1952, by Frederick Lewis Allen. Excerpts reprinted by permission of Harper and Row, Publishers, Inc.
10. Goldman, Eric, *The Tragedy of Lyndon Johnson*, Alfred A. Knopf, 1969, copyright © 1968, 1969 by Eric F. Goldman. Excerpts reprinted by permission of Alfred A. Knopf, Inc.
11. Lasky, Victor, *JFK, The Man and the Myth*, The Macmillan Company, 1963, © Victor Lasky, 1963. Excerpts reprinted by permission of The Macmillan Company.
12. Hughes, Emmet John, *The Ordeal of Power, A Political Memoir of the Eisenhower Years*, 1st ed, Atheneum, 1963, © 1962, 1963 by Emmet John Hughes. Excerpts reprinted by permission of Atheneum Publishers.
13. Gettleman, Marvin E. and David Mermelstein, eds, *The Great Society Reader: The Failure of American Liberalism*, Random House, 1967, © copyright, 1967, by Random House, Inc., © copyright, 1967, by Marvin E. Gettleman and David Mermelstein. Excerpts reprinted by permission of Random House, Inc.
14. Halévy, Élie, *The Era of Tyrannies, Essays on Socialism and War*, translated by R. K. Webb, Doubleday & Company, Inc., 1965, copyright © 1965 by Doubleday & Company, Inc. Excerpts reprinted by permission of Doubleday & Company, Inc.
15. Lippmann, Walter, *The Good Society*, Grosset and Dunlap, 1943, copyright, 1936, 1937, 1943 by Walter Lippmann. Excerpts quoted by permission of Atlantic-Little, Brown and Co.
16. Carson, Clarence B., *Throttling the Railroads*, appearing first in *The Freeman*, May 1970 to Jan 1971, v 20, no. 5 to v 21, no. 1, The Foundation for Economic Education, Irvington-on-Hudson, N. Y.

17. Poole, Jr., Robert, "Fly the Frenzied Skys," appearing in *The Freeman*, May 1970, v 20, no. 5, pp 273–286, The Foundation for Economic Education, Irvington-on-Hudson, N. Y.

18. Hoover, H. C., *The Memoirs of Herbert Hoover* in two volumes, The Macmillan Company, 1951, 1952, copyright 1951, 1952 by Herbert Hoover. Excerpts reprinted by permission of The Macmillan Company.

19. Bernstein, B. J. and A. J. Matusow, *The Truman Administration: A Documentary History*, Harper and Row, Publishers, Inc., 1966, copyright © 1966 by Barton J. Bernstein and Allen J. Matusow. Excerpts reprinted by permission of Harper and Row, Publishers, Inc.

20. Eisenhower, Dwight D., *The White House Years: Waging Peace*, Doubleday & Company, Inc., 1963, copyright © 1963 by Dwight D. Eisenhower. Excerpts reprinted by permission of Doubleday & Company, Inc.

21. Nock, Albert J., *Free Speech and Plain Language*, William Morrow & Co., Inc., Publishers, 1937, copyright 1935 by Albert Jay Nock, © renewed 1965 by S. A. Nock. Excerpts reprinted by permission of William Morrow and Co., Inc., Publishers.

22. Huneker, James Gibbons, *Variations*, Charles Scribner's Sons, 1921, copyright, 1921, by Charles Scribner's Sons. Excerpts reprinted by permission of Charles Scribner's Sons.

23. Saroyan, William, *Days of Life and Death and Escape to the Moon*, The Dial Press, 1970, copyright © 1970 by William Saroyan. Excerpts reprinted by permission of The Dial Press.

24. Mitchell, Edward P., *Memoirs of an Editor, Fifty Years of American Journalism*, Charles Scribner's Sons, 1924, copyright, 1924 by Charles Scribner's Sons. Excerpts reprinted by permission of Charles Scribner's Sons.

25. Villard, Oswald Garrison, *Fighitng Years—Memoirs of a Liberal Editor*, Harcourt, Brace & Co., Inc., 1939, copyright, 1939 by Harcourt, Brace & Co., Inc., copyright, 1967 by Henry H. Villard. Excerpts reprinted by permission of the publisher.

26. LaFollette, Robert M., *LaFollette's Autobiography*, The Robert M. LaFollette Co., Madison, Wisconsin, 1913, copyright 1911, 1913 by Robert M. LaFollette.

27. Ross, Ishbel, *An American Family, The Tafts 1678–1964*, World Publishing Company, 1964, copyright © 1964 by Ishbel Ross. Excerpts reprinted by permission of The World Publishing Company.

28. Ludwig, Emil, *Roosevelt, A Study in Fortune and Power*, The Viking Press, 1938, copyright 1937, 1938 by MacFadden Publications, Inc., copyright 1938 by the Viking Press, Inc., all rights reserved. Reprinted by permission of The Viking Press, Inc.

29. Pringle, Henry F., *The Life and Times of William Howard Taft* in two volumes, Farrar & Rinehart, Inc., 1939, copyright, 1939 by Henry F. Pringle. Excerpts reprinted by permission of Holt, Rinehart and Winston, Inc.

30. White, William Allen, *The Autobiography of William Allen White*, The Macmillan Company, 1946, copyright, 1946, by The Macmillan Company. Excerpts reprinted by permission of The Macmillan Company.

31. Kohlsaat, H. H., *From McKinley to Harding, Personal Recollections of Our Presidents*, Charles Scribner's Sons, 1923, copyright 1923 by Charles Scribner's Sons. Excerpts reprinted by permission of Charles Scribner's Sons.

32. Kerney, James, *The Political Education of Woodrow Wilson*, The Century Co., 1926, copyright, 1926, by The Century Company. Excerpts reprinted by permission of Appleton-Century-Crofts, Inc.

33. Hale, William B., *Woodrow Wilson, The Story of His Life*, Double-day, Page and Co., 1912.
34. Villard, Oswald Garrison, *Prophets True and False*, Alfred A. Knopf, 1928. Excerpts reprinted by permission of The Nation, Inc.
35. Stoddard, Henry L., *As I Knew Them, Presidents and Politics from Grant to Coolidge*, Harper & Brothers, Publishers, 1927, copyright 1927 by Harper & Brothers. Excerpts reprinted by permission of Harper & Row, Publishers, Inc.
36. Smith, Arthur D. Howden, *Mr. House of Texas*, Funk and Wagnalls, Inc., 1940, copyright 1940 by Arthur D. Howden Smith. Excerpts reprinted by permission of the Publisher, Funk and Wagnalls.
37. House, Edward M., *Philip Dru, Administrator*, © 1912 by B. W. Huebsch.
38. *The American Heritage History of World War I*, © Copyright 1964 by American Heritage Publishing Co., Inc. Excerpts reprinted with permission.
39. Thompson, Charles Willis, *Presidents I've Known and Two Near Presidents*, The Bobbs-Merrill Co., 1929, copyright 1929 by Charles Willis Thompson. Excerpts reprinted by permission of the Bobbs-Merrill Company, Inc.
40. Sinclair, Andrew, *The Available Man, the Life Behind the Masks of Warren Gamaliel Harding*, The Macmillan Company, 1965, copyright © Andrew Sinclair 1965. Excerpts reprinted by permission of The Macmillan Company.
41. Fuess, Claude M., *Calvin Coolidge, The Man from Vermont*, 1st ed, Little, Brown and Company, 1940, copyright 1939, 1940 by Claude M. Fuess. Excerpts reprinted by permission of Little, Brown and Co.
42. McCoy, Donald R., *Calvin Coolidge, the Quiet President*, The Macmillan Company, 1967, copyright © 1967 by Donald R. McCoy. Excerpts reprinted by permission of The Macmillan Company.
43. Quint, Howard H. and Robert H. Farrell, *The Talkative President: The Off-the-Record Press Conferences of Calvin Coolidge*, The University of Massachusetts Press, Amherst, Massachusetts, 1964.
44. White, William Allen, *Calvin Coolidge, The Man Who is President*, The Macmillan Company, 1925. Excerpts reprinted by permission of Mr. W. L. White.
45. White, William Allen, *A Puritan in Babylon*, The Macmillan Company, 1938. Excerpts reprinted by permission of Mr. W. L. White.
46. Lyons, Eugene, *Herbert Hoover, A Biography*, Doubleday & Company, Inc., 1964, copyright © 1948, 1964 by Eugene Lyons; copyright 1947 by Reader's Digest Association, Inc. Excerpts reprinted by permission of Doubleday & Company, Inc.
47. Smith, Gene, *The Shattered Dream, Herbert Hoover and The Great Depression*, William Morrow & Company, Inc., 1970, copyright © 1970 by Gene Smith. Excerpts reprinted by permission of William Morrow & Company, Inc.
48. Myers, W. S. and W. H. Newton, *The Hoover Administration: A Documented Narrative*, Charles Scribner's Sons, 1936, copyright, 1936, by Charles Scribner's Sons. Excerpts reprinted by permission of Charles Scribner's Sons.
49. Flynn, John T., *The Roosevelt Myth*, revised edition, The Devin-Adair Company, 1956, copyright, 1948, 1956 by John T. Flynn. Excerpts reprinted by permission of The Devin-Adair Company.
50. Wreszin, Michael, *Oswald Garrison Villard, Pacifist at War*, Indiana University Press, Bloomington, Indiana, 1965.
51. Morgenstern, George, *Pearl Harbor, The Story of the Secret War*, The Devin-Adair Company, 1947.

52. Kimmel, Husband E., *Admiral Kimmel's Story*, Henry Regnery Company, 1955.

53. Bell, Jack, *The Johnson Treatment*, Harper & Row, Publishers, Inc., 1965, copyright © 1965 by John L. Bell. Excerpts reprinted by permission of Harper & Row, Publishers, Inc.

54. Steinberg, Alfred, *The Man from Missouri, The Life and Times of Harry Truman*, G. P. Putnam's Sons, 1962, copyright © 1962 by Alfred Steinberg. Excerpts reprinted by permission of G. P. Putnam's Sons.

55. Allen, Robert S. and William V. Shannon, *The Truman Merry-Go-Round*, The Vanguard Press, Inc., 1950, copyright, 1950, by Robert S. Allen and William V. Shannon. Excerpts reprinted by permission of Vanguard Press, Inc.

56. Albertson, Dean, ed, *Eisenhower as President*, Hill and Wang, 1963, copyright © 1963 by Dean Albertson. Excerpts reprinted by permission of Hill and Wang.

57. Rovere, Richard H., *Affairs of State: The Eisenhower Years*, Farrar, Straus and Company, 1956, copyright © 1956 by Richard H. Rovere. Excerpts reprinted by permission of Farrar, Straus & Giroux, Inc.

58. Goldman, Eric F., *The Crucial Decade—and After: 1954–1960*, Alfred A. Knopf, Inc., 1961, © 1960 by Eric F. Goldman. Excerpts reprinted by permission of Alfred A. Knopf, Inc.

59. Eisenhower, Dwight D., *The White House Years, Mandate for Change*, Doubleday & Company, Inc., 1963, © copyright 1963 by Dwight D. Eisenhower. Excerpts reprinted by permission of Doubleday & Company, Inc.

60. Lincoln, Evelyn, *Kennedy and Johnson*, Holt, Rinehart and Winston, Inc., 1968, copyright © 1968 by Evelyn Lincoln. Excerpts reprinted by permission of Holt, Rinehart and Winston, Inc.

61. Sherrill, Robert, *The Accidental President*, Grossman Publishers, 1967, copyright © 1967 by Robert Sherrill. Excerpts reprinted by permission of Grossman Publishers.

62. Alsop, Stewart, *Nixon and Rockefeller: A Double Portrait*, Doubleday & Company, Inc., 1960, copyright © 1960 by Stewart Alsop. Excerpts reprinted by Doubleday & Company, Inc.

63. Krock, Arthur, *Memoirs, Sixty Years on the Firing Line*, Funk & Wagnalls, Inc., 1968, copyright © 1968 by Arthur Krock. Excerpts reprinted by permission of the publisher, Funk and Wagnalls.

64. Mazo, Earl, *Richard Nixon: A Political and Personal Portrait*, Harper & Row, Publishers, Inc., copyright © 1959 by Earl Mazo. Excerpts reprinted by permission of Harper & Row, Publishers, Inc.

65. de Toledano, Ralph, *Nixon*, Henry Holt and Company, 1956, copyright © 1956 by Ralph de Toledano. Excerpts reprinted by permission of Holt, Rinehart and Winston, Inc.

66. Witcover, Jules, *The Resurrection of Richard Nixon*, G. P. Putnam's Sons, 1970, copyright © 1970 by Jules Witcover. Excerpts reprinted by permission of G. P. Putnam's Sons.

INDEX

CARL A. KEYSER was born in Washington, D. C., but escaped unharmed to New England where he has lived since 1946. During the war he discovered it was just as easy to get seasick in the Mediterranean as in the Atlantic, and no more fun. After the shooting and shouting stopped, he beat his ship into a plowshare and got a job in a shoe factory where there was no shooting but some shouting. His moral decline started when he became an assistant dean of a college. Undaunted, he managed to work himself down to Commonwealth Professor Emeritus and retired in 1968 from the University of Massachusetts when shouting and shooting again seemed imminent. He is the author of several widely used engineering texts, of which one has been translated into Spanish and another into Japanese. Both editions are easier to read than the IRS Instructions for Form 1040. He and his wife and three sons live in Amherst. In between books, he paints, skis, sails and plays a terrible game of golf.